AF663927

VĀMANAVIKRAMA

VĀMANAVIKRAMA

RESEARCH IN INDOLOGICAL STUDIES

(PROF. V. M. KULKARNI FELICITATION VOLUME)

(Vedic Literature, Classical Sanskrit Literature, Poetics, Grammer and Linguistics, Philosophy and Religion, Prakrit and Jainism)

Edited By :

DR. S. Y. WAKANKAR

Deputy Director,
Oriental Institute,
M.S. University of Baroda,
Opposite Palace Gate,
Palace Road,
Vadodara-390001 (Gujarat).

BHARATIYA KALA PRAKASHAN
DELHI (INDIA)

First Edition : 2006

Published by **C.P. Gautam**
BHARATIYA KALA PRAKASHAN
3421-A, IInd Floor, Narang Colony, Tri Nagar,
Delhi-110035. Phone : 27393083, 32967505 (O), 32492129 (R)

ISBN : 81-8090-108-4

Laser Type Setting by
A-ONE GRAPHICS
JD-18C, IInd Floor, Pitampura, Delhi-110088.

Printed by
BDH Printer at Salasar Imaging System, Delhi.

PROF. V.M. KULKARNI

CONTENTS

SECTION-III

VEDIC LITERATURE

SECTION-IV

CLASSICAL SANSKRIT LITERATURE

SECTION-V

POETICS

SECTION-VI

PHILOSOPHY AND RELIGION

SECTION-VII

GRAMMAR AND LINGUISTICS

SECTION-VIII

PRAKRIT AND JAINISM

EDITORIAL

Vāmanvikrama is a Felicitation Volume in honour of Prof. Dr. Vaman Mahadev Kulkarni, an outstanding scholar, teacher, researcher and an administrator. An *Ajātaśatru* and publicity-shy, Prof. Kulkarni made an indelible mark as a sound scholar and a seasoned researcher in the fields of Sanskrit and Prakrit Studies, especially, Poetics, Jainism and Manuscript-related studies. It is a strange co-incidence that though Sanskrit was his most favourite subject, besides English and Mathematics, Destiny willed that this young and budding and promising student should pursue Prakrit Languages, esp. Ardhamagadhi, because, in those days, it was an untapped and neglected field, abounding in rich source material. His friend just suggested to him to offer Ardhamagadhi-a totally new subject-and instantaneously Dr. Kulkarni accepted his proposal and joined the class of Ardhamagadhi. He was singularly fortunate to have a teacher like Prof. Dr. Adinath Neminath Upadhye-a doyen of Prakrit Studies-to guide his Destiny.That decision, taken on the spur of the moment, proved to be highly fruitful in the sense that Dr. Kulkarni rendered yeoman's services to the cause of the study and furtherance of Prakrit Studies, so much so that he considers "PRAKRIT VERSES IN SANSKRIT WORKS ON POETICS" as his *magnum opus* and a life time work, that rightly brought to him international repute. If anybody doubts his decision, he just says that it was "NIYATI" that did this magic of shifting his focus from the favourite subject to a new and much unexplored field at that time.

After perusing this Volume, it will be very evident that Dr. Kulkarni adorned different positions in Academic as well as Administrative fields. His clarity of thought and expression, coupled with his objective attitude, open mind and soft-spoken nature, endeared himself to one and all who happened to come in his contact.

This Volume is a collection of learned articles contributed by his colleagues, students, well-wishers and friends. A look at the contents of this Volume will be sufficient to give a fairly clear idea of the nature of this Volume, as is reflected in the Sections, covering different fields in Indology. The Volume is a Tribute to his diverse interests in research. His amiable manners befriended him to many scholars and intellectuals. Dr. Kulkarni is really a rarity in the sense that he is both-a gentleman as well as a scholar-and never thrusts his scholarship on others.

His introvert attitude must have been one of the reasons, in addition to his being publicity-shy and never blowing his own trumpet, that the idea of his Felicitation Volume did not dawn on anybody's mind. I grabbed this golden opportunity by both of my hands, though, I had never had the fortune to be his student or even a colleague. Despite this fact, he has been showering his affection on me since last thirty five years, goaded as he was by the similar attitude of affection shown to me by his GURU, the late Prof. R.B. Athavale, another doyen in Alaṅkāraśāstra.

Initially, I was helped by Prof. Dr. S.G. Moghe, but, unfortunately, his sudden and saddening death just crippled me and consequently slowed down the momentum. Dr. Moghe, however, before his departure for Heaven contributed an extensive article almost an Academic Biography of Prof. Kulkarni, highlighting his contribution. This vacuum, created by the loss of Dr. Moghe, was ably filled by my younger colleague, Prof. Dr. M.L. Wadekar, who whole-heartedly offered his help and co-operation in every aspect and thus lessened my burden. I have no words to adequately thank Dr. Wadekar for his most-needed help and guidance. I take this opportunity to sincerely thank two colleagues, of mine viz. Ms. Sasvati Sen and Dr. Mrs. Sharmila Bagchi, who did the spade work of correcting the press-copies of some of the articles. Later on, Dr. Bagchi also helped by reading the proof of some one hundred pages. The second proofs, however, were entirely done by me single-handedly. Hence, I beg a pardon of the scholars/readers if any mistakes might have crept in, despite my meticulous efforts and care. Inspite of being a grammarian, I lack in adequate words to thank from the bottom of my heart-the Contributors for favouring me with their papers and also for bearing with me and the unpardonable delay that was due to my lonely and single-handed efforts.

Last but not the least, I sincerely thank my friend, Shri C.P. Gautam, of the Bharatiya Kala Prakashan, Delhi, for undertaking the Publication of this Volume and speedily completing it with his team.

14.3.2006 **Dr. S.Y. WAKANKAR**

NAMES AND ADDRESSES OF CONTRIBUTORS

(1) Prof. Dr. Rewa Prasad Dwivedi, Founder Chairman, Kalidasa Academy, 28, Mahamanapuri, Varanasi-5, U.P.

(2) Prof. Dr. Bhagavatiprasad D. Pandya, 1,A, Gopalakunja Society, Bhairavnath Road, Maninagar, Ahamdabad-380008, Gujarat.

(3) Prof.Sureshchandra J. Dave, 7, Janvishram Society, Behind Sahajanand College, Ambawadi, Ahmedabad-380015, Gujarat.

(4) Dr. N.N. Patil, A-37 Kamalapushpa, Bandra Reclamation, K.C. Marg, Mumbai-400050, Maharashtra.

(5) Smt. Mrudula Prabhuram Joshi, 104, 6-C, Maitri Society, Damodar Park, Ghatkopar (West), Mumbai-400086, Maharashtra.

(6) Smt. Sattvashila Samant, 16, Yashodakunja Society, Tejas Nagar, Kothrud, Pune-411038, Maharashtra.

(7) Late Prof. Dr. S. G. Moghe, B-74, Tatya Gharpure Path, J.S.S. Road, Girgaum, Mumbari-400004, Maharashtra.

(8) Prof. Dr. N.M.Kansara, 17/176, Vidya Nagar Flats, Near Himmatlal Park, Ambawadi, Ahmedabad-380015, Gujarat.

(9) Dr. Majusha D. Gokhale, Block No. 12, Suryaprakash Society, Tekadi Bungalo Road, Naupada, Thane-400602, Maharashtra

(10) Prof. Dr. M.D. Paradkar, 4/11, Shah Building, Bhagat Galli, Mahim, Mumbai-400016, Maharashtra

(11) Prof. Dr. Vijay Pandya, Hon. Professor, L.D Institute of Indology. Near Gujarat University, Navrangpura, Ahmedabad-380009, Gujarat.

(12) Prof. Dr. N.P. Unni, 27/1348, Sreelasyam, Rishimangalam, Vanchiyoor, Thiruvananthapuram-695, 5-Kerala.

(13) Prof. Dr. Vasantkumar M. Bhatt, A-2, Surabhi Apartments, Subhash Society, Vijay Cross Road (East), Ahmedabad-380009-Gujarat.

(14) Prof. Nitin R. Desai, 6, Amul Society, Near New Sharda Mandir, M. Jodhani Road, Ahmedabad-380007-Gujarat.

(15) Dr. Devangana Desai, 1/30, Shanti, 19, Pedder Road, Mumbai-400026-Maharashtra

(16) Prof. Dr. W.K. Lele, A 1/2, Sarvatra Society, Paud Road, Kothrud, Pune, 411038, Maharashtra

(17) Pro.f. Dr. Tapasvi S. Nandi, 4, Professors Colony, Navrangpura, Ahmedabad-380009, Gujarat.

(18) Prof. Dr. Ramesh S. Betai, 103, Savodayanagar-3, Behind Ranna Park, Ahmedabad-380011, Gujarat.

(19) Prof. Dr. S.S. Antarkar, Prof. of Jainology, Dept. of Philosophy, Bombay University, Vidyanagari Campus, Kalina, Santacruz (East), Mumbai-400098, Maharashtra.

(20) Prof. Dr. Shubhada A. Joshi, Department of Philosphy, Bombay University, Vidyanagari Campus, Kalina, Santacruz (East), Mumbai-400098, Maharashtra.

(21) Prof. Dr. Uma Vaidya, Head, Dept. of Sanskrit, Bombay University, Vidyanagari Campus, Kalina, Santacruz (East), Mumbai-400098, Maharashtra.

(22) Prof. Dr. G.V. Tagare, Siddhivinayak, Girinagar Housing Society, Dhankawdi, near Bharatiya Vidyapeetha, Pune-411043, Maharashtra.

(23) Prof. Dr. Esther A.Solomon, Satyagraha Cchavani, Bungalow No. 372, Lane 18, Opposite ISRO, Satellite Road, Ahmedabad-380015, Gujarat.

(24) Prof. Dr. W.R. Antarkar, Jayram Nivas, B-5, 116, Tilak Mandir Road, Parle (East), Mumbai-400057, Maharashtra.

(25) Prof. Dr. K.S. Arjunwadkar, Devangini, 1192, Shakravar Peth, Subhashnagar-3, Pune-411002, Maharashtra.

(26) Prof. Dr. Leela K. Arjunwadkar, Devangini, 1192, Shukravar Peth, Subhashnagar-3, Pune-411002, Maharashtra.

(27) Prof. Dr. Nagin J. Shah, 23, Valkeshvar Society, Ambawadi, Ahmedabad-380015, Gujarat.

(28) Prof. Dr. Mrs. Sindhu S. Dange, Girnar, Gokhale Road, Mulund (East), Mumbai-400081, Maharashtra.

(29) Prof. Dr. Smt. A.B. Bakre, 1/4, Jay Prabhat Society, Sahakar Nagar, Andheri (West), Mumbai-400053, Maharashtra.

(30) Prof. Dr. S.D. Laddu, Pritam Nagar, 2/2, Kothrud, Pune-411029, Maharashtra.

(31) Prof. Dr. M.L. Wadekar, Shriram Complex, Mangal Bazar, Vadodara-390001, Gujarat.

(32) Dr. Gauri Mahulikar, 202, Snehal, 5th Cross Road, Borivali (East), Mumbai-400066, Maharashtra.

(33) Prof. Dr. Siddharth Yeshwant Wakankar, 1/5, Vrindavan Estate, Pashabhai Patel Park, Race Course Circle (South), Vadodara-390007, Gujarat.

Tel: (0265) 2351189 (R) ; (0265) 2425121 (O) ; 9427339942 (M). Fax : (0265) 2357459 ; E-Mail : syw16@rediffmail.com. sywakankar@gmail.com.

BIO-DATA

Name and	:	VAMAN MAHADEO KULKARNI.
Address	:	5, Suruchi Society Dixit Road Extension Vile-Parle (East) Mumbai-400057.
Birth Place	:	AJRA (Dist. Kolhapur) Maharashtra State.
Date of Birth	:	November 22, 1917.
Qualifications	:	B.A., First Class, AMG (Prakrit), Bombay University, 1940 M.A., Second Class, AMG (Prakrit)—Sanskrit, Bombay University, 1942 M.A. Ist Class First, Sanskrit, Benaras University, 1951. Ph. D. in Sanskrit, Bombay University, 1952.
Other Distinctions.	:	(1) A.T. Jain Literature Scholarship (for standing First in AMG at Inter Arts Examination, Bombay University, 1938.) (2) Gangadas Rangildas Scholarship for standing First at the B. A. Examination among all the candidates (Bombay University) 1940. (3) Dakshina Fellowship for 2 years at the Rajaram College, Kolhapur, 1940-42. (4) Springer Research Scholarship for three years.

(5) Silver Medal for Research—The Asiatic Society of Bombay. 1983.

(6) Recipient of President's Award of Certificate of Honour as Eminent Sanskrit Scholar, 1992.

(7) Honorary Fellowship for Life by the Asiatic Society of Bombay. 1993.

(8) Acharya Hemachandrasuri Puraskar (Award) for the work *Prakrit Verses in Sanskrit Works on Poetics* (By B. L. Institute of Indology), Delhi (for 1997), 1998.

GOVERNMENT SERVICE

Joined the Department of Sanskrit and Prakrit, Gujarat College, Ahmedabad — 1942

And Served as an NCC Office, — 1948-1960

(i) Worked as Professor and Head of the Department. — 1956-1961

(ii) Department of Sanskrit, Nagpur Maha-vidyalaya, Nagpur. — 1961-1962

(iii) Professor and Head, Department of Sanskrit, Rajaram College, Kolhapur. — 1962-1967

(iv) Professor and Head, Department of Sanskrit, Vidarbha Mahavidyalaya, Amravati. — 1967-1968

(v) Professor and Head, Department of Sanskrit, Ismail Yusuf College, Jogeshwari (Bombay). — 1968-1972

(vi) Professor of Sanskrit and Acting Principal, Ismail Yusuf College, Jogeshwari (Bombay). — 1971-1972

(vii) Professor and Head, Department of Sanskrit, The Elphinstone College (Bombay). — 1972-1973

(viii) While at the Elphinstone College, was invited by the Government to take up the post of Director of Languages, Maharashtra State, Bombay. — 1973-1975

After Retirement in 1975 worked as :

(ix) Hon. Director, MM Dr. P.V. Kane Research Institute, Asiatic Society of Bombay. — 1976-1981, 1987-1989

(x) Director, B.L. Institute of Indology, Patan (N. Gujarat). 1981-1984

(xi) Editor, Journal of the Asiatic Society of Bombay from 1977 to-date with one or two short breaks in-between. For some years, Dr. Devangana Desai and self have been working as Joint Editors.

STATEMENT OF ORIGINAL RESEARCH WORK

(A) Work for Ph. D.

(1) The Story of Rāma in Jain Literature (as presented in the Sanskrit, Prakrit and Apabhraṁśa languages by the Śvetāmbara and Digaṁbara poets), Doctoral Thesis.

(2) Ph. D. Thesis of Prof. K. H. Trivedi on the Nāṭyadarpaṇa of Rāmacandra and Guṇacandra prepared under my guidance and accepted for the Degree of Ph.D. by the Gujarat University and published by L.D. Institute of Indology, Ahmedabad-9.

(B) Critical Introductions, Editions and Books

(1) Introduction to Paumacariyam (Jain Rāmāyaṇa), published by Prakrit Text Society, Varanasi, 1962.

(2) Kāvyānuśāsana of Ācārya Hemacandra, Second, revised critical edition (in collaboration with Prof. R.C. Parikh), published by Sri Mahavira Jaina Vidyalaya, Bombay, 1964 (pp 83+637).

(3) Jayadeva's Gītagovinda with hitherto unpublished commentary of King Mānaṅka, publ. by L.D. Institute of Indology, Ahmedabad-9, 1965 (pp. xxiv +131)

(4) Śṛṅgārārṇava-candrikā of Vijayavarṇi : A critical edition based on a rare manuscript, publ. by Bharatiya Jñānapitha, Varanasi, 1969 (pp. xi +66+175)

(5) An Anthology of Jain Texts (Sāhityaratnkaośa. Jain Sangraha) publ. by Sahitya Akademi, New Delhi, 1981. (pp. xxxvi + 236).

(6) Critical Introduction (Notes and Appendices) to Mallikā-Makaranda, a Prakaraṇa by Rāmacandra, Text editor, Muni Sri Punyavijayaji, L. D. Institute of IndoIogy. 1983.

(7) Studies in Sanskrit Sahitya Śāstra,: A collection of Research papers relating to Sanskrit Poetics and Aesthetics, publ, by B. L. Institute of Indology.

(8) Edited : Some Aspects of the Rasa Theory : A collection of research papers,

read at the Seminar on the Rasa Theory (organised and) Publ. by B.L. Institute of Indology, Delhi, 1986.

(9) Introduction to Pañcasūtrakam of Cirantanācārya ed. by Muni Sri Jambuvijayaji- B.L. Institute of Indology, Delhi, 1986.

(10). Edited : Vācaka Śrīmad Umāsvāti's Praśamarati-Prakaraṇa, (Translation and Appendices in English by Mahesh Bhogilal) *publ. by* Mrs. Diniben N. Shodhan, Ahmedabad, 1991.

(11) The Story of Rāma in Jain Literature, 2nd edition, (based on the doctoral thesis): Saraswati Pustak Bhandar, Ahmedabad 1990.

(12) Foreword to the Kāvyānuśāsana of Ācārya Hemacandra : A Critical Study by A.M. Upadhyay, M.A., Ph.D. publ. by the Author. Ahmedabad. 1987.

(13) Prakrit Verses in Sanskrit Works on Poetics (in Two Volumes) :—

Vol. I : Text (with Appendixes and Indexes) and

Vol. II : Translation (with Introduction, Glossary and Notes. (Vol. I : pp.1 602+40+129, Vol. II. Introduction pp. 47+ Translation pp. 241+ Glossary pp. 242-286 + Notes pp. 287-699) B.L. Institute of Indology, Delhi. 1988 and 1990

The speciality of this Edition lies in the following respects:

(i) For the first time Prakrit illustrative verses from a score of Sanskrit Works on poetics are presented here as a treasury.

(ii) An effort is made to trace these verses to their sources.

(iii) The texts of a very large number of Prakrit verses have been for the first time restored.

(iv) Only a few verses which have been the editor's despair are left as they are.

(v) Variant readings are noted and discussed in the Notes.

(vi) A considerable number of Prakrit Gāthās, Skandhakas, etc. translated into English for the first time.

(vii) The introduction shows for the first time how the Prakrit verses have greatly influenced Ālamkārikas in their formulation and exposition of their theories of Sanskrit poetry.

(viii) The introduction further provides information at one place about Prakrit poetic works from which the illustrative verses have been drawn.

(ix) Shows how eminent writers have showered praise on Prakrit poetry.

(x) and meets the charge of obscenity against Prakrit poetry.

(14) Bhoja and Harivijaya of Sarvasena :—

(A monograph on the Harivijaya of Sarvasena).

Note : Till recently only four verses from Bhoja's Sarasvatīkaṇṭhābharaṇa were identifiable as Sarvasena's from his Harivijaya, now lost. In Bhoja's Śṛṅgāraprakāśa, I discovered at least forty citations—some of them are repetitions -which are definitely identifiable as Sarvasena's from his Harivijaya. There are other, about one hundred verses, probably identifiable as Sarvasena's from his Harivijaya.

The monograph collects together all available information about the contents of Harivijaya and discusses its structure, technique, language, style, poetic merits and its place in artistic epics (Sarasvati Pustak Bhandar), Ahmedabad,1991

(15) Samarāiccakahā. (Bhava II) of Haribhadrasuri, ed. with introduction, Translation and Notes.

(16) Raghuvaṁśa (cantos VIII and IX) of Kālidasa ed. with Introduction, Translation and Notes.

(17) More Studies in Sanskrit Sahitya Śāstra, pub. Saraswati Pustak Bhandar, Ahmedabad-380001, First Edition 1993.

(18) Five critical Articles in Marathi on Poetics and Poetry (Pāca Pustaka Parīkṣaṇe) pub. Prajna Pathasala Mandala, Wai, 1993).

(19) A Treasury of Jain Tales (ed.) pub. Sharadaben Cimanbhai Educational Research Centre, Ahmedabad-4. 1994.

(20) Usāniruddham of Rāmapāṇivāda, 2nd enlarged edition,Pub. Sharadaben Chimanbhai Educational Research Centre, Ahmedabad, 1996.

(21) Outline of Abhinavagupta's Aesthetics, pub. Saraswati Pustak Bhandar. Ahmedabed-380001, 1998, Price Rs. 200/-.

(22) Nāṭyaśāstra with the Commentary of Abhinavagupta, Vol. II, ed. by late M.

Ramakrishna Kavi. Revised edn. (in collaboration) Oriental Institute, Vadodara, 2001. Price Rs 450/-. GOS No. 68

(23) Nāṭyaśāstra with the commentary of Abhinavagupta, Vol. III Oriental Institute Vadodara-2003 GOS No. 124

(24) Abhinavabhāratī Text Restored And other Articles.

(25) Kūrmaśatakadvayam -Two Prakrit Poems on Tortoise who supports the Earth. Inscribed at Dhara by Mahārājādhirāja Śri Bhojadeva. Epigraphia Indica, Vol. VIII (1905-1906)—L.D. Institute 2003. Rs. 100/- of Indology.

Translated with select Glossary by V. M. Kulkarni, with an Introduction by Devangana Desai.

(26) Studies in Jain Literature (The collected Papers contributed by Prof. V.M. Kulkarni) pub. 2003. Rs. 300/- Sharadaben Chimanbhai Educational Research Centre,—"Darshan", Shahibag, Ahmedabad-380004. 2001. Price Rs. 680/-.

INDEPENDENT ORIGINAL RESEARCH PAPERS

1. Anādiviṁśikā—A Critical Study—AIOC XV—Session, Bombay, 1949 (later published in Jain Antiquary. 1.)

2. The Rāmāyaṇa Version of Saṅghadāsa as found in his Vasudevahiṇḍi- Journal, Oriental Institute, Baroda Vol. I, No. 2, Baroda, 1952,

3. The Rāmāyaṇa of Bhadresvara as found in his Kahāvalī-Journal, Oriental Institute, Baroda- Vol. II, No. 4, June, 1953.

4. Puspadanta's Rāmāyaṇa and its comparison with Vālmīki's Rāmāyaṇa—AIOC, 16th Session, Lucknow, Vol, II. 1953.

5-6. Sanskrit Writers on Plagiarism—Journal, Oriental Institute, Baroda—Vol III No, 4, June, 1954 — Vol. IV No, 1—Sept. 1954.

7. The Problem of Patākāsthānaka—Journal of the University of Bombay, Vol. XXIV (Part 2—Sept. 1955).

8. The Rāmāyaṇa version of Śīlācārya as found in the Cauppanna-Mahāpurisa-Cariya-Annals (Bhandarkar Oriental Research Institute) Vol. XXIV (Part-I and II), Poona, 1955.

9. The Conception of Sandhis in Sanskrit Drama-Journal, Oriental Institute, Baroda, Vol. V. No. 4, June 1956.

10. Sādharmya and Sādṛśya—Journal of the University of Bombay—Vol. XXVI Part. II. Sept. 1957.

11. The Five Sandhis in the Mudrārākṣasa—Gujarat College Magazine (March, 1958).

12. Sītā-Rāvaṇa Kathānaka of Hemacandra—Journal, Oriental Institute, Baroda, Vol. VII, No. 3, March 1958.

13. Sanskrit Rhetoricians on Poetic Conventions—Bulletin. C. G. Vidyabhavan, Surat, August 1959 and 1960 (Nos. 6. 7).

14-15. The Origin and Development of Rāma Story in Jain Literature-Journal, Oriental Institute, Baroda, Dec. 1959. Vol. IX. No. 2 and No.3. March, 1960).

16. Sanskrit Rhetoricians on Poetic Truth—Gujarat College Magazine, (March, 1960).

17-19. Abhinavabhāratī—Text Restored-Journal, Oriental Institute. Baroda. Dec. 1963. Vol. XIII, No. 2, Vol. XIII No. 4. June, 1964, Vol. XIV No. 1. Sept. 1964.

20. A Study in the Saṅketa of Someśvara on Mammaṭa's Kāvyaprakāśa -Journal, Oriental Institute. Baroda Vol. X. No. 4. June, 1961.

21. Bhāmaha on Grammar in relation to Poetry-Śāradā Pītha Pradīpa. Nov. 1962 (Indological Research Institute, Dwaraka.)

22. Someśvara Bhaṭṭa and Hemacandrācārya—Bulletin C.G. Vidyabhavan, Surat, August, 1961, 1962 (Nos. 8 9.)

23. Some Important Quotations from Hemacandra's Kāvyānuśāsana,-Bulletin, C.G. Vidyabhavan, Surat, (No. 10), August, 1963.

24. Sources of Hemacandra's Kāvyānuśāsana—Journal, Oriental Institute, Baroda, Vol. XIV, No. 2 December,1964.

25. The Treatment of Intonation (Kāku) in Sanskrit Poetics-Journal, Oriental Institute, Baroda, Vol. XXVI, No.1, Sept. 1966.

26. Svabhāvavāda (Naturalism): A Study- Shri Mahavira Jaina Vidyalaya, Golden Jubilee Volume, Part-I, Bombay, 1968.

27. Bhoja's Śṛṅgāraprakāśa: Prakrit Text Restored—Shivaji University Journal, Vol. I, Nos. 1 and 2. July, 1968.

28. Some Aspects of Prakrit Verses in Sanskrit Alaṁkāra Works—Journal of the University of Bombay, October 1969, No. 74.

29. Kalpalatāviveka : A Study-Journal, Oriental Institute, Baroda, Vol. XVIII No 4. June, 1969.

30. Prakrit Verses in Kalpalatāviveka-Proceedings of Seminar in Prakrit Studies. University of Poona.

31. Bhoja's Śṛṅgāraprakāśa (Chapter XV.-XXIV)—Prakrit Text Restored-Journal of the University of Bombay, Arts No. Vol.X No. 75, October, 1970.

32. The Śṛṅgāraprakāśa : Prakrit Text Restored, Shivaji University Journal, VoI. IV. 1971.

33. Prakrit Verses in Works on Sanskrit Poetics—Journal of the University of Bombay, Arts No. Vol. XI, No.76, October, 1971.

34. Abhinavabhāratī CH—VII Recovered?—Journal of the Oriental Institute, Baroda, Vol. XX No. 3, March 1971.

35. Fresh Light on Bhāmaha-Vivaraṇa—Sambodhi Vol.I No. 1, April 1972—L.D. Institute of Indology, Ahmedabad-9.

36. Prakrit Verses in Sarasvatīkaṇṭhābharaṇa—Proceedings of the Seminar in Prakrit Studies-University of Bombay, Bombay 1971.

37. Kalpalatāviveka on Abhinavabhāratī-Journal of the Oriental Institute, Baroda,Vol. XXI, (no. 4) June 1972

38. Source of Prakrit Languages—Journal of the University of Bombay, Arts No. Vol. XII No. 77, November, 1972.

39. Neglected Prakrit Verses in Sanskrit Works on Poetics—MM Dr. P.V. Kane Communication Monograph, University of Bombay, 1974.

40. Abhinavaguptācī Śānta-rasa-samīkṣā (Marathi)-Dr. R.S. Valimbe Felicitation Volume, December 1974.

41. The Jain View of Aesthetic Experience—Journal of the Oriental Institute, Baroda, Vol. XXIV. No. 1, 2,1974.

42. Abhinavabhāratī—Text: Restored—Journal of the Oriental Institute, Baroda, Vol. XXV. No. 2. December, 1975.

43. Abhinavabhāratī—Text : Restored—Journal of the Orientel Institute, Baroda, Vol. XXV. Nos. 3,4-March-June, 1975.

44. Bhoja's Śṛṅgāraprakāśa—(Chapter-XXV, XXX) Text Restored-Proceedings

of the Seminar on Prakrit Studies, 1973, L.D. Institute of Indology, Ahmedabad-9.

45. Jaina Contribution to Sanskrit Alaṁkāra Literature—Proceedings of the Seminar on "Contribution of Jainism to Indian Culture"—Motilal Banarasidass, Varanasi, 1975.

46. The Sāhitya Mīmāṁsā: Prakrit Text Restored-The Bulletin of the Chunilal Gandhi Vidyabhavan, August, 1970, No. 15.

47. Bhoja's Śṛṅgāraprakāśa (Chapter- XXXI, XXXVI) Prakrit Text Restored-Sambodhi, Vol. IV. Nos. 3, 4. 1975-76—L.D. Institute of Indology Ahmedabad-9.

48. Sāhitya Mīmāṁsā—Prakrit Text Restored -Sambodhi, Vol.V. Nos. 2,3-July-Oct. 1976- L.D. Institute of Indology, Ahmedabad-9.

49. Bhoja's Śṛṅgāraprakāsa—Prakrit Text Restored—Journal of the Asiatic Society of Bombay-Vols. 47-48/1972-73 (New Series) 1977.

50. The Harivijaya of Sarvasena—Annals, Bhandarkar Oriental Research Institute (Diamond Jubilee Volume) Pune, 1977-78.

51. Bhoja's Śṛṅgāraprakāśa—Prakrit Text Restored—Sambodhi, Vol. 7 (Nos. 1-4) April, 1978-January 1979—L.D. Institute of Indology, Ahmedabad-9.

52. Bhoja's Śṛṅgāraprakāśa—Prakrit Text Restored—Journal of the Asiatic Society of Bombay, Vols. 49,50,51/1974-75-76 (New Series), 1979.

53. Bhoja's Śṛṅgaraprakāśa—Prakrit Text Restored—Journal of The Oriental Institute, VIl. XXIX (Nos. 1-2) September-December, 79, Baroda.

54. Prakrit Verses in Dhvanyāloka with Locana-Sambodhi, Vol. 8 (Nos. 1-4) 1979-80-L.D. Institute of Indology, Ahmedabad-9.

55. Ānandavardhana, Dhanika and Kuntaka on The Abhijñāna-Śākuntala-Proceedings of the All India Oriental-Conference-30th Session -Visva Bharati, Santiniketan, November, 1980.

56. Sanskrit Thinkers on Logic in Relation to Poetry-Studies in Indian Philosophy, June, 1981- L.D. Institute of Indology, Ahmedabad-9.

57. Ratívilāpa, Devīsambhogavarṇana, and Ālaṁkārikas-Anantacharya. Indological Research Institute-Series No. IV—Papers of Seminar on Sanskrit Literature, G.D. Somani School Bullding, Cuffe Parade, Bombay-400 005.

58. Kalpalatāviveka on Bhāmaha's Kāvyālaṁkāra (Chapter-V. vv 5-10) Paper read at the Varanasi Session of the Fifth World Sanskrit Conference, 1981, now published in my Studies in Sanskrit Sāhitya Śāstra, pub. by B.L. Institute of Indology, Pātan (North Gujarat).

59. Prakrit Verses in *Daśarūpaka* (with *Avaloka*) and in Kāvyaprakāśa-Journal of The Asiatic Society of Bombay (MM. Dr. P.V. Kane Birth Centenary Volume) Vols. 52-53/1977-78. New Series, Bombay, 1981.

60. Sanskrit Sāhitya āṇi itar Lalita Kalā (Marathi) Paper read at the Seminar organised by Department of Marathi, University of Bombay, published in Ālocanā (a Marathi Monthly) devoted to criticism of Literature and other Arts), December, 1981.

61. Abhinavagupta on the Alaukika Nature of Rasa-Paper read at the Seminar on "The Rasa Theory" organised by the B.L. Institute of Indology, Patan (North Gujarat), 1982.

62. Bhoja's Śṛṅgāraprakāśā : Prakrit Text Restored-Read before the Prakrit and Jainism Section, All India Oriental Conference, Jaipur Session, October, 1982.

63. Prakrit Poetry and Sanskrit Poetics ... Sambodhi Vol. 10 (Nos. 1-4), April 1981-January, 1982 -L.D. Institute of Indology. Ahmadabad-9.

64. Prakrit Verses in Vyaktiviveka with Ruyyaka's Vyākhyāna and in *Vakroktijīvita*-Journal of The Asiatic Society of Bombay, Volumes-54-55. 1979-80 (Combined) (New Series) 1983.

65. "Gauḍavadha," Eka Prākrit Aitihāsika Kāvya (Marathi), "Abhiruchi" Periodical, Baroda.

66. Usāniruddham : Eka Prākrit Kāvya (Marathi) "Abhiruchi" Periodical, Divali Number, 1949.

67. Jain Rāmāyaṇas and their Source—Paper read at the Rāmāyaṇa Seminar held in Delhi, December 1975.

68. Rasa-Bhāva Vicāra (Marathi)—Translation of Bharata's Nāṭya Śāstra (Chs. VI and VII) by Prof. R.P. Kangle-Review Article in Navabharata, September, 1974.

69. Daśarūpaka-Vidhāna (Marathi) Translation of Bharata's Nāṭya Śāstra (Chs.

XVIII and. XIX) by Prof. R.P. Kangle—Review Article in Navabharata, July 1975.

70. Hemacandrācārya Racita Kāvyānuśāsana in Bhāratīya Sāhitya Vicāra Mañjuṣā, Vol. II (Gujarati) publ. by University Book Production Board, Gujarat State, Ahmedabad. 1977.

71. Jineśvarasūri's Gāhārayaṇakosa, ed. by A.M. Bhojak and Dr. Nagin J. Shah-Review Article in Sambodhi. Vol.VI. Nos. 3-4, October, 1977—January, 1978. L.D. Institute of Indology, Ahmedabad-380 009.

72. Abhinavagupta's Contribution to Rasa Theory-Paper read at the Seminar on "Rasa Theory" held on 19-3-1978 at the Bharatiya Vidya Bhavan (and later published in "Bhāratīya Vidyā"), Vol. XXXIX No. 2.

73. Introduction to Mahimabhaṭṭa's Vyaktiviveka-a monograph by Prof. M.V. Patwardhan in Marathi, to be published by Maharastra Rajya Sahitya and Sanskriti Mandal, Mantralaya, Bombay-400032.

74. Sanskrit Aesthetics, Sambodhi Vol.11.Nos. 1-4 April 1982-January 1983-L.D. Institute of Indology, Ahmedabed-9.

75. Rasa and Its Pleasurable Nature, Sambodhi, Vol. 13—April 1984-March 1985, Nos. 1-4-L.D. Institute of Indology, Ahmedabad-380 009.

76-77. Two Principal Karnik Indological Lectures on "Sanskrit Theory of Beauty" and "Rasa Worldly (laukika) and Extra-worldly (alaukika) were delivered under the auspices of the University of Bombay, on March 19 and 20, 1986.

78. A lecture on Saptabhaṅgi or Syādvāda in a week-long series-arranged by Datta Lakshmi Trust, Pune-2-the lectures are published in a book form (in 1991).

79. Jain Account in relation to Myths of Creation-Paper read at a Seminar on "Myths of Creation" organised by the Department of Sanskrit, University of Bombay, on 17th March, 1985. later published by the University of Bombay, Bombay, 1987.

80. Sacrifice in the Jain Tradition—Papar read at the UGC Seminar on "Sacrifice in India":Concept and Evolution" organised by Department of Sanskrit. University of Bombay, During March 3-5, 1986-later published by Viveka Publications, 3/364, Samad Road, Aligarh-202001-1987.

81. Hemacandra's Treatment of the Alaṁkāra and Rasa Traditions—Lecture

delivered on the occasion of Ācārya Hemacandra Navama Śatābdi Mahotsava-1988—Later published in Sambodhi (Special Issue) Vol. 15. 1990. L.D. Institute of Indology, Ahmedbed-9.

82. Hemacandra on Sāttvika Bhāvas : Paper read at a two-day Seminar on Ācārya Hemacandra-December, 1988—Later published in Sambodhi (Special Number) Vol., 15—L.D. Institute of Indology, Ahmedabad-9, 1990.

83. "Hemacandra—An Assessment" : Lecture delivered at the UGC Seminar organised by the Gujarat University, Ahmedabad, on the occasion of Navamaśatābdi Samaroha of Ācārya. Hemacandra on December 29, and 30, 1988, Sambodhi, L.D. Institute, Ahamdabad, 1989.

84. Criteria for Pṛthag Alamkāratva-Paper contributed to MM Prof. J.H. Dave Felicitation Volume, Bharatiya Vidya, Vol. XLV, XLVI and XLVII, 1985-86-87, 1987.

85. Niyativāda (Predestination, Fatalism, Determinism)—Paper contributed to Mahavira and His Teachings) publ. by Bhagwan Mahavira 2500th Nirvana Mahotsava Samiti, Bombay, 1977, Sole distributor ; L.D. Institute of Indology, Ahmedabad-9.

86. Marriage Rites : Hindu and Jain- Paper read at the Seminar on Dharmaśāstra organised by MM Dr.P.V. Kane Research Institute, a wing of The Asiatic Society of Bombay, Bombay-400023.

87. The Uttarādhyayana Sūtra on Brahmanism-Paper read at the All India Seminar on Jain Canonical Literature held on 16-18 October, 1986, by Prakrit Pali Dept. of Gujarat University, Ahmedabad-9.

88. Abhinavabhāratī : Professor Kangle's Emendations, Paper published in Vāṅmaya, Vol. II., No.1. January 1989, published by Gujarat Sahitya Academy. Gandhinagar (Gujarat State).

89. Jain Aesthetic Concepts—A paper read at the Seminar on Jain Culture and Performing Arts, organised by the National Centre for Performing Arts, later published in Jain Culture And Performing Arts (Proceedings of the Seminar) by the National Centre for the Performing Arts, Nariman Point, Bombay-400021, 1990.

90. Abhinavagupta's Ideas on the Nature of Poetic Beauty (As expressed in his Locana)—Paper contributed to Pt. Bechardas Doshi Commemmoration Volume, publ. in Aspects of Jainology, Vol. 2. by P.V. Research Institute, ITI Road, Varanasi-5, 1990.

91. (Syādvāda) Relativity and Absolutism-Paper read at the Seminar on Jain Philosophy and Epistemology held on 22-25 December, 1990, organised by B.L. Institute of Indology, Delhi.

92. Discovery through Restoration—(Discovery of hitherto unknown works through restoration of corrupt passages on Sanskrit Poetics)—MM Dr. P.V. Kane Memorial Lecture for 1990—Published in The Journal of the Asiatic Society of Bombay 1991.

93. Rājaśekhara, the Critic—Paper contributed to Dr. G.K. Bhat Commemmoration Volume.

94. Dual Nature of Sāttvikabhāvas-Journal, Oriental Institute, Baroda, Vol. 38, Nos, 1-2 (Sept-Dec. 1988) Baroda, 1990.

95. Gāthāsaptaśatī (Uttarārdha) and Śephālikāgāthās 701-1004-Review Article in Navabharata (Marathi) No. 8. May, 1990.

96. Rasa Theory and Puruṣārthas—JASB, Volume 64-66 for 1989-91 (Combined) (New Series) 1993. 97.

97. Abhinavabhāratī Text: Restorod—JASB, Volume 67-68 for 1992-93 (Combined) (New Series) 1994.

98. On Restoring Corrupt Prakrit verses. Vidyopāsanā : Studies in Honour of Dr. H.C. Bhayani, 1999.

99. Mahimabhaṭṭa's views on How Rasas arise and They are enjoyed by Sahṛdayas. JASB Volume-71 for 1996 (New Series) 1997.

100. Bharata's Concet of Bhāva-JASB, Volums-71 for 1996 (New Series) 1997.

101. Abhinavabhāratī Text: Restorod—JASB Volume 72 for 1997 (New Series) 1997.

102. Abhinavabhāratī Text : Restored. (Nāṭyaśāstra Chapter XIX : Sandhi-nirūpaṇa). JASB Volume 73 for 1998 (New Series) 1998.

103. Abhinavagupta's Concet of Kāvya and Nāṭya. JASB, Volume-74 for 1999 (New Series) 2000.

104. Abhinavabhāratī Text : Restored. JASB Volume 75 for 2000 (New Series) 2001.

105. Haribhadra's Viṁśativiṁsikā : An Approach.—N.N. Bhattacharyya (ed.) : Jainism and Prakrit in Ancient and Medieval India : Essays for Jagdish Chandra Jain, New Delhi, Manohar Publishers & Distributors, 1994.

REVIEWS / REVIEW ARTICLES

1. The Daśarūpaka of Dhanañjaya with the commentary Avaloka by Dhanika and the Sub-Commentary Laghuṭīkā by Bhaṭṭa Nrsimha, ed by T. Venkatacharya, reviewed in Journal, Oriental Institute, Baroda, Vol. XIX, No. 3, March 1970.

2. Saptaśatīsāra with Bhāvadīpikā of Vema Bhūpāla, along with *Chappannaya-gāhāo* (Text and Chāyā) by Dr. A.N. Upadhye, Shivaji University, Kolhapur—Reviewed in Journal, University of Bombay, Arts No. Vol. XL, No. 76, October, 1971.

3. Nandisuttaṁ Aṇuogaddārāiṃ, ed. by Muniśrī, Puṇya-vijaya and Pt. A.M. Bhojaka, publ. by Shri Mahavira Jaina Vidyalaya, Bombay 400036, Reviewed in Sambodhi Vol. 2, No.4, Jan. 1974. L.D. Institute of Indology, Ahmedabad—380009.

4. Two Recent works on Sanskrit Aesthetics—Reviewed in Journal, Indian Philosophy, ed. by Bimal K. Matilal, publ. by D. Reidel Publishing Company, Dordrecht, Holland, 1973.

5. Aesthetic Rapture : The Rasādhyāya of the Nāṭyaśāstra (in two volumes)—Reviewed in Ālocanā (Marathi Periodical) July, 1974.

6. A Recent Edition of Dhvanyāloka-Review Article in the Annals, B.O.R. Institute,Vol. LVII, Poona, 1976.

7. A.K. Warder, Indian Kāvya Literature, Vol.I (Literary Criticism) Motilal Banarasidas, Delhi, 1972, pp. xvii, 281—Review in Journal of the Asiatic Society of Bombay, Volumes 47-48/1972-73 (New Series).

8. The Vakroktijīvita of Kuntaka, ed. by Dr. K. Krishnamoorthy, publ. by Karnataka University. Dharwad, 1977- Reviewed in Aryan Path, Jan-Feb. 1978.

9-12. The following four books have been reviewed in the Journal of the Asiatic Society of Bombay, Volumes 49-50-51, 1974-75-76 (New Series), Bombay, 1979.

(1) A Cultural Study of the Niśītha Cūrṇi by Madhusen.
(2) Ānandavardhana's Dhvanyāloka, Critically ed by Dr. K. Krishnamoorthy.
(3) Malayamāruta ed by Dr. V. Raghavan.
(4) The Pādatāḍitaka of Śyāmilaka, Part 2, A Translation by G.H. Schokker.

13. Dhvanyāloka, Ānandavardhanano Dhvani-vicāra (Gujarati) by Nagindas Parekh, publ. by Gujarat Sahitya Parisad, Ahmedabad-380 009, 1981—review in Sambodhi.

14-16. The following three books were reviewed in the Journal of the Asiatic Society of Bombay. MM Dr. P.V. Kane Birth Centenary Volume, Volumes 52-53, 1977-78 (New Series) Bombay, 400023, 1981.

(1) Ṣaṭ-triṁśat-tattva-sandoha with the commentary of Rajanaka Ananda Kavi, by Dr. Debarata, Sen Sharma.
(2) The Hindu Conception of the Deity, by Bharatan Kumarappa.
(3) Kāvyaprakāśadarpaṇa of Viśvanātha ed. by Goparaju Rama.

17-18. The following two Books were reviewed in the Asiatic Society of Bombay, Volumes 54.55/1979-80, Bombay, 1983.

(1) Kṛtyakalpataru of Bhaṭṭa Lakṣmīdhara, Volume IX. Pratiṣthā Kāṇḍa) ed. by K.V. Rangasvamy Aiyangar, Oriental Institute, Baroda, 1979.
(2) Triśaṇkuḥ by D.D. Bahulikar—Rendered into English and Marathi by Arvind Mangrulkar, Pune, 1980.

19. Prakrit Bhāṣāoṅkā Tulanātmaka Vyākaraṇa (evaṁ unmeṁ prāksanskrit Tattva) Sambodhi, Volume 11, April 1982, January 1983.

20. Bharatanu Nāṭyaśāstra, Adhyaya VI with Abhinavabhāratī (Along with translation and commentary in Gujarati) by Dr. Tapasvi Nandi, publ. by Gujarat University, Ahmedabad, 380009, Reviewed in the Annals, BOR Institute, Vol. LXIV, Poona, 1983.

21. Tārāyana (TĀRĀGANA) : An Anthology of Bappabhaṭṭi's Prakrit Gāthās compiled by Śaṅkuka with an Anonymous Sanskrit Commentary ed by Dr. H.C. Bhayani, Prakrit Text Society, C/o. L.D. Institute of Indology. Ahmedabad-380009, 1987. (Review published in Sambodhi, 1998).

22. The Composition of the Nāṭyaśāstra, Srinivasa Ayya Srinivasan, Studien Zur-Indologie Und Iranistic Monographie I, Dr. Inge Wezler Verlag Fur Orientalische Fachpublikationen Reinbek— 1980—Reviewed in Journal of the Asiatic Society of Bombay. Dr. Bhagwanlal Indraji Memorial Volume, Volumes 56-59/ 1981-84 (New Series) Bombay, 400023.

23. Women in Ancient Indian Tales : By J.C. Jain and Margaret Walter, publ., by Mittal Publications. Delhi-110035, 1987—Reviewed for the Journal—Asiatic Society of Bombay—Vol. published in 1991.

24. Rasa Theory and Allied Problems ; by G.K. Bhat, pub. by the M.S. University of Baroda, Baroda, 1984-Reviewed for the Journal- The Asiatic - Society of Bombay, Vol. published in 1991.

25. Paṇḍitarāja Jagannātha (Marathi) by Prof. R.B. Athavale, publ. by Tilak Maharashtra Vidyapeeth, reviewed in Vaikharī, Marathi Periodical.

26. Rājaśekhara's Kāvyamīmāṁśā (Marathi) by Kamal Abhyankar. JASB Volumes 64-66 for 1989-91 (Combined) (New Series) 1993.

27. Studies in Early Jainism (Selected research articles) by Jagdishchandra Jain, JASB Volumes 64-66 for 1989-91 (Combined) (New Series) 1993.

28. A Study of Mahimabhaṭṭa's Vyaktiviveka by C. Rajendran, JASB Volumes 64-66 for 1989-91 Combined) New Series, 1993.

29. Religion and Philosophy of the Jainas by Virchand Gandhi, ed by Nagin J. Shah—JASB Volumes 67-68 for 1992-93 (Combined) (New Series) 1994.

30. Studies in the Dharmaśāstra by S.G. Moghe, JASB Volumes 67-68 for 1992-93 (Combined) (New Series) 1994.

31. Perspectives in the Vedic and the Classical Sanskrit Heritage by G.V. Davane—JASB Volume 70 for 1995 (New Series) 1995.

32. Bharata's Nāṭyaśāstra, Chapters 1-2 (Text only) and 6 (with the commentary Abhinavabhāratī) by T.S. Nandi—JASB Volume 70 for 1995 (New Series) 1995.

33. Vidyāṣṭakam by Muni Shri Niyamasagarji, JASB Volume 71 for 1996 (New Series) 1997.

34. A Transcultural Approach to Sanskrit Poetics by C. Rajendran, JASB Colume 71 for 1996 (New Series)-1997.

35. Śivasūtra, tr. (Marathi) by G.V. Tagare. JASB Volume 71 for 1996 (New Series) 1997.

36. Bharata's Nāṭyaśātra—Chapter VI with the commentary Abhinavabhāratī and Chapters XVI, XVIII and XIX Volume II, Intro. Tr.—Notes in Gujarati by T.S. Nandi, JASB Volume 71 for 1996 (New Series) 1997.

37. Gītārtha Darśana ed by Krishna S. Arjunwadkar. JASB Volume 71 for 1996 (New Series) 1997.

38. Indological Studies by H.C. Bhayani- JASB Volume 72 for 1997 (New Series) 1997.

39. Raghuvaṁśa of Kālidāsa, ed., by Rewa Prasad Dwivedi, JASB Volume 72 for 1997 (New Series) 1997.

40. The Ṛtu-Saṁhāra of Kālidāsa ed by Rewa Prasad Dwivedi-JASB Volume 72 for 1997 (New Series) 1997.

41. Vaidikatva in Indian Philosophy and Religion, ed. S.G. Mudgal, JASB Volume 73 for 1998 (New Series) 1998.

42. Abhijñāna Śākuntala of Kālidāsa by with the com. of by Ghanaśyāma, Ed. Ms. Punam Raval and V.M. Bhaṭt—JASB Volume 73 for 1978 (New Series) 1998.

43. Ānandavardhana's Dhvanyāloka with Abhinavagupta's commentary Locana by T.S. Nandi—JASB Volume 73 for 1998 (New Series) 1998.

44. Ācārāṅga ; Paḍhama Suta-Khandha, Paḍhama Aijhayaṇa (Ācārāṅga : Prathama Śruta-Skandha, Prathama Adhyayana) Ed. K.R. Chandra, JASB Volume 73 for 1998 (New Series) 1998.

45. Isibhāsiyāṁ Kā Prakrit-Sanskrit Śabdakośa, prepared and Edited by K.R. Chandra—JASB Volume 74 for 1999 (New Series) 2000.

46. Sāhityaśārīrakam (Sanskrit) by Rewa Prasad Dwivedi, JASB Volume 74-for 1999 (New Series) 2000.

47. Indological Studies, Volume 2, by H.C. Bhayani. JASB Volume 74 for 1999 (New Series). 2000.

48. Yādavendramahodaya of Nīlakaṇṭha with the commentary of V.S. Ranade, by Siddharth Y. Wakankar, JASB Volume 75 for 2000 (New Series) 2001.

49. Influence of Nyāya Philosophy on Sanskrit Poetics by Sweta Prajapati, JASB Volume 75 for 2000 (New Series) 2001.

50. Sandeśarāsaka of Abdul Rehman, Ed. H.C. Bhayani, JASB Volume 75 for 2000 (New Series) 2001.

51. Jināgamon Ki Mūlabhāṣā, Ed. Acharya Vijayashil Chandramani and K.R. Chandra. JASB Volume 75 for 2000 (New Series) 2001.

52. AMRITA: The Collected Papers contributed by Professor A. M. Ghatage. JASB Volume 76 for 2001 (New Series) 2002.

53. Makaranda (Madhukar Anant Mehendale Festschrift) Ed. M.A. Dhaky, J. B. Shah. JASB Volume 76 for 2001 (New Series) 2002.

SECTION-I

REMINISCENCES

I.1

PROF. V. M. KULAKARNI : AS I FOUND HIM

Prof. Rewa Prasad Dwivedi

In Prof. Vāmana Mahādeva Kulakarṇi, I found both deepest thinking and penetrating insight. Beside the miracle he has done in his two volumes of *'Prākṛta Verses in Sanskrit Works on Poetics'*, he has the credit of the authorship of several learned articles on Sanskrit poetics on some subtle but important subjects as are published in the volume *Studies in Sanskrit Sāhitya Śāstra* (1983,1993, Sarasvati Pustak Bhandar, Ahmedabad). What was thought beyond the reach of the scholars had been made clear in Sanskrita-chāyā also on the obscure/corrupt Prākṛta quotations in Sanskrit-poetics in the first two volumes only by Prof.V.M.Kulakarṇī. By the way Prof.Kulakarṇī has investigated at least up to a considerable extent, the lost text of *Harivijaya* of Sarvasena, referred to by Ānandavardhana and Abhinavagupta. It is Prof. V. M. Kulakarṇi who has the credit to recognise and introduce some passages from the work *Kalpalatāviveka* in the text of lost *Abhinavabhāratī* like Prof. K. Krisnamurthy. So also Prof. Kulakarṇī has consulted and utilised some quotations from Hemacandra's *Kavyānuśāsanaviveka* also in the Edition of Bharata's *Nāṭyaśāstra*. I pay my highest regards to these scholars as this is the only way to procure the lost works and both these scholars have marched vigorously towards it. Sorry to declare my misfortune not to obtain the remaining portions (canto 1 as also 2-4) of Hemādri's *Darpaṇa* on *Raghuvaṁśa* from any source in India and abroad. It is due to lack of investigation.

In Prof.V.M.Kulakarṇī I found a profound knowledge of English language, capacity to express his thoughts in it with an artistic but a balanced way, untouched with भावुकता. Truely he is well educated in the art of essay writing. His monograph on Prof. Śaṅkara Pānduraṅga Paṇḍit, published in the *Bulletin of Asiatic Society Bombay* (1996) is a unique record about the scholar.

Prof.V.M.Kulakarṇī is found habitual of conveying his dislikes into likes if the ground is meritorious. In the eighth decade of twentieth century Prof. V.M. Kulakarṇi wrote me a letter and expressed his view: 'though we do not have much regard for Hindi works in Sanskrit, yet, I appreciate your endeavor in this field'. *(These are not his actual words)*

My Raghuvaṁśa had been published in 1993 by the Sāhitya Akademi, Delhi. In this work I myself had made one serious mistake. It is Prof. V.M. Kulakarṇi who pointed out the same and wrote a letter to me and I at once accepted my mistake. One other change in the text was underlined by him which I explained in a justified argumentation and expressed that, that was my contribution to the *Raghuvaṁśa* edition. That he accepted. The work has been done in Varanasi, published from Delhi, yet corrected by the Bombay scholar is the classic episode in Sanskrit studies of today.

I would like to point that in his outstanding work "*Outline of Abhinavagupta's Aesthetics*" (1998, Sarasvati Pustak Bhandar Ahmedabad) Prof. Kulakarṇī has touched some *significant* points of Sanskrit poetics covering the Rasa theory of Abhinava's philosophical ground wherein he has given much stress to the *'Alaukikatva'* of Rasa experience. Abhinavagupta explains some typical points of poetics otherwise, even though he is regarded as great and unparalleled Ācārya in the field of Poetics. It was Abhinavagupta who came forward to support the Utopian theory of Dhvani introduced and preached as the highest charasteristic in art especially Poetic Art coupled with a function of *Vyañjanā* by Ānandavardhana all of a sudden. Abhinava could come in its support even going against the popular thinking of established philosophies. It was due to the *Alaukikatva* theory also that was meaning "*Dhvani is not available in worldly life, it is a secret of Art alone*", Prof. Kulkarṇī explained the same point in his several articles very clearly.

Mahimabhaṭṭa refuted Dhvani bravely that won admiration from not an ordinary scholar but from one of the sharpest called Śrīsrīharṣa like his predecessor Jayanta Bhaṭṭa. For Dhvani, Śrīhrṣa writes as under which can not be overlooked in any case

दिशि दिशि गिरिग्रावाण: स्वां वमन्तु सरस्वतीं
तुलयत मिथस्तामापात: स्फुरद्ध्वनिडम्बराम्।
स पुनरपर: क्षीरोदन्वान् यदीयमुदीयते
मथितरमृतं खेदच्छेदि प्रमोदनमोदनम्।। नैषधीयचरितम् २२.१५१

The same poet-philosopher writes the immortal lines for Mahima Bhaṭṭa, the famous refuter of Dhvani and the writer of work called *Vyaktiviveka* like this:

दोषं व्यक्तिविवेकेऽमुं कविलोकविळोकविलोचने।
काव्यमीमांसिषु प्राप्तमहिमा महिमाऽऽदृत।। खण्डनखण्डखाद्य (चौखम्भासं० पृष्ठ ७४४, १९७०).

Here the term *vilocana* is noteworthy. It suggests the *abhāva* of Abhinava's *Locana* on *Dhvanyāloka*. No surprise if he indicated *Dhvanyāloka* by the word *loka* in this verse. On the other hand the adjectives used for Mahima Bhaṭṭa are notable in this verse .

Even then Abhinava's stand, in the history of Indian Aesthetics, had been regarded as final word by later poeticians like Mammaṭa in Vedic line and Hemacandra in others. Prof. Kulakarṇī has a soft corner in his mind for both the stands. I think it is Prof. Kulakarṇī's generosity and humbleness towards old writers.

Prof. Kulakarṇī has given due importance to the *Kāvyānusāśana* of Hemacandra. I too regard Hemacandra much more than Mammaṭa. Hemacandra reduced the ten *Ullāsas* of *Kāvyaprakāśa* into eight very successfully. Really he wanted to give the honorable title of *Aṣṭādhyāyī* to a work of poetics. He has given scientific explanation to the theory of *Sāttvika Bhāva*. For a seminar Gujrat University invited both of us. I put my view on Hemacandra, but missed to refer to the theory of *Sāttvika Bhāva*. It was Prof. Kulakarṇi who raised the question who drew my attention to this fact for which I thanked him.

For his deep thinking of important, yet confusing subjects of Sanskrit poetics I extend to Prof.V.M. Kulakarṇī my heartiest honour and think he is second to none in this field.

In the field of Śāstric treatment of very subtle subjects like the *Rasaniṣapatti* in *Sāhitya Śāstra,* Prof. V.M. Kulakarṇī could dare to deal with the stage of *Bhukti* of Bhaṭṭanāyaka like *Alaukikatva* in his several articles wherein he followed the thoughts of Abhinavagupta in toto, yet on the matter of *Dhvanyāloka* 1.5 he was with others who could not follow Abhinavagupta on this point. He invited a paper from me on this subject and appreciated it, though it was not in favour of Abhinavagupta. So also Prof. Kulakarṇi wrote a paper on the concept of 'Bhāva of Mahimabhaṭṭa.'

It is Prof. V.M. Kulakarṇī who pointed out the existence of *Sāmānyaguṇa* noted by a few poeticians like the writer of *Agnipurāṇa*. All the ten *Guṇas* are categorized as *Sāmanyaguṇas* having their ability to realize as the *Guṇas* of *Rasa* in which stage they fall into the category of *Viśeṣaguṇas*.

Even today on the Indian soil there are some scholars who are perfect in every sphere of thought. If I say '*if a work is to be entrusted to a scholar who would finish the same with a standard up to the mark there is only one and he is Prof. V.M. Kulakarṇī* who will always prove himself true to the letters of this statement.'

With these words I wish to write that may long live Prof. V.M. Kulakarṇī and serve Literature, especially Sanskrit coupled with Prākṛta more and more for which he is honoured with the highest award in India "*The Certificate of Honour" by His Highness The President of India* a few years ago, which he deserves in every respect.

यो *वामनोऽपि* हि *महानथ* विद्वद्वरेण्यो भूत्वाऽपि मेदुरितमार्दवभावभव्यः।
नान्यः स केवलमिमं प्रविहाय धन्यधन्यं विवेकनिपुणं *कुलकर्णिवर्य्यम्*॥
जीवेदसौ 'परमभागवतः कलासु', वर्षाणि पङ्कजभुवो गणनातिगानि।
आराधयन् भगवतीं वचसां सवित्रीं वाग्देवतामभिनवैः प्रतिभाप्रसूनैः॥

I.2

महामहिमशालिषु स्वनामधन्येषु पूज्यचरणेषु

–प्रो. डा. श्री वामन महादेव (वी.एम.) कुलकर्णि–महोदयेषु वाक्यपुष्पोपहारः

डॉ. भगवतीप्रसाद पण्डया

भारतदेशीय दक्षिणदिग्भागे समागते कोल्हापुरसंज्ञकनगरपरिसरस्थ 'अजर' संज्ञकग्रामे २२-११-९७ दिनाङ्के लब्धजनुषां मुम्बई-अहमदाबाद-उत्तरगुजरातस्थितपाटनक(पाटणं)स्थानसमागतविद्यासंस्थासु संस्कृत-प्राकृत-भाषयोः प्राध्यापकपदं निदेशकपदं चालङ्कुर्वतां संस्कृतालङ्कारशास्त्रेऽनितरसाधारणं पाण्डित्यं जुषमाणानां, तस्मिन् विषये च चूडामणिभूतग्रन्थजातं प्रपठ्य प्रपाठ्य च सूक्ष्मातिसूक्ष्मसमीक्षणेन लेखन-निर्माणसंशोधनसदृशप्रवृत्तिषु नक्तन्दिवं संलग्नानामनेकानेकग्रन्थ-संशोधनलेखसेवां कृतवतां विपश्चिदपश्चिमानां श्रीराष्ट्रपतिपुरस्कृतानां गुरुवराणां प्रो. डॉ. श्री कुलकर्णिमहोदयानां विषये किं लिखामि? कतमेन प्रकारेण वा लिखामि केन प्रकारेण वा मदीयं स्नेहविशेषं दर्शयामीति वैयाकुलीपूर्णः भावाविष्टचेता अहं स्वल्पं वाक्पुष्पोपहारं समर्पयामि। अत्र प्रथमं तु कैश्चिद्यथामति निर्मितैः पद्यप्रसूनैः तेषां सपर्यामनेन प्रकारेण वितनोमि :–

संशोधनेऽथ कवने च समीक्षणे यः प्राथम्यमाकलयते विदुषां वरिष्ठः।
काव्ये च कोमलमतिर्निकषश्च शास्त्रे नित्यं जयेद् वररुचिः कुलकर्णिसूरिः॥१॥

मान्यो गुणैकनिलयो ध्रुवशक्तिशाली लोकोत्तरप्रथितसद्गुणरत्नमाली।
सत्यार्जवप्रमुदितो मतिकान्तिशोभी जीयाच्चिरं गुरुवरः कुलकर्णिसूरिः॥२॥

यस्यात्मशक्तिरनघा विपुलं च धैर्यं चित्ते समुच्छलति शान्तिमहापयोधिः।
वाग्मी सदोन्नतसुमङ्गलकर्मकारी जीयात्सदा शुभमतिः कुलकर्णिसूरिः॥३॥

आशैशवात्समभवद्धृतिमांस्तितिक्षुः संसारभूमिबहुविघ्ननिराकरिष्णुः।
यः सर्वदा सुरसरस्वतीसेवनाढ्यो जीयाच्चिरं गुरुरयं कुलकर्णिसूरिः॥४॥

प्रकाशशीलश्च मनीषिवर्यो यो वन्दनीयो धृतिभूतिशाली।
यः कर्मयोगी सुपवित्रवृत्तिर्जीयाच्चिरं श्रीकुलकर्णिसूरिः॥५॥

नैसर्गिकानन्दनिधिर्महात्मा विवेकविज्ञानविशुद्धचेताः।
माङ्गल्यसमृद्धिनिकेतनं यो जीयाद् गुरुर्नः कुलकर्णिवर्यः॥६॥

यः संस्कृतं स्वोच्छ्वसितं यथैव संसेव्य नित्यं परिमोदमानः।
माधुर्यसौजन्ययशोम्बुधिर्यो, जीयाच्चिरं श्रीकुलकर्णिसूरिः॥७॥

संस्कृतम्प्राकृतञ्चेति यस्यास्ते लोचनद्वयम्।
सव्यसाची च यः प्रोक्तः कुलकर्णी जयेद् गुरुः॥८॥

अथैकदा क्वचिद् गोष्ठीविशेषे पूज्यतमा अस्मद्गुरुवर्य्याः श्रीरामचन्द्रआठवलेमहोदयाः, तत्रभवतो डॉ. कुलकर्णिमहोदयान् तेषां संस्कृते प्राकृते च भाषासाहित्ये समानाधिकारं निरीक्ष्याकस्मादेव 'सव्यसाचिन्' इति पदेनतान् सम्बोधयामासुः। जानन्ति हि समेऽपि विद्वांसो यत् पाण्डुपुत्रधनञ्जयस्य अर्जुनस्य विषये भगवता श्रीकृष्णेन भगवद्गीतायाम् एकादशेऽध्याये 'निमित्तमात्रं भव सव्यसाचिन्' इति पदं प्रायोजि। सव्येन-वामहस्तेन, सचितुं-शरान् संधातुं शीलमस्येति व्युत्पत्त्या अर्जुनो वामहस्तेनापि शरप्रक्षेपणकर्मणि नदीष्णः इति हि सर्वेषां विदुषां विदितचरम्। ततश्च डॉ. कुलकर्णिमहोदयानां संस्कृते प्राकृते च साहित्ये परमं चरमं च कौशलं निरीक्ष्य, विनोदेन प्रेम्णा च यत्सम्बोधनं एतेषां विषये कृतवन्त इति स्थाने एव।

अथ उपरितनानुष्पुद्छन्दसि यद् गुरुः इति पदं अस्माभिः प्रयुक्तम्, तत्र 'गुरु' पदविषये किञ्चिच्चिन्तयामः। गिरति गिलति शिष्यस्य सविलासमज्ञानबन्धमसौ गुरुः इति व्याकरणदृष्ट्या तौदादिक (षाष्ठगणीय) 'गॄ निगरणे' इत्यस्माद्धातोर्निष्पन्नो गुरुशब्दः डॉ. कुलकर्णिविषये याथार्थ्यं भजते।

अथात्राधुना गुरुपदे समायाते तत्सम्बद्धः शिष्यापरपर्यायः 'छात्र' शब्दोऽपि दृष्टिपदं समायाति। 'छत्र' शब्दात् गुरोर्दोषाणामावरणं शीलमस्येति छात्रः 'छत्रादिभ्यो णः' (4/4/62) इति पाणिनिसूत्रेण 'ण' प्रत्यये विहिते छात्रशब्दः सिध्यति। किन्तु तदीयं विवरणं, अस्य सूत्रस्य वृत्तौ सिद्धान्तकौमुद्यां यद्दत्तं गुरोर्दोषाणां आवरणं शीलं यस्येति तन्नं प्रतीतिकरम्, ततश्च किञ्चिदसङ्गतं तत् प्रतिभाति। वस्तुतस्तु अत्र भगवता महाभाष्यकारेण प्रदत्तं विवरणमेव मह्यं रोचते तच्चानेन प्रकारेण :—यथा छत्रम् आतपादिभ्यः स्वामिनं रक्षति, तद्वत् शिष्योऽपि (छात्रोऽपि) गुरोर्जीवने आच्छादनरूपो भूत्वा, गुरुं सेवते ततश्छात्र इति।

अथेदानीं गुरु-शिष्ययोः सम्बन्धविषये विचार्यमाणे 'षष्ठी स्थानेयोगा' (१/१/४९) इत्येतत्सूत्रोपरितने महाभाष्ये भगवता पतञ्जलिना चतुःप्रकारकाः सम्बन्धा दर्शिताः। ते च (१) आर्थाः (२) यौनाः (३) स्रौवाः (४) मौखाश्चेति। (१) तत्र व्यावहारिके जगति दृश्यमानपदार्थवस्तुविनिमयेन निर्मीयमाणः सम्बन्धः आर्थः (२) पितापुत्रयोः सम्बन्धः शुक्रशोणितजन्यो यौनः (३) वैदिकयज्ञयागकर्मणि स्रुवेण

अग्नौ घृताहुतिं सम्पादयतः ऋत्विजो यजमानेन सहा यः सम्बन्धः सः स्रौवः (४) अथ च गुरु शिष्ययोर्यः सम्बन्धः सः मौखः तथाहि गुरु-मुखान्निष्क्रामतो ज्ञानज्योतिषः शिष्यमुखे प्रवेशेन जायमानः सम्बन्धः स मौख इति। तदेवम् अत्र गुरुपदे विव्रियमाणे आनुषङ्गिकरीत्या शिष्यस्य सम्बन्धस्य च विषये किञ्चिद्विचार्य गुरुवरडॉ.कुलकर्णिनिर्मिते सम्पादिते च साहित्यविषये किञ्चिद् विवक्षुरस्मि।

गुरुवरैनिर्मितानां सम्पादितानाञ्च ग्रन्थानां कृतीनाम्, अथ चैतेर्विलिखितानामनेकानेकसंशोधनलेखानां परममहती सूचिर्विस्तरभिया नात्रोलिख्यते, किन्तु स्थालीपुलाकन्यायेन तत्सामग्रीतः किञ्चिद् उद्धृत्य लिलेखिषुरस्मि।

(१) 'अलङ्कारशास्त्रीयसंस्कृतग्रन्थेषु प्राकृतपद्यानि (Prakrit Verses in Sanskrit Works on Poetics) इत्येतच्छीर्षकेण समलङ्कृतस्य अस्य ग्रन्थरत्नस्य खण्डद्वयम्। डॉ. कुलकर्णिमहोदयैः सम्पादितेऽस्मिन् खण्डद्वये, तैर्विचारिता ये विषयास्ते खलु एतेषामसाधारणं समीक्षापाटवं प्राकृतादिकासु भाषासु एतेषाम् अप्रतियमं वैदुष्यं परिचयन्ति। एतस्मिन् ग्रन्थरत्ने संस्कृतालङ्कारशास्त्रविविधग्रन्थेषु विद्यमानानां, तैस्तैर्लेखकैः समुद्धृतानां १६०० संख्याकानां प्राकृतपद्यानां पाठशुद्धिं विधाय, तत्र दृश्यमानान् लुप्तांशान् संशोध्य, महान्तञ्च परिश्रमं कृत्वा, तन्मूलमन्विष्य, यथार्थपाठप्रदानं-सूचनं वा विहितं तत् न खलु साधारणं कार्यम्। तेषाञ्च पद्यानाम् आङ्ग्लभाषायाम् अनुवादोऽपि एतैरकारि इति सुवर्णे सुगन्धः।

अथ तत्रभवता आनन्दवर्धनेन यस्य सादरं निर्देशः कृतः तेन कविपुङ्गवेन सर्वसेनकविना, रचितस्य प्राकृतभाषायां समुपनिबद्धस्य रिविजयनामकरस्य काव्यस्य साङ्गोपाङ्गमध्ययनं विधाय, एतद्विषयकसर्वाङ्गीणसाहित्यिकसामग्रीपरिचायकः ग्रन्थविशेषः (Monograph) डॉ. कुलकर्णिभि र्लिखितः तत्खलु परमं विशिष्टं कार्यम्। अयं खलु ग्रन्थोऽद्यावधि अदृश्यतां गतः, अप्रकाशितश्चासीत् स हि प्राकाश्यं नीतः। एतद्विषये नूनं डॉ. कुलकर्णिनोभिनन्दनमर्हन्ति।

अथ भोजराजविषये विविधसामग्री प्रदापकः Monograph ग्रन्थविशेषोऽपि गुरुवरैर्लिखितः।

एवमेव प्राचीनालङ्कारिकैः समुपेक्षितानां, श्रीमता राजशेखरेण स्वीय 'काव्यमीमांसायां' विवेचितानां 'काव्यहरण' 'कविसमयादिकानेकेषां' विषयाणां चर्चा श्रीकुलकर्णिभिः स्वलिखिते साहित्यशास्त्रे सिविस्तरं व्यधायि। (अत्र अहमेतन्निवेदयामि यत् मया काव्यमीमांसायाः साङ्गोपाङ्गमध्ययनं कुलकर्णिगुरूणां सविधे विहितमिति मदीयो महान् हर्षः)

अत्रैतदपि सहर्षं निवेदयितुकामोऽस्मि यत्, डॉ. कुलकर्णिमहोदयः स्वीयमातृभाषा-महाराष्ट्र-भाषावत् अथ च संस्कृतप्राकृतविज्ञाः एते गुजराती (गौर्जरीं) भाषामपि साधिकारं वक्तुं समर्था इति आनन्दविस्फूर्जथुर्मे हृदयावच्छिन्नाकारशो बोभवीतीति।

डॉ. कुलकर्णिमहोदयानामेतदपि महत्तरं कार्यं,–यद् 'भरतनाट्यशात्र'स्य षष्ठाध्याये मूलग्रन्थमाश्रित्य श्रीमद् अभिनवगुप्तपादैः लिखितायां अभिनवभारतीटीकायां स्वीयम् अपूर्वं संशोधनम्। 'अभिनव-भारतीटीकायां काल-क्रम-समुपजातलुप्तांशकाः पाठभेदाः, भ्रष्टपाठाः त्रुटिताः खण्डिताश्च, मूलग्रन्थप्रतिलिपि-

कृतप्रमादानवधानदूषिता: तेषां सर्वेषां संशोधनं कुलकर्णिमहोदयै: अनवरतं तदीयमध्ययनं विधाय सशास्त्रं तत्तत्पाठशुद्धिर्विहिता दर्शिता च। एतदर्थञ्च कलिकालसर्वज्ञ श्रीमद्हेमचन्द्रसूरि विरचित-काव्यानुशासनोपरि हेमचन्द्रविलिखितं 'विवेक' आदि टीकाजातं प्रविलोक्य अभ्यस्य च एतद्विषयकानश्च ग्रन्थानभ्यस्य, तत्सम्बद्धसामग्रीजातमन्विष्य या पाठशुद्धिर्विहिता तत्खलु कुलकर्णिनां संस्कृतत्व अलङ्कारशास्त्रे सुमहत्तरम्प्रदानमिति।

(२) इत: परमपि अनेकानि बहुमूल्यवन्ति ग्रन्थरत्नानि एतैर्निर्मितानि। अत्र समग्रतयैतानि लिखितुं न पार्यते किन्तु दिङ्मात्रेणात्र तन्निर्दिश्यते, तद्यथा

(1) Studies in Sanskrit Sāhitya-śāstra.

(2) Some Aspects of the Rasa Theory.

(3) An Anthology of Jain Texts.

(4) शृङ्गारार्णवचन्द्रिका of विजयवर्णी,

(5) जयदेव's गीतगोविन्द with King मानाङ्क's Commentary

(6) आचार्यहेमचन्द्र's काव्यानुशासनम् (सहसम्पादनम्)

(7) वाचक उमास्वाति's प्रशमरतिप्रकरणम् (भाषानुवाद-टिप्पणिभ्यां संवलितम्)

(8) The Story of Rāma in Jain Literature

(9) भोज and the हरिविजय of सर्वसेन (With Introduction, Definitive Text, Translation and Notes)

(10) Outline of अभिनवगुप्त's Aesthetics

(11) More Studies in Sanskrit साहित्यशास्त्र.

तदेवम् इत:पराण्यपि अनेकानि तेषां ग्रन्थरत्नानि अद्यापि साहित्याकाशे प्रकाशं वितन्वन्ति।

अथ गुरुवराणां डॉ. श्रीकुणकर्णिमहोदयानां विविधविषयपराणि संशोधनसमीक्षणपत्राण्यपि अहमदाबाद, वडोदरा, देहली, मुम्बई, पाटण, पुणे सदृश विद्वद्भूमिसंस्थितसुविख्यातप्राच्यविद्यासंस्थानेभ्य: अन्याभिश्च शिक्षणसंस्थाभि: प्रकाशितानि मुद्रितानि पत्राणि दर्शं दर्शं, तदन्तर्गतविपुलसामग्रीं पाठं पाठं जरीहृष्यन्ते अस्माकं स्वान्तानि। एतानि खलु पत्राणि प्रचुरसंशोधनपूर्णानि असंदिग्धानि, सारवन्ति विश्वतोमुखानि वरीवृत्यन्ते।

डॉ. श्रीकुलकर्णिनिर्मितं सम्पादितसाहित्यं च समवलोक्य, एतत्साहित्यं पाणिनि-सूत्र-निर्दिष्ट-'उपज्ञात' साहित्यकक्षामधिगाहते।

अथात्र 'उपज्ञात' साहित्यसन्दर्भे विचार्यमाणे एतत्साहित्यं तादृशं भवति, यत् केनापि विशिष्टेन पूर्वतनाचार्येण लिखितेषु ग्रन्थेषु मौलिकं संशोधनमध्ययनं च विधाय सर्वप्रथमवारमेव तन्निहितं गूढं विचारजातं, विदुषाम्पुरतः, संस्थाप्यते। तत्र तत्र च स्वीया नवनवा युक्तयः नैजा अभिनवा विचाराः प्रस्तूयन्ते।

अथ महर्षिपाणिनेः अष्टाध्याय्यां अन्येऽपि शिक्षासाहित्यविषयिणः शब्दाः प्राप्यन्ते तद्यथा–

(A) 'भासनोपसंभाषा'–(1/3/47) इत्येतत्सूत्रे लभ्यमानं 'भासनम्' इति पदम् (भासनं नाम कस्यापि विषयस्य चमत्कृतं व्याख्यानम्) (B) 'विभाषा विप्रलापे' (1/3/50) सूत्रे निर्दिष्टविप्रलाप इति पदम् (विप्रलापो नाम तत्र तत्रोल्लिखितानां विचारितानाञ्च विविधविषयाणां सम्यगुपन्यसनं तच्चिन्तनञ्च) (c) भासन--(1/3/47) दीर्घसूत्रे निर्दिष्टं विमतिः इति पदम् (विमतिर्नाम कस्मिंश्चिद्-विषये अनेकमतानां विवेचनम्)। तदेवमन्येऽपि संशोधनलेखनादिविषयकाः शब्दास्तत्तत्सूत्रेषु प्राप्यन्ते, किन्तु विस्तरभिया ते नात्रोपदिश्यन्ते।

एवमेव 'वृत्तिसर्गतायनेषु क्रमः' (1/3/38) इति पाणिनिसूत्रेऽस्मिन् दृश्यमानं 'तायनम्' इति पदमपि डॉ. कुलकर्णि-लिखित- साहित्यविषये चरितार्थम् (अत्र 'तायन' नाम सविस्तरं सम्पादनमिति)।

तदेवं कारयित्रीभावयित्रीत्युभयविधप्रतिभासमलङ्कृतानां कस्मिन्नपि विषयलेखने चिन्तने च स्वीयं ताटस्थ्यसंवलितं निर्णयं दत्तवताम् अधीतिबोधाचरणप्रचारशीलानाम् आजीवनम् अलङ्कारशास्त्रादि-महाम्बुधिम्प्रमथ्य तदन्तर्गतं पीयूषं पिबतां पाययताञ्च गुरुवराणां विषयेऽधिकं किं प्रस्तौमि? अतोऽत्रैव विराममभिलषामि।

स्वभावत एव ज्ञानगंभीरान्, सौम्यप्रकृतीन् विगतविकृतीन् आगमस्वाध्यायप्रवचनव्यवहारकालेनेति स्वीयां विद्याम् उपयोजितवतो गुरुवरान् श्री वी. एम्. कुलकर्णिमहोदयान् शतशः सादरं सानुरागञ्च प्रणौमि। साम्प्रतं गायकवाडओरियण्टल सीरिजग्रन्थमालातः प्रकाशितस्य अभिनवभारतीटीकासंवलितस्य भरतनाट्यशास्त्रीयचतुर्थखण्डस्य समीक्षितावृत्तिसम्पादनाय बद्धपरिकरेभ्यः सपरिवारेभ्यो डॉ. श्री कुलकर्णिमहोदयेभ्यो भगवान् भूतनाथो दीर्घायुरारोग्यमैश्वर्यादिकं वितीर्य सर्वथा सर्वदा निरतिशयसुखं वितनुयादिति सम्प्रार्थ्य विरमामि।

I.3

सुधीर्मूर्धन्यः–डॉ० वामन महादेव कुलकर्णी

प्रो० सुरेश ज० दवे

तत्रभवान् स्वनामधन्यः साहित्यशास्त्रकेसरी, प्राकृतवाङ्मयपारदृश्वा, गुणगणालयः करुणावरुणालयः, विद्वन्मण्डनायमानः सौजन्यामन्दमन्दाकिनीमरालः सौम्यभावोल्लसिताननारविन्दः प्रज्ञौदार्यविभूषितः सुचरितस्नेहपीयूषपारावारः सन्ततविद्योपासनयापितजीवनो डॉ. वामन महादेव कुलकर्णिमहोदयः कया रीत्या सभाजनीयः कीर्तनीयो वेति चिन्तने मतिर्मे मुह्यति। 'यस्मान्नोद्विजते लोको लोकान्नोद्विजते च य' इति भगवद्गीतासु भगवता कृष्णचन्द्रेणोपदिष्टं सत्पुरुषलक्षणं यस्मिंश्चरितार्थतां याति तथा च तेनैव कारणेन निजप्रातिभौजसा जनमन्यमन्धीकर्तुं न कदापि कामयमानेन तेन स्वसारस्वतपुरुषार्थोऽमाकं संस्कृतप्राकृतसाहित्यनिहित–प्राचीनपरम्परा–प्रकटीकरणाय तल्लाभलब्धोल्लासं लोकं तस्यावलोकनं कारयितुमेव योजितः। अस्मिन्नेव कर्मणि तेन निजकर्मसिद्धिः समीहिता।

महाराष्ट्रप्रदेशे कोल्हापुरमण्डले अजरग्रमे १९१७ तमे ख्रिस्तहायने नवेम्बरमासि लब्धजन्मनः तत्रभवतः डॉ कुलकर्णि–महोदयस्य प्रथमं दर्शनं मम महाविद्यालयीयाध्ययनकाले अहमदाबादनगरे गुजरातकॉलेजाख्ये विश्रुते महाविद्यालये जातम्। संस्कृतार्धमागधी–विषयावध्यापयत् सः। कुलपरम्परया उताहो केनाप्यज्ञातकारणेनाहं महाराष्ट्रीयविदुषः प्रति महत्तरं समादरं धारयामि। तत्रापि गुजरातकॉलेजे डॉ. कुलकर्णिमहोदयं संस्कृताध्यापनकर्मसंलग्नं दृष्ट्वा मनसि मे हर्षोल्लासः समजायत। महाविद्यालयस्यास्य तृतीयवर्षे (Sr. B.A.) संस्कृतमर्धमागधीं च विषयद्वयं प्रधानगौणरूपेण स्वीकुर्वाणेन मया डॉ कुलकर्णिमहोदयः साक्षात् गुरुपदे स्थापितः। अनेन तेन सह नैकट्यं जातमेव किन्तु तस्य ज्ञानस्नेहामृत–वर्षणस्य भूयान् लाभोऽपि संप्राप्त इत्यमन्दसौभाग्यं मम। काव्यप्रकाशमध्यापयता तेन साहित्यकर्तव्य–मुद्बोधयता यद् भणितं तस्य सारजातमधुनापि मम चेतश्चमत्करोति। तेन निरूपितं यत् साहित्यं वर्तमान–समयस्य दर्पणं भवेदिति न पर्याप्तम्। साहित्यं वर्तमानस्य प्रतिबिम्बमात्मसात्करोति तत्परावर्तते च। अतः साहित्यं लोकस्यादर्शः। एतावतैव साहित्यकर्म समाप्तिं न याति। लोकः कीदृशो भवेदित्यपि साहित्य–कारेण चिन्त्यम्। साहित्याद्दीपदर्शनमप्यपेक्ष्यते। अनेन साहित्यस्यापरो दीपधर्मोऽपि मनोभूमिं नेयः। दीपधर्ममुररीकुर्वत्साहित्यमुपदेशकक्षायां पदं न न्यसेदित्यर्थं कविना सावधानेन भाव्यम्। नो चेत् साहित्यतत्त्वस्य हानिर्जायते।'

छात्रत्वकाले तदनन्तरं चापि सुदीर्घकालं डॉ कुलकर्णिमहोदयस्याध्यापनयात्रासाक्षिरूपेणाहं कथयितुमुत्सहे यत्तस्य सत्त्वकुसुमं स्वत्वसुमनश्च गुर्जरदेशे अहमदाबादनगरे प्रफुल्लतां प्राप्तम्। गुजरातकॉलेजाख्यो महाविद्यालयश्चात्र गौरवग्रहणाधिकारी। तत्पुष्परिमलो न केवलं तस्य छात्रद्विरेफकदम्बैराघ्रातोऽपि तु अत्रस्था गुजरातराज्यस्था एतद्देशीया अन्ये विद्वांसोऽपि तन्मकरन्दलाभाय समाकृष्टाः।

न केवलं संस्कृते प्राकृतेऽपि कुलकर्णिमहोदयस्य पाण्डित्यं जाजागर्ति। एतेन महोदयेन नूनं निजाध्ययनकाले प्राकृताय प्राथम्यं दत्तम्। एम्. ए. इत्युपाधिरुपार्जितः। परन्तु वाङ्मयस्य पूर्णरूपेणावगाहनाय केवलमिदमपर्याप्तमिति सम्बुध्य जेगीयमानपूर्णतया तेन संस्कृतविषयमवलम्ब्यानुस्नातकोपाधिरप्युपार्जितस्तेजस्वितया विद्योपार्जनमिदं तेनाध्यापनसेवां तन्वतैव कृतं यत्र भास्वत्साफल्यमप्यधिगतमिति तस्य क्षुरधारातुल्यशेमुषीं प्रथयति। इदमपि हर्षास्पदमत्र यदेको विषयो विषयमन्यं नावारुणत् का वार्ता तस्य हननस्य? संस्कृतप्राकृतयोर्मध्ये तेन प्रशंसार्हा समतुला स्थापिता। प्राकृतग्रन्थानां तस्याध्यापनं तथैव गहनतया सूक्ष्मेक्षिकया सर्वतोमुखं चासीद्यथा संस्कृतकृतीनाम्। अत्र तावत्तस्य शीलमेव प्रवर्तते। तस्य विद्यासाधना ज्ञानप्रेप्सायां परिणतवती ज्ञानं च छात्रवृन्देन साकं विद्वज्जनकलापसमीपनयनफलवच्चावर्ततेति हन्त महीयान् गरीयांश्चादानप्रदानयोगः।

विद्याफलं मानसिकशीलरूपेण बाह्याचरणरूपेण चेति द्विधा दरीदृश्यते। शीलवृत्तफलं श्रुतमितीयमुक्तिः डॉ कुलकर्णिमहोदयस्य जीवने चरितार्थतां याति। तस्य स्नातक–अनुस्नातक–पी.एच.डी. कक्षानामनल्पश्छात्रसमुदायोऽद्यापि वर्तते, स्वजीवन उन्नतपदमधिरुह्य तद्विभूष्य च स्वस्य स्वगुरोश्च यशःपताकां फर्फारायत इति कस्य सचेतसो मनो न प्रह्लादयेत्? दृष्ट्वा ज्ञात्वा चैतत् डॉ. कुलकर्णिमहोदयः सन्तुष्टिं लभतेतरामिति नितान्तं योग्यम्। अध्यापको बलिष्ठः सहिष्ठो युवेत्युपनिषद्वचनमत्र स्मृतिपथमायाति।

शिक्षाक्षेत्रं व्यवसायत्वेन स्वीकुर्वन् जनः पठनपाठनपरायणस्तु भवत्येव। लेखनी तस्य फलं बलं चास्ते। डॉ कुलकर्णिमहोदयः केवलमेतावत्यैव प्रवृत्त्या तुष्टिं नाभजत। कोमलधियां जनानामुपास्यत्वेन प्रथितस्य साहित्यशास्त्रस्य गहनान्तस्तलं सूक्ष्मेक्षिकया। गाहमानेन तेन शास्त्रोपासनेन साकं शस्त्रचालनकौशलमप्यधिगतमितीदं वैशिष्ट्यमुपेक्षां नार्हति। अहमदाबादे गुजरातकॉलेजे National Cadet Corps इत्यस्य प्रभारिप्राध्यापकरूपेण तेन शस्त्रविद्याधिगता दीर्घकालपर्यन्तं तज्ज्ञानं छात्रेषु वितीर्णं च। कर्मेदं वितन्वता तेन (Major) मेजरपर्यन्तं पदमधिरूढम् एन्.सी.सी. छात्रेभ्यः संरक्षणजागृतिः प्रबोधिता। शास्त्रोपासनायाः शस्त्रचालनस्य च कर्मद्वयं सममेव समाचरतां लघुसंख्यकसंस्कृताध्यापकानां मध्ये डॉ. कुलकर्णिमहोदयस्य नामाङ्कनमादिमपङ्क्तौ राराजत इत्यहो विद्योपासनायां शस्त्रविद्याजिघृक्षायां च कौशलाप्तिरतिः। कर्मेदं तस्यानुगामिनां नैकेषां कृतेऽनुकरणार्हमिति नाज्ञातं सचेतःकदम्बानाम्।

पाठनमेवाध्यापकस्याद्यो धर्मः। किन्तु पाठनमात्रकर्मरतत्वमेकाङ्गित्वं निमन्त्रयति। सन्तताध्ययनपरायणोऽध्यापकः स्वाध्यायजन्यनूतनराद्धान्तानन्येषां लाभार्थमुपयुञ्जेतेत्यपेक्ष्यते। एवम्प्रकारेणाध्ययननिरतस्याध्यापकस्य चिन्तनं संशोधनफलं च वर्तमानागामिविद्योपासकानां लाभाय कल्पते। डॉ कुलकर्णिमहोदयेन प्राकृतग्रन्थं पउमचरियमवलम्ब्य 'जैनसाहित्ये रामकथा' इतिविषयको गवेषणात्मको महानिबन्ध आङ्ग्लभाषायां विलिखितो येन स पी.एच्.डी. उपाधिमुपार्जितवान्। विषयोऽयं तस्य च वैदुष्यपूर्णं प्ररूपणं विद्योपासकानां विद्वज्जनानां न केवलं भारतदेशे अपि तु देशान्तरेष्वपि प्रशस्तिवचांस्यचूचुरत्। प्राकृतमस्य प्रथमो वरणविषयो भवतु नाम। किन्तु गच्छता कालेन तेनानुस्नातकोपाधिर्यशःप्रदायी यथा

भवेत्तथा, संस्कृतविषयमवलम्ब्य समधिगतः। एतौ विषयावेव तस्य स्वाध्यायकर्मणि केन्द्रवर्तिस्थानमलभेताम् यस्य फलरूपेण पारेशतं शोधपत्राणि गवेषणापूर्णनिबन्धाः प्रकाशतामियुः। शोधपत्राणीमानि प्राच्य-विद्या-परिषदि स्तुतिवचनाधिकारीणि जातानि। अमूनि स्वीयमुखपत्रस्यालङ्करणं भवेयुरित्यर्थं विविधविश्वविद्यालया अहमहमिकया पस्पर्धुस्तानि सम्प्राप्य गौरवं च बभ्रुरित्यहो कुलकर्णिमहोदयस्य कृते निरतिशयं समादरं विवर्धयति।

विद्वल्ललामभूतस्यास्य डॉ. कुलकर्णिमहोदयस्य गवेषणामतिः संशोधनपत्रलेखनमात्रे समाप्तिं नाप्नोति। प्राकृतसंस्कृतक्षेत्रे समावृत्य तेन सुवर्णकल्पा ग्रन्था विद्वज्जगत उपायनीकृताः। ग्रन्थानामेतेषामध्ययनं संस्कृतकाव्यनाट्यक्षेत्रे प्राकृतवाङ्मये च तत्कर्तुः सिद्धहस्तत्वं प्रत्याययति। इदमप्यवगम्यते यदस्मिन् काव्यनाट्यक्षेत्रे डॉ. कुलकर्णिमहोदयस्य विशेषः पक्षपातः प्रवर्तते। महानुभावोऽयं गुजरातकॉलेजे भवेत्, महाराष्ट्र-राज्यस्थविविधमहाविद्यालयेषु स्यात्, महाराष्ट्रस्य भाषानियामकपदमलङ्कुर्यात्, गुजराते पाटणपत्तनस्थभोगीलाल-लहेरचन्द-संशोधन-संस्थाया नियामकपदं विभूषयेदाहोस्वित् पूर्णनिवृत्तिकालं यापयेत्, तस्य काव्यनाट्यशास्त्रादिसेवा कदापि क्षीणतां न यातेति हन्त सदैव जागृतिं धारयति तस्यान्तरिकं सत्त्वम्। सर्वदा गहनशास्त्रीयग्रन्थानालोड्य तत्तत्त्रुटीः संशोध्य ताः संशोधितरूपेण प्रकाश्य, विद्वन्मण्डलीमुपकुर्वाणः स समयं सम्यगुपयुनक्तीति महदादरास्पदम्। ग्रन्थानामेतेषां नामश्रवणेनाप्यात्मानं धन्यं मन्वाना बहवो विद्वांसोऽपि पुनन्तितरां निजस्वान्तम् का वार्ता तत्पठनेन ज्ञानलब्धिं कुर्वतां सचेतसनाम्। ग्रन्था इमे डॉ. कुलकर्णिमहोदयस्य संस्कृतप्राकृतयोः संतुलितचिन्तनोपासनां, स्फटिकसमां सुस्पष्टां, तलवेधिनीं च दृष्टिं परिचाययन्ति। ग्रन्थानामेतेषां पाण्डित्यपूर्णं सर्वतोमुखं सत्त्वं साहोभावं स्वागतीकृतं विवेचकवृन्देन। डॉ. कुलकर्णिमहोदयेन अन्यान्यसमये विविधानि पारितोषिकानि तु प्राप्तान्येव चन्द्रका अपि अधिगताः। किन्तु तस्य वैदुष्यं प्रमाणयता भारतस्य राष्ट्रपतिनाप्याजीवनपुरस्कार (Certificate of Honour) प्रदानेन सम्मानितोऽयं सारस्वतशिरोमणिरित्यहो स्थाने सम्मानः। अत्राधो निरूप्यते तत्रभवता रचितानां केषाञ्चिद्ग्रन्थानां मज्ज्ञानानुसारिणी सूचिः।

(i) The Story of Rāma in Jain Literature
(ii) Introduction to Paumacariyam
(iii) Kāvyānuśāsana of Hemacandra
(iv) Jayadeva's Gītagovinda with the commentary of King Mānāṅka
(v) Śṛṅgārārṇava-candrikā of Vijayavarṇi
(vi) An Anthology of Jain Texsts
(vii) Critical Introduction to Mallikāmakaranda
(viii) Studies in Sanskrit Sahityaśāstra
(ix) Some Aspects of the Rasa Theory
(x) Introduction to Pañcasūtrakam of Cirantanācārya
(xi) Vācaka Śrīmad Umāsvāti's Praśamarati

(xii) Prakrit Verses in Sanskrit Works on Poetics (2 volumes)

(xiii) Bhoja and Harivijaya of Sarvasena

(xiv) More Studies in Sanskrit Sāhityaśāstra

(xv) Outline of Abhinava's Aesthetics

(xvi) Kūrmaśatakadvayam

(xvii) Abhinavabhāratī Text Restorted and Other Articles

(xviii) Studies in Jain Literature

एतावन्महिमचयसंभृतः सैन्यानुशासननियमानुपालने सुबद्धपरिकरोऽयं प्रकृत्या कठोरतां धारयेदिति शङ्कितुं चेतश्चेष्टेत चेत्, तर्हि तन्न समीचीनम्। तदानीन्तने काले शासकीयमहाविद्यालये सेवां वितन्वानाः प्राध्यापकाः छात्रसंसर्गाद्विमुखीभूय व्यचरन्। तैः सह संलापः संवादो वा कल्पनागोचरः । एतादृश्यां स्थितौ विद्यमानेनापि डॉ. कुलकर्णिमहोदयेन सा सरणिर्नोररीकृता। छात्रैः सहोचितमन्तरं रक्षन्नसौ स्वजनवद् व्यवजहार समेषां चेतांसि च जिगायेति समुचितमनुकरणीयं चाचरणं परेषां कृते। नैके छात्रा आत्मीयत्वमप्यनुबभूवुः। डॉ. कुलकर्णिमहोदयस्तेषां गुरुरूपेण स्वजनः समजायतेति परमं सौभाग्यं तत्तच्छात्रस्य। इतोऽप्यधिक, तस्य धर्मपत्नी सुश्री शालिनीदेवी येदानीं नामशेषा सती दिवं भूषयति साऽपि निजगृहोपगतच्छात्रेषु मातृवदस्निह्यत्। डॉ. कुलकर्णिमहोदयः अल्पपरिचये जातेऽपि गुरुमात्मीयत्वं प्रदर्शयति तनोति च। न केवलं छात्रेष्वपि तु संस्कृतसेवां कुर्वतीषु संस्थास्वपि तस्य समभावः समदृश्यत। अहमदाबादस्था श्री बृहद् गुजरात संस्कृत परिषद् तास्वेकतमा वर्तत इति महत्सौभाग्यम्।

करुणायाः साक्षादुदधिः श्रद्धायाः समुन्नततरुरयं विद्यागुणविभूषितान् सरस्वतीसमुपासकान् दृष्ट्वा जरीहृष्यते, तैः सह चर्चाप्रसङ्गे निगूढविषयान् विवृणुत इति हन्त समुल्लसति देवी शारदा। तस्यार्जवं, गुणानुरागित्वं, समर्चनीयेषु विनयं, यथालाभसन्तोषं, मितभाषित्वं, प्रियवादित्वं, शास्त्रसमन्वयरूपं जीवनसारसञ्चयत्वं च स्मारं स्मारं कस्य गुणग्राहिणो मनो न नन्नमीति? एतादृशो विद्यासुधाम्बुधिविलास-परायणो नाम्ना वामनस्तथापि कर्मणा विराटो, विद्वन्मानसराजहंसः, छात्रकैरवकदम्बमार्तण्डोऽधीति-बोधाचरणप्रसारणपरः सुधीर्मनीषी महादेवरावतनुजः कुलकर्णीत्यवटङ्कः वामनरावो ममामन्दप्रेममन्दाकिनीं प्रवाहयन् गुरुरासीदास्त आसिष्यते चेति गौरवमावहामि। कथमपि भुवनेऽस्मिन् सन्ति सन्तः कियन्तः।

गीर्वाणसाहित्यमहार्णवस्य पारङ्गतः प्राकृतवाङ्मयस्य।
उपास्य साहित्यगतं च तत्त्वं जातः स मूर्धन्यसुधीर्नदीष्णः।।
ध्यायं ध्यायं धवलयशसः पाठनं सारभूतं
पायं पायं रसिकवचसो वाक्सुधां चापि दिव्याम्।
स्मारं स्मारं हृदयनिहितं सागरं तद्गुणानां।
छात्रा आहो नवनवमुदा सन्नताः सन्ति नित्यम्।।

बिभ्रतेऽस्मै गुरुवर्याय जीवनपथि भद्रं वितरतु, सर्वतोमुरवं मङ्गलं तनोतु, सुस्वास्थ्यं दीर्घमायुश्च ददात्विति प्रार्थये।

I.4

DR. V. M. KULKARNI—SOME HAPPY ASSOCIATIONS

Dr. N. B. Patil

My mind goes back to the labyrinth of memory lanes and I visualize my first meeting with Dr.V.M. Kulkarni in August 1971. I was then a Deputy in the Directorate of Languages, Government of Maharashtra, Mumbai. Dr. W.N. Pandit was the Director and my services in the Education Department were placed at the disposal of the Directorate. The Directorate was engaged in the implementation of the Maharashtra Official Language Act, 1964. In a few years after my joining the department, Dr. Pandit was elevated as a member of All India Council for Translation of Central Acts in regional languages. He left for Delhi and Shri K.M. Aradhye, then a Joint Director was promoted as Director. After a year or so, Shri Aradhye also retired and there was a big void in the department. The Government judiciously thought of appointing Dr. V.M. Kulkarni as the Director of Languages. He was then Professor of Sanskrit at the prestigious Elphinstone College, Mumbai and a senior member of the Maharashtra Education Service, class I.

When his posting orders were received in our Directorate, I was very happy. I myself was a student of Sanskrit and was therefore glad to know that Dr. Kulkarni would be heading our Department. After the retirement of Shri Aradhye, I was holding the charge of the Director. I was eager to hand over this burden to its rightful owner.

I went to the Elphinstone College to meet Dr. Kulkarni. I waited in the Common Room as Dr. Kulkarni was engaging his class. The bell rang and Dr. Kulkarni returned to the Common Room where I was waiting for him. He was tall and well built and a bit stern. I was seeing him for the first time, though I had heard about him and his scholarship. We exchanged greetings and I told him that we in the

Directorate of Languages were anxiously waiting for him. In a week or so, he was relieved from the Elphinstone College and assumed the office of the Director of Languages, Maharashtra.

Dr. V.M. Kulkarni, apart from being a good scholar and a professor, was a good administrator as well. He soon grasped the working of the Language Directorate. I briefed him about the activities and the projects that were on the anvil. He acquainted himself with the staff at all the levels. The Directorate soon regained its rhythm of work.

The Directorate had many wings. One wing was taking care of legal and legislative work; the other wing was catering to the needs of the various Government Departments in the *Mantrālaya.* This wing attended all administrative translations. But the bulk of the translation staff was engaged in evolving administrative, commercial, financial, scientific and technical terminologies. The work of administrative terminology was almost over and the rough draft of *Shasan Vyavahar Kosh* was already circulated among various Government Departments, litterateurs, the Press for their comments. We received a volley of comments from the various sections of the society. These comments were to be placed before the Language Advisory Board, for its consideration. This was done and various objections received were valued and a corrected press copy of *Shasan Vyavahar Kosh* was prepared by the Directorate.

Dr. V.M.Kulkarni saw to it that this *Kosh* was out of the press soon. He set dates for various operations and we did the job to his satisfaction. Dr. Kulkarni also took great interest in speeding up the work of Marathi terminology in various science subjects such as Physics, Chemistry, Mathematics, Botany, Zoology and Commerce and Agriculture. The procedure in this regard was all laid down by earlier Directors. The various subjects committees consisting of professors from various universities in Maharashtra, and representatives of Marathi Vijnan Parishad used to meet periodically and scrutinize the information culled by the Directorate from various sources. Marathi terms for various scientific words were discussed, new terms were coined, and arranged in alphabetical forms which were later printed in book forms. Meetings of such committees were held mostly in Mumbai and occasionally in various university centers in Maharashtra. One of the senior professors used to chair such meetings and Dr. V.M. Kulkarni used to convene these meetings. His serene presence at such meetings was always welcome. His grammatical insight and his profound knowledge of Sanskrit, Pali, Prakrit and Marathi were of immense help in arriving at the right Marathi equivalents of scientific and technical terms.

I had the pleasure of accompanying him on a number of occasions to such meetings held at University head quarters. He was a man of few words and would talk in the meeting rarely. He would intervene only when he would notice that the discussion is going astray. During the five years, he was the Director, he successfully led a number of projects to completion.

The Director of Languages, as a part of General Administration Department, was directly under the Chief Minister and Deputy Minister in charge of G. A.D. There were a few bitter occasions when the minister would not grasp the significance of his sane suggestions, but, he never swerved from giving the right advice. He was upright in his dealings and extremely conscious of his responsibilities.

His research activities continued even when he took over as the Director of Languages and a number of research papers were published in those years. He continued to attend the Oriental and other conferences in those years and I was with him on one or more such occasions. I remember that Dr. Iravati Karve has made an honourable mention in her book of Dr. Kulkarni's research on *Jain Rāmāyaṇas*.

After retirement in 1975, Dr. Kulkarni associated himself with the Asiatic Society of Mumbai as the Honorary Director of its MM. Dr. P.V. Kane Institute. He is also the Fellow of the Society and the recipient of its Silver medal. He is also editing the Journal of the Society, jointly with Dr. Devangana Desai. Dr. Kulkarni scrutinizes meticulously the research papers that are received for publication. He has made the Journal prestigious.

His contribution in the field of Sanskrit and Prakrit studies and in Poetics has been appreciated at the national and international levels and the President of India has honoured him as a National Sanskrit Scholar.

I feel myself blessed to have come in contact with such a profound Pandit. I pray for his long and active life.

I.5

MY HIGHLY RESPECTED 'GURU'

Mrudula Prabhuram Joshi

My association with Dr. V. M. Kulkarni is quite recent compared to that of many others. He never taught me in College but has become my 'Guru', philosopher and guide, and I consider it my proud privilege to be called his associate and in a way his student.

In 1996, I was calld by Dr. Kulkaeni and Dr. Devangana Desai to assist them in the production of the prestigious annual *Journal of the Asiatic Society of Bombay* of which they were the Executive Editors. I was required to be the copy-editor and proof-reader for thc volume. As the text of the Journal contained diacritical marks, the copy-editing had to be done with utmost care and at the stage of reading the proofs, a certain level of perfection was supposed to be reached. Although I had vast experience of doing similar work behind me, both the editors had not known me before and hence were initially rather skeptical about my abilities. But soon I earned their confidence and as a result, I have been assisting them in this job ever since.

By the time I started working with Dr. Kulkarni, he had almost lost sight in one eye and had reached an age where not much physical activity was possible. But I was amazed to find him working on ever new projects and keeping himself totally immersed in academic, scholarly pursuits round the clock, his weak eyesight notwithstanding.

It has been a matter of great pleasure for me to sit at his feet and learn many things. One thing that is very very evident is that he wears his scholarship very lightly. He does not want to throw his weight around and in that he is a typical *'Vidwan'* who is self-effacing, publicity-shy and in essence, a gentleman. Anyone who is a keen student of Sanskrit, Prakrit, Jainism or Buddhism can approach him for guidance and Dr. Kulkarni never tires of giving all the requisite references, showing the necessary books from his vast personal treasure. He is the 'Quintessential Teacher' and hundreds have benefited from his scholarly munificence.

Apart from the *Journal of the Asiatic Society of Bombay,* I have had the good fortune to assist him in the production of his books like *Outline of Abhinavagupta's Aesthetics, Studies in Jain Literature* and *Abhinavabhāratī Text: Restored and Other Articles.* I have learnt a great deal in this process. The pioneering work that he has done in restoring the lost *gāthās* is simply mindblowing. I am not equipped to comment on his scholarship but having worked closely with him for more than 8 years, I can certainly vouch for the way he spares no pains while doing his research. In fact, research is the 'mission of his life'.

Since he cannot go out, everyone who wants to meet him has to visit him at his home. Here, one sees him as the perfect host. He showers his tender care, love and personal warmth on the visitor. Himself a lover of good food, Dr. Kulkarni enjoys treating his guests to tasty homemade delicacies. Here, one also sees him as a loving father and a doting grandfather, in short, a 'happy householder'. With age, he has become a 'wise old man'. His stature as a profound scholar, a learned professor, author of several path-breaking books, erstwhile Director of Languages of Maharashtra State does not intimidate anyone. In fact, he wins over anyone with his soft-spoken ways and endearing attitude. For many like me, he has become a father-figure. It's not often that one comes across such a unique personality. Personally I am indebted to him for enriching my life and I pray to the Almighty to give him a long, healthy life to be able to give us more and more of his books and scholarship.

I.6

कुटुंबवत्सल ज्ञानयोगी

–सत्त्वशीला सामंत

१९७१-७२ च्या सुमारास डॉ. वा. म. कुलकर्णी हे नवे भाषा संचालक म्हणून आमच्या भाषा संचालनालयात रुजू झाले. अर्धीअधिक हयात अध्यापन क्षेत्रात घालवल्यानंतर उतारवयात ह्या गृहस्थांना सरकारी खात्यातील प्रशासन कसें जमणार आणि कामचुकारपणात मुरलेली नोकरशाही ह्यांना कितपत जुमानणार अशी सर्वांच्याच मनांत शंका होती. पण आमच्या कार्यालयात येताक्षणीं, 'तो आला, त्याने पाहिलें. व त्याने जिंकलें' अशा थाटात त्यांनी कसलेल्या घोडेस्वाराप्रमाणें आमच्या चौखूर उधळलेल्या घोड्यावर पक्की मांड ठोकली आणि अल्पावधीतच त्यांनी या उनाड घोड्याला वठणीवर आणलें मागाहून आमच्या कानांवर आले कीं, एकेकाळीं एन्.सी.सी. मध्यें वरिष्ठ अधिकारीपदावर असलेल्या डॉ. कुलकर्णींनी 'इस्माईल युसूफ' सारख्या बेशिस्त महाविद्यालयावर आपली पुरती जरब बसवली होती. उंचीपुरी, भरदार देहयष्टी व कांहीसा करडा चेहरामोहरा यांमुळें त्यांचा लष्करी बाणा प्रथमदर्शनीं नजरेत भरत असे. कोणत्याहि कार्यालयातील वरिष्ठ अधिकारी हे कांही मौलिक कार्य करण्यासाठीं नसून नुसतेच मुकादमगिरी करण्यासाठीं नेमलेले असतात हा (अप)समज त्यांनी प्रथम मोडून काढला आणि सर्व वरिष्ठ अधिका-यांना ख-या अर्थाने कामीं लावलें आणि कनिष्ठ कर्मचा-यांसमोर एक आदर्श ठेवला.

पण डॉ. कुलकर्णी हे नुसतेच रांगडे लष्करगडी नव्हते. भाषा संचालनालयाने नेमलेल्या विविध विद्वज्जन समित्यांच्या बैठकांमध्ये कार्यालय प्रमुख म्हणून ते जेव्हा सहभागी होत तेव्हा, त्यांच्या विद्वत्तेचा प्रखर प्रकाश पडत असे व इतर विद्यापीठीय प्राध्यापकांचेहि ते नेतृत्व करीत असत. तास न् तास वायफळ पंडिती चर्चा करण्यातहि त्यांना रस नव्हता. ज्याअर्थीं, सरकार विद्वानांना मानधन देऊन कोशकार्यासाठीं बोलावतें त्याअर्थी विद्वानांनीदेखील काळ, काम व वेग यांचे भान ठेवून कांहीतरी उपयुक्त फलनिष्पत्ति करावी यावर त्यांचा कटाक्ष असे. भाषा संचालनालयाच्या कारभाराची विस्कटलेली घडी पूर्ववत् बसवून व एक कुशल प्रशासक अशी आपली प्रतिभा ठसवून, १९७५ साली ते सेवानिवृत्त झाले व पुन्हा आपल्या विद्याव्यासंगात रममाण झाले. १९७५ सालापासून ते १९८६ सालीं मी नोकरीतून स्वेच्छानिवृत्त होईपर्यंत त्यांचा-माझा फारसा संपर्क झाला नाही.

मध्यंतरीच्या काळात त्यांच्या वैयक्तिक जीवनाला हादरा देणा-या दोन दुर्घटना घडल्या. १९७७ सालीं पुण्यात जक्कल नांवाच्या गुंडाने घडवून आणलेल्या अभ्यंकर-हत्याकांडात त्यांचे परमपूज्य गुरु म. म. काशीनाथशास्त्री अभ्यंकर यांचा दारुण अंत झाला आणि १९७९ सालीं त्यांच्या सुविद्य व सुस्वभावी प्रेमळ पत्नीचें मधुमेह विकाराने अकाली निधन झाले. त्या दोन्ही प्रसंगी मीं त्यांना पत्राने व समक्ष भेटून माझी सहानुभूति कळवली होती. एवढाच काय तो संपर्क घडला. पण त्यावेळीं, काळजातली जखम अतिशय संयमाने झाकून, समाचारासाठीं आलेल्या मंडळींशीं ते अतीव सौजन्याने बोलत, तेव्हा मला त्यांच्या धीरोदात्तपणाचें दूरदर्शन घडलें होते.

१९८६ सालीं मी स्वेच्छानिवृत्त झालें तेव्हा, आला रिकामा वेळ उपयुक्त कामांत कसा घालवायचा हा माझ्यापुढें यक्षप्रश्न होता. त्यावेळीं पहिल्याप्रथम मला डॉ. कुलकर्णींची आठवण झाली वमीं त्यांच्याशीं संपर्क साधला. त्यानंतर त्यांनी मला त्यांच्या संस्कृत-प्राकृत संशोधनपर ग्रंथांच्या मुद्रितशोधनाचीं कामें देण्यास सुरुवात केली. या कामाच्या निमित्ताने मी त्यांच्या निकट संपर्कात आस्यामुळें मला त्यांच्या व्यक्तिमत्त्वाच्या विविध पैलूंचें समीपदर्शन घडलें. मी उपस्थित केलेली कोणतीहि शंका-मग ती कितीहि किरकोळ वा क्षुल्लक का असेना-ती त्यांनी कधीं फेटाळून लावली नाही, तर माझ्या प्रत्येक शंकेचें त्यांनी निरसन केलें. 'बालादपि सुभाषितम्' असें मानून त्यांनी माझ्या प्रत्येक शंकेचे स्वागत केलें. एवढेंच नव्हे तर, तिहाइताने शंका व्यक्त केल्याने विद्वान व्यक्तींचा कमीपणा होत नाहीं, उलट चुकून एखादी त्रुटि राहून गेली असल्यास, ती दूर होऊन आपली संहिता अधिक सुधारते अशी त्यांची धारणा होती. त्रुटि दूर करण्यासाठीं आवश्यक ते संदर्भग्रंथ धुंडाळणें, त्यांचे पुन्हा परिशीलन करणें व जरूर तर दुरुस्ती करणें हा त्यांचा नित्यक्रम होता. त्याचप्रमाणें, आपणास साहाय्य करणा-या मदतनीसांना त्यांच्या कामाचा योग्य तो मोबदला देण्याबद्दलहि ते आग्रही होते.

१९९३ सालीं एक पेचप्रसंग उद्भवला. डॉ. कुलकर्णी व डॉ देवांगना देसाई ही दोघें Journal of Asiatic Society of Bombay या वार्षिकाचे संपादन करीत. त्याचे नेहमी मुद्रितशोधन करणा-या व्यक्तीकडून कांही अडचणींमुळें त्या वर्षीं त्या कामास नकार मिळाला. तोवर मला संस्कृतविषयक इंग्रजी ग्रंथांचें मुद्रितशोधन करण्याचा बयापैकीं सराव झाला होता. म्हणून डॉ. कुलकर्णींनी ते काम माझ्याकडे सोपवलें. त्यानंतर १९९५ सालीं मुंबईहून पुण्याला कायमकरता स्थलांतर करीपर्यंत मीं सलग तीन वर्षे ते काम केलें आणि डॉ. कुलकर्णी यांची मर्जी संपादन करून मीं त्यांची विश्वासू सहायक बनलें.

याच काळात कामाच्या निमित्ताने मी वारंवार त्यांच्या घरीं जाऊं लागलें. माझी तेवढी लायकी नसतानाहि अधूनमधून त्यांच्या पंक्तीला बसून जेवण्याचाहि योग आला. अनेकदा त्यांच्या सारस्वती पाहुणचाराचाहि आस्वाद घेतला. त्यांच्या कुटुंबीयांशीमुलगा, सून, मुलगी, नातवंडे, इ.-यांच्याशीहि माझा परिचय झाला. तेव्हा स्वतः डॉ. कुलकर्णींनी विधुरावस्थेतहि आपल्या कुटुंबीयांशीं किती प्रेमाचें, स्नेहाचें नाते जपलें आहे हें मीं जवळून अनुभवलें. कुटुंबीयांवर आपल्या व्यक्तिगत दुःखाचें

सांवट पडूं न देतां व तरुणांच्या संसारात अनावश्यक ढवळाढवळ न करतांहि, त्यांच्यावर मायेचें छत्र कसें धरावें याचा आदर्श नमुना म्हणजे डॉ. कुलकर्णी. त्यामुळेंच कुटुंबीया त्यांची अडगळ झाली नाही, त्यांना ते भारभूत झाले नाहीत, उलट ते त्यांचे आधारवड बनले.

सेवाकाळात महत्त्वाचीं पदें भूषवूनहि किंवा सेवानिवृत्तीनंतर आपल्या विद्याव्यासंगात मग्न राहूनहि, डॉ कुलकर्णी कधीं प्रसिद्धीच्या प्रखर झोतात आले नाहीत, एवढेंच नव्हे तर त्यांनी आडवळणानेहि तसा प्रयत्नदेखील केला नाहीं. तरीहि, १९९२ सालीं त्यांचा मंद कीर्तिसुगंध थेट दिल्लीपर्यंत दरवळत गेला व त्यांना संस्कृत-प्राकृतचे व्यासंगी विद्वान म्हणून राष्ट्रपतींचे प्रशस्तिपत्रक (Certificate of Honour) बहाल करण्यात आलें. न हि कस्तूरिकामोदः शपथेन विभाव्यते।–गुणीजनांचा गुणसुगंध शपथेवर सिद्ध करावा लागत नाहीं. तसेंच, न रत्नमन्विष्यति, मृग्यते हि तत्' या न्यायाने १९९८ सालीं त्यांच्या Prakrit Verses in Sanskrit Works on Poetics या द्विखंडी ग्रंथाबद्दल त्यांना ५१,००० रु. चा आचार्य हेमचंद्र पुरस्कार मिळाला.

(माझ्या दृष्टीने अभिमानाची गोष्ट अशी कीं, या ग्रंथाचें मुद्रितशोधन करण्याची अमूल्य संधी मला मिळाली होती.)

पण 'पिकतं तिथं विकत नाही' ही म्हण मात्र खरी आहे. त्यामुळेंच सांस्कृतिक नगरी म्हणून प्रसिद्ध असलेल्या विलेपार्ल्याच्या नागरिकांना या पुरस्काराबद्दल त्यांचा सत्कार करण्याचें हि सुचलें नाही. डॉ. एच्. सी भायाणी नामक पंडिताने Journal of Asiatic Society of Bombay या वार्षिकात डॉ. कुलकर्णींच्या उपर्युक्त ग्रंथाचें इंग्रजी परीक्षण लिहिले होतें. मी त्याचा मराठी अनुवाद करवून घेतला व एका ख्यातनाम भाषाविषयक मराठी नियतकालिकाकडे तो पाठवला. तत्कालीन संपादकांनी प्रथम तो लेख स्वीकारला व त्याची अक्षरजुळणीहि केली. अंतिम टप्प्या तो सर्व मजकूर, त्यावर अखेरची नजर टाकण्यासाठीं संस्थापक-संपादकांकडे गेला आणि काय आश्चर्य, ऐन वेळीं तो लेख वगळण्याचा निर्णय झाला. (या घटनेचीं पाळेंमुळें भूतकालात रुजलेलीं असल्याचें मला मागाहून समजलें. वाईच्या 'प्राज्ञपाठशाळा मंडळा' ने प्रकाशित केलेल्या डॉ. कुलकर्णींच्या 'पाच पुस्तकपरीक्षणे' या अभ्यासपूर्ण टीकाग्रंथात त्यांनी सदर संपादकांच्या एका पुस्तकाचें परीक्षण करून खंडन केलं होते. त्याची प्रतिक्रिया म्हणून डॉ. कुलकर्णींच्या ग्रंथावरील परीक्षणलेख वगळला गेला हें उघड आहे.)

त्यानंतर, मीं सदर अनुवादित परीक्षणलेख महाराष्ट्रातील एका नामवंत परंतु गंभीर व विद्वज्जड मासिकाकडे पाठवला. त्या मासिकाच्या संपादकांनी सदर लेख तर नाकारलाच, पण त्यांनी कळवलेलें नकाराचें कारणहि मोठें विलक्षण होतें. तें वाचून तर मी हतबुद्धच झालें. याला म्हणतात महाराष्ट्रातीळ मराठी माणसांचा करंटेपणा. थोडक्यात काय, तर 'बोद्धारो मत्सरग्रस्ताः।' (याउलट, डॉ. सिद्धार्थ वाकणकर या बृहन्महाराष्ट्रातील एकलव्य शिष्याने डॉ. कुलकर्णींच्या गौरवग्रंथाचा घाट घालावा ही गोष्ट खरोखरी कौतुकास्पद आहें।)

एवढें होऊनहि, डॉ. कुलकर्णी यांच्या मनात कोणाबद्दलहि कटुता नाही वा आपली उपेक्षा होत असल्याबद्दल विषादाची भावनाहि नाही. ते सर्वार्थांनी समचित्त व समदर्शी आहेत. त्यांच्या एका डोळयाची दृष्टि गमावलेली असल्याने शब्दशः ने 'एकाक्ष' असले तरी, दुस-या एकमेव डोळयावर भिस्त ठेवून आज वयाच्य। ८८ व्या वर्षींहि अखंड ज्ञानयोग चालू ठेवण्याइतपत ते 'चाणाक्ष' आहेत कामाच्या शिस्तीबाबत ते 'वज्रादऽपि कठोर' असले तरी, भोवतालच्या परिवारातील माणसांच्या सुखदु:खांविषयीं त्यांच्या मनान 'कुसुमादपि मृदु' असा जिव्हाळा आहे खाजगी कुटुंबाबरोबरच आमच्यासारख्या शिष्यपरिवारावरहि ते प्रेमाचा वर्षाव करीत असतात. 'मीपण ज्यांचे पक्व फळापरि सहजपणाने गळलें हो, जीवन त्यांना कळलें हो' अशा महनीय व्यक्तींमध्यें डॉक्टर कुलकर्णींची प्रामुख्याने गणना करावी लागेल. त्यांच्या या गौरवग्रंथाच्या निमित्ताने, त्यांना दीर्घायुरारोग्य लाभावें व त्यांचे ज्ञानपूत जीवन सुफळ, संपूर्ण व्हावें ही शुभकामना!

SECTION-II

1. INDOLOGY

2. REVIEWS OF VMK'S BOOKS

II.1
PROFESSOR DR. V.M. KULKARNI'S CONTRIBUTION TO INDOLOGY

Dr. S. G. Moghe

Here is a modest effort on the part of the present writer to evaluate the contribution of Dr. V.M. Kulkarni (VMK) to the domain of *Alaṁkāra-Śāstra*, Prakrit studies, *Rasa-Siddhanta* and others. VMK is an octogenerian scholar and has devoted more than 50 years of his life to the studies of the above subjects. Before, however, coming to the contribution aspect proper, it would be just in the fitness of things to point out the background to correctly appreciate the work of VMK.

In the last century, it appears, that most of the Sanskrit scholars like MM. Dr. P.V.Kane, Dr. S.K.De, Dr. V. Raghavan, Dr. K. Krishnamoorthy and others have completely ignored the study of the Prakrit language. In fact, it would be more correct to state they have given neglected treatment to the studies of the Prakrit languages. Those who studied Prakrit languages did not concentrate on the *Alaṁkara-Śāstra* and those who studied *Alaṁkāra-Śāstra* completely ignored the importance of the Prakrit languages. VMK is the only scholarly person who mastered both the *Alaṁkāra-Śāstra* and the Prakrit languages and made significant contribution to the study of the *Alaṁkāra-Śāstra*. It must be stated here that Dr. Kane, Dr. De and Dr. Raghavan are regarded as the *munitraya* of the *Alaṁkāra-Śāstra*. But the later two did not,however, realise the importance of the Prakrit languages. Hence whatever imperfections remained in the works of Dr. De and Dr. Raghavan and even others could be removed only by a scholar proficient in both the branches of learning like the *Alaṁkāra-Śāstra* and Prakrit Studies. This valuable work is done by Dr. VMK with perfect ease and with assiduous efforts.

A sincere effort therefore is made in the present paper, to highlight the contribution of VMK from the points of view of translation, restoration, emendation, critical editions, novel views, his relation with the other scholars etc. It must be stressed here that VMK' s attitude is mostly impartial, studious and never harsh.

I. As an editor of the works:—

(i) Dr. VMK has edited the work on the *Alaṁkāra-Śāstra* known as *Śṛṅgārarṇava-candrikā* of Vijaya-varṇī. This is published by the Bhāratiya Jñānapīṭ ha in the year 1969. It must be stated here that this work is based on a solitary manuscript. The speciality of this work lies in that it deals with all the aspects of Sanskrit poetics including the *Rasa* and the Dramaturgy. This work has the basis of Jainism. In this work, one finds by way of the illustrations, the stanzas connected with the life of the king Kāmīrāja, of Baṅgavādī in Karnataka. This king is said to have flourished at the end of the 13th century A.D.

It seems that Vijayavarṇī was the pupil of Munīndra Vijayakīrtī, an ardent follower of the *Syād-vāda*. At the request of the king Kāmīrāja, Vijayavarṇī composed the work otherwise known as *Alaṁkāra-Saṁgraha*. VMK has made a lot of discussion on the date of King Kāmīrāja and has concluded that he came on to throne in 1264 A.D.

He further remarks that this work comes near to another work entitled *Alaṁkāra-Saṁgraha* by Amṛtānandayogin.

This work *Śṛṅgārārṇava-candrikā*. contains simple enumeration, definition and exposition.

The word *Śṛṅgāra* means or denotes the *Rasa*. *Arṇava* means the ocean and *candrika* means the moon-light. The title thus means the moon-light to the ocean of *Śṛṅgāra*. VMK further[1] adds that it may also mean the work imparting special knowledge about poetics and covers *Śṛṅgāra* and other topics. It thus implies the inclusion of other less important topics.

Here the text covers pp.1-120. Several appendices are added to it. In the Introduction, VMK has given a detailed account of the work and has noted the important points raised by Vijaya-varṇī. Some of these deserve mention here—(1) He holds that the *Karuṇātmaka*[2] *Vipralaṁbha* can be shown if one of the lovers passes away. (2) In the list of the friends of the hero such as Vidūṣaka and others, he adds the Nāgarika. (3) His definitions of *śayyā* and *Pāka* are in close agreement with those of Vidyānātha. (4) VMK has pointed out some aspects of Vijayavarṇī's work in comparison with other writers on *Alaṁkāra-Śāstra*. He has also shown the sources of the work. (5) Vijayavarṇī follows Mammaṭa in some respects including the *Doṣas*. He discusses 33 *Alaṁkāras* in keeping with Rudraṭa. In the treatment of

Vṛtti, he follows Vidyānātha as a model. Among the *Rītis,* he drops the Lāṭī in the ten *guṇas,* and in some respects, he follows Daṇḍin and occasionally Vāmana. Here, it may be pointed out that the concept of *Rasābhāsa* as clarified by Vijyavarṇī in the tenth chapter in. stanza No. 183 deserves specific mention.

(ii) Dr. VMK brought out a critical edition with Prof. R.C. Parikh of the *Kāvyānuśāsana* by Hemacandra. This is edited with two commentaries *Alṁkāra-Cūḍāmaṇi* and *Viveka* and published by Shri Mahāvīra Jaina Vidyālaya, Mumbai in the year 1964.

Here, the text with two commentaries covers pages 1-466 and the Index of the stanzas in the two commentaries covers pp.467-504 and the Sanskrit C*hāyā* of the Prakrit prose and poetry covers pp.505-513. There is another Index of the *Sūtras* of *Kāvyānuśāsana,* covering pp.514-521 and the Index of the works and authors quoted in the work covers pp.522-528. There is further the Index of technical terms covering pp.529-566 and there are further appendixes.

VMK has given us the information about the personality of Hemacandra in the light of his works, such as *Śabdānuśāna*, *Abhidhānacintāmaṇi-kośa. Deśīnāma-mālā, Triṣaṣṭi-Śalākā-Puruṣacaritam, Yogaśāstra, Dravyāśraya, Chandonuśāsana, Kāvyānuśāsana, Pramāṇa-Mīmāṁsā,* and *Vītarāga-stotra.*

In the Introduction, VMK has also discussed the chronology of the works of Hemacandra even including the work *Siddha-hemacandra-vyākaraṇa.*

VMK has also subjected to criticism the view of Dr. Jacobi on the point of the relation of Hemacandra with Siddharāja Jayasiṁha and the Cālukya King Kumārapāla. He has also fixed the date of Hemacandra as 1145 A.D. to 1229 A.D. This date of Hemacandra is also accepted[3] by Dr. P.V.Kane in his *History of Sanskrit Poetics.'*

Here instead of giving other points in the edition, I prefer to make a reference to the article of Dr. Kalkarni on 'The Sources of Hemacandra's *Kāvyānuśāsana.'*

Here, he has given the tables[4] showing the subject-wise sources of *Kāvyānuśā-sana* by referring to *Kāvyaprakāśa, Kāvya-mīmāṁsā*, *Locana* on *Dhvanyāloka,* Vāmana's *Kāvyālaṁkāra* and *Śṛṅgāra-prakāsa* of Bhoja (ii) Besides, Hemacandra has given the comments of Bhoja on some *Gāthās*. These are six in number and these passages are also found in *Dhvanyāloka, Locana, Nāṭyaśāstra*. For the *Kāvya-doṣa-vivecana,* Hemacandra has taken portion from the *Kāvyaprakāśa, Kāvyamī-ṁāmsa, Dhvanyāloka* and *Locana*, Mahimabhaṭṭa's *Vyaktiviveka*, and Vāmana's *Kāvyālaṁkārasūtra*. When Dr. Raghavan states that Hemacandra has completely reproduced discussions on *guṇas*, definitions and examples from the *Śṛṅgāraprakāśa* chapters XI and XII Dr. Kulkarni points out that a reference to the chapter XII of the *Śṛṅgāraprakāśa* is not clear as this chapter is devoted to the structure and technique of the drama. Dr. Kulkarni further adds that Hemacandra has reproduced faithfully his masters' views in their own words, though at some places, he has said *'vayam tu brūmaḥ'* etc.

The greatest merit of the work of Hemacandra lies in this that he has brought within the compass of a single work the portion from the poetics and dramatics. In this respect, he has followed the lead taken by Bhoja in his *Śṛṅgāra Prakāśa*.

It is further clear that Hemacandra has taken these sources indirectly from the sources utilised by him in writing the *Kāvyānuśāsana*.

The charge of plagiarism levelled against Hemacandra is also dismissed[5] by Dr. Kulkarni by stating that while writing a work on any scientific subject, there is nothing wrong if any author quotes such works. If we do so, we will be only betraying our poverty of imagination and scant respect for the intelligence of Hemacandra.

He has shown his sense of discrimination[6] in rejecting three *Kāyaprayojanas* mentioned by Mammaṭa in his *Kāvyaprakāśā*. He holds that *Lakṣaṇā* is based on *Prayojana* only not on *Rūḍhī* or *Prayojana* as held by Mukulabhaṭṭa and Mammaṭa. He further rejects *ubhaya-śakti mūla-dhvani* mentioned by Mammaṭa. Hemacandra further criticizes Dhanika for describing Jīmūtavāhana as the *Dhīrodātta nāyaka* of the drama. Mammaṭa's division of eight *Madhyama kāvyas* is rejected by Hemacandra and he has accepted only three types of *Madhyama-kāvyas*. Further, Hemacandra's treatment of the *Guṇas* in the fourth chapter of the *Kāvyānuśāsana* reminds one of the similar treatment given by Rājaśekhara in his *Kāvyamīmāṁsā*. He has compiled several passages from different sources into one organic whole-adding his own remarks in between. This is abundantly clear from the discussion based on the *Vyakti-Viveka* and *Vṛtti*, *Dhvanyāloka* and *Locana* at the proper place.

Here it may be noted that the contribution of Hemacandra lies in preserving the passages from the *Locana* and *Abhinavabhāratī* and this has helped Dr. Kulkarni to purify many corrupt passages from the *Abhinavabhāratī*. This importance of the work of Hemacandra has escaped the notices of Dr. Kane and Dr. De and even other scholars.

(iii) Another critical edition by VMK is popularly known as *"Sāhitya-ratnakośe—Jainasaṁgrahaḥ"* published by the Sāhitya Academi, New Delhi, as Vol. VIII in the year 1978. This contains selections from the poems, plays, *subhāṣitas*.

Here VMK has dealt with the *Āgama,* Logic, Metaphysics, religious disciplines and Puranic literature on the *Tīrthaṁkaras.*

In this book, there is also the inclusion of the chapter on "A Survey of the Jaina Literature (in the Sanskrit and Prakrit languages) covering pages i to xxxii.

This collection is divided into three parts. (1) *Caraṇānuyoga*, (2) *Dravyānuyoga* and (3) *Kathānuyoga*. Here some passages are taken from the works such as *Bṛhatkathākośa, Ādipurāṇa, Uttarādhyayana sūtra. Triṣaṣtiśalākāpuruṣacaritam* etc. Another significant aspect of this collection is that the passages are taken from the works of both the śvetāṁbara as well as the Digaṁbara sects.

Here, in the introduction, VMK modestly states that the passages selected here may not be the best but will illustrate the quality and quantity of the Jaina Literature.

One will have to note here that there is a significant addition of the section on *'Stotras'* pp. XVIIII-XIV which however, has no place in the introduction to the survey in the '*Treasury to Jain Tales*,' published by VMK in the year 1994 on behalf of Chimanbhai Educational Research Centre, Ahmedabad

Incidentally, it may be noted that the survey of the Jain Literature is again published by VMK in a '*Treasury of Jain Tales*', dropping the *Stotra* Portion.

In passing, it may be added that this Anthology of the Jaina Texts covers printed 236 pages and the lengthy introduction covering xxxiii pages and the Bibliography covers two pages.

iv) *Jayadeva's Gīta-govinda with the Commentary of the King Mānāṅka* is edited by VMK and is published by the L.D.Institute of Ahmedabad, in the year 1963.

In the introduction to this work, VMK has discussed the problems such as Jayadeva's date, the popularity of the *Gīta-govinda.* other works of Jayadeva, brief summary of the chapters, form of the poem, origin and mystical significance of the title and the position of the *Gīta-govinda* as a lyrical and devotional poem.

He has further discussed the date of the King Mānāṅka and the nature of his commentary and his position as a commentator.

VMK adds[7] that Rādhā here stands for human soul and Kṛṣṇa stands for God. This is the love of human soul for God. It must be added here that eroticism is a part of the *Bhakti*, It seems that Jayadeva is a poet of true love and a great devotee of Viṣṇu.

The flaws in the writings of Jayadeva are noted by Paṇḍitarāja Jagannātha in his *Rasagaṅgādhara*. However, the meed of praise is showered on Jayadeva by the foreign and Indian scholars like A.B. Keith. Winternitz, De and Dasgupta and others.[8]

As regards the commentator King Mānāṅka, the question arises regarding his identity. Dr. V.V.Mirashi held that the commentator Mānāṅka cannot be the founder of the early Rāṣṭrakūṭa dynasty as the latter flourished in the 13th century A.D. He, therefore, may be identical with the king Mānasiṁha of Bundelkhaṇḍa.

Dr. D.R. Mankad, however, is inclined[9] to identify Mānāṅka with Mānasiṁha, the king of Jayapur.

VMK has placed Māṅānka between 12th and 14th century A.D. He points out that Mānāṅka is quoted by Rāyamukuṭa in his commentary on the *Amaruśataka*. This author Rāyamukuṭa flourished in 1431 A.D. and his commentary is known as *'Ṭippaṇī'*.

VMK has pointed out in his introduction that this *Ṭippaṇī* of the king Mānāṅka is not a sub-commentary; but, it directly explains the text of the *Gīta-govinda*. Mānāṅka uses the expression *mayā ṭippaṇikā kṛtā*. He gives word by word explanation, cites grammatical *sūtras* from the *Kātantra-vyākaraṇa,* quotes dictionaries like *Amara,* and shows the synonyms for the expressions used in the text. It is further worthy of interest that Mānāṅka does not give the metre of the stanzas, no discussion on the readings. He simply wrote a gloss and his commentary is not learned like that of the *Rasikapriyā* commentary on the *Gīta-govinda* of Jayadeva.

For the critical edition of this work, VMK has utilised the three manuscripts out of which 2 are borrowed from the L.D. Institute of Ahamedabad and the third from the Bhandarkar Oriental Research Institute, Pune. It must be noted here that VMK has also added the extracts from another commentary *Bhāvaprabodhinī*. on the *Gīta-govinda* and this commentary is not published so far. It is particularly to be noted[10] that VMK has also quoted the *sūtras* from the *Kātantra-vyākaraṇa* in the Appendix No.2. Infact, VMK has made every attempt to make the work as complete as possible.

(v) VMK has also edited the text ' *Praśamarati-Prakaraṇa* by Vācaka Srīmad Umāsvātī. This text contains 313 stanzas. This text is translated into English by Mahesh Bhogilal (14-3-1938 to 27-5- 1983). This work is published by Mahesh Bhogilal Memorial Trust Bombay in the year 1991.

This is a treatise on the joys of peace of the soul and a religious philosophical work. It deals with the duties of a house-holder and of a monk, 12 *Bhāvanās, Kṣapaka-Śreṇī*, six substances, nine concepts of reality, *Saptabhaṅgī* and the way to *Mokṣa*. This is a Jain work. Although Mahesh Bhogilal was born as a Jain, he believed with Samadarśī Ācārya Haribhadra whose couplet may be quoted in the foot-note.

There are in all six Appendixes. In the first Appendix we have the benefit of the explanatory notes. In the second Appendix, the concept of *Leśyā* is explained with references to the verses 37-38 of the text with the help of three stories. The third Appendix gives the concept of a *Tīrthaṅkara* referred to in the verse No.12. This is followed by three stories. In the fourth Appendix, we have the detailed classification of different typical conditions of a *Jīva* referred to in the verse Nos. 196-197. In the fifth Appendix, the nature of a Real thing otherwise known as *Saptabhaṅgī* referred to in the verse No. 204 is adequately explained. In the Sixth Appendix, five-fold classification of the Right Conduct is explained and this is referred to in the verse Nos. 228-229.

In passing, it may be added that the text contains an English translation. Besides, as pointed out in the Bibliography, there are two references[11] to the Gujarati Translation of the text with the explanation by Pūjya Muni Śrī Rājaśekharavijayajī and the same text with the long commentary by Pūjya Muni Śrī Bhadraguptavijayajī is published. This edition is indeed a sincere service of VMK to the publication of a Jain work.

(vi) VMK has also edited *'A Treasury of Jain Tales'* and this is published by Sharadaben Chimanbhai Educational Research Centre, Ahmedabad in March 1994.

With the help of other scholars like the late Prof. S.T. Nimkar, Mrs. Nirmala Chedda, the late Dr. G.S.Bedagkar, R.P. Nipanikar, Dr. M. Upadhye and J.C. Jain, VMK has presented here the English version of 124 Jain tales. It may be remarked here only incidentally that most of the bulk is the work of Nimkar.

Here, there is a division of Jain tales with different heads. Legends of famous persons cover pp. 6 to 115, Biographical Sketches cover pp.119-146, Tales of Wit and Wisdom cover pp.147 to 290 and the Voyage tales occupy the tales of Mākandī brothers and other tales pp.295-395.

This is followed by critical notes and appendix and the list of contributors and select Bibliography.

This narrative literature is prefaced by a note of VMK on the brief survey of the Jain Narrative Literature covering pp. XV to XXXVI.

On page xxxvi, VMK has given the characteristics of the Jain tales such as pages devoted to the past and future births, inexorable law of *Karman* playing a very conspicuous role, sermons with dogmatic details, parables and illustrative tales, here and there. Lastly, it must be noted that 'the spirit of asceticism is writ large throughout the text and almost as a rule every hero retires from the world to attain better status in the next life.'

It must be incidentally noted that VMK has also added the note of the learned scholar Dr.G.S.Bedagkar[12] indicating his reaction on the Jaina tales particularly in comparison with the tales in English literature. Here it will not be out of place to quote one paragraph. The story of the Mākandī brothers' voyage should find a worthy place in the voyage literature of the world by the side of Haklyut's voyages and many other Spanish and Italian accounts, the Indian woman mentioned in this story,the tribal woman who charms sailors by her beauty and youth but, destroys them by her demands, has her counter-part in Homer's Circe.

The story also works up a fabulous atmosphere which clearly sends ripples of Arabian Nights in our minds. The survey presented by VMK is based on the *'History of Indian Literature"* Vol. II by Dr. Winternitz, published at Calcutta in the year 1933. Here VMK has dealt with the canonical literature (pp.xvi-xxiv), Commentaries on the Canonical works (pp.xix to xxi) *Bhāṣyas and Mahābhāṣyas* p. xxi, *Cūrṇīs*, *Vṛttis* pp. xxii. xxiv, and the counterparts of the *Rāmāyaṇa, Mahābhārata*, and *Mahāpurāṇas,* and 63 *Śalākā-Puruṣas* p.xxvii to xxx, and further the counter part of *Bṛhatkathā*, quasi—Historical *Prabandhas*, *Dharmakathās* Campūs, Ornate poems, *Kathā, Kośas* (pp. xxxiv-xxxvi)

It is significant to add here that at the end, scholarly notes[13] are added by VMK on the Jain tales in this collection and the views of the scholars like Dr.A.M. Ghatage and others are quoted.

In fact, one will be tempted to remark that VMK has surely rendered a valuable service to the Jaina Narrative literature by the present volume.

(vii) *Uṣāniruddham of Rāmapāṇivāda*—This critical edition is brought out by VMK and is published by Sharadaben Chimanbhai Educational Centre, Ahmedabad-380004 in the year 1996.

This edition will have to be regarded as an improvement upon the earlier editions of the *Usāniruddham* brought out by other scholars.

Here one may note that the Sanskrit *Chāyā* of the text is procured by VMK from the Oriental Institute, Madras. This manuscript is nothing but the transcript of the original manuscript. Here the text of the Sanskrit *Chāyā* covers pp.1-79, This is followed by an English Translation covering pp. 81-126.

Further, the modern students have the benefit of the mythological notes given by VMK covering pp.127-134.

The value of the book is further heightened by adding glossary of the words and the select Bibliography.

This book gives us the lengthy introduction of 32 pages. VMK observes that at the end of the Second canto, the scribe has repeated some thirty verses presenting other readings. Thus, the manuscript gives us the double version of the texts. These readings VMK has relegated to the foots, with the word 'Also'. This peculiarity we notice on pages 48-56.

VMK has placed the work entitled' *Uṣāniruddham'* to the middle of the 18th century A.D. He further suggests that another work *Kaṁsavaho* seems to have been composed by the poet at the advanced age and it is thus clear that it is written after the *Uṣāniruddham.*

Some of the views[14] of VMK as regards the use of the Prakrit language in the drama deserve mention. The appearance of Prakrits in the drama is coterminous with the beginning of the Ancient Indian drama so far known. After Aśvaghośa, Bhāsa has used *Prakrits* in all his plays except the *Dūtavākya*. It is further clear that for most of the writers after Kālidāsa, the writing of Prakrit became mechanical and was as good as the conversion of the Sanskrit sentence into Prakrit. VMK further observes that the whole performance of the Prakrit composition was a prosaic affair. By the time of *Mahānāṭaka* or *Hanumannāṭaka*, Prakrit lost its conventional ground in the Sanskrit plays. He further adds that originally the manuscripts of the plays were written without Sanskrit *Chāyā,* but, by the time of Rājaśekhara, the practice of adding the Sanskrit *Chāyā* had come into vogue. Here the view-point of A.B. Keith is referred to by VMK. But, as regards the position of the Prakrit in the *Uṣāniruddham* is concerned, VMK categorically holds that the Sanskrit *Chāyā* was written first and then followed the Prakrit verses.

In this introduction, VMK has also discussed the other problems of the style of the poem and metres in the poem. Incidentally, it may be remarked here that the English Translation of the text is in keeping with the idiom of English language and not the old-fashioned[15] English translation of the works previously given by Dr. S.K. Belvalkar, R.D. Karmarkar. A.B. Gajendragadkar and others. Herein lies the novelty of the English Translation of the *Uṣāniruddham.* for whichVMK has best utilised the help of Dr.G.S. Bedagkar.

VMK has also pointed out the originality of Rāmapāṇivāda in the opening setting *(Uṣāniruddha* I.1-16), the dramatic and dainty addresses in the mouth of

Citralekhā in response to the observations of Uṣā and Aniruddha (I.36-38 and 42 to 45). He further adds that Rāmapāṇivāda has followed the *Bhāgavata-Purāṇa* and for the references to Gāndharva form of marriage, Kottavī and not Kottara indicate his use of the *Harivaṁśa*.

By this critical edition, VMK has created an honourable place for himself in the field of textual criticism.

(viii) VMK has to his credit another work on '*Some Aspects of the Rasa Theory'* published by B.L. Institute of Indology Delhi, (extension Centre, Patan) in the year 1986. This book contains a collection of eleven articles on the different aspects of *Rasa* written by the renowned scholars. H.C. Bhayani wrote on 'The Basic Modes of Poetic Expression (pp.1-4) "Germs of the Later *Rasa* Doctrine in Bharata's *Nāṭyaśāstra* (pp5-12) by M.V. Patwardhan, R.B. Patankar, the author of *Saundarya-mīmāṁsā* threw light on "Śaṅkuka—A defence (pp.13-27)", VMK clarified the position of the "*Laukika* and *Alaukika* nature of *Rasa*", (pp.28-42). T.S. Nandi brought to light "Worldly Nature of *Rasa"* (pp.43-53), There are three articles on the *'Rasa* theory and the *Darśanas'* written by K.S. Arjunavadkar, P.R. Vora and Bhagavati Prasad Pandya covering pages 54 to 71. P.N. Virkar, however, concentrated on the *Rasa* Theory and its relation to the fine Arts' (pp,72-80), K. Krishnamoorthy discussed the "Relevance of the '*Rasa* Theory to the modern Literature' covering pp.81-96. C.N. Patel dealt with' Catharsis and *Rasa,* in five pages. There are two further articles published in the Appendix I and II on the 'Relevance of Sanskrit Poetics to Contemporary Practical Criticism' by Umashankar Joshi (pp.101-109). R.B. Patankar has dealt with the topic 'Does the *Rasa* Theory have any modern relevance?' (pp.110-120). This bunch of articles is prefaced by a small note of VMK. It would not be out of place to remark that VMK's treatment of the *Rasa* will be dealt with later on by devoting a special section for the *Rasa Siddhānta*.

ix) Another critical edition to the credit of VMK is the Second Volume of Abhinavagupta's commentary on *Bharata's Nāṭyaśāstra* originally edited by the late Ramakrishna Kavi. and revised by Dr. V.M.Kulkarni and Prof. Tapasvi Nandi and published by the Oriental Institute, Baroda.

In this Critical edition, one finds the chapters VIII to XVIII of Bharata's *Nāṭyaśāstra* with the *Abhinavabhāratī* of Abhinavagupta.It must be mentioned here that the text of *Abhinavabhāratī* on the *Nāṭyaśāstra* is hopelessly corrupt and this is purified by Dr. V.M.Kulkarni, by utilising the other works like Hemacandra's *Kāvyānuśāsana, Nāṭyadarpaṇa* of Rāmacandra and Guṇacandra and the *Kalpalatā*. It should be noted here that Dr. Kulkarni has published so far a series of articles on this aspect of the restoration of the corrupt text of the *Abhinavabhāratī* and his attempt is appreciated by M.V. Patwardhan and Masson and even by Dr. K. Krishnamoorthy.

Some of the peculiarities of this second revised edition may be noted here for the attention of the scholars.

1. In his introduction, Dr. Kulkarni has quoted the passages from the *Abhinavabhāratī* and *Kāvyānuśāsana covering* pp. ii to vi to show how the *Kāvyānuśāsana* of Hemacandra is highly useful for correcting the corrupt text of the *Abhīnavabhāratī*. Here, attention may be drawn to *Abhinavabhāratī* p. 445 with Hemacandra's *Kāvyānuśāsana* p. 441, *Abhinavabhāratī* p. 206 with *Kāvyānuśāsana* p. 108, *Abhinavabhāratī* p. 208 with the *Gāthā-Saptaśatī* III. 59 etc.

2. There is further the utilisation of the new manuscript called '*N*' (Nepal). This manuscript shows a number of absolutely new variants coming to the figure 366, 136 readings out of which agree with the other manuscript.

3. Some misisng portion of the *Abhinavabhāratī* on chapter XVIII is supplied by Hemacandra in his *Kāvyānuśāsana* p. 441 *Abhinavabhāratī* p.445. Similarly *Abhinavabhāratī* p. 266 agrees with *Kāvyānuśāsana* p. 108. Dr. Kulkarni remarks that Hemacandra presents consistent, convincing and satisfactory meaning of the word (p.iii) and presents true and original and genuine readings of the passages of *Abhinavabhāratī*. Also Compare further *Abhinavabhāratī* p. 209 with the *Kāvyānuśāsana* p. 419.

4. Dr. Kulkarni has suggested some emendations at some places. For example, p. 412.

5. For the explanation of '*Kāku*' Dr. Kulkarni has quoted Abhinavagupta' s *Locana* commentary on the *Dhvanyāloka* of Ānandavardhana III,38 on page 389 of the *Nāṭyaśāstra*.

6. He has also shown the *prakṣipta* portion of the *Abhinavabhāratī* p.348.

7. On page 344, Dr. Kulkarni has identified the stanza from Vāmana's *Kāvyālaṅkāra* III. 1. 25. Also see p. 332.

8. Dr. Kulkarni has shown on page 336 that the idea in the *Abhinvabhāratī* is found in the *Raghuvaṁśam* III.70. This is only for showing the similar idea.

9. Dr. Kulkarni has also explained the word *'paridevanam'* in the *Nāṭyaśāstra* p.

320 by quoting the explanation from Bhoja's *Śṛṅgāraprakāśa* which illustrates the idea by the example from the *Ratnāvalī* Act. III. Incidentally, he has also referred to the view point of Śāradātanaya on *Parivāda* as *mṛṣā-doṣaḥ.*

As usual, there is an index of the works and authors quoted in the *Abhinavabhāratī* covering two pages and the index of the stanzas in the text.

Looking at this scholarly edition of the *Nāṭyaśāstra* Vol. II, one will be almost tempted to observe that by his rich and varied experience, Dr. Kulkarni has sufficiently enhanced the value of the work with the rare insight of a seasoned scholar.

(II) As a translator of the technical work :—

VMK has rendered good services to the subject. Some of the interesting points in connection with this role as a translator deserve mention here.

(i) It VMK has translated into Marathi, the portion from the *Abhinavabhāratī* of Abhinavagupta particularly connected with the *Śānta-Rasa.* He has contributed this article to *Prof. R.S. Walimbe Felicitation Volume* brought out under the title *'Sahitya and Nāṭya-Kāhī Samasyā'.* This volume is published in the year 1974. Here VMK's translation covers pp.70 to 90. Incidentally, it may be noted here that on some doubtful passage, VMK sought the explanation from Bālaśāstrī Khuperakar, the learned Śāstrī from Kolhapur. The article of VMK is followed by the explanation of the learned Śāstrī and this shows that VMK's thirst for knowledge is adequately satisfied and his doubts are properly removed by the learned Śāstrī. In passing, it may be added that in the foot-note No.16 on page No.90, VMK has added a paragraph stating that though he has made proper use of the works of Dr. V. Raghavan *'The Number of Rasas'* and *'Śāntarasa and Abhinavagupta's Philosophy of Aesthetics'* by J.L. Masson and Prof. M.V. Patwardhan, yet, at some places, the readers will experience a difference in translation between VMK's work and the above-mentioned two scholars.

In his foot-note No.13 on page 86, VMK has also given corrupt passage purified by him. But in the foot-note No.14, VMK has remarked that the sentence *'sattvabhāvo hi hāsyarasaḥ/* is unintellibile. In the foot-note No.12, Hemacandra's reading *'na śāstravirodhī/* is preferred by VMK as compared to the reading accepted by M.V.Patwardhan and J.L.Masson. Further, in the foot-note No.10, VMK has expressed a doubt whether the words *'Khaṇḍa* and *Muṇḍa'* in the text of *Abhinavabhāratī* stand for the varieties of bulls like Dhavalya and Pavaḷya or these are the names of the bulls.

Anyway, on reading the translation of VMK of the *Śāntarasa,* one is tempted to observe that he has made a very close study of the discussion of Abhinavagupta and has added new material to the appreciation of the *Abhinavabhāratī.*

(ii) VMK has also expressed his indebtedness to the learned Professor M.V. Patwardhan by quoting his translation of the *Pratāparudrīya of Vidyānātha with the commentary Ratnāpaṇa* of Kumāraswāmī in the Appendix II pp. 97-201 in the book *'More Studies in Sanskrit Sāhitya Śāstra'* published by Sarasvati Pustak Bhandar, Ahmedabad in the year 1993. Secondly VMK has also quoted some portion of *sāttvika-bhāva's* translation by Prof. M.V. Patwardhan in the Appendix I of the above mentioned book. Here M.V. Patwardhan has translated some portion of the *Kāvyānuśāsana* of Hemacandra dealing with the portion of the *Sāttvikabhāvas.* This covers pages 191 to 196. Thirdly, VMK has also quoted Prof. M.V. Patwardhan's translation of the Alaṁkāracūḍāmaṇi on pages 90-92 in the book '*More Studies in Sanskrit Sāhitya Śāstra.*

(iii) VMK has also reproduced the translation given by Dr. S.K. De in his *'History of Sanskrit Poetics'* of 'Rājaśekhara's Theory of *Pāka*'. This translation, VMK has quoted in his chapter on 'Rājaśekhara: The Critic' published in the book *'More Studies in Sanskrit Sāhitya Śāstra*', pp. 110-111.

(iv) VMK has restored another work entitled *'The Harivijaya of Sarvasena'*. In this book, he has translated into English, about 25 stanzas which are definitely ascribed to *Harivijaya.* In the first Part, he has reproduced the stanzas with Sanskrit *chāyā* and added scholarly notes. So far as the second part is concerned, VMK has collected about 95 stanzas which are probably drawn from *Harivijaya,* by Bhoja in his *Śṛṅgāraprakāsa* and *Sarasvatīkāṇṭhābharaṇa.*These 95 verses are also translated by him with proper Notes. In the Notes, he has cited extracts from the *Śṛṅgāra-prakāśa* and the *Sarasvatī-kaṇṭhābharaṇa.* In the Appendix to this work, VMK has discussed the sources of the *Harivijaya-* such as the *Viṣṇu-Purāṇa* and the fourth part of the *Bhāgavata-Purāṇa.* Incidentally, however, VMK has also quoted some portion of the translation of the *Viṣṇu Purāṇa* by H.H. Wilson, published in the year 1961 p. 462 He has consulted the translation of the *Bhāgavata Purāṇa by* Dr. G.V. Tagare.

(v) Another enormous work done by VMK is the '*Prakrit Verses in Sanskrit Works on Poetics.'* In the first part of this work, he has taken into consideration the works of 20 authors and the Prakrit verses quoted in them. These figures may be stated here:-

1.	Rudraṭa's *Kāvyālaṁkāra*	15	Verses.
2.	*Dhvanyāloka* with *Locana*.	59	"
3.	*Vakroktijīvita*	28	"
4.	*Daśarūpaka* with *Avaloka*.	25	"
5.	Vyaktiviveka.	29	"
6.	*Śṛṅgāraprakāśa*	1655	"
7.	*Sarasvatī kaṇṭhābharaṇa*.	383	"
8.	*Kāvyaprakāśa-*	64	"
9.	*Alaṁkārasarvasva* with *Jayaratha's Vimarsinī*.	56	Verses
10.	*Sāhityamīmāṁsā*	121	"
11.	*Vāgbhaṭālaṁkāra*	12	"
12.	*Kāvyānuśāsana*.	80	"
13.	*Kalpalatāviveka*.	122	"
14.	*Alaṁkāra-mahodadhi*.	79	"
15.	*Vāgbhata's Kāvyānuśāsana*.	23	"
16.	*Sāhitya-darpaṇa*.	27	"
17.	*Rasārṇavasudhākara*.	26	"
18.	*Alaṁkāra-ratnākara*.	168	"
19.	*Rasagāṅgādhara*.	103	

VMK has also added an Appendix I showing 69 Apabhraṁśa passages corrected by Dr. H.C. Bhayani. In the Appendix II, the Apabhraṁśa passages corrected by Dr. H.C. Bhayani come to about 20. In all, in this work, one comes across the 3164 Prakrit passages, presented with Sanskrit *Chāyā*.

This work in two parts is published by B.L. Institute of Indology, in the years 1988 and 1990.

As regards the treatment, it may be said that VMK has tentatively restored some verses, some are partially restored and some are left as they are. It may be remarked here that in restoring the verses, VMK has also disclosed sources of the verses immediately side by side with the verses. The second part of this work is devoted to the translation, introduction and glossary and notes of the verses. Here again some interesting points may be noted in connection with the second volume.

1. He has utilised the translation of some verses as done by others. M.V. Patwardhan's translation of verse No.201. He has also utilised the translation by K.K. Handiqui on pages 194 and 233.

2. He has added significant foot-notes on some pages -141, 217, 216,, 141 etc.

3. On page 119, VMK corrects the *chāyā* for stanza No.1258

4. In Vol. I, verse No.1243 is declared as corrupt and therefore obscure. But in Vol. II on page 117, VMK has given the *gāthā* with the Sanskrit *chāyā*. On page 490, he remarks that this *gāthā* is tentatively restored.

5. The verse No.1199 given in the Vol I page 262, is left untranslated by VMK, as it is incomplete and obscure.

6. In Vol. I, on page 274, we have the verse No.1258 which is quoted from the *Gāthāsaptaśatī* In his translation of the verse 1258 in Vol. II, p.119, VMK gives a hint for the correction of the *chāyā* as *'kṣīyata ahamiva*-But, in his Notes on this verse No. 1258, VMK further suggests that for *roditi rudatya maya* one should read *rudatyām mayi.* This clearly shows that VMK took pains to correct the *chāyā* not only in the translation part but further in the notes part too.

7. He has left some verses untranslated such as 1127, 1099, 1103, 1104, 1023, 1021, 1063, 1065. 1066, 1035, 1925, 802, 694, 640, 646, 641, 654 etc. thereby giving opportunity to the future scholars of *Alaṁkāra-Śāstra* to complete this work.

8. At times, it is noticed that only half of the verse is translated and half left untranslated, for example, verse No 964.

9. In the foot-note on verse No. 820, VMK has given the different meanings of the word *Puṇḍarīka.*

10. In Vol. I verse No. 674 was left by VMK as corrupt and obscure. But in the Vol. II p. 73, he has reconstructed the *Gāthā* which was originally not intelligible to him. In his notes on page 416, he has frankly admitted that this *gāthā* is tentatively restored.

11. For the verses 21 and 24 of the *Sāhityadarpaṇa,* VMK has consulted the material of Dr. A.M. Ghatage. For the verses in the *Alaṁkāra-Ratnākara,* he also consulted the works of C.R. Deodhar, K.V. Abhyankar and Prof. R.D. Wadekar.

12. Verse No. 98 of Bhoja's *Śṛṅgāra-prakāśa,* is translated by VMK in the Vol.-II p. 23 with the remark in the foot-note that this *gāthā* is cited to illustrate the poetic blemish called impropreity.

    Finally, a word about the notes to these verses. Some remarks are only given. his notes are critical, wrong readings are pointed out, and corrected, different translation of the verses is given in view of the emendation in the reading originally accepted but later on revised, Commentaries on the works are quoted and the research papers of the scholars on the particular aspect are best utilised by VMK. In fact, one will be very happy to observe here that this work in two volumes will have to be regarded as the best contribution of Dr. Kulkarni to the Prakrit verses in the *Alaṁkāra* works. It must be admitted that the study of this *Śāstra* cannot be said to be complete without the correct grasp of the Prakrit passages quoted by almost all the writers on Sanskrit *Sāhitya Śāstra* and hence this aspect can hardly be ignored.

13. Incidentally, it may be worth mentioning here that Dr. Kulkarni in his reviews on some books has made the translation of some corrupt passages and thereby purified the text and corrected the translation. But such places, I reserve for further discussion.

III. Restoration of the lost passages can be regarded as the significant contribution of VMK for the *Alaṁkāra-Śāstra*. It may be noted here that this principle of restoration is also utilised by Dr. Kane for the *Kātyāyanasmṛti* and *Śaṅkha Likhita Dharma-Sūtra*. Dr. Moghe used it for the reconstruction of the *Vyāghrasmṛti* and *Ṛṣyaśṛṅgasmṛti*. Dr. M.L. Wadekar employed this principle for the reconstruction of the *Devala Smṛti*. In the *Abhinavabhāratī of Abhinavagupta* on the *Nāṭyaśāstra,* many passages are hopelessly corrupt and these passages have baffled great scholars like Dr. V. Raghavan, Dr. K. Krishnamoorthy, Ramkrishna Kavi and others. Dr. Kulkarni deserves credit for removing this obstacle of corruption by the Principle of Restoration. He has published an article on 'Discovery through Restoration', in *the Journal of the Asiatic Society of Bombay,* Vols.60-61, for 1985-86 (New series) and this has also appeared in his book *'More Studies in Sanskrit Sāhitya Sāstra*, pp.170-190. Here, it would be proper to quote the principles[16] he adopted on the point of Restoration for the future benefit of the scholars.

(i) One must hunt the source for the corrupt passage. If the source is traced, the emendation becomes universally applicable or acceptable.

(ii) If, by chance, the corrupt passage is found quoted in order to illustrate different points of poetics at two or more places in one and the same work to reconstruct it by comparing the corrupt texts at different places.

(iii) If the source is irretrivably lost, to try to find out if the passage under consideration is cited in another work on poetics or metres or Grammar.

(iv) If it is not so traced, to try to find out if the verse in quotation is included in a later anthology, or any other work of poetics by way of a quotation.

(v) If no internal or external evidence be available, to take into consideration the immediate context and emend the text in consonance with the metre and general or overall purport.

(vi) To take into consideration parallel ideas found in other works on Sanskrit and Prakrit and emend the text accordingly.

(vii) To take especial care that the emended text is as far as possible very akin to the printed letters or words in the corrupt verse /passage.

(viii) Failing all these alternatives, to emend the text using one's own (creative) imagination (*pratibhā*), keeping in mind the immediate and the larger context, the metre and the tenor of the concerned verse.

(ix) To take particular care that the proposed emendation keeps arbitrariness to the minimum.

(x) To consult, wherever possible, the manuscripts on which the printed text is based; if the editor of the printed text has read a word or quarter of a verse or part of it wrongly, the consulting of manuscripts may help one to recover the correct reading.

In this context of the Restoration of the Corrupt Passages in the *Abhinavabhāratī* of Abhinavagupta, Dr. Kulkarni contributed a series of Research[17] papers which are listed in the foot-note. He made the adequate use of the *Kāvyānuśāsana* of Hemacandra, the commentary *Viveka* on the same, the *Nāṭyadarpaṇa* of Rāmacandra and Guṇacandra and the *Kalpalatā-viveka* and restored the passages and purified the same.

Incidentally, it may be noted that VMK has also stated that the corrupt passages in the *Kalpalatā* can also be purified by the help of the *Abhinavabhāratī* of Abhinavagupta.

Here it deserves to be mentioned that Dr. Kulkarni has restored about 93 passages from the *Abhinavabhāratī* in five research papers contributed to the *Journal of the Oriental Institute*. Baroda. These papers have also appeared again in his book '*Studies in Sanskrit Sāhitya-Śāstra*.' pp. 37-70. There is one more paper of Dr. Kulkarni on '*Abhinavabhāratī* Chapter VII Recovered?' originally published in the *Journal of the Oriental Institute*, Baroda, Vol. xx No.3, March 1971. This paper is again published in the above volume on pages 71-77. For elucidating 33 *vyabhicāribhāvas,* Dr. Kulkarni has quoted the passages from Hemacandra's *Kāvyānuśāsana* side by side with *Kalpalatā-viveka* for 9 passages and the passages from the *Nāṭyadarpaṇa* side by side with the *Kalpalatā-Viveka* for 11 passages. By citing these tables, Dr. Kulkarni has legitimately come to the conclusion that the *Kalpalatā-viveka* has preserved[18] a major portion of the *Abhinavabhāratī* on the *Bhāvādhyāya* i.e. the sixth chapter of the *Nāṭyaśāstra*.

Dr. Kulkarni further states that since the portion dealing with *Sattva* and *Sāttvika -bhāvas* does not find place in the *Kalpalātaviveka,* probably, it has dealt with this topic in the *Kalpalatāpallava*. For this view of Dr. Kulkarni, attention is drawn to the foot-note on Page No. 77 of *Studies in Sanskrit Sāhitya Śāstra*. It deserves to be added here that VMK has purified more than 3000 passages of the Prakrit verses quoted in the *Alaṁkāra-Śāstra* and also the important portion of the *Bhāvādhyāya* and *Rasādhyāya* of the *Abhinavabhāratī* and has thus rendered valuable service to the studies of *Alaṁkāra-Śāstra* and the *Nāṭya-Śāstra*.

The importance of the *Harivijaya* of Sarvasena is admitted by Ānandavardhana in his *Dhvanyāloka* III. 11, 12, Abhinavagupta in his *Locana* on *Dhvanyāloka* p. 335 and Kuntaka in his *Vakroktijīvita* p. 71 (S.K.De's edition). This text was held as irretrivably lost by the scholars through the passage of time. But by the effective weapon of Restoration, Dr. VMK has brought to light the verses of *Harivijaya* and thereby rendered important service to the field of research.

In his introduction[19] to the *Harivijaya of Sarvasena,* Dr. Kulkarni refers to the view point of Handiqui that it may be doubtful if the *Harivijaya* was a mature product. Dr. Kulkarni simply observes that this is rather harsh and unfair to Sarvasena. He further adds that just as the plays of Bhāsa are eclipsed by the plays of Kālidāsa, in the similar manner, Pravarasena's *Setubandha* might have eclipsed Sarvasena's *Harivijaya*.

Attention may be drawn to the important passage from the *Abhinavabhāratī* vol. I p. 339, reconstructed by Dr. V. Raghavan in his book '*The Number of Rasas*' p. 115. Dr. Kulkarni, however, keeps in mind the reading in the *Kalpalātaviveka* and the text of the *Abhinavabhāratī* and restores the text and seeks confirmation to it from the *Abhinavabhāratī* pp. 340-341. Here the reading of the *Kalpalatā-viveka* reads *antarmukhatalābhena* and *Abhinavabhāratī* proposes the reading '*antarmukāvasthābhedena*.' It is thus clear that Dr. Kulkarni has made improvement upon the reconstruction of the passage proposed by Dr. V. Raghavan with convincing evidence. For this discussion, attention of the readers is drawn to the article on '*Kalpalatāviveka* on *Abhinavabhāratī*' originally published in the *Journal of oriental Institute,* Baroda, Vol. XXI No.4, June 1972 and also published in the volume '*Studies in Sanskrit Sāhitya Śāstra*' p. 68. One may refer also to the page No. 53 for the correction of the bald reading in the *Abhinavabhāratī*.

(IV) Emendations:—

Generally it is a practice of the scholars to emend the corrupt text only to bring a connected and coherent sense of the passage under discussion.

It would be equally interesting to see how Dr. Kulkarni has used this technique in respect of the passages from the *Abhinavabhāratī* and the allied texts.

(i) In his article '*Abhinavabhāratī* Text- -Restored' Dr. Kulkarni quotes the passage from the *Abhinavabhāratī* Vol. I p. 338. Dr. V. Raghavan adds the word into the bracket. Dr. Kulkarni cites a passage from the *Kāvyānuśāsana* p. 122 which has preserved the passage from the *Abhinavabhāratī*. He simply remarks that the passage from the *Abhinavabhāratī* is quite intelligible and hence the emendation suggested by Dr. Raghavan of the word (*na*) (in the bracket) is quite unnecessary and further the passage is flawless. Here it should be noted that the suggested emendation is generally to be put into the bracket. Also see page No. 58 of the book *'Studies in Sanskrit Sāhitya-Śāstra'* for the wrong case of emendation.

(ii) Dr. Kulkarni has accepted the emendation suggested by Prof. R.P.Kangle in the *Abhinavabhāratī* Vol. I. 272 (Baroda edition) by suggesting *kālāttu māndyadarśanam* for *Kālāttanumāndyadarśanam* in the *Abhinvabhāratī*. In accepting the emendation of Prof. Kangle, Dr Kulkarni remarks that the reasoning given by Prof. Kangle is acceptable at all level. This discussion is available on p. 47 in the book *'Five-Book Reviews'* published in the Marathi by Kulkarni.

(iii) When Prof. Kangle suggests emendation to the corrupt passage of the *Abhinavabhāratī* Vol. I p. 275, in his *Rasa-bhāva-vicāra* p.142, Dr Kulkarni supports the same by quoting the authority of Hemacandra. Here the question arises as regards the correct reading *kāvyamupacitakākuprabhṛtyupaskareṇa'* in the text of the *Abhinavabhāratī*. Prof. Kangle suggests the reading *'Kāvyamu-*

citakākuprabhṛtyupaskāreṇa. Here he suggests *ucita* for *upacita* for the text. This is accepted by Dr. Kulkarni by quoting a passage from the *Kāvyānuśāsana* of Hemacandra p. 95. This discussion takes place in the book *'Five- Reviews'* in Marathi pp. 47-48.

(iv) Prof. Kangle suggests the reading *'Rāvaṇakāvye* for *Rāvaṇavākye'* in the *Abhinavabhāratī* Vol. I p. 296. Here, Prof. Kangle observes that the editor of the *Abhinavabhāratī* has suggested the emendation as *'Rāvaṇavākye'*. But, the reading *'Rāvaṇakāvye'* is the correct reading found in some manuscripts and it is also supported by Abhinavagupta's *Locana* commentary on the *Dhvanyāloka*. On this point, Dr. Kulkarni lends further support to Prof. Kangle's emendation by quoting a sentence from the *Kalpalatā-viveka* p. 127 which also prefers the reading *'Rāvaṇa-kāvyākarṇane'*. It is thus clear that Dr. Kulkarni gives additional support[21] to the reading emended by Prof. Kangle in the light of the manuscript and the *Locana*.

(v) At one place, Prof. Kangle emends the reading in the *Abhinavabhāratī* passage Vol. I p. 286 in his *Rasabhāva-vicara* p. 180. Here for the reading *'vaktrāṁbujanmāsavaḥ'* Kangle suggests the emendation such as *vakrāmbujasyāsavaḥ*. Kulkarni points out that the emendation suggested by Kangle is unnecessary as the word *'aṁbujanman,* for *Aṁbuja'* is the reading supported by the commentary *'Bālapriyā'* on the *Dhvanyāloka-Locana* p. 277. Here, the emendation is treated as unacceptable on the basis of the commentary[22] on the *Dhvanyāloka-Locana*.

(vi) When Prof. Kangle introduces major changes in the *Abhinavabhāratī* Vol. I p. 344, in his discussion in the *Rasa-bhāva-vicāra* P. 368, so as to bring out the spirit of the passage, Dr. Kulkarni does not favour this emendation. He points out that when the suitable passage is found in Hemacandra's *Kāvyānuśāsana* P,124, it is not desirable to make emendation of a major type. For the discussion on this passage, the attention of the readers is drawn to the book *'Five-Reviews'* pp. 53-54. It must be noted here that Dr. Kulkarni has relied upon the *Kāvyānuśāsana* for a better and clear reading of the line.

(vii) When the question arises whether the reading *lakṣaṇaḥ* or *vilakṣaṇaḥ* is correct in the passage from the *Kalpalatā-viveka* p. 307, Dr. Raghavan's emendation as 'Vilakṣaṇaḥ in Bhoja's *Śṛṅgāra-prakāśa* p. 480 is uncalled for. He gives the reason for the same by showing that the reading *lakṣaṇaḥ* is supported by Hemacandra's *Kāvyānuśāsana* p. 96 and the *Abhinavabhāratī* p. 277.

The above discussion leads one to the conclusion that Dr. Kulkarni has judiciously employed the technique of emendation either to support the text or to discard the emendation and to show how it is unecessary in the particular context.

In passing, it may be noted that the emendations and purifications suggested by Dr. Kulkarni in the *"Abhinavabhāratī* Chapter VII Recovered', were accepted[23] by Dr. Krishnamoorthy as a genuine part of the *Abhinavabhāratī* Chapter VII in the fourth edition of the *Nāṭyaśāstra* (Vol. I), Vadodara, 1992. This is, indeed, a great honour conferred on Dr. Kulkarni for his sound work in the matters of Restoration and Emendations.For this, attention may be drawn to the page vii of the second Volume of the *Abhinavabhāratī* revised by Dr. V. M. Kulkarni and Dr. Tapasvi Nandi.

V. *Sanskrit Sāhitya Śāstra;* Dr. Kulkarni has written two volumes contributing his views on some aspects of the *Sanskrit Sāhitya Śāstra*. It would be, therefore, proper to give some idea of some of his papers published in the two books *'Studies in Sanskrit Sāhitya Śāstra,* and *'More Studies in Sanskrit Sāhitya Śāstra'*.

(i) In his paper 'Sanskrit Rhetoricians on Poetic Convention' Dr. Kulkarni has shown[24] that poetic conventions are of three types- celestial, terrestrial and infernal things. This has again sub-varieties. Here he has taken survey of the works of Rājaśekhara, Hemacandra's indebteaness to *Rājaśekhara, Arisiṁha* and Amaracandra, Deveśvara, Viśvanātha adding few more conventions, Vāgbhaṭa borrowing from *Kāvyamīmāṁsā* and *Kāvyānuśana,* and *Keśavamiśra* and Kṛṣṇakavi (later than 1600 A.D.). He further notes the silence of Bhāmaha and Daṇḍin and Vāmana's[25] laying down the rules in relation to Grammar, Gender, Metre and Syntax. Dr. Kulkarni adds that Keśavamiśra's attempt to widen the province of *Kavisamaya* is not quite successful. He has failed to make any distinction between Poetic Convention and conventional poetry. Being close to natural phenomena, they i.e. the poets have selected[26] the symbols purely based on lively imagination. Hence,they have given colours to things, they indulged in Romantic imagination, symbols of birds and animals, black colour to defamation, white colour to fame and laughter etc. It is Rājaśekhara who made significant contribution to the concept of *Kavisamaya* i.e. poetic convention.

(ii) In his paper[27] on 'The treatment of Intonation (*Kāku*) in Sanskrit Poetics' Dr. Kulkarni has utilised the material right from the works of *Nāṭyaśāstra,* Abhinavagupta, Rājaśekhara, Bhoja, Mammaṭa, Vidyānātha, Viśvanātha, Appayya Dīkṣita and notes the points that *Kāku* can be *sākāṅkṣā*, this is again three-fold *Ākṣepagarbhā*, *Praśnagarbhā* and *Tarkagarbhā*. The *Nirākāṅkṣā Kāku* is either *vidhirūpā*, *Uttararūpa* and *Nirṇayarūpā,* The *Kāku* construction is looked upon as a case of *Guṇībhūta-vyaṅgya Kāvya.* It is not a figure of speech according to Rājaśekhara. Mammaṭa, however, treats it as a *Śabdālaṁ-*

kāra and Ruyyaka goes to the extent of treating intonation as an *Arthālaṁkāra*. Śrīdhara, however, holds that it is both *Śabdālaṁkāra* and the *Arthāṁkāra*. Abhinavagupta gives us the etymology of *Kāku*, its varieties and subject-matter and shows freshness of approach and originality. In this article, Dr. Kulkarni has also discussed the examples of *Kāku* from the Sanskrit dramas and has thrown more light on this topic which is lightly touched by others.

(iii) In his paper on 'The conception of *Sandhis* in the Sanskrit Drama' he has ransacked material from the works on the *Nāṭyaśāstra,* discussed five *artha-prakṛtis*, five *kāryāvasthās*, the five *sandhis* and has taken pains to explain 64 *saṅdhyaṅgas* connected with *Mukha-sandhi*, *Pratimukha-sandhi* etc,. To illustrate these *sandhyaṅgas*, Dr. Kulkarni has given illustrations from the Sanskrit dramas like the *Veṇīsaṁhāra,, Ratnāvalī, Uttararāmacaritam*. He has also explained the use of the *Sandhyaṅgas* and the sixfold purposes at the back of the *Sandhyaṅgas*. He has specifically pointed out that Bharata's analysis of the *Sandhis* and *Sandhyaṅgas* reveals that he was conscious of the principle of *Aucitya* (propriety) essential to the *Rasa* in particular. The point of Propriety[28] is highly developed by Kṣemendra and the later authorities display distinctive power of logical analysis and practical acumen. He simply concludes that the later dramatists were not tightly bound by the rules, rather rigid rules, of dramatic rules and have shown freedom in the thought—process.

(iv) In his article on 'The Problem of *Patākāsthāna*,' Dr. Kulkarni has discussed the definitions of the *Patākāsthāna* with the help of the Sanskrit commentator *Rāghavabhaṭṭa* and given proper illustrations of the *Patākāsthāna* which simply means the foreshadowing of the future incident in a drama. Incidentally, he has also shown a distinction[29] between *Gaṇḍa* and *Patākāsthāna*. *Gaṇḍa* is always ominous and is rather abrupt; while the *Patākāsthāna* serves to accomplish the desired object. In this article, all the four varieties of the *Patākāsthāna* are discussed and for the etymological explanation of *Gaṇḍa*, there are quotations from the *Daśa-rūpaka* III. 18 and the *Nātya-darpaṇa* p. 137. Further the *Patākāsthāna* is based on equivocal situation and equivocal speech.It is further to be noted that in the *Patākāsthāna,* the ambiguous situation may result in bringing about the aim of the hero. Dr. Kulkarni simply concludes that the device of the dramatic irony was duly taken into consideration by the Sanskrit playwrights.

(v) In his article on 'Sanskrit rhetoricians on Poetic Truth,' Dr. Kulkarni has consulted the works on Sanskrit Poetics like the *Kāvyaprakāśa, Sāhitya-darpaṇa, Kāvyamīmaṁsā* and the *Dhvanyāloka* and concluded that the rhetoricians were fully aware of the distinction betwen the scientific truth and the poetic turth. They also knew[30] that the *śāstras* are concerned with the scientific truth and the poetic truth is the concern of the poeticians. Further, in the name of poetic truth, they do not grant the licence of scientific ignorance or inaccuracy of detail to the poet. In fact, the principle of *Aucitya* or propriety enunciated by them embraces all the aspects of poetic truth, such as emotional, imaginative truth and poetic conventions and the law of probability.

(vi) Another interesting paper of Dr. Kulkarni's is on 'Criteria for separate *Alaṁkāra* (*Pṛthagalaṁkāratvam*).' In this article, he has noticed the tendency of the writers in increasing the number of *Alaṁkāras* and also in decreasing the number. But a figure is to be regarded as separate, if it produces charm of a different kind from that produced by some other accepted figure. It must be remembered that this test is applied by both Jayaratha and Jagannātha. Some times, one is constrained to regard a particular figure as a sub-variety of another figure. It must be further borne in mind that if there is slight strikingness and one goes on imagining another separate figure of speech, there would be no end to it. Jagannātha has gone to the extent of treating the training and poetic sensibility of the *sahṛdaya*[31] as the final authority, on this point Dr. Kulkarni has quoted five places from Jagannātha's *Rasa-gaṅgādhara* (pp.434, 451, 497, 613 and 703 Nirnaya Sagar edition, Bombay).

(vi) In his paper 'Rājaśekhara: The Critic', Dr. Kulkarni has shown that the modern scholars like Drs. Kane, De and A.B. Keith have not given any importance to Rājaśekhara and his work *Kāvyamīmāṁsā*. He pinpoints the contribution of Rājaśekhara on the concept[32] of *Pāka,* his views on Poetic Truth, poetic conventions and plagiarism. Rājaśekhara has further introduced four types of poets, the principle of Adaptation and his indebtedness to Bhāmaha and Ānandavardhana is brought to light by Dr. Kulkarni. His treatment of poetic truth is indeed noteworthy and he has dealt with this topic fully and it is to his credit that he should have fully and sympathetically dealt with the topics which are slightly touched by others. Herein lies his novelty.

(vii) Another thought-provoking paper of Dr. Kulkarni is on 'Hemacandra's Treatment of *Alaṁkāra* and *Rasa* Tradition.' In this article, Dr. Kulkarni refers to the view point[33] of Prof.R.B. Athavale on the inclination of Hemacandra towards reducing the number of *Alaṁkāras*. He finds fault with Hemacandra. Dr. Kulkarni answers this point by noting the tendency of the *Ālaṁkārikas* in increasing and decreasing the number of *Alaṁkāras* and finally refers to the authority of Jagannātha who treats *Sahṛdayas* alone as the authority on this point. Dr. Kulkarni also dismisses the charge of plagiarism levelled against Hemacandra by the ancient and modern critics. He holds that in a scientific text, if one quotes complete passages or illustrations to illustrate the point, it cannot be regarded as a case of plagiarism. In fact, the text of the *Kāvyānuśāsana* of Hemacandra comes to the level of the *Kāvyaprakāśa* of Mammaṭa and the *Sāhitya-darpaṇa* of Viśvanātha. Dr. Kulkarni has also noted the supreme importance of the work of Hemacandra. He points out that whatever are the corrupt passages in the commentary *Abhinavabhāratī* on the *Nāṭyaśāstra,* the same can be properly corrected with the help of Hemacandra's *Kāvyānuśāsana.* In this work, Hemacandra has preserved original passages of *Abhinavabhāratī*, *Dhvanyāloka-Locana, Vakroktijīvita, Sarasvatī-kaṇṭhābhara*, *Śṛṅgāraprakāśa, Bhāmahavivaraṇa* etc. When the primary source of the manuscript of these works fails, one has naturally to depend upon the secondary but valid source of Hemacandra's *Kāvyanuśāsana* and *Nāṭyadarpaṇa* of Rāmacandra and Guṇacandra. Incidentally, he also refers to the view of Prof. D.D. Kosambi who finds fault with Hemacandra for writing on the topic of erotic experience. Dr. Kulkarni simply remarks that Prof. Kosambi is harsh on Hemacandra. Finally, it is concluded by Dr. Kulkarni that Hemacandra does not claim any originality as regards any new theory of poetics. But he claims his originality in his method, manner and the treatment of the subject-matter and in preserving the original passages of the works on poetics. Herein lies the utility of Hemacandra and this utility can hardly be denied by any responsible worker on the subject.

(viii) It is to be significantly noted that his paper on 'Ānandavardhana, Dhanika and Kuntaka on the *Abhijñānaśākuntala*' is more interesting. Dr. Kulkarni has shown how the stanzas from the *Śākuntalam* are quoted by these rhetoricians to illustrate some aspect[35]. Ānandavardhana in his *Dhvanyāloka* III. 1-2, quoted the famous line *'kimiva hi madhurāṇām* maṇḍanam *nākṛtīnām'* to show that the word *'madhura'* is here suggestive. He further quotes the *Śākuntalam* III.23, to illustrate how the *nipāta* is suggestive. Dhanika quotes the '*Śākuntalam svasukha-nirabhilāśaḥ*' as an example of the term *vijigīṣu* 'hero. He further quotes the famous stanza '*medaschedakṛśodaram*' to illustrate *mārdavam* i.e. mildness in which faults are considered as merits and merits as faults. Kuntaka,however, in his *Vakroktijīvita* II.29, quotes the famous line '*vayam tattvānveṣān madhukara hatāstvam khalu* kṛtī' to show the charm of *sāṁkhyā-vakratā*. Here instead of *'aham'* Duṣyanta uses the expression *'vayam'* which suggests that he is in fact, a stranger. Here, we get *tāṭasthyapratītiḥ*. He further quotes the stanza from the *Śākuntalam* I.7 as the example of realistic and graphic description of *jāti* (species). In this way, Dr. Kulkarni has given other illustrations only to show how the writers on *Sāhityaśāstra* appreciate the beauty of the drama '*Śākuntalam*' perhaps in a manner different from the regular commentators of the *Śākuntalam*, He finally concludes[36] that the criticism levelled against Kālidāsa by the Western scholars, is certainly unjust and unfair.

(ix) In his article on 'Sanskrit writers on Plagiarism,' Dr. Kulkarni points out the authors who have not dealt with this topic. He has also referred to the view-point of Rājaśekhara that one poet is a creator, another an adapter, *(parivartaka)*, the third one is *'acchadaka'* and still one is *'samvargaja'* i.e. collector. He further holds that there is no poet who is not a thief.He has made a lot of discussion on this topic. But, in his Critical Remarks, he has pointed out that borrowing without beautifying is plagiarism. But, all plagiarism is not improper. If a later poet transmutes into his own precious metal the less refined one of the other poets, it is not plagiarism. Dr. Kulkarni further adds that the charge of plagiarism is valid only where borrowing is deliberate without creating new thought and new effects. He gives the view point of the Western scholars on the point of plagiarism. 'Colourable[37] imitation constitutes plagiarism. Taking a substantial part of the original work is a literary theft. 'Substantial' does not refer to quantity alone but also to the importance of the part taken in relation to the whole. Dr. Kulkarni adds in a foot-note No.37 on page 18 that there is nothing in the works of Sanskrit writers that would correspond to such thoughts of the Western writers in this paragraph. Lastly, he adds that if a poet makes what is ancient his own by his assimilative skill, we cannot damn him as a plagiarist. Even great poets have done that and there is no harm in that. Dr. Kulkarni holds[38] that Sanskrit writers have not given deep thought to this problem of plagiarism and have failed to observe some subtle aspects of it, yet, it must be recorded that their contribution to this very interesting subject is sufficiently rich.

(x) In his learned paper on 'Some aspects of Prakrit verses in the Alaṁkāra-works', he has shown[39] that a lot of Prakrit passages are quoted in the *Alaṁkāra-śāstra*. The Sanskrit writers write in both the languages-Sanskrit and Prakrit with perfect ease. There was no compartmentalisation but integration of Sanskrit and Prakrit studies. The writers on *Alaṁkāra Śāstra* have clarified the concept of obscenity. The use of the words which rise to the feelings of shame or disgust or convey the sense of inauspicious are treated as taboo in cultured and polite society. They have denounced obscenity even in particular combination of letters giving rise to words meaning the names of the private parts of the human body. The Prakrit poetry is generally declared as obscene and giving expression to the immorality or clandestine unions of the lover and beloved. But the *Ālaṁkārikas* preferred a moral approach, They did not denounce immorality, but, whatever was bad in aesthetic sense or taste. They further held that eroticism was most appealing. Later on, however, aesthetics and ethics came to be combined. Finally it must be borne in mind that life in all its aspects has a place in literature. It is for the poet to present it in a beautiful form. Elsewhere, Dr. Kulkarni held that it would be proper on the part of the readers to appreciate the poetry irrespective of its immoral or obscene aspect. It is left to the law-givers to take action against such descriptions. We must not mix up law with the art of appreciation.

(VI) The Study of Prakrit Language:—

I have already referred to some of the works of Dr. Kulkarni on the Prakrit studies. In the present section, I have decided to enlighten the readers on his Prakrit works left untouched so far.

(i) VMK has written a Ph.D.[40] thesis on 'The Story of Rāma in the Jaina Literature'. This thesis covers 13 chapters. In the first chapter, Dr. Kulkarni has given the character of Jain mythology. Here he has pointed out that the Jain mythology is indebted to Hindu mythology and the writers of Jain literature have disfigured Hindu mythology and have introduced changes in it so as to suit their own requirements and particularly to put forth the principle of *Ahiṁsā* and becoming a monk. In the second chapter, he has discussed the *Paumacariya* of Vimalasūri. In dealing with this work, he has discussed at length the other relevant topics such as date of the poet, his life, his other works, his position as a poet, the form of the poem, the title of the poem, its extent, his aim at the back of the writing, his conception of Rākṣasas and Kinnaras, language of the work and metres and the social life as reflected in this work. This kind of treatment he has followed in respect of the other works of Ācārya Raviṣeṇa, *Rāmāyaṇa* version of Sanghadāsa, *Rāmāyaṇa* version of Guṇabhadra, *Rāmāyaṇa* version of Silācārya, *Rāmāyaṇa* version of Ācārya Hariṣeṇa,Puṣpadanta, Dhaneśvara Sūri, Bhadreśvara, Ācārya Hemacandra, the origin of the Rāma story in Jain literature, Vimalasūri's indebtedness to Vālmīki's *Rāmāyaṇa,* and his attack on the *Rāmāyaṇa* and the Development of Rāma story in the Jain Literature. The main intention of the Jain authors is to purge the story of Rāma of its Brahmanical atmosphere. This story is introduced in the *Rāmāyaṇa* to create Jain atmosphere and specially for propagating the doctrines of Jainism such as *Ahiṁsā*, attack on the institution of sacrifice . For achieving this aim, they have omitted some portion from the original *Rāmāyaṇa* of Vālmīki and added some new matters which have no place in it. Incidentally, it should be noted that Rāvaṇa is painted as a noble person in Jain literature. VMK has also discussed the Digaṁbara version of Guṇabhadra and has compared the Jaina *Rāmāyaṇas* with the *Rāmāyaṇa* of Vālmīki.

All these features of the Ph.D. thesis show that VMK has made a thorough study of the story of Rāma in the Jain literature. Incidentally, he has also discussed the views of scholars in this work and expressed his opinion in that respect. For the present, I have to remain contented by noting only the important changes made by the Jain writers in the original Rāma story of the *Rāmāyaṇa*. (1) Raviṣeṇa introduced Suprabhā as the fourth queen of Daśaratha. (2) The image of Janaka is destroyed by Bibhīṣaṇa. (3) Vajravarta and Sagaravarta are the names of the two bows bent by Rāma and Lakṣmaṇa at the time of the Sītā-*svayaṁvara*. (4) Bharata's wife is known as Lokasundarī. (5) In the *Ātithya* episode, Rāma assumed the role of a dancing girl. (6) Hanumat sides with Lava and Kuśa against Rāma in the battle. (7) The god Meṣa-ketana helps Sītā in her fire-ordeal. (8) Puṣpadanta states that Indrajit was older than Rāvaṇa. (9) The arms of Lakṣmaṇa were long and unbending. Bibhīṣaṇa is described as a long-lived (*cirañjīvin*). (10) Hemacandra states that after marriage with Kaikeyī, Daśaratha goes to Rājagṛha and returns to Ayodhyā after a long time. (12) Aparājitā experienced four dreams and Sumitrā experienced seven dreams indicative of the birth of two mighty sons. (13) Khara is described as the husband of Candranakhā and Dūṣaṇa and Triśiras were his younger brothers. (14) Hemacandra refers to the four Mahādevīs of Daśaratha but does not refer to the 8000 wives of Daśaratha. (15) Hemacandra describes that Rāma went in search of Sītā and returns home to perform her *śrāddha*. (16) Rāma personally collects the news of the scandal about Sītā and then gets it confirmed by his investigating spies. (17) Bhadreśvara introduces the picture motif to convince Rāma that Sītā still yearns for Rāvaṇa.This trick is played by other two queens of Rāma. (18) He also shows the motif of jealousy of the two queens of Rāma to draw the feet of Rāvaṇa in a picture. (19) Vimalasūri holds that Khara and Dūṣaṇa are not two persons but this refers to a single individual. (30) Vālin's victory over Rāvaṇa has no place in Vimalasūri's *Paumacariyam*.

In this context, the originality[41] in the work of Dr. Kulkarni may be stated. (1) He has made a critical and comprehensive study of Jain *Rāmāyaṇas*. (2) He has taken an all-embracing review of the various aspects of the problem of Rāma story. (3) He has discussed the problem of Rāma against the background of Jain mythology. (4) He has also given us the literary appreciation of the Jain versions. (5) He has also made the interpretation of the Jain versions and comparative study of Jain works with the *Rāmāyaṇa* of Vālmīki.

Besides, the different tables indicating the comparison of the works introduced by Dr. Kulkarni on pages 148-151, 205-211, 142-143, 133-135, 109-113. 92-97 are indicative of his critical mind and systematic study. He has also discussed the Religion and Mythology of the Jains, covering pages 1-14.

All this survey simply reveals that Dr. Kulkarni has drunk deep in the fountain of Jain literature connected with the *Rāmāyaṇa* and Vālmīki's *Rāmāyaṇa*.

(ii) Dr. Kulkarni's monumental work '*Studies in Jain Literature* (Collected papers of Prof. V.M.Kulkarni) is a recent publication of the year 2001 on behalf of the Shresthi Kasturbhai Lalbhai Smārak Nidhi, Ahmedabad. A glance over this work, at once, reveals that this collection of the papers of Dr. Kulkarni reveals the contribution of Jain authors to the *Alaṁkāra-Śastra*, his reviews on some important Jain works, his discussion on the Jain mythology, exposition of VMK of the Jain philosophy, Narrative literature of the Jains, Anthology of *Tārāyaṇa (Tāragaṇa)* of the Jain verses in Prakrit and the comparative study of the *Gītā* and the *Uttarādhyayana-sūtra* and comparative study of some works like *Nandīsuttam* and *Anuogaddariraim,* and types of stories in Jain literature, the Jain concept of aesthetics and the brief survey of the Jain narrative literature and Women in Ancient Indian Tales. These topics discussed in this work further reveal Dr. Kulkarni's deep knowledge of the Jain literature which helped him sufficiently in restoring the corrupt Prakrit verses in the *Alaṁkāra-Śāstra*. However, for the benefit of the readers, I intend to give here some interesting points from this book. In his paper[42] on '*Uttarādhyayana-sūtra* and Brahmanisms, Dr. Kulkarni has rightly concluded that though there are differences in the Brahmanism, Jainism and Buddhism, yet we can easily notice the cultural unity on the points of a life of self-control and the liberation can be achieved through right knowledge of the reality. In another paper[43] on 'The *Bhagvad-gītā* and *Uttarādhyayana-Sūtra*—A Comparative Study', Dr. Kulkarni has pointed out that the *Uttarādhyayana-sūtra* condemns the views of the *Gītā,* rejects the view that god is a creator of this universe, downright condemnation of the system of sacrifice in which the beast is a victim. As the Jainism believes more in *Ahiṁsā*, there is no place for war, sacrifice etc. in it. In explaining 'The eschatological ideas in Jain Tradition,' Dr. Kulkarni has correctly explained[44] *Nidāna* as bartering away one's austerities for sensual pleasures in a future birth, which are denied to him in the present birth or for avenging for insults or personal injuries in the subsequent births. This is illustrated by the example[45] of Draupadī who believes in the Principle of *Nidāna* explained above. Incidentally, Dr. Kulkarni refers to twenty *viṁśativiṁsikā* on page 128 while discussing an approach to the work of Haribhadrasūri. In his other paper on 'Veda and Jain Texts,' Dr. Kulkarni explains the *Gaṇadhara-vāda* on p.93 which is concerned with the conversion of Indrabhūti

Gautama, Agnibhūti and nine other very learned Brāhmaṇas to Jainism. Thus, the converted persons were later on known as *Gaṇadharas*, chief disciple of Mahāvīra. In his review on 'Women in Ancient Indian Tales', Dr. Kulkarni has noted that the Prakrit Jain narrative literature is rich in folklore and the women painted here are shown as maintaining their chastity at whatever cost, and women messengers prominently figure in these tales. Here we have the picture of courtesans, women messengers, wealthy merchants and princes. They delight and at the same time teach. Dr. Kulkarni has reviewed the anthology in the Prakrit language otherwise known as '*Tārāyaṇa (Tārāgaṇa)* edited by Dr. H. C. Bhayani, with an anonymous Sanskrit commentary. The importance[46] of this Anthology is pointed out by Dr. Kulkarni by stating that one *Gātha* from Bhoja's *Śṛṅgāraprakāśa* vol. III. verse 3, left untouched by him on account of its corrupt nature and obscurity, is restored by him with the help of *Tārāgaṇa* verse no. 171 (p. 70) and made the *Gāthā* intelligible. Dr. Kulkarni further presents a table of the verses common to both the *Tārāgaṇa* and *Gāhārayaṇakośa*, and makes a conjecture that a few more verses from the last portion of the *Tārāgaṇa* may have been cited by Bhoja in his two works and by Jineśvarasuri in his *Gāhāraṇyaūakośa*. From the point of restoration of the Prakrit verses, the source of this Anthology of Bappabhaṭṭi will have to be regarded as supreme. The first six articles of this volume dealing with Rāma story in the Jain literature have appeared in his Ph.D. thesis. Dr. Kulkarni has made a thorough study of the work '*Samarāiccakahā* (*Bhāva* II) of Haribhadrasūri. Here he has discussed the age, the life of Haribhadra, his other works, summary of the contents of the work, the parable of the man in the well, the position of the work as a *Dharmakathā*, language and style of the work and the society depicted in this work. Here on page 415, one finds that festivals in honour of Madana were performed, and the festival of Yakṣa Dhanadeva was celebrated. People believed in rebirths and doctrine of inexorable *Karma* or fatalism served as a consolation at the time of distress. One further comes across the good and bad omens and belief in Astrology and influence of stars had a firm hold upon the people. The second *Bhāva* of this work gives us a good description of marriage ceremony, This description on page 416 reminds one of the Hindu customs of Marriage, with slight modifications.

Dr. Kulkarni has further attempted the appreciation of the drama 'Mallikā-makaranda' by Rāmacandra, the Jain author, summary of the acts, Ramacandra as a dramatist, Mandakulastrī[47] as the heroine of the *Prakaraṇa*. She is not a lady of great family or a lady whose character is not above reproach, or a courtesan. Discussing the style of Rāmacandra, Dr. Kulkarni on page Nos 444-445 gives the examples of *Arthāntaranyāsa* in the play of Rāmacandra. He also explains some dramatic technical terms like *Nāndī*, *Sūtradhāra, Nepathya* etc.

In his treatment of the types of *Dharma kathās*, on page No.156, Kulkarni has made a distinction[48] between *Kathā* and *Vikathā*. In the *Dharma-kathā*, *dharma* is the main theme which treats of the virtues like forgiveness, humility, straight-forwardness, freedom from greed, self-control, truthfulness, purity, celibacy and other religious matters like the five lesser vows. While *Vikathā* is so called because it is opposed to the *Kathā* and deserves to be shunned. In *Vikathā*, one finds the stories of women, food, country, king or a ruler. A *Vikathā* is marked by tenderness and pity and compassion. This kind of *kathā* is so influencial that it affects man's right faith and right conduct.

(VII) Dr. Kulkarni and Aesthetics :—

On the topic of Aesthetics, otherwise known as literary criticism, Dr. Kulkarni has written a series of papers which deserves special mention here with the points clarified by him.

(i) In his paper 'Sanskrit theory[49] of Beauty', Dr. Kulkarni has made a discussion covering 17 pages and has raised the points that beauty is subjective, it is objective also, beauty is that which gladdens the eyes and sense organs, the suggested sense or *Vyaṅgyārtha* is powerful and delightful than the *abhidhā* or *lakṣaṇā*. It is the *pratibhā* of a poet that adds to the beauty of a thing. Ānandavardhana and others treat *Alaṁkāra* as beautiful provided it embellishes the suggested sense. The *pratibhā* of a poet gives aesthetic delight and *cārutva-pratīti* presupposes the existence of objective beauty. He further quotes the opinion of Ānandavardhana that if we judge the poetry with the help of *pramāṇas,* it would simply lead to ridicule. Both Ānandavardhana and Abhinavagupta hold that emotions are the central theme and content of the *Kāvya*. In this article, Dr. Kulkarni has quoted many authorities and one *subhāṣita* states that thing alone, to which one is attached, is a pleasant or agreeable thing to him.

(ii) In his other paper 'Bharata's concept[50] of *Bhāva*', Dr. Kulkarni points out that *Vibhāvas* and *Anubhāvas* are not to be treated as *Bhāvas*. 2) The *Sāttvika*, *Sthāyī* and *Vyabhicāri* alone deserve to be called *Bhāvas*. 3) *Sāttvika bhāvas are* both *Vyabhicāribhāvas* and *Anubhāvas* . 4) *Vyabhicāribhāvas* cannot be attended by other *Vyabhicāribhavas* . 5) *Bhāvas* are so called because they suggest or manifest the *Kāvyārtha* i..e the *rasa* connected with the dramatic presentation. The word *Bhāva* is derived from the root *bhū*. to cause to be, i.e. to bring about or create. and to pervade. The first meaning brings about the *Rasa* and the second meaning shows that they pervade the minds of the spectators as any smell does. The commentary *Bālapriyā* holds that the body of the spectator is pervaded by the *Rasa* as the drywood by fire, that is why the *Vibhāvas* are the external manifestation of the *Sāttvikabhāvas* like the *romāñca* or *pulaka*, *sveda*. But Dr. Krishnamoorthy states that connoisseur's appreciative response to poetry was not called *rasa* by Bharata or his early interpreters. They rightly term it as *'hṛdaya-saṁvāda*. While clarifying the position of *Rasa*, *Dr.* Kulkarni states that of many *rasas* which are used in the same work, the one whose form is of large compass, alone should be considered the *(sthāyin) rasa*, the others are *sañcārin rasas*. As per the *Yoga-Sūtra* IV. 10, it is quite evident that the correspondence between Memory, *Saṁskāras Dharma*and *Vāsanas* is endless as the desire of a man is endless. In the *Rasa* concept, the position of the *sthāyī* is supreme among all the *bhāvas* as is the position of a king among people and a teacher among the pupils. Further, the eight— *Sāttvikabhāvas* are regarded external manifestations and physical attributes.

(iii) In his paper[51] 'Dual nature of the *Sāttvikabhāvas.*' Dr. Kulkarni points out that *sthāyibhāvas* come as *Vyabhicāribhāvas*. Secondly *vyabhicāribhāvas* are treated as *sthāyibhāvas*. The distinction between the two is very slender. Besides, the *Sāttvikabhāvas* are both *vyabhicāribhāvas* and *anubhāvas*. In addition to this, the *Sātvivabhāvas* are both internal and external. The *Sāttvikabhāvas* are eight in number such as paralysis, perspiration, horripilation, faltering voice, trembling, loss of colour or paleness, tears and fainting. The different meanings of the term *Sattva* are given. Abhinavagupta takes it as concentration of mind. The authors of *Nāṭyadarpaṇa* take that when the mind is attentive, it is called *sattva.* For, if the mind be inattentive, it is not possible for the actor to act as per the *sāttvikabhāvas* like *svarabheda*. Hemacandra takes *Sattva* as *prāṇātmakam vastu* (vital energy). It is so called because the mind dwells in it and there is predominance of *sattvaguṇa* in it. And the *Sāttvika-bhāvas* arise from it. Viśvanātha in his *Sāhitya-darpaṇa* III. 134-135 understands *sattva* as a certain inward disposition which spontaneously reveals the repose of one's soul where it does not interfere to modify the indication. And the *Sāttvikas* are changes in human being. They are involunarary or honest and spontaneous, which arise from *Sattva.* In the *Rasa-ratna-pradīpikā, Sattva* means extreme readiness of the actor's / or spectactor's heart to appreciate the sorrows (or joys) of another (the original character) and it arises from a concentrated mind. VMK finally concludes that Abhinavagupta's theory of external and internal *Sāttvikabhāvas* involves the *Sāṁkhya* and *Vedānta* concepts. This is favoured only by Hemacandra, Naraharisūri and Kumārasvāmin, the illustrious son of the commentator Mallinātha. But, others have not favoured this view of Abhinavagupta. This paper is scholarly and VMK has consulted a lot of authorities but in the above discussion only interesting points are noted by me.

(iv) In his paper '*Rasa Laukika*' Dr. Kulkarni has made an indepth study[52] of the commentary of Abhinavagupta and the and *Nāṭyadarpaṇa,* and has shown that 'All *Rasas* are pleasurable'. 2) Some hold that only some *rasas* are pleasurable and others are not pleasurable (*duḥkhātmaka)*. 3) Poets exhibit richness of imagination in depicting the sentiments. 4) Some scholars accept only four *rasas* and reject the other four *Rasas*.

Rudrabhaṭṭa in his *Rasakalikā* agrees with the author of *Nāṭyadarpaṇa* and states that the *rasa* of *Karuṇa* is of a peculiar kind and is particularly due not to the nature of the emotion itself, but, to our contemplation of the Art with which an actor presents it. Here, incidentally, one may refer to Abhinavagupta's use of the *Sāṁkhya* view in deciding the nature of *Rasa*. The worldly objects are capable of producing pleasure and pain and are external, but the—*Sthāyins* awakened by the external objects are internal and of the nature of either pleasure or plain. According to *Sāṁkhyas*, the *rasa* is of dual nature- of amphibian nature- of pleasure or pain.

v) In his other paper[53] '*Rasa-Alaukika*' Dr. Kulkarni seems to have made a very thorough study of the commentary *Locana* on the *Dhvanyāloka*. He has also made the best use of the commentary of Abhinavagupta on the *Nāṭyaśāstra*. He points out that the *Rasa* is *alaukika* because when the spectator goes to the theatre he becomes so much engrossed in what he sees at and is so carried away by an overpowering sense of wonder that he identifies him with the principal character and sees the whole world as the latter saw it. Abhinavagupta points out the step in the aesthetic experience, the attitude of a true spectator, the generalised nature of what he sees on the stage and extraordinary non-worldly nature of the cognition of *rasa,* absence of any physical activity on the part of the spectator, and presence in him of a contemplative attitude. Abhinavagupta further adds that *rasa* is capable of being suggested by alliteration, gentle or harsh, which is devoid of any denoted sense. This is an additional proof of the *Alaukika* nature of the *Rasa*. Abhinavagupta adds that the Vibhāvas etc. are *alaukika* and they make it possible for the *rasika* to relish *rasa*. These *vibhāvas* etc. are not causes of cognition (*jñapti-hetus*), they are also the causes of production (*niṣpatti-hetu*). This position of the *Vibhāvas* strengthens the position of the *siddhānta* that the *rasa* is *alaukika*. The ancient thinkers like Bharata and others make a distinction between the real world and the world of a drama or a *Kāvya*. It must be noted here that the poet transforms the things of real life by the magic touch of his divine *pratibhā*- creative imagination. This aesthetic sense is not universal. So, the poet needs a *sahṛdaya* or a sensitive spectator to appreciate the things of beauty and joy, the poet has created by his *pratibhā*. The Poet's creations are wholly impersonal and have no reference to anybody in particular. Hence the aesthetic experience is free from the limitations of ordinary pleasure, arising out of narrow attachment such as envy. The sensitive spectator enjoys a unique kind of delight that has no parallel in day to day life. It is further clear that *Rasa* is achieved from other worldly process or mundane (*alaukika*). It is achieved by the power of suggestion which is peculiar only to poetry. It is further to be noted that both Abhinavagupta and Ānandavardhaa accepted full-fledged autonomy of the poet or a dramatist. They, i.e. the poets and dramatists, are autonomists. The term autonomy is used in Indian Aesthetics in a wider and popular sense. It may be further noted that Kant has used the term antonomy in a narrow sense. Hence Abhinavagupta will have to be described as an exponent of the *Alaukikavāda*. Incidentally, it may be noted that Abhinavagupta is in agreement with Śaṅkuka and not with Bhaṭṭatauta on the point of the *Alaukikavāda* of the *Rasa*.

(vi) In his paper on '*Rasa* and its *Āśraya* (Location, seat)', a question is raised whether the *Rasa* arises in a poet, or actor, or in the composition of a poet or in the mind of the *Sahṛdaya* i.e. sensitive spectator. Abhinavagupta holds that the *Rasa* does not arise in an actor. In this respect, Jagannātha has followed the lead of Abhinavagupta. Rāmacandra and Guṇacandra, the authors of *Nāṭyadrapaṇa,* take an opposite view and hold the *Rasa is* experienced by an actor or a singer. Bhaṭṭa-Nāyaka is of the view that the *Rasa* is actually experienced by the spectator. Bhaṭṭa-Lollaṭa, however, takes the stand that the *rasa* is located in the character that is portrayed (*Anukārya*). Incidentally, it may be remembered that according to Abninavagupta, the dramatic poem is like a tree. The dramatic representation by the actor is like flower etc. The spectator's aesthetic enjoyment is like the fruit. Consequently, everything is full of *Rasa*. Bhaṭṭa-Tauta held that the aesthetic experience is the same in the case of a hero of a poem or a play, the poet himself, the reader of the poem, or spectator of a play when recited or acted respectively. Bhoja in his *Śṛṅgāra-prakāśa,* as observed by Dr. Raghavan, holds that the *rasa* is in the character, in the poet, in the actor and in the composition.

(vii) In another paper '*Rasa* Theory and *Puruṣārthas*', Dr. Kulkarni has pointed out that generally in the case of a poet or dramatist, the acquisition of the four goals of human life is the aim. Now the question arises whether for the *Rasa*, there is any connection of the *Puruṣārthas-Dharma, Artha*, *Kāma* and *Mokṣa*. For this purpose, Dr. Kulkarni has consulted the particular portions from the *Abhinavabhāratī* on the *Nāṭyaśāstra* VI. 15, VI. 31, VI. 39. 41, XVIII. 10 and the concluding verse of the *Nāṭyaśāstra,* Chapter XVIII, and has demonstrated that the *Rasas* are concerned with the four *Puruṣārthas*. He Has also referred to the view-point of Pratihārendurāja that the nine *rasas*, *Śṛṅgāra* and others, are the means of acquiring four goals of human life. This is particularly evident from the discussion in the *Laghu-vṛtti* on the *Kāvyālaṁkāra-sāra-saṅgraha* pp. 52-53. Abhinavagupta has shown that *rati* is conducive to *Kama* and *Dharma* and ends in *Artha*. *Krodha* is conducive to *Artha* and ends in *Kama* and *Dharma*. The *Bībhatsa* and *Śānta rasas* are concerned with the *puruṣārtha* known as *Mokṣa*. Further, Abhinavagupta has linked the six types of drama : *Nāṭaka*, *Prakaraṇa*, *Samavakāra*, *Ḍima*, *Vyāyoga*, and *Īhāmṛga* with the *Puruṣārthas*.

(viii) In his paper on 'Mahimbhaṭṭa's views on How *Rasas* arise and they are enjoyed by *Sahṛdayas*', Dr. Kulkarni has summed up the position[57] of Mahimabhaṭṭa on this point. (1) *Rasādis* are of the nature of their corresponding *sthāyibhāvas,* relation between the *sthāyibhāvas* and their corresponding *rasa* is that of the *Biṁba-pratibiṁba-bhāva*. (2) There is further the sequence between *vibhāvādi-pratīti* and *rasādi-pratīti*. (3) The *Vibhāvādi- pratīti,* is the *sādhana* (means) and *rasādi-pratīti* is the *sādhya* (the end). (4) Although the *vibhāvādis* are artificial and the mental states like *rati* etc. be unreal, the enjoyment of *rasa* is very much real. (5) Things directly seen do not delight so much as they do when described by a gifted poet. In the similar manner, the things inferred from *hetvādis* in our real life do not delight us as they do when inferred from the *vibhāvādis*. Likewise, the expressed meaning does not delight us so much as does the implied meaning. (6) In passing, it may be noted that Mahimbhaṭṭa does not accept the function of *Vyāñjanā,* but, holds that *rasa-pratīti* is possible by *Anumāna*. The question also arises whether Mahimabhaṭṭa is indebted to Śaṅkuka. It is the view of Śaṅkuka that the *rasa* exists only in the drama and not in the characters to be portrayed etc. This view of Śaṅkuka is also referred too by Mammaṭa. Dr. Kulkarni further points out that by combining the two views, Mammaṭa seems to have attributed *Citra-turaga-nyaya* to Śaṅkuka. Dr. Kulkarni finally decides the point that the claim of Mahimabhaṭṭa to originality in connection with view on *Rasas* is not sustained. Dr. Kulkarni closes this discussion by pointing out another view[58] of Abhinavagupta that the drama alone gives complete *Rasāsvāda* and the same is the case with the *Muktakas,* when the reader is able to supply appropriate context. In passing, it may be added that Dr. Kulkarni has given adequate explanation[59] to the point raised by Dr. C. Rajendran in his '*A study of Mahimabhaṭṭa's Vyaktiviveka*' p. 118 that Mahimabhaṭṭa possibly could not have read *Abhinavabhāratī* for the view of Śaṅkuka., Dr. Kulkarni has pointed out that Mahimabhaṭṭa has read the portion of the *Locana* on the *Dhvanyāloka* and decided the above point very cleverly.

(ix) In his other paper '*Rasa* and its pleasurable nature', Dr. Kulkarni refers to the view-point of Rāmacandra and Guṇacandra, the authors of the *Nāṭyadarpaṇa*, that the mysterious delight is seen to result from these painful *rasas* due to the poet's creative imagination and the actor's skill in acting. Here they give credit to the excellence of the art of the dramatist and the skill of the good actors. Viśvanātha follows Abhinavagupta and holds that in the drama, the *alaukika* joy is produced from the *Vibhāvas* etc. which are *alaukika*. Jagannātha also holds that the role of *Vyañjanā* (suggestion) is supreme; that even things like sorrow, although unwelcome in themselves, when portrayed in creative literature, produce extraordinary joy or delight. Dr. Kulkarni also refers to the discussion in the *Locana* III p.510 and states[60] when Abhinavagupta compares *Rasāsvāda* with 2 *parabrahmāsvāda,* it is a case of mere *Arthavāda* (praise or eulogy) with a view to glorifying *rasa*. Dr. Kulkarni also refers to the view-point of modern thinkers who may not accept the position that in aesthetic experience, one enjoys one's own consciousness that consists of a compact mass of bliss.

(xi) In his paper on 'Hemacandra and *Rasa* Tradition', Dr. Kulkarni refers to the view-point[61] of moderns including the view of Siddhicandra, the commentator of the *Kāvyaprakāśa*. They regard that aesthetic pleasure is on par with ordinary pleasures of the senses as only (*laukika*). ii) They further hold that there are only four *rasas*- the erotic, the heroic, the comic and marvellous (*Adbhuta*). iii) They reject the claim of the pathetic, furious, the terrifying and the disgusting to the title of *Rasa*. From this, it would be clear that Siddhicandra, a modern thinker, has gone a step further in bringing the *rasa* to the *laukika* level. It should be noted that both Hemacandra and Siddhicandra are the Jain authors who held such peculiar views in the matter of the *Rasa*-enjoyment. xii) One may refer here to another article of Dr. Kulkarni on 'The Jain view of Aesthetic Experience.' In the Jain text[62] '*Anuyogadvārasūtra,* there is the mention of 9 *rasas*. Here, instead, of *Śānta*, there is the mention of the *praśānta Rasa*. It deserves to be added here that there is no place for the *Bhayānaka rasa* in this work; but the author has given place to the *Vrīḍānaka* (with *vrīḍā* or *lajjā* as its *sthāyībhāva*. The commentator of this work remarks that the *bhayānaka-rasa* is included under *raudra*. In this work, the prominence is given to the *Vīra-rasa* and not to the *Śṛṅgāra rasa*. This change is certainly significant.

The authors of the *Nāṭyadarpaṇa* hold that the *sthāyibhāva* when developed by *vibhāvas* etc. and manifested by the *anubhāvas* etc. is to be called *rasa*. This view of the nature of *rasa* is identical with the *Utpattivāda* or *Puṣṭi-vāda* of Bhaṭṭa Lollaṭa and Daṇḍin.

Further the authors of the *Nāṭyadarpaṇa* do not subscribe to the view[63] later on expressed by Jagannātha and previously expressed by Dhanika, the *miśrānandavāda*. They also hold that the *rasa* is present in the hero (Rāma, Duṣyanta etc.), in the spectator and some times in the actor.

Namisādhu,[64] the commetator of the *Kāvyālaṁkāra* of Rudraṭa, looks upon *rasas* as innate *guṇas* like *saundarya* of the *Kāvya*.

Dr. Kulkarni concludes this discussion by saying[65] that it is rather shocking that none of the Jain commentators has taken note of the '*nava-kāvya-rasā-pannata*' passage found in their sacred text called '*Anuyogadvāra-sūtra*.'

In passing, it may be noted that other Jain authors like Maladhārī Narendra-prabha, Vāgbhaṭa II and Vijayavarṇī and the autnors of *Alaṁkāramahodadhi*, *Śṛṅgārārṇava-candrikā* have nothing to say about *rasa*.

(xii) Dr. Kulkarni further notes in his paper on 'Hemacandra on the *Sāttvikabhāvas*', that the psychic states, when they enter into the predominantly earth-allied element in the vital force (*sattva*), give rise to *stambha* (the blocking of sensation), when they enter or affect the water-allied element in the vital force, they give rise to tears. As *tejas* is intimately allied to the vital force either intensely or in a feeble manner, it gives rise to perspiration and paleness of the body. Perspiration due to the infusion of *tejas* into the water dominated element of the vital force, for example, is illustrated in the commentary *Viveka* p.146. But the physical paleness or loss of colour due to infusion of *tejas* into water dominated element of the vital force in a feeble manner, is illustrated in the commentary *Viveka* by quoting a stanza '*sañcariṇī dīpaśikheva rātrau*' from the *Raghuvaṁśa*. This contribution of Hemacandra to the *sāttvika-bhāvas* has no parallel in the entire *Alaṁkāraśastra* literature or in the works on dramaturgy. Herein lies the greatness of Hemacandra.

(VIII) Dr. Kulkarni and some Introductions :—

(i) Here it may be stated that he has written introduction to the *Paumacariya* of

Vimalasūri, published by the L.D. Institute of Indology, Ahmedabad. the points of which are covered in his book' *The Rāma story in the Jain literature.*

(ii) Dr. Kulkarni has written a scholarly introduction[66] to the edition of the *Vyaktiviveka of Mahimabhaṭṭa* by Prof. M.V. Patwardhana, published by the Maharashtra Sahitya Sanskriti Mandala, Bombay, in the year 1998. Some of the points of introduction deserve notice here.

(1) He enumerates on pages 11-12, the critics or the opponents of *Dhvanivāda* of Ānandavardhana such as Bhaṭṭa-Nāyaka, the author of the commentary *Hṛdaya-darpaṇa*, quoted by Ruyyaka. Dhanika has accepted the *Bhāvya-bhāvakabhāva* instead of the *Vyaṅgya-vyañjaka-bhāva* of Ānandavardhana. Kuntaka includes *dhvani* in his *vakrokti,* Jayantabhaṭṭa in his *Nyāya-mañjarī* and Dhanika in his *Avaloka* commentary on the *Daśarūpaka* favour *Bhāvyabhāvaka-bhāva*. It is rather surprising that Mahimabhaṭṭa made no attempt to attack the criticism of Ānandavardhana against the *anumitivāda.*

Bhāmaha gets credit[67] for introducing the *Pratyakṣa* and *Anumāna pramāṇas* in the *Sāhityaśāstra*.

It may be noted that Mahimabhaṭṭa does not refer to Śaṅkuka to support his view-point. His *doṣa-mīmāṁsā* has become acceptable.

It deserves notice that Mammaṭa in his *Kāvya-prakāsa* has criticised Mahima-bhaṭṭa, particularly towards the end of the fifth chapter.

Though the *Anumāna-pramāṇa* is accepted by Mahimabhaṭṭa, Viśvanātha and Jagannātha, yet it did not stand the test of the *Nyāyaśāstra*.

Dr. Kulkarni points out that though the *Anumitivāda* of Mahimabhaṭṭa is not favoured by the later writers on *Sahitya-śāstra*, yet Mahimabhaṭṭa deserves credit as a critic and introduction of his *Anumitivāda* against the *Dhvanivāda* of *Anandavar-dhana*.

It deserves to be noted that Prof. M.V. Patwardhan holds that the *gamya-gamaka bhāva* is a synthetic view in the matter and the *bhāvas* like *kārya-kāraṇa-bhāva, Anumāpaka-anumāna* and *Vyaṅgya-vyañjakabhāva* etc. are the examples of analytical views. These views have surely enriched the Sanskrit *Sāhitya Śāstra*. In this context, one may remember the Upaniṣadic-statement or example *'vācāraṁ-bhaṇam vikāro nāmadheyam mṛttikā etyeva satyam:*

Dr. Kulkarni has praised the efforts of Prof. M.V. Patwardhana and his sound scholarsnip and has admitted his indebtedness to him. This can be further proved by the fact that Dr. Kulkarni has shown admiration for Prof. M.V. Patwardhan and

J. L. Masson by dedicating his book *'Outline of Abhinavagupta's Aesthetics* to these scholars.

(IX) Dr. Kulkarni and some Reviews:—

(i) He has reviewed the *Saptaśatīsāra with the commentary Bhāvadīpikā of Vemabhūpāla* edited by Dr. A.N. Upadhye, in the *Journal of the University of Bombay* vol. XL No.76, 1971, pp. 257-258. Here Dr. Kulkarni points out that only one hundred *gāthās* from the *Gāthasaptaśātī* are selected by Vemabhūpāla. He further shows that some readings in the text do not agree with the readings presented in the Sanskrit commentary.

He also adds that Vemabhūpāla seems to have been influenced by the works such as *Śṛṅgāraprakāśa,* and *Sarasvatīkanṭābharaṇa*. Dr. Kulkarni further adds that the Sanskrit *chāyā* to the text is personally added by Dr. A.N. Upadhye.

The importance of this work likes in that it is a work on Sanskrit poetics, as this commentary shows the *Dhvani* aspect of the poetics.

(ii) His review on the '*Vakroktijīvita*' edited by K. Krishnamoorthy and published[68] in the *Aryan Path,* January-February 1978 is a novel one.

Dr. Kulkarni adds that this edition of Dr. Krishnamoorthy is an improvement upon the earlier edition of this work by Dr. S.K. De. The simple reason at the back of this edition is that it has presented fresh material and presented complete and pure text. The text covers pages 283.

Dr. Kulkarni further points out the mistakes and misprints in giving the precise source of the verses.

As regards the translation of this work, Dr. Kulkarni simply remarks that though it is not literal, it keeps as close to the words of the text. It is lucid, elegant and idiomatic.

He further shows that there is a discrepancy in the translation with the words in the foot-notes and the words in the accepted text.

It is significant to add that Dr. Kulkarni suggests better readings for the words in the text and helps to identify the text. Attention is drawn to the page 135, verse 17 from Bhāmaha's *Kāvyālaṁkāra.*

For suggesting a better reading, he quotes several authorities and rejects the reading *rakṣitam* and accepts the reading *lakṣitam.*

(iii) Dr. Kulkarni has reviewed the book *'Rasa Theory and Allied Problems,* by Dr. G.K. Bhat, 'in the *Journal of the Asiatic Society of Bombay* Vols. 60-61 for 1985-86. Here he points out that some of the passages relating to Bhaṭṭa Lollaṭa's view and its criticism by Śaṅkuka are wrongly interpretated by Dr. G.K. Bhat, because of accepting the corrupt[69] readings.

He significantly remarks that Dr. Bhat should have better consulted Gnoli's excellent edition *'The Aesthetic Experience according to Abhinavagupta'*, while presenting the views of Śaṅkuka and others.

He further adds that the idea of intensification introduced by Dr. Bhat simply leads to obscurity. There is further gross misunderstanding of the objection raised by Śaṅkuka and Dr. Kulkarni clarifies the point of Śaṅkuka in a better manner. He further states that for each grade of love there should be different grades of intensity and lastly welcomes the attempt of Dr. Bhat.

(iv) He has reviewed the edition of the *Kāvyānuśāsana* edited by Dr. T. S.Nandi, in the *Journal of the Asiatic Society of Bombay.* Vol.76, p. 146 for 2001. In his review on this work Dr. Kulkarni points out, in the first place, the misprints on pp. 4, 92, 117, 366. Then he shows the mis-statement on p. 20 and mistake in the Translation on page 365.

Dr. Kulkarni points out that the present edition by Dr. Nandi is an improvement upon the edition of Hemacandra's *Kāvyānuśāsana* brought out by Prof. R.B. Athavale. It must be noted here that Prof. Athavale translated only the first two chapters of the work in Gujarati. The novelty in the work of Dr. Nandi is that he has translated all the 8 chapters of the *Kāvyānuśāsana* and has also criticized the view-points of the towering personalities like Dr. Kane, S.K. De and V. Raghavan.

(v) Dr. Kulkarni has also reviewed a book *'Sandeśarāsaka* of *Abdul Rahaman'* in two parts with Text and commentary and Introduction and Translation by Dr. H.C. Bhayani, in the *Journal of the Asiatic Society of Bombay* Vol.75 for 200, pp. 192-193.

Here, Dr. Kulkarni notes that Abdul Rahaman was a weaver of the Muslim community and the first Muslim to write in Prākrit language (Prakrit Apabhraṁśa). He belonged to the latter half of the 13th century or first half of the 14th century A.D.

It appears that the author Abdul Rahaman seems to have received proper training on traditional base and intimate knowledge of Sanskrit, Prakrit and Apabhraṁśa masterpieces.

It should be noted that this *Kāvya* is both a *Khaṇḍa-Kāvya* and also a *Dūta-kāvya*. Dr. Kulkarni has further noted the carelessness on the part of the Assistant in carrying out blindly the instruction of the author and not the matter.

(vi) *Jināgamon ki Mūlabhāṣā*. edited by Acarya Vijayashilachandramuni and K.R. Chandra, Prakrit Society, Ahamedabad, is reviewed by Dr. Kulkarni for the *Journal of the Asiatic Society of Bombay* Vol. No. 75 for 2000, pp. 194-196, Here the controversy arises as regards the original language of the Jain canonical literature. Whether it is Ardhamāgadhī or whether it is Śaurasenī.

Chandra concludes that Śaurasenī is posterior to Ardhamāgadhī. Dr. Sangam Jain adds that the Ardha-māgadhī is the language of the Aśoka's inscriptions and not Śaurasenī.

Dr. Kulkarni concludes quoting the view-point of Dr. A. M. Ghatage that the classification of the languages is based on a firmer foundation and is more comprehensive. To the older stage, belong the various inscriptions- Pālī, Ardhamāgadhī and Paiśacī. A later stage is formed by Śaurasenī, Māgadhī and Jain Mahārāṣṭrī and Jain Śaurasenī. A still developed form is seen in Mahārāṣṭrī-*kahanaya Tigaam*. In this article, incidentally, Dr. Kulkarni has also referred to the view-points of other scholars which are passed over here. He further adds that it is in the Ardhamāgadhī language that the Lord Mahāvīra gave his religious sermons.

(vii) Dr. Kulkarni's '*Five Book reviews*' in Marathi deserves mention here. He has reviewed[70] the works of Prof. R.P. Kangle on the *Rasabhāva-vicāra and Daśarūpaka-vidhāna,* emended readings of the *Abhinavabhāratī* by Prof. Kangle, and *Prācīna Bhāratīya Sāhitya-Mīmāṁsa* by Prof. Ashok R. Kelkar and the *Gāthāsaptaśatī* : *Uttarārdha* and *Śephālikā—Gāthās* 701-1004. This book is published by the Prajna Pathasala, Wai, in the year 1993. Regarding the restoration and emendation preferred by Prof. Kangle, I have already noted the view-points of Dr. Kulkarni. In his review on the *Gāthāsaptaśatī* and *Śephālikā*, Dr. Kulkarni has given the list of the books he has consulted on page 80. In explaining the *Gāthā* No. 768, Dr. Kulkarni has reproduced the translation of the *Gāthā* according to Prof. M.V. Patwardhan; for the *Gāthā* Nos. 778, 784, 786, Dr. Kulkarni quotes the work *Gāhāikosa* i.e. *Gāthākośa* by Bhuvanapāla and corrects the reading and also gives the translation. For the *Gāthā* No. 951, Dr. Kulkarni draws attention to the *Kāvyānuśāsana* P. 54 of Hemacandra and further quotes the commentary of Vemabhūpāla to clarify the sense of the word '*gṛhapati'* in the *Gāthā*. He further points out that *Gāthā* No. 958 is found quoted in the *Prabandha-cintāmaṇi* P. 11 No.12 and also the *Subhāṣita gāthā saṅgraha* No. 70 and simplifies the entire discussion as such. He closes this review by complimenting Joglekar and Mangalurkar for their efforts to explain the text and simply remarks that the discussion in the light of the authorities and commentaries would certainly help to understand the *gāthā* correctly and the excellent suggested sense at the back of the *gāthās*. Suffice it to remark that the similar treatment he has extended to the work of Prof. Ashok Kelkar. One would be constrained to remark here that by these five book reviews. Dr. Kulkarni has modestly shown the limitations of the works of other scholars and enlightened the intelligent readers of the subject on the different aspects of restoration, emendation, choice of correct reading, correct translation of the *gāthās* and the source material that he has quoted here and the journals he has referred to. For this scholarly work of Dr. Kulkarni, no praise would be too high. I only hope that the scholars would correctly appreciate the value of this work and further endeavour in the direction he has shown in this work.

(vii) He has reviewed the work *'Yādavendramahodaya of Nīlakaṇṭha with Sanskrit Commentary* of *V. S. Ranade*, edited by Dr. S.Y. Wakankar; for the *Journal of the Asiatic Society of Bombay,* Vol. No. 75 for 200, pp.188-189. He has whole heartedly appreciated the work of Dr. Wakankar and made the suggestion that Kṛṣṇa's many-sided personality is of perennial interest to all. It would be good if the various theories, advanced by eminent scholars, are discussed and a flood of light is thrown on his personality. He also adds that the finest verses of Nīlakaṇṭha should be translated and their literary or aesthetic beauty should be unfolded.

(viii) Though the article 'A recent edition of *Dhvanyāloka*, by Dr. K. Krishnamoorhy is not reviewed by Dr. Kulkarni and published Annals a paper-in the of the Bhandarkar Oriental Research Institute, Pune, LVII of 1976 covering pages 129 to 138, I look upon it as a review. In the first place, Dr. Kulkarni declares that the present edition ranks high among the various editions now available. Secondly, he adds that about forty verses from the Prakrit literature are quoted by Ānandavardhana in his *Dhvanyāloka*. Some of these verses were already discussed by Dr. H.C. Bhayani in the *Journal of the Gujarat University.* However, they are not pressed into service by Dr. Krishnamoorthy. He further remarks that this kind of failure on the part of that scholar resulted into the errors in translation. Fourthly, he shows that though Dr. Krishnamoorthy consulted other works, he has completely ignored the importance of the *Kalpalatā,* particularly its Prakrit verses. He further cautiously remarks that one may be tempted to agree with Dr. Krishnamoorthy in holding that Rudraṭa is prior to Ānandavardhana. But for this position, one will have to wait for more substantial evidence. He further points out that the learned editor has not considered the article of Masson and Patwardhan pointing out the striking ideas common to both Vākpatirāja and Ānandavardhan. This article of the two scholars is published in *Kosambi Commemoration Volume* under the caption 'Science and Human Progress', covering pages 176-183.

Dr. Kulkarni further quotes the pages from the edition of *Dhvanyāloka* of Dr. Krishnamoorthy, indicating whether words or lines have either been left out in the translation or wrongly translated; such places are pages 23, 40, 60, 108, 134, 142, 218, etc.

He has further drawn attention of the scholars to the stanza on page 44 and remarks that this stanza is found explained in Hemacandra's *Kāvyānuśana* pp. 164-165 even by Vāmanācārya Jhalakikar in his *Bālabodhinī* p. 458. and this is at once convincing.

He significantly points out that stanza on p. 82 though translated by the editor, does not bring out the sense intended to be conveyed by Abhinavagupta on *Locana* p. 247. He also shows that some times the translation is partly inaccurate. He also points out that the reading *rakṣitam* to preferred *lakṣitam* by Dr. Krishnamoorthy is wrong. Hemacandra and *Vakroktijīvitakāra* have preserved the reading *lakṣitam* which is to be accepted.

He finally adds that for the benefit of the Post-Graduate students, it would have become necessary to quote the relevant passages from the *Locana* and translation of the same is also a must.

Looking at the several points raised against this edition, one is tempted to observe that this is not a paper, but, a review on the work of Dr. K. Krishnamoorthy.

(ix) Dr. Kulkarni has further written a paper on the '*Gauḍavaho*—a historical poem'. In this paper, Dr. Kulkarni has pointed out the poetic qualities of Vākpatirāja and remarked that the criticism of Dr. A.B. Keith on this *kāvya* is unfair. Keith held that 'Nor does it normally reach any high standard of merit'. This is the view expressed in the work *'The Sanskrit Drama* p. 150. He further added that this remark of Keith is doing injustice to Vākpatirāja. He points out that looking to the qualities of Vākpatirāja no one can take away his position to rank in the list of the great poets like Kālidāsa, Bhavabhūti and others. If any one attempts in this direction, then it would be an insult even to the Goddess or Sarasvatī. This is the opinion Dr. Kulkarni has expressed[71] in the Marathi Journal *Abhiruci* for *Dec.* 1950 covering pp. 263-270.

(x) Finally, the review of Dr. Kulkarni on the '*Aesthetic Rapture*' by Masson and Patwardhan deserves to be noted for interesting points. Here also a review on '*Śāntarasa and Aesthetic Rapture*' by these two authors is given in the *Journal* of *Indian Philosophy* (1973) pp. 138-144 published at U.S.A. Here only the interesting points of the review are given.

Dr. Kulkarni has shown that the translation of Masson and Patwardhan is decidedly better than the translation of Prof. Gnoli, of the two verses of Abhinavagupta. Here the concerned reference is to pp-5-6. Dr. Kulkarni supplied a correct reading found in the *Kalpalatā-viveka* of the first verse (a) *dhigatagamitvam'* to *dhiganagamitvam'*-. This reading Prof. Patwardhan accepted and gave the tentative translation of the verse. Dr. Kulkarni also consulted Prof. R.B. Athavale for the correct translation of the verse and the translation is quoted by Dr. Kulkarni on p. 139. Further Prof. Patwardhan revised his translation in the light of the comments in the *Kalpalatā-viveka*, on which Dr. Kulkarni remarks that in my opinion this is more faithful and original.

He has also noted the places of the wrong translation of Prof. Gnoli and the improvement of Masson and Patwardhan on the same.

Dr. Kulkarni further states that the remark of both the scholars is not acceptable. 'The description may be obscene but not vulgar on page 10 of 1.16. Dr. Kulkarni adds that both vulgarity and obscenity are the *doṣas* for the Sanskrit literary critics. The description of *Devī-sambhoga* is a case of impriety according to Ānandavardhana. This impropriety is, however, only for the time being, not noticed by the reader who is lured away by the wondrous *pratibhā* i.e. inspiration.

He further points out the discrepancy of the two scholars on account of their statements at p. 239 and 142 can be adequately understood if we take *abhinayopayogitari* as referring to the preceding part of the sentence on page 116. Therefore, in the case of Śānta, the advice of the practice of *yama, niyama*, *īśvarapraṇidhāna* etc. is useful for acting. This position stands to reason.

Dr. Kulkarni also notes the places where the translation of the scholars needs correction, particularly in Vol. II Note 148, p. 22 and Vol. II, Note. 16, P. 3.

He further adds that the emendation *'samanvitaḥ'* suggested by the two scholars is unnecessary and seeks support from the *Kalpalatā-viveka* p. 301, 11, 21-22).

While concluding the review, Dr. Kulkarni observes significantly that the presentation of these scholars is highly or refreshingly novel and reveals a penetrating insight, an analytic attitude, vast scholarship, and a first-hand study of an enormous variety of Sanskrit texts.

(X) Reviews on Dr. Kulkarni's works :—

Only some important reviews on the works are introduced here.

(i) *The Gīta-Govinda* edition of Dr. Kulkarni is reviewed by Dr. K. Krishnamoorthy for the *'Aryan*[72] *Path'*,—May 1967, p. 226. He appreciates the work of Dr. Kulkarni and observes that in the introduction, Dr. Kulkarni should have stated that the commentary is a work of King Lakṣmaṇasena adjusting his court poets and a tabular indication of the *rāgas* as recorded by different commentators for the particular songs should have found a place in the introduction.

(ii) Dr. Kulkarni's other work *'Bhoja and Harivijaya of Sarvasena'* is reviewed by Dr. H.C. Bhayani for the *Journal of the Asiatic Society of Bombay,* vols. 67-68 for 1992-93 pp. 265-267. Dr. Bhayani here appreciates Dr. Kulkarni's efforts and his imagination combined with a sound knowledge of the conventional style and mode of expression.

So far as the second part of the work is concerned, Dr. Bhayani suggests five different readings at five places.

Dr. Bhayani has drawn attention of Dr. Kulkarni to a stanza in the *Śṛṅgāra-prakāśa* of Bhoja, Vol. I p. 234 which has escaped the notice of Dr. Kulkarni.

It is evident that for this work, Dr. Kulkarni has used two manuscripts in which two verses are not identical. The manuscripts belong to different streams and Dr. Bhayani adds that this problem should be dealt with systematically.

(iii) Dr. Kulkarni's work *'Outline of Abhinavagupta's Aesthetics'* is reviewed by Dr. Tapasvi Nandi for the *Annals of the Bhandarkar Oriental Institute* Vol. LXXIX-1998 pp. 287-288. Here Nandi agrees with Dr. Kulkarni that Mahimabhaṭṭa is neither a *Naiyāyika* nor a *Pratyabhijñāvādin* like Hemacandra… Mahimabhaṭṭa is clear in whatever he has not seen. So perhaps he could not have missed *Abhinavabhāratī*.

He compliments Dr. Kulkarni for the real appreciation of the commentaty—the work not done by both Dr. Raghavan and Dr. Krishnamoorthy.

Dr. Nandi observes that Dr. Kulkarni had the opportunity to use the Hindi edition of the *Vyaktiviveka* by Revaprasad Dvivedi.

(iv) His work '*Studies in Sanskrit Sāhitya Śāstra*' is reviewed by Dr. Chitra Shukla for the Journal of the Oriental *Institute/Baroda,* Vol. XXXIII, No. 3-4, March June 1984 pp. 366-368. She observes that Dr. Kulkarni has defended Kālidāsa against the attack of Ānandavardhan on the point of obscenity.

She holds that the network of the *Sandhyaṅgas* is alarming and leaves little scope for the freedom of the dramatist.

She further remarks that Kulkarni is at his brilliant best in restoring the lost text of the *Abhinavabhāratī*.

Before closing this article, let me express my views on the work of Dr. Kulkarni, knowing fully well my limitations in this branch of learning.

i) In criticising the view of Prof. D.D.Kosambi that Hemacandra's writing on erotic topics is objectionable, Dr. Kulkarni simply states that he is harsh on Hemacandra. But it may be added here that Kosambi has not taken a correct view of the works of hermits, both Hindu and Jain. Here it may be pointed out that Pūrṇasarasvatī (the hermit) has written a commentary on the *Mālatīmādhava* of Bhavabhūti and also a commentary on the *Meghadūtam*. Dr. T. G. Mainkar has brought out the poetic qualities of Pūrṇasarasvatī in his book *'Studies in Sanskrit Dramatic Criticism*' pp. 19-37, published by Motilal Banarasidas, Delhi in the year 1971. Recently Vāsudevānanda Sarasvatī (1854-1914) has written a *Kāvya* known as *Tri-śatigurucaritrakāvyam*'. There are many such *saṁnyāsins* who have written on the erotic topic and *kāvyas*. Hence the criticism of Prof. Kosambi displays only his lack of knowledge of the life of hermits only. On this point, I feel like completely agreeing with Dr. Kulkarni. Besides, the objection of Prof. Kosambi is already answered by Abinavagupta in his *Locana*. p. 488.

ii) In the field of research, it is always believed that one should try to make the discussion as upto date as it is possible for the author. This principle of up-dating the matter has escaped the eagle eye of Dr. V.M. Kulkarni. In his *'Studies in Sanskrit Sāhitya Śāstra*', Dr. Kulkarni has published the article on 'The conception of Sandhis in the Sanskrit Drama' in the year 1983. It must be noted here that this article is originally published in the *Journal of the Oriental Institute,* Baroda, Vol. V. No. 4, 1956. In the meanwhile, in the year 1960, Dr. T.G. Mainkar published his Ph.D. thesis on '*The Theory of the Sandhis and Sandhyaṅgas*' in the year 1960.

There is no reference to this book at least in the foot-note of the above article written by Dr. Kulkarni. Besides, the writer of this note has also published an article on 'A comparative Study of the Sandhyaṅgas in the commentaries on the *Śākuntalam*' published in the *Journal of the University of Bombay,* Vol. XLII (New Series) No. 78, October 1973. There is also no reference to this article. In addition to this, Dr. Moghe has also written a paper on 'Abhinavagupta on the Sandhyaṅgas in the *Śākuntalam*' in the *Journal of the Oriental Institute,* Baroda, Vol. XXXIV Nos. 3-4, March-June 1985 covering pages 155-160. One may understand that this article is published after 1983 and hence there can not be a reference to it in the paper of Kulkarni. I have mentioned this article only to fulfil the principle of updating the matter.

Further, Dr. Kulkarni has published the edition of the *Uṣānirudham* of Rāma Pāṇivāda with critical introduction and English Translation in the year 1996. He has failed to make an entry of the article of this writer in the Bibliography on pages 143-144. Dr. Moghe has published a paper on 'The descriptions of the moon in the Uṣāniruddham and indebtedness of Rāma Pāṇivāda to the Sanskrit poets' published in the *Proceedings of the Seminar on Prakrit Studies* arranged by Dr. T. G. Mainkar, in the University of Bombay, during October 27-30, 1971. Here Dr. Moghe's article covers pp. 172-177. In passing, it may be added that Dr. Kulkarni's article on the Prakrit verses in the *Sarasvatī-kaṇṭhābharaṇa* has also appeared in the same volume pp. 134-145. Incidentally, it may be noted that this principle of Updating the matter is followed by Dr. P.V. Kane in his *History of Dharma-Śāstra* and Dr. R.N. Dandekar in his works.

In conclusion, one will have to admit that Dr. V.M. Kulkarni is a sound scholar of *Alaṁkāra-Śāstra* and Prakrit language. He made signficant contribution to the studies of both the branches by his critical edition, accurate translations, emendations, restorations, criticism of the views of Gnoli, Kosambi, S.K. De, Dr. Krishnamoorthy and others with research bent of mind and without any spirit of jealousy. His criticism is generally very mild and not harsh or exhibiting his authoritative tone, as is the case with some scholars. His criticism certainly befits his writing. Dr. Kulkarni has also shown highest regards for the scholars like Dr. Kane, Prof. R.B. Athavale, Abhinavagupta and others and while referring to them he always uses significant adjective like 'great'. As Dr. Kulkarni's personality is dominated by innate humility, he has taken chance to exhibit his indebtedness to scholars like J.L. Masson, M.V.Patwardhan, Pandit Bālācārya Khuperkar and others. His enduring contribution to the restoration and emendations particularly for the *Abhinavabhāratī* commentary will be permanently remembered by the scholars and he has laid the future scholars of *Alaṁkāra-Śāstra* and Prakrit studies under his deep obligations. In his reviews, one notices his close reading of the book, noting the merits and demerits of the work and suggestions for the emendations of the work. His reviews generally show his deep scholarship and one does not feel that the book is reviewed by a reader who is shallow in the subject; or has not read the book completely. In there reviews he also points out the names of the books which should have been consulted by the author. One would be very happy to note that his works are appreciated by the towering persons like Dr. H.C. Bhayani, Dr. Krishnamoorthy, Prof. Athavale, and others. One may remember here the words of Dr. Krishnamoorthy that Dr. Kulkarni has made a considerable progress or advancement over those places of the Studies on which the scholars like Dr. A.M. Ghatge and others have failed. Herein lies the true greatness of the work of Dr. Kulkarni. With these remarks, I wish Dr. V.M. Kulkarni, a long and happy and healthy life to make further progress in the subject and incidentally to win many more laurels.

FOOTNOTES

1. Kulkarni V. M. *Śṛṅgārā ṇavacandrikā,* p. 8.
2. *Ibid.* P. 16.
3. Kane P. V. *History of Sanskrit Poetics,* p. 290.
4. Kulkarni, V. M. *Studies in Sanskrit Sāhitya-Śāstra,* pp. 149-152.
5. *Ibid.* p. 153.
6. Kulkarni, V. M.—*Jayadeva's Gīta-govinda,* p. xiii.
7. *Ibid.* pp. xx-xxi.
8. *Ibid.* pp. xx-xxi.
9. *Ibid.* p. xxi.
10. *Ibid.* pp. 121-123.
11. Kulkarni, V. M. *Praśamarati-Prakaraṇa.* Appendix VI.
12. Kulkarni, V. M., *A Treasury of Jain Tales*-Introduction, p. xxxvii.
13. *Ibid.* Story No. 1 to story No. 124.
14. Kulkarni, V.M. *Uṣāniruddham.* Introduction, pp. ?8-29.
15. Gajendragadkar, S. N. *Brahma-Sūtra-Śāṅkarabhāṣya-II. ii.* (published by University of Bombay, 1965) pp.
16. Kulkarni, V. M. *More Studies in Sanskrit Sāhitya-Śāstra*, pp. 174-175.
17. Kulkarni, V.M. Paper on Bharata's *Nāṭyaśāstra* and the commentary *Abhinavabhārati*.

(1)	JAS. Bombay,	Vols.	64-65	for	1989-91.
(2)	"	Vols.	67-68	for	1992-1993.
(3)	"		71	for	1996.
(4)	"		72	for	1997.
(5)	"	"	73	for	1998.

(6) " " 74 for 1999.
(7) " " 75 for 2000.
(8) " " 76 for 2001.

18. Kulkarni, V. M. *Studies in Sanskrit Sāhitya Śāstra,* p. 77.
19. Kulkarni, V. M. *Harivijaya of Sarvasena*—Introduction, p. 5.
20. Kulkarni, V. M. *Five Book Reviews* (In Marathi), pp. 1-101.
21. Kulkarni, V. M.,—*Ibid.* p. 49.
22. Kulkarni, V. M.,—*Ibid.* p. 49.
23. Kulkarni, V. M. and T. S. *Nandi—Nāṭyaśāstra with the Commentary of Abhinavagupta,* Vol. II refers to p. vii for the view of Dr. K. Krishnamoorthy expressed in the Introduction to Vol. I of the above volume.
24. Kulkarni—V.M., *Studies in Sanskrit Sāhitya Śāstra,* p. 26.
25. *Ibid.* p. 27.
26. *Ibid.* pp. 20-26.
27. *Ibid.* pp. 28-36.
28. *Ibid.* p. 107.
29. *Ibid.* p. 112.
30. *Ibid.* p. 191.
31. Kulkarni, V. M. *More Studies in Sanskrit Sāhitya Śāstra,* p. 110.
32. *Ibid.* pp. 111-113.
33. *Ibid.* p. 128.
34. *Ibid.* p. 133.
35. *Ibid.* pp. 129-145.
36. *Ibid.* P. 142.
37. Kulkarni, V. M. *Studies in Sanskrit Sāhitya Śāstra,* p. 18.
38. *Ibid.* p. 18.
39. *Ibid.* pp. 155-161.
40. Kulkarni, V. M. *The Story of Rāma in Jain Literature,* pp. 1-247.
41. *Ibid.* p. ix.
42. Kulkarni, V. M. *Studies in Jain Literature,* p. 82.
43. *Ibid.* pp. 83-88.
44. *Ibid.* pp. 125, 161, 505.
45. *Ibid.* p. 125.
46. *Ibid.* pp. 559-560.
47. *Ibid.* p. 436.
48. *Ibid.* p. 156.
49. Kulkarni V. M. *More Studies in Sanskrit Sāhitya Śāstra,* pp. 1-21.
50. Kulkarni, V. M. *Outline of Abhinavagupta's Aesthetics,* pp. 18-28.
51. *Ibid.* pp. 29-39.
52. *Ibid.* pp. 46-52.
53. *Ibid.* pp. 53-69.
54. *Ibid.* p. 68-

55. *Ibid.* pp. 81-87.
56. *Ibid.* pp. 69-80.
57. *Ibid.* pp. 95-105.
58. *Ibid.* p. 105.
59. *Ibid.* pp. 101-102.
60. *Ibid.* p. 79.
61. Kulkarni, V. M. *More Studies in Sanskrit Sāhitya Śāstra,* p. 132.
62. Kulkarni, V. M. *Studies in Sanskrit Sāhitya Śāstra,* p. 180.
63. *Ibid.* p. 182.
64. *Ibid.* p. 182.
65. *Ibid.* p. 183.
66. Patwardhan, M. V. *Mahimabhaṭṭa's. Vyakti-viveka*—Introduction by V. M. Kulkarni, pp. 19-20.
67. *Ibid.* 22-23.
68. Kulkarni V. M. *Aryan Path*—Jan-Feb 1978.
69. *Journal of the Asiatic Soceity of Bombay* Vols. 60-61-for 1985-86 p.
70. Kulkarni, V.M.—*Five Book Reviews,* pp. 1-52.
71. Kulkarni, V. M. *Gauḍavaho—A Historical Kāvya—in Abhiruci-(*Marāthi*)* for Dec. 1950, pp. 263-270.
72. Krishnamoorthy K. *The Aryan Path*- Vol. XXXVIII No. 5, p. 226.
73. *The Mālatī-mādhava- with commentary of Pūrṇa-sarasvatī.*

REVIEWS

II.2.1

STUDIES IN SANSKRIT SĀHITYA-ŚĀSTRA

M.V. Patwardhan

Dr. V.M. Kulkarni, M.A., Ph.D.

The present volume covering two hundred pages of double crown size and published by the Bhogilal Leherchand Institute of Indology, Patan (Gujarat) as No. 1 of the B.L. Series, contains 16 selected papers contributed by the learned author to oriental journals over the last 25 years and dealing with a variety of problems relating to Sanskrit poetics and dramaturgy and to some Sanskrit works on poetics. Fourteen out of these papers deal with problems relating to Sanskrit poetics, while two (Nos. 14 and 15) deal with Prakrit verses cited in works on *Alaṁkāra-Śāstra* and with Sarvasena's *Harivijaya,* a lost epic poem in Prakrit describing poetically the life and exploits of Śrīkṛṣṇa and preserved only in the form of citations in Sanskrit works on poetics. No. 16 deals with the Jainistic view of aesthetic experience as gathered from Jaina canonical works and from works by Jaina authors on poetics and dramaturgy. Nos 1, 2 and 3 deal with plagiarism (*saṁvāda*), poetic conventions (*Kavisaṅketa*) and intonation or voice modulation (*kāku*). Nos. 7 and 8 are devoted to a consideration of the concepts of *Sandhis* and *Patākāsthāndkas* in Sanskrit dramaturgy. No. 12 deals with the views of Sanskrit poeticians on *Rativilāpa* and *Devīsambhoga* in Kālidāsa's *Kumārasambhava.* No. 9 is concerned with an exposition of Bhāmaha's views on grammar in relation to poetry as presented by him in his *Kāvyālaṁkāra*. Nos. 4 and 6 devote themselves to the restoration of some portions in Abhinavagupta's commentary on Bharata's Nāṭyaśāstra, with the help of Hemacandra's *Kāvyānuśāsana* and the anonymous commentary called *Kalpalatāviveka*. No. 10 shows how the *Kalpalatāviveka* helps us in the understanding of some difficult stanzas in Bhāmaha's *Kāvyālaṅkāra,* Chapter-V. while No. 11

shows how the same anonymous commentary throws fresh light on Udbhaṭa's lost commentary called *Vivaraṇa* on Bhāmaha's *Kāvyālaṅkāra.* No. 13 deals with the nature and sources of Hemacandra's *Kāvyānuśāsana.* In the appendix, the author has printed his article on the view of Sanskrit rhetoricians on poetic truth.

All these papers bear eloquent testimony to the author's patient work on the problems concerned, his insight in them and his sober, balanced and dispassionate judgement marked by his deep study of those problems. The author's claim in the preface that the papers included in the present volume deal with problems that have not yet received adequate attention at the hands of Sanskrit Scholars, is more than justified and legitimate; witness the papers on plagiarism, poetic conventions, voice-modulation *Sandhis and Patākāsthānakas.* The paper throwing fresh light on *Bhāmahavivaraṇa* is the outcome of the author's penetrating study on the anonymous commentary, *Kalpalatāvivekaḥ* Dr. Kulkarni examines eleven passages from *Kalpalatāviveka* and from Hemacandra's *Kāvyānuśāsana* and shows how these passages contain situations from the lost *Bhāmahavivaraṇa* and throws light on mutilated lines from that work as presented by the Italian Scholar Gnoli in his work on *Bhāmahavivaraṇa* published in 1962. The papers *Kalpalatāviveka* on *Abhinavabhāratī* (No.5) and *Abhinavabhāratī (*Chapter VII) recovered (No.6) and *Kalpalatāviveka* on Bhāmaha's *Kāvyālaṁkāra* clearly demonstrate the author's careful study of the *Kalpalatāviveka,* which has proved to be a veritable *open sesame* in Dr. Kulkarni's hands in solving knotty problems connected with works on Sanskrit poetics.

The paper (No. 14) on "Some aspects of Prakrit verses in Alaṁkāra works" underlines the purely aesthetic and strictly amoral approach of Sanskrit *Ālaṅkārikas* in citing Prakrit stanzas some of which are blatantly erotic in their contents and justly exculpate *Alaṁkāra* writers from the charge of gloating over obscene situations depicted in them.

Dr. Kulkarni deserves the gratitude of students of Sanskrit *Sāhitya Śāstra* for placing in their hands in neat, handy and nicely printed volume the fruits of his lucubrations on many a problem in Sanskrit poetics—the fruits that till now were lying scattered in several issues of oriental journals published during the last twenty-five years.

II.2.2

STUDIES IN SANSKRIT SĀHITYA ŚĀSTRA

K. Krishnamoorthy

By V. M. Kulkarni, Bhogilal Leherchand Institute of Indology, Patan [North Gujarat], 1983; pp. 200 Price Rs. 60-00.

Dr. V. M. Kulkarni is one of the few scholars in India today dedicated to text-critical studies of *Alaṁkāra* texts in general and to Prakrit citations by major theorists like Ānandavardhana, Abhinavagupta and Bhoja in particular. His keen insight and unrivalled mastery over the entire area of *Sahitya-Śāstra* have illumined many a dark corner in our masterpieces like the *Locana, Abhinavabhāratī,* and *Śṛṅgāraprakāśa.* He has published a number of papers well over these three decades, devoted to the explication of concepts mostly ignored by doyens like S. K. De, P. V. Kane, and V. Raghavan—*kavisamaya, kāku, haraṇa,* to name a few—and more importantly, in providing indepth critiques of text-readings proposed by earlier scholars in the light of *testimonia offered for the first time by generally neglected Jaina authors as unoriginal framers of compendia of disparate unacknowledged material from various source books*.

Thanks to scholars like R. C. Parikh and Dr. V. M. Kulkarni, the world of *Alaṁkāra*-scholars soon came to realise the inestimable value of Hemacandra's *Kāvyānuśāsana* (with auto-commentary) in restoring the right readings of many a puzzling passage in important texts like the *Abhinavabhāratī*. But the gold mine presented by the anonymous *Kalpalatāviveka* published by the L. D. Institute, Ahmedabad, remained to be tapped. The present reviewer was rewarded by it beyond measure in reconstructing portions of Kuntaka's *Vakroktijīvita* text, though its editor showed no awareness of it. In like manner, Dr. V. M. Kulkarni has succeeded in recovering the right readings of the *Abhinavabhāratī* in some of the most crucial passages including the chapter of *Rasa* (i.e. VI), passages which had baffled even eminent specialists like R. Gnoli, V. Raghavan, J. L. Masson, and M. V. Patwardhan. Among the sixteen papers collected in this Volume, those papers (4 to 6) are of intrinsic excellence and constitute an all-time contribution.

No less important are the papers that broaden the horizon of Sanskrit literary studies by giving us for the first time most substantial material from Udbhaṭa's *Bhāmaha-vivaraṇa* bearing on logical and literary issues, the published fragments by Gnoli being virtually unreadable with vast lacunae.

Though quite a few books have been published on the *sandhis* and *sandhyaṅgas* of Sanskrit drama, one's ignorance is such that one is unable to apply it straight to the plot of any drama, say even the *Śākuntala,* with confidence. Dr. Kulkarni's penetrating presentation of the essentials is still relevant and welcome.

But a major break-through achieved by Dr. Kulkarni is in piecing together the lost threads of a large number of Prakrit citations that lie scattered in *Alaṅkāra*-works-*Dhvanyāloka, Locana, Śṛṅgāra-prakāśa, Sarasvatīkaṇṭhābharaṇa,* etc. For the first time Dr. Kulkarni traces them to their sources like Sarvasena's *Harivijaya* and Pravarasena's *Setubandha,* with well—documented and convincing evidence. Even when such tracing is not possible, he succeeds in restoring right readings even in cases left as most intractable by earlier scholars. There are instances where Dr. Kulkarni succeeds where even Dr. A. N. Upadhye and Dr. A. M. Ghatage had their trial without much success.

Finally, discussions of the author on divergent views of theorists regarding erotic descriptions in Kālidāsa, dramatic devices like the *Patākāsthāna* and uniquely novel ideas of Jaina writers on *Rasa* are of wide general interest. The papers are replete with all research documentation needed and the present review need not go into details, since they are all published earlier and familiar to scholars.

This is a book of abiding relevance which no student of Indian poetics who wants to be up to date can afford to miss.

II.2.3

PRAKRIT VERSES IN SANSKRIT WORKS ON POETICS

H. C. Bhayani

Volume I—Text (With Appendices and Index), Volume II—Translation (With Introduction, Glossary and Notes), by V. M. KULKARNI, published by B. L. Institute of Indology, Delhi, 1988, 1990; 24 X 18 cm. Vol. I, pp. 12 + 602 + 40 + 130; Vol. II, pp. 13 + 47 + 702. Price not mentioned.

Here wc have the mature product of several years' stupendous scholarly labour and patient exemplary diligence in the area of Classical Prakrit Studies. After Weber's *Saptaśatakan des Hāla* (1881) and Handiqui's *Prvarasena's Setubandha* (1976), it will be rather difficult to name a few comparable contributions to Prakrit textual and literary scholarship.

In the first volume, Kulkarni has given the corrected or restored text, along with the Sanskrit *Chāyā,* of some three thousand Prakrit verses which occur as illustrative citations in twenty well-known Sanskrit works on Poetics and their commentaries. These are as follows : *(1)* Rudraṭa's *Kāvyālaṅkāra* and Namisādhu's *Ṭippaṇa, (2) Dhvanyāloka and Locana, (3) Vakroktijīvita, (4) Daśarūpaka and Avaloka, (5) Vyaktiviveka, (6) Śṛṅgāraprakāśa (7) Sarasvatīkaṇṭhābharaṇa, (8) Kāvyaprakāśa, (91 Alaṁkāra-sarvasva* and Jayaratha's *Vimarśinī, (10) Sāhityamīmāṁsā, (11) Vāgbhaṭālaṁkāra, (12)* Hemacandra's *Kāvyānuśāsana (13) Kalpalatāviveka, (14) Alaṅkāramahodadhi, (15)* Vāgbhaṭa's *Kāvyānuśāsana (16) Sāhityadarpaṇa (17) Rasārṇavasudhākara, (18) Alaṅkāra-ratnākara, (19) Rasagangādhara,, (20) Alankārakaustubha.*

The citations, as far as could be identified by Kulkarni, have been taken by the authors from famous Prakrit works like Hāla's *Saptaśataka,* Sarvasena's *Harivijaya,*

Setubandha, Gaūḍavaha, Mahumahavijaa,Līlāvaīkahā, Viṣamabāṇalīlā, Karpūramañjarī and from a few well-known Sanskrit dramas. But a very large number of citations remains untraced as the source texts are lost to us. Now due to increasing decline in the knowledge of Prakrit language in later centuries, the text of the citations has suffered a lot in transmission. Numerous corruptions, careless omissions, arbitrary interpolations, violent alterations have marred the text of the Prakrit verses to such an extent that at times we are faced with meaningless jumble of letters. The task of restoring these highly corrupt texts so as to have at least a semblance of meaningful verbal and metrical structure involves heroic scholarly efforts while the achieved result is likely to be uncertain or doubtful. Kulkarni has spared no pains in accepting and accomplishing as far as possible this daunting task. And his untiring efforts can be said to have been richly rewarded in that he has rescued a considerable mass of excellent Prakrit lyrical poetry that remained so far obscure or incomprehensible.

The second volume of the work contains the translation of all the verses, notes and introduction. The translation is careful and perceptive. It strives, moreover, successfully to catch the literary merits of the original lyrics, and hence it will be found quite enjoyable even by the non-specialist lovers of poetry. Critical notes discuss competently and meticulously various points and specific issues relating to the restorations and interpretations. Kulkarni's extensive knowledge of Sanskrit Poetics has been brought to bear on the discussion of various passages and thus they form a significant contribution to Prakrit textual exegesis. In his introduction, Kulkarni has pointed out the fact that Sanskrit and Prakrit poetry were accorded equal status by poets and poeticians in the Classical Indian tradition. He has shown with apt illustrations that the praises showered on Prakrit poetry by the poets and *rasikas* as having high literary excellence were not just *cāṭuvāda* and *arthavāda*.

The lion's share of Prakrit citations goes to the two encyclopaedic works of Bhoja viz, the *Śṛṅgāraprakāśa* (1654 citations) and the *Sarasvatīkaṇṭhābharaṇa* (383 citations)

In a way, we can look upon the present work by Kulkarni as an extensive and representative anthology of choicest Prakrit lyrics from a vast abundance produced during a span of some fifteen centuries. Thus it illuminates for us an important area of unbelievably and inexhaustibly rich Indian Classical poetry.

An invaluable by-product of Kulkarni's researches in this subject is the partial rescue from oblivion of a lost *kāvya-ratna,* viz, Sarvasena's *Harivijaya,* which is the earliest known *Mahākāvya* in Mahārāṣṭrī. Bhoja has quoted it extensively in his

Śṛṅgāraprakāśa and in view of its importance, Kulkarni has separately brought it out in the form of a monograph.

This wealth of citations is important from another point of view also. They make available numerous variants for the passages from the known Prakrit works. This is helpful in numerous cases in improving their text. So also the Apabhraṁśa citations in both the *Alaṁkāra* works of Bhoja serve the purposes of providing us with a glimpse of the Apabhraṁśa poetry of the eighth to the tenth century with its metrical variety as also some hints about the likely sources of the Apabhraṁśa illustrative citations in the Apabraṁśa section of Hemacandra's *Siddhahema-Śabdānuśāsana*.

A considerable number of the cited Prakrit verses still defy efforts of textual restoration and ascertaining their meaning. With patient efforts and the guidance available from already restored verse texts, we may hope to succeed in a number of these tough cases. An attempt to deal with some of the tough cases will be made in a separate paper.

Even though the vigorous tradition of Classical Prakrit scholarship has regrettably suffered a serious decline in recent years, we can be optimistic that a work like the present one which maintains in its depth and breadth high standards of Indological research may yet inspire and activate some researchers of younger generation to take interest in Prakrit Studies.

II.2.4

OUTLINE OF ABHINAVAGUPTA'S AESTHETICS

Tapasvi Nandi

V. M. Kulkarni; Pub. by Saraswati Pustak Bhandar, Ahmedabad 380001; 1998 ; Pp. viii + 110; Price : Rs. 200/-

Dr. V. M. Kulkarni's (VMK) book viz. "*Outline of Abhinavagupta's (A.) Aesthetics*" consists of ten valued articles on topics concerning Indian Aesthetics in general and A.'s approach to the same in particular.

Before writing anything about this work, I will hazard to suggest a new title for it such as, "*An Indepth Study of A.'s Aesthetics*," for that exactly it is. This happens to be VMK's third collection of research articles. I know Prof. VMK as a great scholar, so thorough, hard working and meticulous in his approach to any problem that falls within the range of Sanskrit *Alaṅkāraśāstra* in general. He exhibits an unbiased and balanced application and dedication to whatever he picks up for a close study, be it in Sanskrit or in Prakrit. His expressions, in keeping with his conclusions, are clear and unbiased like his thinking, as has been evident in his three earlier publications. I count him as one of the greatest modern *Ālaṅkārikas* in company with Dr. Rewaprasad Dwivedi, Dr. K. D. Tripathi, the late Drs. R. C. Dwivedi, Raghavan, K. Krishnamoorthy, and Pundit Viśveśvara, Prof. R. B. Athavale. Prof. R.C. Parikh, Dr. Hiriyanna, and also Drs. Gnoli, Masson, M. V. Patwardhan and Kunjunni Raja. The chief merit of his approach is that he goes to the root of a given problem from many angles, is open to all suggestions, tries to interpret the given author, quoting all relevant passages from his writing and then takes a critical and unbiased view, acceptable to all. In this respect, I would place him with the great Jagannātha Paṇḍita of the *Rasagaṅgādhara* fame, the difference being that VMK is all humility. For sure, the present study of A. is meant only for those who justifiably claim to have a closer acquaintance with A.

The first article "Sanskrit Theory of Beauty " (pp. 1-17) gives a critical and comparative study of the concept of beauty in east as well as in west. "Bharata's Concept of *Bhāva*" (pp. 19- 98) presents the view of Bharata on *Bhāva* in his famous *Nāṭyaśāstra (NS).* VMK clearly explains the terms *vibhāva, anubhāva, sthāyibhāva, sāttvikabhāva* etc. in the light of *NS*. VMK quotes from *Locana* at relevant places and supports his observations. On p. 23 VMK goes to observe : "After it is activated there takes place *hṛdayasaṁvāda (*sympathetic response)." We may feel that perhaps this fact of *hṛdayasaṁvāda* should precede *sādhāraṇīkaraṇa,* because in its absence, the first *rasa* viz. *sambhāvanāviraha* has a chance. Again A. goes to observe on *Śāntarasa* ; *na sarvasya sarvatra hṛdaya-saṁvādaḥ* Then. VMK critically considers the nature of *Vyabhicāri-bhāva-s* (pp. 24-25) and *Śāttvikabhāva-s* (p. 26).

In the next article VMK discusses the "Dual nature of *Sāttvikabhāva"*. It is obvious that the *sāttvikabhāva-s* partake the nature of both *vyabhicārins* and *abhinayas*; and *sāttvikas* such as '*stambha*' '*vaivarṇya*' etc. stand for the internal feelings that are not manifested. We fail to agree with Dr. Raghavan's observation (ft. n. 9, p. 31), because the *sāttvikas*, when they partake of the nature of *vyabhicārins*, are to be taken as '*a-jaḍa*', and therefore they are to be separated from '*abhinaya*' or mere external acting. VMK (pp. 33) also explains Hemacandra's (HC) approach critically and also explains the views of Śaradātanaya, Kumārasvāmin, *Rasataraṅgiṇī, Rasa-ratna-pradīpikā, Rasa-pradīpa,* Masson & Patwardhan etc. (pp. 36-38). VMK again refers to Raghavan's understanding about '*sattva*' (pp. 35), with which we fail to agree.

VMK (p. 41) explains carefully the views of HC., in "Hemacandra on Sāttvikabhāvas". The next topic "*Rasa-laukika"* presents the views of those who feel that *rasa*-experience can be equalled with worldly feelings. P. 53 gives the next topic "*Rasa-Alaukika."* VMK has quoted from *A. bh.* and *Locana.* The next article "*Rasa* and its pleasurable nature" follows as a natural corollary from the earlier article. We generally agree with VMK's observations in the next article "*Rasa and its Āśraya*" (pp. 80-89).

The last article on "*Mahima*" is a great achievement. VMK could have also utilized Dr. Rewaprasad's Hindi Edn. In our humble opinion, Bhoja could have echoed Mahima' s views for the latter was a greater genius. Mahima may not be a *'naiyāyika'* as observed by VMK, like Hemacandra who was not a *pratyabhijñāvādin*. Mahima is clear in whatever he has not seen. So perhaps he could not have missed *A. bh.*

VMK could have obliged by giving a select bibliography at the end. It is clear that VMK alone has, for the first time, coherently presented and critically appreciated all relevant references on all topics from A. Neither Raghavan nor K. Krishnamoorthy has done this. We welcome this valuable work of VMK.

SECTION-III

VEDIC LITERATURE

III.1

PREREQUISITES FOR PROPER VEDIC INTERPRETATION[1]

Prof. (Dr.) N.M. Kansara

The *Ṛgveda* is the *magnum opus* and the original basis of all the Vedas and their recensions. It is under the *Ṛgveda* that all the original *mantras* of all the Vedas and their recensions had come up. The mutual individual differences were chiefly phonetic and about the technical vocabulary. When they separated, some variations in the readings occurred in the *mantra* portion, too, as and when it was necessary. And, along with it, somebody laid emphasis on some name in the ritualistic rite, while some other gave importance to some other name. But, this difference was verbal, of interpretation, but not of the essence itself. Hence, in all the Vedas the central subject is everywhere the same. However, there arose so much difference of opinion in the technical vocabulary that it is difficult, if not impossible, to keep a count of it. One and the same order of creation has been evolved into numerous streams due to different technical terms, and interpretations. The task of decoding and explaining these Vedic terms, their interpretations and their relative underlying truth demands a Herculean effort. Numerous historical and Purāṇic *Gāthās* were prevalent prior to the revelation of the *Vedas*. Their language had already become rich in those days. As regards the language of the Vedic *mantras*, it has been specifically mentioned in the *Rgveda* itself that they had sifted the language in the cultural sieve and produced the *mantras* after having measured them in the *Sabhās* and *Saṅgoṣṭhīs*.[2] It is to this end that the traditional Vedic seers propose that there resides in their speech, the Goddess of Prosperity *(lakṣmī)* or the splendor *(pratibhā)* in their speech. The Vedic language is upright and mature. Its maturity is testified by the fact that in the very same *mantra* there is found to be ingrained the genius of incorporating the triad of history, philosophy and ritual. The full knowledge of constellations, signs of zodiac, months, seasons, fortnights, equinoxes, the two turns of galaxy, the planets of solar system, and those beyond it had been already obtained. The Ganges of knowledge had been flowing in thousands of streams in the form of sparks of lightning. The wonderful stage of drama in the form of sacrificial ritual had already been presented. The sacred thread *(brahma-sūtra),* as a symbol of 27 basic elements of the pure *Brahman,* had already adorned the neck of every cultured Indian then. The education in the form of the creative philosophical faculty *(prātibha-darśana)* had already been revealed as also the sciences explaining the names and forms, such as word combination, euphonic coalescence and metrics. Today people say that *Śikṣā, Kalpa, Vyākaraṇa, Nirukta, Jyotiṣa* and *Chandas* are the auxiliaries of the Vedas. But it does not mean that they have evolved or have been derived from the Vedas. On the contrary, the Vedas is the golden flower that has grown up as a result of all these sciences combined. These sciences had already been developed before the *Vedas* came to be revealed. Hence, the Vedic literature is the veritable Primordial Cosmic Golden Egg *(hiraṇya-garbha)* containing the upright and mature sciences, philosophies, folk traditions, history, sacrificial ritual, astronomy, metrics, etymology, grammar and interpretative techniques. The highest extent of revealed knowledge had arisen in the Vedas.

To reach to the shore of the ocean of the proper knowledge of the Vedic *mantras,* a long missionary walk is essential. The very first prerequisite for the one who wants to grasp the meaning of the Vedas, and interpret them, is that he must be fully equipped with the knowledge of the philosophy, the *Śikṣā* or the *Prātibha-darśana* or the science of the principles of language. The science of language is not a particular system, like the modern Linguistics; at least for the study of the Vedas, the *Prātibha-darśana* has been almost lost. For the one who does not know the philosophy, the *Śikṣā* or the *Prātibha-darśana,* it is simply impossible to acquire the knowledge of the *Akṣara Brahman,* and it would be mere wild goose race if he adventures to take up the Vedas for study. He would be unable to do anything with the Vedic *mantras;* he would find nothing in them. The Vedic seers have themselves declared in the Vedas that the knowledge of the *Akṣara Brahman* would be attainable only by those who have mastered the *Prātibha-darśana.*[3] The Vedic seers have prohibited those devoid of the knowledge of the *Prātibha-darśana,* because they have raised up the spinal chord of the Vedic philosophy in two forms.—*Akṣara* means two types of *Akṣara*, viz., (1) Undefined spiritual or *anirukta ādhyātmika,* and (2) Defined material or *bhautika nirukta.* In both of them, the eighteen thousand million (18,000,000,000) monosyllabic mystic vocables *(bījākṣara),* or the divinities *(deva)* are gradually defined. Without the insight into the chief aspects of the Vedic spiritual vision, like the *Gāyatrī-brahmasūtra,* the understanding of the musical tunes of the *Sāmaveda,* the nature of the accents of the Ṛg*veda* and the *Yajurveda,* the discussion of the words and sentences through *sphoṭa,* the *sapta-paridhayaḥ, catvāri vāk-parimitā padāni,* it is simply impossible to plunge into the true knowledge of the Vedas. The *Prātibha-darśana* is a *Śikṣā-darśana,* which has been called the very nose of the Knowledge in the form of Man.[4]

The second prerequisite for the interpreter of the Vedas is the knowledge of the *Kalpa,* which is but an imagination. The imagination is effected in two ways, in accordance with the roles to be played and the procedure of the sacrificial ritual. The mixed operation of both these is called *karma-kāṇḍa.* The foundation of the *kalpa* or the imagination had been laid by keeping in view the various interpretations of the 50 basic elements of the development of the Brahman. Whatever subtle prescription and invariable prescription has been laid down in the sacrificial ritual, each of them is connected with the subtlest interpretation of each of the basic elements. All actions are commenced with the *svasti-vācana*, and the invocation and prayer of the basic element concerned. With the *mantra 'brahma jñānaṁ prathamaṁ purastāt'*[5] the prayer of Viṣṇu and Rudra along with that of the Brahman, the whole of the cosmos is invoked in the form of Gaṇapati The *ṣoḍaśa-mātṛkā* and the *ṣoḍaśa-kalā-brahman* is the Brahmic interpretation. The *nāndī-śrāddha,* and the *Brahmans* of the third and fourth *saptaka* are worshipped in the form of the *Pitṛs*, i.e., the manes or ancestors. After the *kalaśa-sthāpanā,* the *sad-brahma* is invoked in the form the *Hiraṇya-garbha*, and after putting in it, as the representatives of the seeds of the entire cosmos, the food grains, the twigs of palāśa etc., the plants like haridrā, and the diamond etc, the *Catuṣpāda* (four-faced) Brahman is installed, and in it the *pañcāmṛta* of the pañca-*tattvas* as also the nine oblations *(navāhuti)* are offered. The *kuśa-kaṇḍikā* plays the living role of the creation of the development of the *eka-pād, dvi-pād, and tri-pād Brahmas*. Thereafter, the *graha-yāga* takes, through the oblation of the juices of the *catuṣ-pād Brahmas* the first half of the sacrifice, to the development of the 33 gods of the *brāhma-sṛṣṭi.* In other sacrifices, single aspects are enacted, as for instance, in the *gāyatrī-yāga* during the *upanayana* ceremony, the *brahma-jñāna-jyoti* of the sacred thread is enacted by keeping the pigtail *(śikhā).* Secondly, the sacrificial ritual that only the selected few popular Vedic *mantras* have been adopted, and they have been used in such appropriate situations that the Vedic vision automatically gets clear. Hence, it is impossible to know the Vedic *brahma-jñāna* for the one who knows nothing of the sacrificial ritual. Any way, the enacting of the second stage of the Vedic *brahma-jñāna* has to be seen from the viewpoint of *brahma-jñāna.* Thirdly, as regards the use of the Vedic *mantras*, some say that the *mantras* are meaningless and useless, since they do not grasp the affinity of the common meanings of *kṣīram, dadhi, ājyam, madhu, śarkarā, sūrya, candra, bhauma, budha, guru, śukra, śani, rāhu* and *ketu,* in the *mantras* pertaining to them. These *pañcāmṛta* and the *grahas* are utilized symbolically, but not by keeping in view the material things like milk, yogurt, boiled butter, honey, sugar, and the planets like, the Sun, Moon, Mars, Mercury, Jupiter, Venus, Saturn, etc. These *pañcāmṛta* and the *grahas* are the source of our microcosmic and macrocosmic universe. The *pañcāmṛta* are the basic elements of the first four *saptakas,* and the *grahas* are the eight chief *Brahmas* of the first *saptaka*, and their enactment is effected by symbolizing the planets of the Solar System in the same way as the *Gāyatrī brahmas* is worshipped by symbolizing it through the Sun. Neither is *Gāyatrī* the Sun, nor is the worship of the Vedic *graha-yāga* the sacrifice of the planets, nor it is the milk etc.; on the other hand,these things are only the symbols for the enactment, and all the *mantras* pertaining to them are explanatory of the elements of the *brahma-sṛṣṭi*.

The third prerequisite for the Vedic interpreter is the profound knowledge of the *Nirukta.* It has to be admitted that generally all the commentators, translaters and critics have definitely studied, and are studying, Yāska's *Nighaṇṭu* and *Nirukta.* But it is unfortunate that even during the times of Yāska himself there prevailed the blind tradition of taking the Vedic *mantras* as denoting the ritualistic sense only. Yāska has analysed and classified the deities—gods and goddesses—in accordance with the blind tradition of sacrificial ritualism, and wherever he has sought to give even the spiritual *(ādhyātmika)* significance, he has totally left out the Upaniṣads, and has failed to grasp the secrets of the Brāhmaṇas and the Āraṇyakas. For instance, while explaining the *mantra 'aditer dakṣo ajāyata, dakṣād u aditiḥ pari'*[6], he asks *'katham itaretara-janmānav iti?'* and answers *deva-dharmeṇa itaretara-prakṛti* and that is all. While explaining the *mantras 'ṛco akṣare parame vyoman',*[7] *tisro vāco irayanti*[8] and *'catvāri vāc parimitā padāni',*[9] even after mentioning the sacrificial, grammatical, *Nirukta*, etc., viewpoints, he has not been able to show for certain as to what really the words *'akṣare', 'tisro vāco'* and *'catvāri padāni* signifies. It was, therefore, quite insufficient for him to have taken recourse to the *Nirukta,* for discovering the sense of the Vedic *mantras*. It seems, the knowledge of the Vedic vision had already been lost by those days. It was for this reason that he has tried, at the conclusion of the *Nirukta,* to give the popular version of the *Sāṅkhya-Yoga* in trustworthy form, and after that he has also tried to give a somewhat spiritual interpretation to about 10/15 *mantras* pertaining to the *soma-brahman,* which indicates that even in the days of Yāska the impression that there is some, full or incomplete philosophy, was not totally lost. The importance of the *Nirukta* as the work as presenting the meaning of words and the collection of some excellent *mantras,* has of course been duly recognized. Possibly, Vārṣyāyaṇi and Śākapūṇi, the predecessors of Yāska, may have given some spiritual interpretations of the *mantras*; but no work of them is extant now. Hence, it is not possible to discover the significance of the Veda with the help of the *Nirukta,* even if it is considered authentic in explaining the Vedic words.

The fourth requisite for the Vedic interpreter is the knowledge of '*vyākaraṇa*'. But, by *'vyākaraṇa,* it is feared, people take it to be the same as the 'Śabdānuśāsanam', i.e., Grammar. But, the *Vedāṅga* Vyākaraṇa was a part of the *Prātibha-darśana.* In those days the *Śikṣā-darśana* discussed the nature of the sounds, their development and the accentual stress on the sounds, while the *'vyākaraṇa'* discussed minutely the sentences, the coalescence in the metrical construction and its stress of the accent. In those days Sanskrit was a living language of common parlance. Hence, there was no *Śabādnuśāsanam* like that of Pāṇinī. which taught the usages, like *bhavati, gacchati, rāmaḥ, rāmau, rāmāḥ,* etc., nor was it necessary then. In those days all the words were got automatically formulated by minimum grammar, and that part is the most difficult, which even the highly expert modern grammarians do not know. In modern times, that part has been incorporated in the *Prātibha-darśana.* Bhartṛhari has in his *Vākyapadīyam* shown that same grammar as the best one among the ancient philosophical systems. It belongs to the class of the *Śikṣā-darśana* or the *Prātibha-darśana.* Due to the remark of Bhartṛhari, some people have an illusion that the Pāṇinian Grammar was a philosophical system *(darśana);* on the contrary, it was merely a *Śabdānuśāsana,* or a grammar, meant for the formulations of word and sentences. In the modern age, the knowledge of the ancient grammar is highly essential for understanding the Vedas.

The fifth requisite for the Vedic interpreter is the knowledge of the Vedic Astrology. In Astrology, however, the knowledge of the mathematical procedure and prediction is a must. The *brahma-darśana* of the Vedic seers is fundamentally based on the principle of *Aho-rātra.* In this *Aho-rātra-darśana*, the following problems are dealt with: What is the day? What is the night? On what element is the beginning of the day based? What is meant by the Sunrise (*sūryodaya*)? What is meant by the Moonrise (*candrodaya*)? What are the planets *(graha)* and those beyond them (*ati-graha*), constellations (*nakṣatra*)? The knowledge about the system of constellations (*nakṣatravāda*) is connected with the *ahorātravāda.* Of the 50 elements, each one of them has been mentioned by the name of the constellation or its presiding deity (*svāmī*). First of all, one has to determine as to where the *Aśvinī* should be placed, or is situated. This determination should be such as would correspond mathematically with the *saṁvatsaravāda* or the *ṛtuvāda* which is a part of the *saṁvatsaravāda,* which is the third aspect of the *ahorātravāda.* There is an *ayanavāda* and the *pakṣavāda* in the *saṁvatsaravāda.* Both these *ayanas* and the *pakṣas* should be set mathematically in the 50 elements. One who cannot do this cannot hope to get the knowledge of the *brahma-darśana.* The explanation of these six aspects of the *Ahorātra* principle has been definitely sought to be given, to some lesser or greater extent, by the works like *Brāhmaṇa, Āraṇyaka, Upaniṣad, Gītā, Smṛti, Mahābhārata and Purāṇa.* Hence, in the absence of this knowledge of Vedic Astrology, it is not at all possible to obtain the Vedic vision. And, without the Vedic Astrology there can be no *brahma-vāda,* nor *aho-rātra-vāda,* nor *nakṣatra-vāda,* nor *saṁvatsara, ṛtu, māsa, ardha-māsa, pakṣa* and *ayana-vāda.* There is a *kalāvāda* included in the Astrology of the Vedic seers, according to which the 50 elements have been divided into two aspects, viz., the *pūrvārdha* or *śukla* and the *uttarārdha* or *kṛṣṇa.* These aspects are different from the two groups of six months of the *saṁvatsara-vāda.* The aspects of these *brahmans* have been divided into the *ṣodaśa-kalā brahmans.* The first aspect has been also called *guhā.* All these concepts cannot be understood without the proper knowledge of the Vedic astronomy. The *catuṣkalā brahman* that has been explained in some works is also called *pādavāda.* It is in no way connected with the aspect called *kalāvāda.*

The sixth prerequisite for the Vedic interpreter is the full understanding of the tradition of the use of the Science of Vedic Metres *(chandaḥ-śastra).* It is not a difficult discipline. But the Vedic seers have utilized the syllables of the metres in the form of the elements *(tattva),* and their quarters as the steps of the First Creation *(ādi-sṛṣṭi).* The *gāyatrī-brahmāda,* however, has been fully cast into the syllables and quarters of the *chandaḥ-śāstra.* Here this *chandaḥ-śāstra* has been utilized as the representative phonetic syllables of the ṛco *akṣare'* of the *sikṣā-darśana* or the *prātibha-darśana. The brahman* has been called *eka-pād, dvi-pād* and *tri-pādī,* in accordance with the three quarters of the eight syllables each of the *gāyatrī-chanda,* representing the twenty-four *brahmans.* The twenty-fourth *brahman* is the first *brahman* of the fourth *saptaka.* The *tri-sapta samidhaḥ* of the *Puruṣa-sūkta*[10] *are* not 21, but are 24 *samidh*; that is why they are not mentioned as *eka-viṁśati,* but rather as *tri-sapta,* i.e., the three *saptakas* or quarters of eight syllables. The twenty-fifth *brahman* is the *sūrya* or *cakṣu,* which is invoked here. On this the *Aitareya-brāhmaṇa*[11] remarks as follows: *'Devatā akṣarabhājaḥ karoti akṣaram evaitad-devatā anu prapibanti, deva-pātreṇa (chandasā) eva tad-devatās tṛpyanti yaṁ kāmayetānāyatavānt syād ity avirājāsya yajet gāyatryā vā triṣṭubhā vā anyena vā chandasā vaṣaṭ kuryād anāyatanavantam evainaṁ tat karoti.* Thus, in the 32 syllables of the *Anuṣṭubh-chandas* each one of the syllables is a *brahman*, and in these 32 syllables the Brahmic creation *(brahma-sṛṣṭi)* is completed. The 33 elements of this same creation have been called the *raudra-sṛṣṭi*, by the three-quarters of the 11 syllables. The four quarters of 12 syllables each of the *Jagatī* are utilized for representing the full creation *(pūrṇa-sṛṣṭi)*. The *virāṭ* with its twelve syllables represents the *virāṭ puruṣa* of 40 elements. This is the knowledge of the *akṣara brahman* through the syllables of the Vedic metres. To this day no author of a *bhāṣya, ṭīkā, ṭippaṇī,* translation or criticism has ever thought of this type of the knowledge of the *akṣara brahman* through the syllables of this important Science of Vedic Metres *(chandaḥ-śāstra)*. The *Brāhmaṇas*, the *Āraṇyakas* and the *Upaniṣads* have explained the *chandaḥ-śāstra* numerous times in this way at every step; and further, the metres are called the animals or beasts (*paśu*).[12]

The seventh prerequisite for a Vedic interpreter is that he should be a great scientist and a philosopher. Here by 'great scientist' and 'philosopher', what is meant is that he should be one whose beliefs are supported by mature thinking based on personal experimental experience; not the one who is satisfied by quoting others. Even for such a great scientist -philosopher the profound study of all the *Brāhmaṇas, Āraṇyakas, Upaniṣads* and the *Bhagavad-gītā* is of course essential. Along with it, the deep knowledge of the Indian systems of philosophy, viz., ancient *Sāṅkhya* and *Yoga* is also expected.

The Vedic interpretation will not be complete merely by presentation of these seven prerequisites. It is highly required that he should keep before himself a clear picture of the Vedic background. May be the *Brāhmaṇas,* the *Āraṇyakas* and the *Upaniṣads* were compiled at the time when the significance of the ancient *gāthās* was getting lost or forgotten, but, their complete skeleton was already formulated well before the compilation of the *mantra* portion, which is but a metrical version of the *Brāhmaṇas,* the *Āraṇyakas* and the *Upaniṣads.* The original complete Veda is the *Brāhmaṇas,* the *Āraṇyakas* and the *Upaniṣads*. The exposition that was remaining to be presented in them is incorporated in the *Purāṇas* and the *Mahābhārata.* The declarations *'bhāratam pañcamo vedaḥ'* and ; *purāṇam pañcamo vedaḥ* are to this effect. The *Mahābhārata* is the real source of the *Purāṇas*.

Other important fact to note is that the age in which the Vedas were compiled, the Vedic seers had kept before them the full outline of the Vedic philosophical vision. While the elements were called by different names, their places were fixed and determined. They have given the serial number of each of the elements very clearly in the *Brāhmaṇas* etc., as for instance, *'prathamo'yam agniḥ, dvitīyaṁ parijāta-vedāḥ, kumāro navamo rudraḥ, indro ha ṣoḍaśī, saptadaśo'yaṁ prajāpatiḥ, ekonaviṁśo* 'yam, viṁśo'*yam, caturviṁśaṁ mahāvratam, ekatriṁśo'yaṁ puṣaḥ, catuṣ triṁśo'yaṁ prajāpatiḥ, catvāriṁśo'yaṁ virāṭ, aṣṭacatvāriṁśo'yam jāgataḥ puruṣaḥ,* Till now, the attention of nobody has been drawn to such references. The *Brahman* is *sapta-padī,* and the *sapta-vāda* is of many types, and these are the seven stages of the Brahmic philosophical vision. And, in each of these stages, there are seven, in some eight, or six *śaḍ-aṣṭakas or aṣṭa-ṣaṭka.* Nobody has thought about this, too. The *saṁvatsara-brahma-vāda,* however, is an all round extensive Wish-fulfilling tree of the Vedic path of Yoga.

FOOTNOTES

1. The author of this article does not claim any originality, since the endeavour here is to acquaint the Indologists of all the countries of the world with the ideas expressed by Pandit Harishankar Joshi of Hindu Vishva Vidyalaya, Varanasi, in his Hindi book *"Vaidika Viśva-darśana"* Vol.1, Chapter 3 (pp.28-34). N.M.K.
2. RV., 10.71,2 : *Saktum iva titaunā punanto yatra dhīrā manasā vācam akrata /*
   Atrā sakhāyaḥ sakhyāni jānate bhadraiṣāṁ lakṣmīr nihitādhi vāci //
3. RV., 10.164.39 : *Ṛco akṣare parame vyoman yasmin devā adhiviśve niṣeduḥ /*
   Yas tan na veda kim ṛcā kariṣyati ya it tad vidus ta ime samāsate //
4. YVl3.3. *Śikṣā ghrāṇaṁ tu vedasya /*
5. RV. 10.72.4c.
6. *Ibid.,* 1.164.39a
8. *Ibid.*, 9.97.34a.
9. *Ibid.*, 1.164.45a.
10. RV. 10. 90.
11. Ait. Br. 3.2.22.
12. Śat. Br. 4.3.5.1: *paśavo vai devānāṁ chandāṁsi /*
    Te yathedaṁ paśavo yuktā manuṣyebhyo vahanty evam
    chandānsi yuktāni devebhyo yajñaṁ vahanti//

III.2

ṚGVEDA, X.85.40 : A STUDY

Dr. M.D. Gokhale

Ṛgveda, X.85 is well known as *Sūryāvivāhasūkta*. Sūryā is the divine ideal of human brides and the ceremony of her marriage is the prototype of human marriage prevailing through ages. Many of the *mantra-s* from this hymn have been incorporated in the rituals of marriage. The fortieth *mantra* of this hymn is as follows:-

Somaḥ prathamo vivide gandharvo vivida uttaraḥ /
Tṛtīyo agniṣṭe patis turīyas te manuṣyajāḥ //

The *mantra* with slight variations occurs in the *Atharvaveda*, XIV.2.3.[1] Soma is here considered to obtain the girl first, then Gandharva obtained her. Agni was her third *pati* and human being was the fourth. The very next verse continues the idea and says that Soma gave her to the Gandharva, he, in his turn, gave her to Agni and it is Agni who bestowed her to the bridegroom.

The root *vid* (6th conjugation) means to obtain, to possess, to take to wife or to marry. *Vid* (2nd conjugation) means to know or to understand—perhaps suggestive of the carnal knowledge. The Atharvavedic *mantra* consists of the word '*jāyā*' which is derived from the root *jan* and is suggestive of procreation. Sāyaṇa while commenting on *AV*.II.36.2, specifically uses the word '*upabhoga*' *(Somādidevatātrayopabhogānantaram kanyāyā mānuṣapatisambandhaḥ śṛtyantare samāmnāyate)*. The word '*pati*' means the owner, the governor, the husband or the protector. Thus it can be obviously noticed that versatile ideas are involved in the *mantra* and those are of possession, protection, and procreation. Hence the *mantra* can be viewed from various angles. The paper presents a humble attempt to explore possible explanations for this *mantra*.

The *mantra* may indicate the necessity of protection for a woman. Aryans had colonized a foreign land. They had non-Aryan rivals; at the same time, there were clashes among the Aryan clans. It was perhaps a time when a woman was certainly exposed to much danger. Aryans had a constant urge for male children and a female was primarily viewed as potential mother. Her claim to the protection which she required is well recognised in the *Ṛgveda*. She was shielded, no doubt, by the strength of her father and brothers; still the divine protection was thought to be required. Hence the deities like Soma, Gandharva and Agni were considered to possess the maidens. Then it becomes their responsibility to protect their possessions. Soma is considered to afford protection from foes. He is goblin-slayer and slayer of a wicked.[2] Agni being domestic priest *(purohita)* is the custodian of maidens (*kanīnām patiḥ*)[3]. He is '*rakṣohan*' burns and dispels evil spirits and hostile magic.[4] Gandharva, according to Grassman and Griffith, is the protector of virginity. (In the *Mahābhārata*, Sairandhrī assures Sudeṣṇā that she would be protected by her *Gandharva-patis*.)[5]

The *mantra* may be suggestive of polyandry prevailing in the period much prior to the *Ṛgveda*, when society was formed by large patriarchal families (*kula-s*). The *kula-s* primarily required jointness and co-operation, based on kinship ties in order to ward off enemies and to carry out agriculture. In the words of G. Sontheimer, 'it may be necessitated by mere pressure of an inhospitable environment where it even may lead to polyandry'.[6] Hence the maiden obtained through marriage belonged to the whole family and not to the bridegroom personally. *Āpastamba Dharmasūtra* and *Bṛhaspatismṛti* are aware of this fact.[7] The *kulamukhya* had the first right on the bride. Then in peculiar conditions, with his due permision, she was allowed to have conjugal relation with others to procure a son. The Bālhīka tribe is referred to in *Śatapatha Brāhmaṇa* and *Mahābhārata* to be polyandrous.[8] Yudhiṣṭhira has justified the marriage of all the brothers with Draupadī saying that they are following the path of the ancients. Kapadia has mentioned that the *Khas*-s, the Himalayan tribes, who, in their features and language show themselves to be Aryans, practised polyandry. When the elder brother marries, his wife is regarded as the wife of his younger brothers also. If a younger brother wants to marry a particular girl, the elder brother goes through the marriage ceremony and he may assign the bride to the particular brother.[9] This fact seems to correspond with the Vedic concept that the bride first belongs to the three deities and they assign her to the human bridegroom. Thus though polyandry was rejected and condemned in later Vedic tradition, it was prevalent in pre-Vedic period and it may have remained symbolically in the *mantra*.

Though marriage is seen as a flourishing institution in the Ṛgvedic society, especially though the marriage-hymn shows that the institution of marriage had already taken deep root, these particular verses may call to memory the ancient age, when marriage had not become binding on men and women. The dialogue between Yama and Yamī as well as some references in the *Mahābhārata* indicate such age when a maiden was free to consort with men as per her wish.[10] Women had more liberty and were not confined as in later times. (The word *'kanyā'* is derived from the root *kam,* i.e. to long for.) The Ṛgvedic poets observe that the mind of a woman is ungovernable and her temper fickle.[11] The reference to Soma and Gandharva may indicate her relations with males prior to her marriage.[12] The reference to Agni as her third lord who gives her to the bridegroom may indicate that at the time of marriage she was purified by Agni. The fire is quite well known as the purifier. (Even Sītā was purified by the fire to destroy the default of staying at Rāvaṇa's place). Thus finally it was Agni who handed the *'pariśuddhā'* bride over to the bridegroom. Dange refers to a custom of purifying the bride before the marriage ceremony takes place.[13] The ritual of *lājāhoma* may indicate that Agni prevents her from unrestrained behaviour and leads her to permanent monandrous union. The *mantra* involved therein *'sa imām devāḥ preto muñcatu'* indicates her detachment- physical as well as emotional- from previous relations.

The Vedic seers believe that all their desired objects primarily belonged to the Gods. The human beings have to obtain their desired objects from the Gods. In order to please them, they perform the rituals along with the *mantra-s* and fulfil their desires with the help of the Gods. A seer-poet prays that Pūṣan would provide the maidens to him.[14] The *mantra* may be observed from this point of view. The bride is in the possession of the Gods. She is to be obtained from them. Hence Aryamā, Varuṇa and Pūṣan are approached with the mantra *'sa imām devaḥ preto muñcatu nāmuta svāhā'* The *mantra* is separately uttered for each one of the three.[15]

The three oblations of roasted grains are perhaps given as the symbol of compensation. Moreover, in order to release her completely from the acquisition of the gods, *Gṛhyasūtra-s* prescribe a *vidhi* called *śikhāmocana* which includes the *mantra 'pra tvā muñcāmi varuṇasya pāśāt' etc.*[16]

The words *'preto muñcāmi nāmutaḥ* as well as *'pra tvā muñcāmi'* may suggest that the bridegroom is releasing the bride from the gods forever. The gods may take a note that hereafter she belongs to the bridegroom and cannot be separated from him. The bridegroom is humble but firm when he warns that he is not stealing the girl *(na steyam asmi);*[17] on the other hand, he is officially releasing her from the pāśas of Varuṇa.

Rajwade thinks that men had to rescue those maidens perforce from the Gods which were snatched away by them.[18] But it seems that the transfer of possession takes place smoothly without any bitterness or dispute between the Gods and the human beings. Moreover, the Gods are her well-wishers and they find a bridegroom for her.[19] The maiden obtains her husband with their good wishes and permission. AV.II.36.2 says- *dhātur devasya satyena kṛṇomi patívedanam.* Sāyaṇa comments here as follows. *Devasya satyena anujñārūpeṇa devatāvyatiriktasya manuṣyarūpasya patyurlabhakam karomi*.

There is another important point to be noted. The Vedic Aryans have always considered the Gods to be their ideal. They have tried whole heartedly to follow them with faith and respect. They perform the rituals in the same way as the Gods have performed.[20] Even the tradition of wedding is considered to be founded by the Gods. AV.X1V.2.32 says, 'the Gods in the beginning lay with their spouses.' The *ṛṣi* asks the girl to get united with her husband as Sūryā did.[21] Thus Sūryā is the heavenly proto-type of human bride. She was obtained by Soma in the heaven, hence the human bride is considered to be obtained by Soma first. Then the Gods hand her over to the Gandharva who dwells in the *antarikṣa* or middle region.[22] When she reaches the earth, it is Agni who takes her charge in the capacity of being the main deity in the earthly region and the mediator between Gods and human beings. Then finally she is obtained by the human husband. Thus the bride is the heavenly gift that has descended to the earth for the well-being of human beings.

It would be interesting to observe the significance of the mention of these three in particular, viz. Soma, Gandharva and Agni. AV.II.36.2 mentions Soma, Brahmā and Aryamā in similar context. But Sāyaṇa deliberately equates Brahmā to the Gandharva as well as Aryamā to Agni (*Somadevena sevitam brahmaṇā parivṛdhena gandharveṇa ca juṣṭam atrāryamāśabdena vivāhāgnir ucyate)*.

Dange observes that Soma has a well-set rain-background in the Vedic context.[23] It is the semen of the sun *(ayam somo vṛṣṇo aśvya retaḥ)* that comes down to the earth in the form of rain.[24] The bride is always viewed as the field in the Vedic tradition.[25] As Parjanya sprinkles seed in the womb of the field, Soma also should endow the bride with profound ability of conception (*Somo rājā suprajasām kṛṇotu).*[26] There was a ritual of sprinkling *soma*-juice, yellowish golden in colour, on the ploughshare before ploughing the field. Similarly, there was a custom of besmearing the bride with *soma*-juice. Afterwards the soma-juice was replaced by *haridrā* (turmeric), which has similar golden yellow colour. Moreover, there is a ritual called '*suryajalābhiṣiñcana*' which endows the bride with lustre as well as the offspring.[27]

Ṛgveda speaks of the three fires of the three regions i.e. sun, lightning and sacrificial fire as the three sprinklers of semen.[28] The lightning is associated with the Gandharva.[29] The Gandharva seems to be the personification of the fire of the sun.[30] Being '*somasamrakṣaka*', he guards the '*retas*' of the Sun and brings it safely to the earth and hands it over to the *vivāhāgni*. That is why perhaps the *vivāhāgni* is brought to the abode of the bridegroom and *gṛhapraveśanīya-homa* is performed with it. Agni is considered as '*puruṣa-tattva*' and is therefore called '*kanīnām patiḥ.*' It is Agni who deposits the divine semen with the bride. Agni gives to the bridegroom the bride who now possesses the wealth in form of the power of procreation. Now she is capable of being called as '*jāyā*. Her '*jāyātva* thus depends upon Soma, Gandharva, and finally upon Agni. It seems that her '*jāyātva*' is emphasised in these *mantra-s*. Hence '*patitva*' primarily goes to Soma, then respectively to Gandharva. Agni and finally to human being.

Vedic matrimonial rituals consist of fire as very important factor. Agni is the centre of the family-life of the Aryans. Compared to any other deity, Agni is more closely associated with human life and activities. He is the promoter and protector of human clans. He is *viśpati'* as well as *gṛhapati*. Hence it is his duty to protect and to supervise the continuity of human life. Moreover, being the mediator between men and gods, he brings the divine semen to the humans. Hence '*lājāhoma'* seems to be the first among the main rituals performed by the woman.

It is a point of dispute whether the Soma means the moon. As MacDonell refers to in his *Vedic Mythology*, many scholars consider that Soma is the name for the moon so far as the earliest hymns of the *Rgveda* are concerned.[31] Especially in the case of X.85, Velankar, Muir and Keith opine that Soma here means the moon.[32]

Hence it should be observed whether this meaning throws any light on the fortieth *mantra*. The moon is said to be born of the mind of the '*puruṣa* (*candramā manaso jātaḥ*)[33] and it is strongly believed that *candramā* governs the mind; especially the females are overpowered by the moon. According to medical science, emotional development of a female child is faster and more prominent up to nine years age.

The feminine traits are obvious more in her emotional expressions, rather than in her physical form. Therefore, it can be said that in this stage a girl is dominated by Soma, i.e. the moon. Afterwards her secondary sexual characteristics get developed and secretions of Follicle Stimulating Hormone and Luteinizing Hormone become prominent. As a result, her physical form changes speedily as well as sexual attractions occur prominently in her mind. At this stage an adolescent girl is dominated by the Gandharva. The Gandharva in the Vedic tradition is fond of beauty and passionate love. He is aggressive, hostile and jealous in nature. (Even *Avestā* speaks of '*gandareva*' as destructive demon.)[34] Gandharva Viśvāvasu is regarded as the rival of the bridegroom in the first days of wedlock.[35] He is not ready to set the girl free from his clasp. Hence the *Gṛhyasūtra-s* speak of '*trirātra-vrata*.'[36] The marriage is not consummated for three nights after the arrival of bride at husband's house. Between them at night a staff is placed which is clad in a garment. According to Keith, it is a symbol of Viśvāvasu who is then worshipped, praised and asked to go to the mid-region and rejoice with the Apsaras-s. The *vrata* is completed by offering oblations into Agni. It is remarkable that the oblations are offered to Sūrya, Candra, Gandharva and Agni.[37] AV.XIV.2.33 mentions that the young maiden dwelling in her father's house is the share assigned to him. This reference corresponds with '*gandharvo vivida uttaraḥ*.'

The later texts consider that the Gandharva-s have grcat attraction for human maidens and have a mystic power over them. They preside over fertility and are worshiped for obtaining off-springs.

The reference to Agni as the third *pati* may suggest the third stage in the development of a girl, i.e. the cognitive development. Agni is '*jātavedas*', '*vipaścit*' and '*vayunavat*'. In capacity of the respectable, knowledgeable, elderly member of the family, Agni teaches her the ancient norms of behaviour, makes her aware of her rights as well as her duties as a mistress. According to Psychiatry, the development of a human child as a mature person consists of three aspects, viz. emotional, physical and cognitive. Thus the maiden, perfectly developed in all respects (i.e. emotional, physical and cognitive), is now bestowed to the husband to adorn the seat of a *gṛhiṇī* or rather *samrājnī*.

Thus the *mantra* can be viewed from various angles. It seems that it is very difficult to determine any one of such explanations as the only suitable explanation for this *mantra*. Hence it appears that the charm lies not in concluding, but in continuing the exploration.

FOOTNOTES

1. *AV*.XIV.2.3—*Somasya jāyā prathamam gandharvas te aparaḥ patiḥ/*
   Tṛtīyo agniṣṭe patis turīyas te manuṣyajāḥ)/
2. *RV*.IX.49.5 ; 28.6
3. *Ibid*. 1.116.10
4. *Ibid*. III.15.1;X.87.1,2,5,14
5. *Mahābhārata* BORI, IV.8.27:31
6. Sontheimer Gunther, *The Joint Hindu Family*, New Delhi, 1977, p. 13.
7. Joshi Laksmanashastri, *Vaidic Sanskriticha Vikas*, Wai, 1972, p. 231
8. Sontheimer G., *Op. Cit*., p.14
9. Kapadia K. M., *Marriage And Famiy In India*. 2nd edn. Kolkata, 1958, p. 63,68
10. *Mahābhārata,* BORI, I.I 113.4.5.7
11. *RV*.VIII.33.17.
12. One may remember here Satyavatī and Kuntī. Their virginity is considered to remain unhampered.
13. Dange S.A., *Ashvatthachi Pane,* Nagpur, 1974, p.5
14. *RV*.IX.67.10.
15. *Āśvalāyana Gṛhyasūtra,* 1.7.13
16. *lbid*.I.7.16-17.
17. *AV*.XIV.1.57.
18. Rajwade S.R., *Nāsadiyasūktabhāshya,* Vol.II, Pune, 1874, p.1372
19. *AV*.XIV.1.17-*Aryamaṇam yajāmahe subandhum pativedanam* /
    Ibid.XIV. 1.59-*Dhātā vipaścit patim asyai viveda* /
20.. *RV*.X.90.16
21. *AV*.X1V.2.32
22. *RV*.VIII.66.5; *AV*.XIV.2.34
23. Dange S.A. *Field And The Divine Fructification,* Bombay, 1971, pp. 191-2
24. *RV*. I. 164.35
25. Dange S.A. *Op. Cit*.
26. *AV*.XIV.I.49
27. Dange S. A. *Ashvatthachi Pane,* p. 44
28. *RV*.V.69.2; VII.33.7
29. Macdonell A., *Vedic Mythology*, p. 136
30. *ṚV*
    Dowson John. *A Classical Dictionary of Hindu Mythology and Religion,* New Delhi, 1992, p. 105
31. Macdonell A., Vedic Mythology, p. 112
32. Velankar H. D., *Ṛksūktavaijayantī*, p. 365
    Keith A *B.,The Religion and Philosophy of the Veda and Upanishads,* 1st Indian

reprint, New Delhi, 1970, p. 377; J. Muir *Original Sanskrit Texts on the Origin and History of the People of India,* New Delhi, 1976, part V, p. 270
33. *RV.*X.90.13
34. *Vedic Mythology,* p. 137
35. *ṚV*
36. *Āśvalāyana Gṛhyasūtra*. 1.9.11
37. Keith, *Op. Cit*.

SECTION-IV

CLASSICAL SANSKRIT LITERATURE

IV.1

ENVIRONMENTAL AWARENESS IN THE RĀMĀYAṆA

Dr. M. D. Paradkar

It has to be appreciated that our ancients looked at life as a connected whole and the idea of cosmos was at the basis of all their undertakings . The holistic approach of our ancient thinkers made them aware of the essential rapport between nature and man. Vālmīki, the first poet of this land, has been responsible for providing exquisite touches of true poetic feeling with which *Rāmāyāṇa* abounds. Monier Williams rightly said that *Rāmāyaṇa* is a spacious and delightful garden teeming with fruits and flowers watered by perennial streams and even its most tangled thickets are intersected with delightful pathways.

Rāma's descriptions of natural scenery occurring in only *Ayodhyākāṇḍa* also for that matter show that princes in those early days were not mere bookworms and did not study nature at second hand, but completed the intellectual as well as aesthetic parts of their culture by studying nature in nature's favourite haunts. Thus the Gaṅgā described in the 50th *Sarga* of *Ayodhyākāṇḍa* speaks of

जलौघाट्टट्टहासोग्रां फेननिर्मलहासिनीम्।
क्वचिद्वेणीकृतजलां क्वचिदावर्तशोभिनीम्।

the realistic touch evincing his interest in the glory of the river. He has words of appreciation for the *Haṁsa* as well as *Sārasa* along with सदामत्त विहगs and was really in love with सुमहानिङ्गुदीवृक्ष: who was full of flowers and sprouts due to vicinity and he asks the charioteer to choose this spot for their sojourn. In the 95th *Sarga* of the *Kāṇḍa* he spoke of Mandākinī in the words

विचित्रपुलिनां रम्यां हंससारससेविताम्।
कुसुमैरुपसंपन्नां पश्य मन्दाकिनीनदीम्।।

It is significant to note that मृगयूथनिपीतानि कलुषाम्भांसि सांप्रतम् have also made the alluring for him रतिं संजनयन्ति मे. Rāma of Vālmīki enjoys मारुतोद्धूतशिखरैः प्रनृत्त इव पर्वतः and lovingly attracts the attention of Sītā in the eloquent words

निर्धूतान् वायुना पश्य विततान् पुष्पसंचयान्।
पोप्लूयमानानपरान् पश्य त्वं तनुमध्यमे।।

No wonder that with such an interest in the beauty of nature, *Rāmāyaṇa* teems with descriptions of almost all seasons; namely हेमन्त in16th *Sarga* of *Araṇyakāṇḍa* (रविसंक्रान्तसौभाग्यस्तुषारारुणमण्डलः। निःश्वासान्ध इवादर्शश्चन्द्रमा न प्रकाशते।।), वसन्त or the spring in *Kiṣkindhākāṇḍa Sarga* 1 (मत्त कोकिल सन्नादैर्नर्तयन्निव पादपान्। शैलकन्दरनिष्क्रान्तः प्रगीत इव चानिलः)---पम्पातीररुहाश्चेमे संसिक्ता मधुगन्धिनः etc. The description of शरत् in अभिवृष्टा महामेघैर्निर्मलाश्चित्रसानवः। अनुलिप्ता इवाभान्ति गिरयश्चन्द्ररश्मिभिः। In fact this is reminiscent of the words of the English poet L'Allegro viz "Mountains on whose breast, the labouring clouds rest." The 28th *Sarga* in *Kiṣkindhākāṇḍa* appreciates the music of Nature in

षट्पादतन्त्रो मधुराभिधारं प्लवङ्गमोदीरितकण्ठचातम्।
आविष्कृतं मेघमृदङ्गनादैर्वनेषु संगीतमिव प्रवृत्तम्।।

It will not be proper to say that all these descriptions can be explained on the basis of the moods of Rāma. The words like सागरं चाम्बरप्रख्यमम्बरं सागरोपमम्। सागरं चाम्बरं चेति निर्विशेषमदृश्यत।। in the *Yuddhakāṇḍa* (*Sarga* IV) speak of innate interest in Nature irrespective of likes and dislikes of a human being. The moon in full glory will appeal like हस्तीव जाम्बनदबद्धशृङ्गो विभाति चन्द्रः परिपूर्णशृङ्गः only to a poet of high order who has innate love for appreciating the luminary, a part and parcel of nature. In *Araṇyakāṇḍa* (Canto LXXV) Rāma says to Lakṣmaṇa—We have seen the wonderful hermitage of Mātaṅga. In it deer and tigers are roaming without fear. There they saw big trees rich in flowers and sonorous with chirpings of the Koyasti (Lapwring), Arjunaka (a kind of peacock) and Satapara (woodpecker) and the whistling of the bambos called Kīcakas. In *Kiṣkindhākāṇḍa* (*Sarga* 1) nature in the region of Pampā is feelingly and picturesquely described by Rāma after his painful separation from his beloved wife. He says, "the breeze blows gently in this spring season and wafts the fragrance of flowers all around and is filled with the music of bees and cuckoos, to the melody of which trees agitated by the gentle wind dance merrily."

The learned and chaste Anasūyā of Vālmīki has graphically described to Sītā the approach of the evening at her hermitage near the borders of the *Daṇḍakāraṇya* (CXIX 3-9) "The sun has set, the auspicious evening has come, birds having spent the whole day in wandering in search of food are repairing to their nests and chirping before their sleep." Hanumān's description of *Aśokavana* also deserves mention from the point of view of variety of flowers. Even the giant Kabandha appears to be suscceptible to the influence of Nature (*Araṇyakāṇḍa* LXXIII). No wonder that Rāma, Lakṣmaṇa and the *Vānara* army enjoyed Nature's beautiful scenery in the region of Sahya-*parvata*. The description of the sea, which the *Vānara*-army sees for the first time, is beautiful and sublime at the same time; the boundless watery expanse is convulsed by the wind and is full of fierce sea-animals; the sea laughs with its foam and dances with its high waves, the moonrise swells it and fills it with its image." *Vānaras* of Vālmīki were charmed by the beautiful scenery of Laṅkā (Laṅkākāṇḍa). If ornaments enhance the beauty of men, beautiful and fragrant flowers as well as fruits increase the charm of the forest.

Rāmāyaṇa is full of indications of the poet's shrewd knowledge of various aspects of life. The shark and the whale (Mahājhaṣa) piercing through the ocean, is present here. Reference to the irrigation of an unwatered field form and through a watered field (केदारस्येव केदारः सोदरस्य निदइकिः। उपस्नेहेन जीवामि जीवन्ती यच्छृणोमि ताम्।। *Yuddhakāṇḍa* VII) Words like नवमासधृतं गर्भं भास्करस्य गभस्तिभिः। पीत्वा रसं समुद्राणां द्यौः प्रसूते रसायनम्।। *Kiṣkindhākāṇḍa*-13) speak of close observation coupled with a live interest in the natural phenomena.

Really speaking, Vālmīki is peerless among Indian poets of Nature. According to Indian philosophical thought, Nature and life are twin blossoms of the tree of Creation. Life is incomplete without the link with Nature; the latter is incomplete without being linked with life; both are incomplete without their relation or association with God i.e. Love and Law or *Ṛta* of the Vedic *Ṛṣis*. This is the reason why ग्रहनक्षत्रचन्द्रार्कतारागणविभूषिते। विताने जीवलोकस्य विमले ब्रह्मनिर्मिते।। (*Sundarakāṇḍa,* 168, 170) happens to be his expression. ततोऽस्तमगमत् सूर्यः सन्ध्यया प्रतिरञ्जितः poetically describes the wonderful hues and harmonies of Indian sun-set; the calm of the Indian nights is gloriously described in *Kiṣkindhākāṇḍa* XXVIII-58. In *Sundarakāṇḍa,* we come across a wonderful outburst of poety descriptive of the calm radiance of the moon.

The poet is equally at home in describing the terrestrial phenomena i.e. mountains and forests. The famous verse in *Ayodhyākāṇḍa* (XCTV-3) Viz.

न राज्याद्भ्रंशनं भद्रे न सुहृद्भिर्विनाभवः।
मनो मे बाधते दृष्ट्वा रमणीयमिमं गिरिम्।।

in which Rāma clearly talks of forgetting his exile and loneliness in the company of hills rightly evoked the admiration of Ravindranath Tagore who wrote his poem आमि कोन छले जाबो घाटे। शाखा थरथर पाता मरमर छाया सुशीतल बाटे and maintained that a true admirer of Nature ought to have innate liking for शाखा थरथर पाता मरमर not cabined and confined to the meeting of the loved one. One is also reminded of wonderful descriptions of the mountains from which Hanumān jumped to Laṅkā and back from Laṅkā in the verse सृजतां पुष्पवर्षाणि तोयं तोयमुचामिव' certainly has wonderful naturalness and appositeness. The words *prabhā*, *varṇa* and *prasāda* in the verse ताराणामिव सुव्यक्तं महतीनां शुभचिन्तनम्। प्रभावर्णप्रासादाश्च विरेजुस्तत्र योषिताम्।। *Sundara-kāṇḍa* IX-44) can only come from the facile pen of a master poet. It is also opportune to point out the difference in the lavish description of spring-time in case of Rāvaṇa and Rambhā, this great poet is able to kindle the impure and unholy lust while the description of the same season in *Uttarakāṇḍa* XXVI is full of pure and holy passion as well as pining of Rāma for Sītā.

This paves the way for the description of the 'mutual responsiveness of Nature-scenes and human moods.' Vedantic bent of the Indian mind always realises human life as enblossommed in the life of Nature. Nature not only charms and awes the human being but it also consoles, purifies and uplifts their minds. This is the reason why Rāma's departure from Ayodhyā makes nature also weep as is clear from व्यसृजन् कवलान्नागा गावो वत्सान् न पाययन् (XLI-10)अपि वृक्षाः परिम्लानाः सपुष्पाङ्कुरकोरकाः (LIX-4). No wonder that Sītā while being abducted by Rāvaṇa appeals to the hills and the trees to inform Rāma about the tragedy that befell her

आमन्त्रये जनस्थाने कर्णिकारान् सुपुष्पितान्।
क्षिप्रं रामाय शंसध्व सीतां हरति रावणः।।

Araṇyakāṇḍa LX-6 has spoken of

रुदन्तमिव वृक्षैश्च म्लानपुष्पमृगद्विजम्।
श्रिया विहीनं विध्वस्तं सन्त्यक्तवनदेवतम्।।

Rāma in grief asked the trees, animals and birds about the tidings of Sītā and Nature did give a silent but eloquent reply

एवमुक्ता नरेन्द्रेण ते मृगाः सहसोत्थिताः।
दक्षिणाभिमुखास्सर्वे दर्शयन्तो नभस्तलम्।।
मैथिली ह्रियमाणा सा दिशं यामन्वपद्यत।
तेन मार्गेण धावन्तो निरीक्षन्ते नराधिपम्।। *Araṇya*-LXIV 17-18.

It has to the remembered that Nature silently consoled Sītā when she was abducted by Rāvaṇa

नलिन्योद्ध्वस्तकमलास्त्रस्तमीनजलेचराः।
सखीमिव गतोच्छ्वासामन्वशोचन्त मैथिलीम्।। *Araṇya* (LIII—3)

Thus it has to be admitted that Nature in Vālmīki becomes one with the human being in weal and woe as the two form an integral part of the universe who in the eyes of the sage was a cosmos. Vālmīki also laid down the norm for the description of Nature in and by and for herself thereby providing an example to poets like Bhavabhūti and Tagore who are in love with all her forms, agreeable as well as disagreeable. Oneness of Nature and man really represents a balance between the two. This sense of balance is also indicated in his vision of a society in which groups are harmonised and learn the lesson of interdependence where life is based on duties than rights and in which wealth is not sought to the exclusion of righteousness and enjoyment. It is also true that righteousness is also not sought to the exclusion of wealth and enjoyment.

For appreciating this in Vālmīki's immortal poem, one can start by what Rāma asks Bharata in *Ayodhyākāṇḍa* c. 63, 64.

कच्चिदर्थेन वा धर्ममर्थं धर्मेण वा पुनः।
उभौ वा प्रतिलोभेन कामेन च न बाधसे।।
कच्चिदर्थं च धर्मं च कामं च जयतां वर।
विभज्य काले कालज्ञ सर्वान् वरद सेवसे।

This really speaks of harmony of aims that existed then in case of the individuals and of societies. In the *Rāmāyaṇa*, man is shown not only in and for himself but also in action in the family and in the society. He has to realise himself in and for and through the society. Rāma's life also enblossommed in the loving maternal arms of Nature. His life began on the banks of Sarayu, goes to the bank of Gaṅgā, enters many hills and forests and societies and sovereignties and comes back to Sarayu again before it is funded back into 'the imperial palace & whence it came.' Rāma though unequalled in power has the goodness to embrace Guha, Sugrīva and Hanūmān as well as Bibhīṣaṇa and meet them on an equal level. This is why Sugrīva and Bibhīṣaṇa were back in their Kingdoms after seeing Rāma-*rājya* established in Kosala.

Contrasted from this stands the conquest by Rāvaṇa described in the *Uttarakāṇḍa* through pride and war and destruction. The significance of वीर्योत्सेकेन बाधसे (*Bālakāṇḍa* XV.22) should not be lost sight of. Really speaking Rāvaṇa became a *Lokakaṇṭaka* i.e. the injurer of the world by upsetting the balance of life everywhere. Is it not significant to note that Viṣṇu was not asked by the Gods to rule the world but only to free the world from Rāvaṇa? In fact, Vālmīki has depicted three types of family life; the Āryan household of king Daśaratha of Ayodhyā, the *Vānara*-household at Kiṣkindhā ruled by Vālin first and Sugrīva later and the third is the Rāvaṇa-establishment at Laṅkā. In the household of Daśaratha all proprieties are maintained, a sense of the fair and the just prevailed, men and women of all classes and kind have personal feeling for the king and queen as well as Rāma. The news of conferring *Yauvarājya* on the deserving prince gives rise to rejoicings in the town-night and day—which really makes a pleasant reading. All the people are uniformly struck with sorrow on hearing the sudden turn of events. Duties to friends, *Gurus*, parents and relations between king and his subordinates, behaviours in the *Āśrama* are all well understood. That speaks of tradition and culture springing from an innate sense of discipline. Courtesies between Janaka and Daśaratha in connection with the marriage are picturesque and full of dignity.

The description of Laṅkā is rich and colourful. The luxury and abandon described in this city are really unmatched in Sanskrit literature. In fact Rāvaṇa is a powerful adversary to Rāma. Really speaking, Rāvaṇa had developed a whole system of life that had organised into a mighty destructive force. Rāvaṇa gives that famous cynical advice of his grand uncle in, एष मे सहजो दोष: स्वभावो दुरतिक्रम: No wonder when Bibhīṣaṇa makes himself bold to pass strictures on Rāvaṇa's conduct, he is upbraided and ordered to go out of Laṅkā. It must however be admitted that Rāvaṇa never thought of harassing his wife and children in his absence and this befits his pedigree.

Vānaras of Kiṣkindhā speak of third type of family where Vālin is the strongest warrior and adopts an unnecessarily cruel and vindictive behaviour with Sugrīva. Laxity in morals appears to be the characteristic. These people fight with trees and stones, with nails and teeth indicating perhaps there शाखामृगत्व which also explains their fickleness. It is only when Sugrīva, Aṅgada and Hanumān work together, that *Vānara*- force can achieve great results. Presence of Nala and Suṣeṇa as well as of Jāmbavān give a guarantee of wisdom and experience.

It is true that characters in the *Rāmāyaṇa* tend to be idealistic but they have provided the norm of behaviour to people of this land. It is true that he is "an ancient of the world", still he can be said to be "in the morning of the times." His idea of कुटुम्ब or family is based on a wider canvass and is not restricted to the husband and wife and their children. The forces of world-domination are now let loose; sanity and sweetness appear to be on the wane. The world has certainly become one but it is yet full of bleeding wounds inflicted by man on man and by nation on nation. Is it not true that in our society egoism is rampant ? Is it not a fact that inside the family the graces and refinements and sanctities of the earlier age seem to have gone never to return ? Not only men but women have also joined in this general scramble. The principle of life has become. "they shall take who have power and they shall keep who can."

Vālmīki belonged to an age where co-ordination of individual discipline and social harmony is not captured and imbalance is allowed to rule, there is little hope of recovery. May the pure and purifying Gaṅgā of poesy coming from the serene and sovereignfill top of Vālmīki and flowing into the ocean of Rāma's grace shower on the world purity and prosperity, power and perfection rooted in balance of man and environment. This may lead the world to peace.

वाल्मीकिगिरिसंभूता रामसागरगामिनी।
पुनातु भुवनं पुण्या रामायणमहानदी॥

SELECT BIBLIOGRAPHY

1. *Studies in the Rāmāyaṇa*—K. S. Rāmaswāmi Shastri
2. *Vālmīki Rāmāyaṇa*—V. Sitarerriah
3. Rāmakośa (Marathi) -Amarendra Gadgil, Vol. I

IV.2

CANONISATION OF RĀMA-KATHĀ AS APOTHEOSIZED IN THE CHARACTER OF SĪTĀ

Dr. Vijay Pandya

As we know, the *Rāma-kathā*, the story of Rāma enshrined in the earliest available Sanskrit work *Vālmīki-Rāmāyaṇa,* has assumed the status of a canon in the Indian society. Its hold upon the minds of millions of Hindus in unparalled in the history of India. As A. A. Macdonell, a well-known indologist specifically avers Probably no work of world literature secular in origin has ever produced so profound an influence on the life and *thought* of a people as the *Rāmāyaṇa*.[1]

And we know that when such a work has exercised such an influence upon the minds of the Indian people then it means that it has acquired the status of a religious scripture or the position of a canon. And the *Rāmakathā* over the centuries or millenia has undergone this process of canonisation. While analysing the process of canonisation, Heinrich Von Steiteneron elucidates the process, "If (a work) itself becomes endowed with an aura of sacredness which derives both from the original seers, *ṛṣis*, prophets or teachers who formulated the message and from the external truth which is thought to be encapsulated in the text of canonical scripture, Canon is a continuous source of self-awareness and self-definition. It provides meaning and direction to the community as a whole and to each individual member by representing both the ultimate truth and the means of attaining it.[2]

It is very interesting and edifying to study and analyse this process of canonisation of *Rāmakathā* which in itself is a very complex thing, a culmination of several socio-cultural-religio-ethical forces at work over a vast expanse of time of centuries or millenia.

At the very outset it may be observed that in the Rāma-story, as narrated in the *Vālmīki-Rāmāyaṇa* this process is visible.

The *Vālmīki-Rāmāyaṇa* which sets out to tell the story of Rāma, begins in this way.

Vālmīki asks Nārada, a popular mythological character and in this way the Rāma-story commences.

"Is there a man in the world today who is truly virtuous? Who is there who is mighty and yet knows both what is right and how to act upon it? Who always speaks the truth and holds firmly to his vows? Who exemplified proper conduct and is benevolent to all creatures? Who is learned, capable and a pleasure to behold? Who is self-controlled having subdued his anger? Who is both judicious and free from envy? Who when his fury is aroused in the battle, is feared even by the gods? This is what I want to hear for my desire to know is very strong. Great seer, you must know of such a man.[3,4]"

What is important in this Query is Vālmīki wants to know about a man (नर). But there is a catch in it. A man he should be, but, endowed with extraordinary qualities.

And Nārada, also in reply to Vālmīki's inquiry, says 'The many virtues you have named are hard to find---. Hear now of a man who has them all.[5]

So *Rāmakathā* is a story of a man, although a man of exceptional abilities.

Thus, the heroic saga of a man gets rolling on the vast canvas of time and in its long journey it gets canonised, seeds of which were inherent in the story of an extraordinary man itself.

Gradually the man gets divinised or apotheosized. So the story of the *Rāmakathā* is a tale of human beings getting divinised over a long period of time.

The hero of the *Vālmīki-Rāmāyaṇa*, Rāma is identified with Viṣṇu, one of the highest trinity of the Hindu pantheon. This identification is mainly discernible to a student of *Vālmīki-Rāmāyaṇa* in the *Bālakāṇḍa* and the *Uttarakāṇḍa*, the first and last books of the *Vālmīki-Rāmāyaṇa*. We shall not enter into the question of interpolation[6] here as that does not concern us here in the present context of the canonisation. However, it would not be amiss here to remark that even interpolations also reflect the socio-cultural-religio-ethical forces of the day.

So, though *Rāmakathā* began as a story of a man but eventually ended with a story of a man getting divinised and along with the process some other characters connected with the hero of the epic also basked in the glory of divinity. To be more precise, other characters also did get their share of divinity. To wit, Lakṣmaṇa is an incarnation of the serpent Śeṣa, the monkeys who helped Rāma in exterminating the demon-king Rāvaṇa were also incarnation of the gods who descended upon the earth to render assistance to Rāma in his subsequently divinely ordained task of destroying the demons. In this way, the *Rāma-kathā* gets divinised.

And it is not difficult to see the connection between canonisation and apotheosis. So over millenia, *Rāmakathā* was completely canonised. So when a Sanskrit work on poetics *Kāvyaprakāśa* (11th century A.D. Circa[7]) remarks रामादिवद्वर्तितव्यं न रावणादिवत्.[8] one should behave like Rāma, not like Rāvaṇa', the *Rāmakathā* is considered to have attained the status of a canon, which has crept into even a work of Sanskrit poetics.

Thus, in the *Vālmīki-Rāmāyaṇa,* there is a very delightful interplay between the divinity and humanity of Rāma. This trait of the character of Rāma is indeed a source of canonisation of the *Rāmakathā*.

Similarly the character of Sītā to some extent, shares this trait of Rāma's character. We know that Sītā has been the role-model for millions of Hindus in India since time immemorial, or since the days of the *Rāmakathā* which is as old as hills so to say. This phenomenon is as much as a culmination of the canonisation and apotheosis of Sītā through the traverse of time of millenia. This happens due to the complex characterisation of Sītā and also, due to her connection being a spouse of Rāma, who is regarded as an incarnation of the Lord Viṣṇu.

Sītā, like Rāma in the *Vālmīki-Rāmāyaṇa*, is extremely human and her character is very artistically though poignantly unfolded by the great artist Vālmīki.

When Sītā is kidnapped by the demon Rāvaṇa, Vālmīki without any inhibition, depicts the moment thus.

'Rāvaṇa clasps Sītā's thinghs with his right hand and with the left hand seizes her hair and then throws her into the chariot.[9]

And then Sītā was kept in captivity by Rāvaṇa for about a year.

The Indian society has never been able to reconcile to this tragic incident which has taken place in the conjugal life of Rāma and Sītā. It has given a poignant dimension to the character of Sītā too.

The war is over. The demon Rāvaṇa is slain. Funeral rites for Rāvaṇa have been performed. Now Sītā has come to know about the happy turn of events and is eager to see Rāma.

She has been brought into the presence of Rāma on the battlefield. There is a commotion among the crowd comprising bears, monkeys and demons as Sītā is being brought on the battlefield. To make way for Sītā these crowds are being cleared but Rāma stops that and says that there is really no harm in their witnessing Sītā directly, for, women can be seen in the eventuality of disasters, wars, a choice marriage, sacrifices and weddings. But Lakṣmaṇa, Sugrīva and Hanumān, got apprehensive hearing such words of Rāma. Looking at Sītā, Rāma experienced the conflicting emotions of joy, misery and anger.[10]

"Sītā stands before him covering her face with an end of her sari. She was weeping and addressing the *Āryaputra.* She had raised her face to see the face of her Lord. But instead of joyful reunion, Rāma starts speaking overwhelmed with anger in his heart.

'So I have won you back having defeated my enemies. I have acted as a man should act wiping out the insults to my honour. Today I have fulfilled my vow and now I am in full control of life. That fickle demon had kidpapped you from me. That was the fault of fate which a mortal has overcome."

Sītā hearing such feelingless words started weeping profusely. Rāma looks at her and gets angrier. Again Rāma launches an onslaught upon her saying that she should know that he did not do anything for her. But in order to remove the stigma to himself and to his family, he undertook the efforts. Now here is a doubt regarding her character and hence she is repugnant to him like a lamp to a person whose eyes have a disease.

Rāma continues

"you can go in any of the ten quarters. I have got nothing to do with you. How can I accept you who are directly from the lap of Rāvaṇa and pollute my family greatly. I have no attachment to you now, go anywhere as you please. You can accept Lakṣmaṇa or even Bharata or the king of monkeys Sugrīva, or even the king of demons Vibhīṣaṇa.

Rāvaṇa could not have resisted you staying in his house.[11]

Sītā was terribly pained. She was much ashamed and her limbs were as if entering into her. Then she started speaking.

'Why are you speaking to me so callously and inappropriately like a common man to a common woman. I am not as you take me to be, you must believe me. I speak on an oath. Because of the conduct of some lowly women you cast doubt on the entire sex. Cast aside this doubt if I am tested."

Now she utters most heart-rending and ominous words.

'If my body was touched by another it was because I was helpless and not because I had some carnal desire. Fate is to be blamed. The thing which is under my command is my heart and that is always with you. If my limbs are in the clutches of somebody else, what can I having no control over myself' do?[12]

These words have a too ominous ring for any male to stomach but Sītā in her disarmingly straight-forward attitude does reveal her heart.

To continue the narrative, she was ready to face the fire-ordeal. As she got ready to enter into fire, the gods appeared on the scene and they reminded Rāma of his divinity. Gods told him that he was not a mere mortal. These gods break into praise of Rāma as the Supreme God. Some scholar has opined that Sītā's trial by fire is actually more a testing of Rāma than of her.[13]

That may be. But in the fire-ordeal lies the apotheosis of Sītā's character which again goes to contribute to the canonisation of the work.

The incident of fire-ordeal is very important in the sense that at this moment the divinity of Rāma is revealed. Rāma is reminded of his divinity but Rāma says.

"I consider myself to be a man, the son of Daśaratha, Rāma and you may point out who am I whence am I and so on.[14]"

Agni appears in an embodied form holding in his hands the radiant gold-hued Sītā, unscarred with her garlands and ornaments as shining as before. Agni vouchsafes for Sītā's purity and asks Rāma to accept her which ultimately Rāma does.

Fire-ordeal is a very momentous moment in the life of Sītā.

But one has to admit that, the Indian society in its heart of the heart is very uncomfortable with the fact that Sītā stayed for about a year in captivity at an enemy's place. The Indian society is at pains to come to terms with this fact that purity of Sītā's remained unsullied though she stayed in captivity at an adversary's place.

The *Vālmīki-Rāmāyaṇa* itself tries to wriggle out of this ugly situation by way of divine intervention.

But even then it continued to rankle in the *Vālmīki-Rāmāyaṇa* and in the psyche of Indian society.

In the *Vālmīki-Rāmāyaṇa* again, there was a calumny spread about Sītā and Rāma abondoned her. Sītā is again asked to attest for her fidelity before she is accepted by Rāma and Sītā utters an oath

"Since I have never thought of any man but Rāma, let the Goddess Mādhavī (the earth) split open before me."[15]

As Sītā speaks, the earth, her mother, splits open and gives her refuge.

This is the tragic end of Rāma-Sītā's conjugal life.

But where is end? There is no end.

It is a festering wound in the Indian psyche.

Further, during the course of centuries and millenium, there arises another way of coming to terms with Sītā's purity remaining unblemished.

The *Adhyātma-Rāmāyaṇa* (of the 13th century AD circa) offers another version of the *Rāmakathā*. It is interesting to see how this version of the *Rāmakathā* handles abduction-incident which is at the root of the agony of the Indian psyche.

Meanwhile complete divinisation has taken place, in the *Adhyātma-Rāmāyaṇa*. Hence, when the day of kidnapping Sītā neared, Rāma told Sītā in privacy.

"Rāvaṇa shall come to you in the guise of a mendicant. You enter the cottage having placed a shadow of yourself outside. You live in the fire unseen by my order for a year. On Rāvaṇa having been killed, you shall come to me.' Hearing such words uttered by Rāma, Sītā did as she was told and having placed an illusive Sītā outside, entered the fire.[16]

Then in the narrative, whatever happens to Sītā is not to real Sītā, but an illusive Sītā to whom calumny would not stick. We can understand that this is also an attempt to maintain Sītā's purity and to believe in it.

Immediately in succession follows another *Adbhuta-Rāmāyaṇa*, which has been influenced by the *Adhyātma-Rāmāyaṇa*.

In *Adbhuta-Rāmāyaṇa*, the character of Sītā is completely divinised without any semblance of pretensions to her being human.

Adbhuta-Rāmāyaṇa is given the Śākta-orientation[17]

Here in the *Adbhuta-Rāmāyaṇa* Sītā is depicited as a primordial matter, *Mūlaprakṛti* the root of the whole creation. The sages absorbed in the Brahman, meditate on her as *vidyā* as well as *avidyā,* she is beyond *guṇas* and so on. The *Brahman* and the universe emerge from her. She is the cause of all causes. She is the nature as well as modification. She is *cinmayī* as well as one who delights the mind.[18]

In this *Rāmāyaṇa,* there are two Rāvaṇas viz. one is ten-headed and another is thousand-headed. Rāma has been able to slay the ten-headed Rāvaṇa but to exterminate the thousand headed Rāvaṇa is beyond the capacity of Rāma. That task is accomplished by Sītā. Sītā, assuming a terrible form, attacked the thousand headed Rāvaṇa and severed all the heads with the sword. The bellies of some other demons were torn open by Sītā. She started roaring and playing like ball with the heads of Rāvaṇa. At that time mothers appeared out of the pores on the surface of her body.[19]

Apotheosis of Sītā is complete.
That may be
Is the gnawing of the heart over?
Is the ranking in the heart stopped?
Do not know.

REFERENCES

1. Quoted by Robert Goldman in his translation of the *Vālmīki-Rāmāyaṇa,* General Introduction, p. 3 Vol. I, Pub. by Princeton Uni. Press, 41 New Jersey 1984.
2. *Charisma and Canon*, ed. by Vasudha Dalmia, Angelika Malinar Martin Christof, Oxford University Press, Oxford Indian Paperbacks 2003, p. 14.
3. Translation by Robert Goldman, *Vālmīki-Rāmāyaṇa, Bālakāṇḍa,* Vol. I, Pub. Princeton Uni. Press, 41, New Jersey, 1984.
4. को न्वस्मिन्सांप्रतं लोके गुणवान्कश्च वीर्यवान्।
धर्मज्ञश्च कृतज्ञश्च सत्यवाक्यो दृढव्रतः।।
चारित्रेण च को युक्तः सर्वभूतेषु को हितः।
विद्वान्कः कः समर्थश्च कश्चैकप्रियदर्शनः।।
आत्मवान्को जितक्रोधो द्युतिमान्कोऽनसूयकः।
कस्य बिभ्यति देवाश्च जातरोषस्य संयुगे।।
एतदिच्छाम्यहं श्रोतुं परं कौतूहलं हि मे।
महर्षे त्वं समर्थोऽसि ज्ञातुमेवंविधं नरम्।।१-१-२ to 5
Vālmīki-Rāmāyaṇa Text as constituted in its Critical Edition, Oriental Institute, Vadodara (India), First Edition 1992. For textual references, this edition is referred to.

5. बहवो दुर्लभाश्चैव ये त्वया कीर्तिता गुणाः।
   मुने वक्ष्याम्यहं बुद्ध्वा तैर्युक्तः श्रूयतां नरः।। Ibid.
6. But when a new view as the conception of the identity of Viṣṇu with Rāma appears in the texts the same remains restricted to the interpolated portions and does not pervade the entire poem, p. 47, Dr. Herman Jacobi, Dr. S. N. Ghosal, 1960.
7. *History of Sanskrit Poetics,* S. K. De, Reprint, 1988, p. 147.
8. Gujarati Edn. of *Kāvyaprakāśa,* ed. by Naginders Parekh, First Edn. 1987, pub. by Gujarati Sāhitya. Parishad, p. 4.
9. वामेन सीतां पद्माक्षीं मूर्धजेषु करेण सः।
   उर्वोस्तु दक्षिणेनैव परिजग्राह पाणिना।। ३-४७-१६.
10. तामागतामुपश्रुत्य रक्षोगृहचिरोषिताम्।
   हर्षो दैन्यं च रोषश्च त्रयं राघवमाविशत्।। ६-१०२-१६
11. तां तु पार्श्वे स्थितां प्रह्वां रामः संप्रेक्ष्य मैथिलीम्।
   हृदयान्तर्गतक्रोधो व्याहर्तुमुपचक्रमे।।
   एषासि निर्जिता भद्रे शत्रुं जित्वा मया रणे।
   पौरुषाद्यदनुष्ठेयं तदेतदुपपादितम्।।
   गतोऽस्म्यन्तममर्षस्य धर्षणा संप्रमार्जिता।
   अवमानश्च शत्रुश्च मया युगपदुद्धृतौ।।
   अद्य मे पौरुषं दृष्टमद्य मे सफलः श्रमः।
   अद्य तीर्णयतिज्ञत्वात् प्रभवामीह चात्मनः।।
   या त्वं विरहिता नीता चलचित्तेन रक्षसा।
   दैवसंपादितो दोषो मानुषेण मया जितः।।
   संप्राप्तमवमानं यस्तेजसा न प्रमार्जति।
   कस्तस्य पुरुषार्थोऽस्ति पुरुषस्याल्पतेजसः।।६.१०३.१ to 6
   इत्येवं ब्रुवतस्तस्य सीता रामस्य तद्वचः।
   मृगीवोत्फुल्लनयना बभूवाश्रुपरिप्लुता।।
   पश्यतस्तां तु रामस्य भूयः क्रोधोऽभ्यवर्तत।
   प्रभूताज्यावसिक्तस्य पावकस्येव दीप्यतः।।
   स बद्ध्वा भ्रुकुटिं वक्त्रे तिर्यक् प्रेरितलोचनः।
   अब्रवीत्परुषं सीतां मध्ये वानररक्षसाम्।।
   यत्कर्तव्यं मनुष्येण धर्षणा परिमार्जिता।
   तत्कृतं सकलं सीते शत्रुहस्तादमर्षणात्।।६-१०३-१० से १३
   विदितश्चास्तु भद्रं ते योऽयं रणपरिश्रमः।
   स तीर्णः सुहृदां वीर्यान्न त्वदर्थं मया कृतः।।
   रक्षता तु मया वृत्तमपवादं च सर्वशः।
   प्रख्यातस्यात्मवंशस्य न्यङ्गच परिमार्जिता।
   प्राप्तचारित्रसंदेहा मम प्रतिमुखे स्थिता।

दीपो नेत्रातुरस्येव प्रतिकूलासि मे दृढम्।।
तद्गच्छ ह्यभ्यनुज्ञाता यथेष्टं जनकात्मजे।
एता दश दिशो भद्रे कार्यमस्ति न मे त्वया।।
कः पुमान्हि कुले जातः स्त्रियं परगृहोषिताम्।
तेजस्वी पुनरादद्यात्सुहल्लेखेन चेतसा।।
रावणाङ्कपरिभ्रष्टां दृष्टां दुष्टेन चक्षुषा।
कथं त्वां पुनरादद्यां कुलं व्यपदिशन्महत्।।
तदर्थं निर्जिता मे त्वं यशः प्रत्याहृतं मया।
नास्ति मे त्वय्यभिष्वङ्गो यथेष्टं गम्यतामितः।।
इति प्रत्याहृतं भद्रे मयैतत्कृतबुद्धिना।
लक्ष्मणे भरते वा त्वं कुरु बुद्धिं यथासुखम्।।
सुग्रीवे वानरेन्द्रे वा राक्षसेन्द्रे विभीषणे।
निवेशय मनः सीते यथा वा सुखमात्मनः।
न हि त्वां रावणो दृष्ट्वा दिव्यरूपां मनोरमाम्।
मर्षयेत चिरं सीते स्वगृहे परिवर्तिनीम्।। ६.१०३.१५ to २४

12. एवमुक्ता तु वैदेही परुषं लोमहर्षणम्।
राघवेण सरोषेण भृशं प्रव्यथिताभवत्।।
सा तदश्रुतपूर्वं हि जने महति मैथिली।
श्रुत्वा भर्तृवचो रुक्षं लज्जया व्रीडिताभवत्।।
प्रविशन्तीव गात्राणि स्वान्येव जनकात्मजा।
वाक्शल्यैस्तैः सशल्येव भृशमश्रूण्यवर्तयत्।।
ततो बाष्पपरिक्लिष्टं प्रमार्जन्ती स्वमाननम्।
शनैर्गद्गदया वाचा भर्तारमिदमब्रवीत्।।
किं मामसदृशं वाक्यमीदृशं श्रोत्रदारुणम्।।
रूक्षं श्रावयसे वीर प्राकृतः प्राकृतामिव।
न तथास्मि महाबाहो यथा त्वमवगच्छसि।।
प्रत्ययं गच्छ मे स्वेन चारित्रेणैव ते शपे।।
पृथक्स्त्रीणां प्रचारेण जातिं त्वं परिशङ्कसे।।
परित्यजेमां शङ्का तु यदि तेऽहं परीक्षिता।
यद्यहं गात्रसंस्पर्शं गतास्मि विवशा प्रभो।।
कामकारो न मे तत्र दैवं तत्रापराध्यति।
मदधीनं तु यत्तन्मे हृदयं त्वयि वर्तते।।
पराधीनेषु गात्रेषु किं करिष्याम्यनीश्वरा।। ६-१०४-१ to ९

13. Shulman David, *Many Rāmāyaṇas, The Diversity of a Narrative Tradition in South Asia,* ed. by Paula Richman, Delhi, Oxford University Press, p. 93.

14. आत्मानं मानुषं मन्ये रामं दशरथात्मजम्।

    योऽहं यस्य यतश्चाहं भगवांस्तद् ब्रवीतु मे।। ६-१०५-१०

15. यथाहं राघवादन्यं मनसापि न चिन्तये।

    तथा मे माधवी देवी विवरं दातुमर्हति।। ७.८८.१०

16. रावणो भिक्षुरूपेण आगमिष्यति तेऽन्तिकम्।

    त्वं तु छायां तदाकारां स्थापयित्वोटजं विश।।

    अग्नावहइयरूपेण वर्षंस्तिष्ठ ममाज्ञया।

    रावणस्य वधान्ते मां पूर्ववत्प्राप्स्यसे शुभम्।।

    श्रुत्वा रामोदितं वाक्यं सापि तत्र तथाकरोत्।

    मायासीतां बहिः स्थाप्य स्वयमन्तर्दधेऽनले।।

    (*Adhyātma-Rāmāyaṇa, Araṇyakāṇḍa*) 17-2-3-4.

17. V. Raghavan, *Sanskrit Rāmāyaṇas other than Vālmīki's. The Adhhuta Adhyātuna and Ānanda Rāmāyaṇas* Gita Press, Gorakhpur 23rd Edn. Samvat 2052, First Edn. 1998, p. 4.

18. जानकी प्रकृतिः सृष्टेरादिभूता महागुणा।

    तपःसिद्धिः स्वर्गसिद्धिर्भूतिर्भूतिमती सती।।

    विद्याविद्या च महती गीयते ब्रह्म वादिभिः।

    ऋद्धिः सिद्धिर्गुणमयी गुणातीता गुणात्मिका।।

    ब्रह्मब्रह्माण्डसंभूता सर्वकारणकारणम्।

    प्रकृतिर्विकृतिर्देवी चिन्मयी चिद्विलासिनी।।

    Gujarati Ed. by Dr. Jashwanti Dave, First Ed. 2000

    अद्भुत-रामायणम्-१-१३ to १५ए

19. *Ibid.*, 23rd Canto

IV.3

DŪTAGHAṬOTKACA
A FRESH ASSESSMENT

Dr. N. P. Unni

THE DISCOVERY

The short one-act play entitled *Dūtaghaṭotkaca* was discovered in 1909 by T. Ganapati Sastri, the Curator of the Travancore Government Manuscripts Library among the thirteen plays located by him in Maṇalilkkara maṭhom near Padmanabhapuram. It was published by him for the first time in the Trivandrum Sanskrit Series as the eighth in the '*Bhāsanāṭakacakra*'[1]. The learned editor could procure only one manuscript as the basis of his edition. As in the case of other works the name of its author is not mentioned anywhere in the play. The editor attributed all the thirteen plays to Bhāsa who is renowned as the author of *Svapnavāsavadatta* which incidentally forms one of the dramas included in the codex.

As the title suggests the story deals with the messengership of Ghaṭotkaca. Abhimanyu the son of Arjuna was murdered by Kauravas in a fight. Kṛṣṇa deputes Ghaṭotkaca to the side of Duryodhana to carry the message that the next day Arjuna is going to wreak his vengeance upon them. The story is only an invention of the poet to a large extent.

Curiously enough the short play is not at all found mentioned by such authors who have referred to Bhāsa as a dramatist. Surprisingly, the work, if it was really composed by him, was lying in oblivion until the hands of the Trivandrum Series editor sought for it. It was subsequently found that *Abhijñānaśākuntalacarcā*[2] by an anonymous author who probably belonged to the 15th century contains several references to the work[3]. Nowhere else the work is referred to even by name.

Manuscripts of the work are extremely rare and hence the Trivandrum editor's efforts to secure more manuscripts for his edition proved fruitless. Prof. C.R. Devadhar who has re-edited the work claims to have used another manuscript belonging to the Bhandarkar Research Institute[4]. The whereabouts of the second manuscript are not known to the present writer and he could not find any reference to it in the descriptive catalogue published from the institute.

A survey of the so-called Bhāsa manuscripts undertaken by the present writer could establish the existence of at least seven manuscripts of *Dūtaghaṭotkaca* of which only two have been utilised by the two editors of the work. All other editions are mere reproductions. Editors often introduce changes at their will and such conjectural emendations mislead the readers. For an instance of such emendation the colophon given as *'Dūtaghaṭotkacam nāmotsṛṣṭikāṅkam samāptam"*[5] is not found in any manuscript so far available. The manuscripts simply state *"Dūtaghaṭotkacam avasitam"*. Another colophon of the work is referred to as *"Dūtaghaṭotkacāṅkam."*[6] This reference again is unsupported by manuscript evidence though it is quite possible since the play was put on the Kerala stage along with other plays.

Some Technical Defects

The authorship of the play assigned to Bhāsa has all along been a subject of controversy. The lack of technical perfection evident in some of the thirteen plays has raised serious doubts with regard to the authorship of Bhāsa who is renowned to be a great dramatist and worthy enough to be mentioned by Kālidāsa and Bāṇabhatta. The protagonists of the Bhāsa theory have tried to save "Bhāsa" from this predicament by placing the blame on those who preserved these manuscripts by maintaining a long stage tradition. "This may be due to the mangling by some Cākyār, into whose hands these plays fell". The shortcomings of the author are lightly dealt with once it was supposed that Bhāsa is the author and that he preceded Bharata who gave shape to the rules of dramaturgy through his *Nāṭyaśāstra*. One explanation along these lines suggests that "the fact of Bhāsa's plays not conforming to the rules of *Nāṭyaśāstra* was taken to indicate that either Bhāsa preceded the extant *Nāṭyaśāstra* or followed a different tradition'. Another explanation is that "an older recension of the present *Nāṭayaśāstra* may have been lacking in strict observance of the rules.'

However, Winternitz has criticised the play as a "patch-work" and observes that "the message of Kṛṣṇa which he (i.e. Ghaṭotkaca) brings in the final verse (taking the place of *Bharatavākya*) is quite out of place." The play ends rather abruptly.

The manuscripts of the play so far discovered do not contain the *Bharatavākya* and in this respect differ from other plays.

Abhijñānaśākuntalacarcā referred to earlier has pointed out some defects in the play. In order to illustrate the point that sometimes the *Sūtradhāra* alone is made to introduce the play, *Dūtaghaṭotkaca* is mentioned by the anonymous author of the commentary. The absence of *Naṭi* and the lone appearance of the *Sūtradhāra* characterises the *Sthāpanā* of the play. This feature is common to *Svapnavāsavadatta, Bālacarita, Pañcarātra* and some other plays. Sometimes the dramatist introduces the *Sūtradhāra* as belonging to the time and place of the action in a drama. Again the play is referred to as an illustration[7]. Here he is running away from the vicinity of Arjuna after having succeeded in killing Abhimanyu, The kings have lost their moorings having been wounded by the arrows of the young prince. They are described as running away to find shelter in their homes. The commentator remarks that it is not possible to say that the *Sūtradhāra* has witnessed the scene though he describes it closely. Is it possible that he might have seen the actors donning the costumes of the kings? The answer is no. The commentator concludes that the *Sūtradhāra* is only visualising the scene in his mind,[8] in order to introduce the scene to the audience and to prepare them for the action which is to follow.

The commentator holds that the characters mentioned by the *Sūtradhāra* are usually expected to appear on the stage. That is the usual course ordained by the rules of dramaturgy.[9] But in *Dūtaghaṭotkaca* the kings mentioned by the *Sūtradhāra* do not enter the scene.[10]

It is improper on the part of the dramatist that the characters are not introduced soon after the announcement of the *Sūtradhāra*. The question will arise that how is it possible to introduce a number of kings at the same time. It will be difficult as in the case of stage directions like 'then enter a hundred monkeys'. So it is not proper to mention the entrance of many characters at once. How can one know that *Sūtradhāra* has indicated them? It is clear since he has referred to them before his departure from the scene. Hence this kind of reference made by *Sūtradhāra* is improper and it shows the weakness of the dramatist.

Yet another technical impropriety on the part of the dramatist is also discussed here. It is with regard to the entrance of a *Bhaṭa* who is not mentioned by the *Sūtradhāra*.[11] What he has mentioned is only the flight of the kings after having murdered Abhimanyu. He has failed to indicate the entrance of the *Bhaṭa* in order to report the slaying of Abhimanyu to king Dhṛtarāṣṭra. This is not the usual practice, for only such characters who are mentioned in the prologue are introduced by the dramatists. Hence there is neither justification for this exception nor is it supported by authorities.

Thus we are able to notice that some of the improprieties on the part of author of *Dūtaghaṭotkaca* is severely criticised. Can we expect such a lack of general knowledge in dramaturgy from a pastmaster like Bhāsa who is the reputed author of *Svapnavāsavadatta?* Is it worth justifying him after ascribing the authorship of *Dūtaghaṭotkaca* to him when there is not even a shred of evidence either literary or textual for such an ascription? Will the hypothesis[12] of Bhāsa's pre-Bharatan existence hold water when the technical merits of *Svapnavāsavadatta* and *Dūtaghaṭotkaca* are compared dispassionately? Or, will the laxity of rules in a supposed different version of *Nāṭyaśāstra* come to the aid of an author of lesser merit from whose pen the present play must have originated? These are some of the questions baffling a dispassionate reader. What other proof can a protagonist of the Bhāsa theory advance in this connection except that this play happened to be found in a codex in which *Svapnavāsavadatta* was discovered. In the light of the criticism levelled by the above mentioned commentator, arguments like similarity in technique, situation etc., will fade into background.

It is evident that the play was put on the Kerala stage by the professional actors as one of a serial in the *Mahābhārata* saga though stage manuals dealing with the details of the performance are not available at present. It seems that the play was referred to as *Dūtaghaṭotkacāṅkam* and some take it to mean that the play belongs to the type called *Utsṛṣṭikāṅkam*[13]. The play had got another peculiar feature. The manuscripts so far discovered do not contain the *Bharatavākya* forming the epilogue. This has prompted some scholars to postulate that "the poet might have added something more towards the end which is now lost."[14] But the last verse of the play forming the message of Janārdana is suggestive of the completion of the work and any further stanza will be redundant.

FOOTNOTES

1. TSS No. 22, Trivandrum, 1912.
2. TSS No. 195, Trivandrum, 1961.
3. Unni N.P., 'The Trivandrum plays and Abhijñānaśākuntalacarcā', *Vishveshavaranand Indological Journal,* XIII, 1975.
4. Devadhar C.R., *Plays ascribed to Bhāsa,* Poona, 1962.
5. *Ibid,* p. 474.
6. JBRAS, 1925, p. 141.
7. *Ibid,*p. 22: nanu dūtaghaṭotkace sthāpanāyām sūtradhāra āha......... dhāvantītyuktiḥ.

8. *Ibid*, p. 23:*Evam ceha anubhāvayamānena smaraṇena 'yāntyarjune'-tyādi vacanamanupapannam, na mukhyadarśanena.*
9. *Nāṭyaśāstra: Sūcayet vastu bījam vā mukhyam pātram athāpi vā.*
10. *Carcā*, p. 24: *Sūtradhāreṇa sūcitānām rājñām apraveśo nopapannaḥ. Nanu katham bahūnām rājñām yugapat praveśah; tadā 'tataḥ praviśati vānaraśatam' itivad vilambanam syāt.Pātraistricaturairaṅkaḥ' iti bahupātrasūcanam na kartavyam. Katham ete sūtradhāreṇa sūcitā iti jñāyate. Niṣkrāntapadātpūrvam abhihitatvāt jñāyate.*
11. *Ibid*, p. 25: *Api ca, atra asūcitasya bhaṭasya praveśo'anupapannaḥ. Katham asya asūcanam iti. Naipathyaśravaṇena jñātvā abhimanyurnihata iti abhidhitā narādhipā bhayena nivartante ityuktam; na punar dhṛtarāṣṭrāya abhimanyuvadham nive-dayitum āgatasya bhaṭasyāyam śabda iti abhihitam. Ato asūcanam. Sūtradhārasū-citasyaiva sarvasthāpanāntarapraveśo dṛśyate, na asūcitasya. Na ca atropapattiḥ prāmāṇikavacanam vā.*
12. Pusalker A.D., *op, cit.*, p. 198.
13. Devadhar C.R., Poona Oriental Series 54, p. 474, gives the colophon: *Dūtaghaṭotkacam nāmotsṛṣṭikāṅkam samāptam.*
14. Pusalker, *op.cit.*, p. 167.

IV.4

बुद्धचरित–विडम्बनासिद्ध महाकाव्य

वसन्तकुमार भट्ट

सुप्रसिद्ध आलङ्कारिक डॉ राधावल्लभ त्रिपाठीजी ने 'बुद्धचरित' का साहित्यिक मूल्यांकन करते हुए लिखा है कि 'रसोद्रेक में रससांकर्य या रसमिश्रण महाकवि अश्वघोष की दुर्लभ विशेषता है। भयानक रस के उपयुक्त निरूपण में बुद्ध का शांत विग्रह निरन्तर उनकी दृष्टि में हैं; अतः शांत का प्रवाह भयानक के साथ साथ बहता चला आता है।. . . सुन्दर वस्त्रों तथा कोमल चमड़ी के आवरण में छिपी वीभत्स वास्तविकता का बोध जिस तरह अश्वघोष कराते हैं, वह संस्कृत महाकाव्यसाहित्य में दुर्लभ हैं'।[1] परन्तु यह दुर्लभ रससांकर्य रूप कविकर्म की आधारशिला –नींव की पत्थर–क्या है, कहाँ पर है? यदि उसकी समीक्षा नहीं की जाती तो इस काव्य के साफल्य का रहस्योद्घाटन नहीं हो सकेगा। इस 'बुद्धचरित' के महाकाव्यत्व की सिद्धि करने वाला जो विडम्बना तत्त्व (Irony) है, वही तो प्रथमतया सिद्धार्थ को बुद्धत्व की ओर ले जानेवाला तत्त्व है। विडम्बना रूप इस दार्शनिक परिमाण ने ही सिद्धार्थ को महाभिनिष्क्रमण के लिए उत्तेजित किया है, और कवि ने भी उसी को कविकर्म के रूप में पूरे काव्य में घुलामिला दिया है। उसी को बिना पहचाने अश्वघोष के कविकर्म की भी सही पहचान नहीं हो पायेगी। अतः प्रस्तुत आलेख में, 'बुद्धचरित' का अद्यावधि अनुल्लिखित रहा जो रचना-गत विडम्बना-तत्त्व है, और जो अनेक वैविध्यों के साथ समग्र कृति में सुव्याप्त है, उसका निरूपण किया गया है।

पाश्चात्य साहित्यकारों ने 'हास्य' के जो विभिन्न प्रकार बताये हैं, उसमें विनोद (Humour) २. नर्म-मर्मयुक्त उक्ति (wit), ३. कटाक्ष या व्यङ्ग्य (Satire) ४. टोना या ग्राम्य कटाक्ष (Sarcasm) के साथ में ५. (नाट्यात्मक) वक्रोक्ति/विडम्बना (Dramatic Irony) का भी परिगणन किया था। लेकिन कालान्तर में, इस 'नाट्यात्मक वक्रोक्ति या विडम्बना की' व्यापक झलक पर भी विचारणा होने लगी। क्योंकि इस नाट्यात्मक वक्रोक्ति में किसी की छद्मपूर्ण विडम्बना होती देखकर सदैव हास्य ही निष्पन्न होता है, ऐसा नहीं है। कदाचित् 'छद्मपूर्ण

विडम्बना' अथवा 'संगोपनपूर्वक की विडम्बना' से करुण का भी अनुभव होता है। मनुष्य को जब इस छद्मपूर्ण विडम्बना का साक्षात्कार होता है, तब वह विरोधों या विसंगतियों से भरे जीवन का गहरा अनुभव पाता है। जिसके कारण वह निर्भ्रांत होता है, जीवन की संकुलता से बाहर निकलता है और परम सत्य का दर्शन करके शान्ति का भी अनुभव करता है। अतः आलोचकों की दृष्टि में यह Irony-जिसको हम 'संगोपनपूर्वक' की गयी विडम्बना 'या' छद्मपूर्ण विडम्बना करेंगे,–उसका ख्याल (विभाव-concept) अभी भी विकसनशील है।[2] और इसके परिणाम स्वरूप, साहित्यिक कृतियों की रचना-प्रक्रिया में प्रयुक्त होनेवाली विभिन्न युक्तियों में से एक युक्ति (structural device) के रूप में भी यह Irony—विडम्बना तत्त्व-का स्वीकार हुआ है।

'बुद्धचरित' में महाकवि अश्वघोष ने जो बुद्ध का जीवन दर्शन प्रकटित करके मोक्षार्थ-गर्भा कृति का प्रणयन किया है, वह दर्शन के मूल में 'इदंप्रथमतया' विडम्बना तत्त्व ही है। जैसे कि–'संवेगोत्पत्ति' नामक तृतीय सर्ग में, राजकुमार सर्वार्थसिद्ध नगरयात्रा के दौरान एक ओर जरा, व्याधि एवं मृत्यु को देखते हैं। दूसरी ओर जनसमुदाय को इस जरा, व्याधि-एवं मृत्यु की ओर गजनिमीलिका करके हर्षोन्माद के साथ जीवन व्यतीत करते भी देखते हैं। तब वह अपने जीवन में प्रथम बार ही एक मूलगामी विडम्बना का साक्षात्कार करता है। :–

इदं च रोगव्यसनं प्रजानां, पश्यंश्च विश्रम्भमुपैति लोकः।
विस्तीर्णम् अज्ञानमहो नराणां, हसन्ति ये रोगभयैरमुक्ताः॥३-४६॥

"प्रजाओं की यह रोगरूप विपत्ति देखते हुए भी संसार विश्वस्त (निर्भीक) रहता है। अहो, (कितना) विशाल अज्ञान है (इन) मनुष्यों का, जो रोगभय से अमुक्त हो कर भी हँस रहे हैं?"[3] इस तरह मृतशरीर को देखने के बाद सिद्धार्थ फिरसे यही विडम्बना महसूस करता है :–

इयं च निष्ठा नियता प्रजानां प्रमाद्यति त्यक्तभयश्च लोकः।
मनांसि शङ्के कठिनानि त्व नृणां, स्वस्थास्तथा ह्यध्वनि वर्तमानाः॥ (३-६१)

"प्रजाओं का यह विनाश नियत है और संसार भय छोड़कर असावधानी बरत रहा है? मनुष्यों के मन, मैं सोचता हूँ, कठोर है। क्योंकि (मृत्यु के) मार्ग में रहते हुए वे उस प्रकार सुखी-स्वस्थ बैठे हैं।"

राजकुमार सिद्धार्थ जब बालक था, बाद में किशोर हुआ और आज नवयुवक है और विवाहित होकर एक पुत्र का पिता भी बना है, तब पहली बार उसे मालूम हो रहा है कि मनुष्य जीवन में 'जरा' भी है, 'रोग' भी है, और अन्त में मौत भी निश्चित है। पिता ने उसे इस अवश्यंभावी भयों से अद्यावधि अज्ञात रखा-यह कैसी वञ्चना? और नगर के प्रजाजन भी यह अनिवार्य दुर्घटनाओं को जानते हुए भी उसकी ओर आँख-मिचौनी करके जी रहे हैं–यह कैसी विडम्बना? इस वैश्विक

विडम्बना (Cosmic Irony) के दर्शन ने ही उनके मन में संवेग उत्पत्ति की है और बुद्धत्व प्राप्ति का मार्ग प्रशस्त किया है।

बुद्धत्व की प्राप्ति में निमित्तभूत बने इस विश्वव्यापी विडम्बना तत्त्व की पहचान को एक काव्य में यदि उजागर करना हो तो, किसी भी कवि के लिए यह आवश्यक है कि इस विडम्बना तत्त्व को ही अपने कविकर्म का अनिवार्य भाग बना दे। अर्थात् काव्य की निर्मिति में भी एक रचना-गत युक्ति (Structural device) के रूप में उसका प्रयोग करना चाहिए। और यदि ऐसा सफलतापूर्वक किया जाता है तो वह कृति सही अर्थ में बुद्ध के जीवनदर्शन को बड़े प्रभावक ढंग से प्रस्तुत कर पायेगी, और 'महाकाव्य' पद की दावेदार बना सकेगी।

अश्वघोष के 'बुद्धचरित' में एक रचनागत युक्ति के रूप में विडम्बना तत्त्व कहाँ कहाँ पर और किस तरह विलसित हो रहा है उसको कुछ उदाहरणों के जरिये हम देखेंगे :–

(१) शाक्याधिपति शुद्धोदन और महिषी मायावती के घर पुत्र जन्म होने पर तपोवन से आये महर्षि असित ने कहा था कि–यह (पुत्र) राज्य को छोड़कर, विषयों में अनासक्त रह कर तीव्र प्रयासों से ज्ञानमय सूर्य का प्रकाश करेगा, और जगत् का मोहान्धकार नष्ट करेगा इत्यादि। (१-६१ से ७७) लेकिन, "मेरा यह पुत्र निःश्रेयस् के मार्ग पर चलेगा और कदाचित् वन में भी चला जायेगा" ऐसा सोचकर राजा ने उसको कामासक्त करने के प्रथम उपाय के रूप में 'यशोधरा' नामक एक वामा के साथ उसका विवाह करवा दिया। (१-२५-२६) दूसरे उपाय के रूप में, कुमार के मन में किसी भी तरह का क्षोभ उत्पन्न न हो इस लिए उसको महल में ही रखने की सूचना दी गई। कुमार को भूमि पर फिरने की अनुमति नहीं थी।[4] तीसरे उपाय के रूप में, सर्व ऋतु में सुख देने वाले नृत्य-गीत-संगीतादि का प्रबन्ध किया गया। (बु २.२९) चतुर्थ उपाय के रूप में–उस कुमार को कामोद्दीपन में पण्डित एवं रति क्रीड़ा में निपुण हो ऐसी वाराङ्गनाओं से परिवृत कर दिया गया।[5] पिता के इन उपायों को वर्णित करने के बाद कवि ने उस पर नुक्ताचीना करते हुए लिखा है कि

रिरक्षिषन्तः श्रियमात्मसंस्थां रक्षन्ति पुत्रान् भुवि भूमिपालाः।
पुत्रं नरेन्द्रः स तु धर्मकामो ररक्ष धर्माद्विषयेषु मुञ्चन्॥२-५५

"पृथिवी पर अपनी राजलक्ष्मी की रक्षा चाहनेवाले अन्य भूमिपाल जब अपने पुत्रों की (विषयोपभोग से) रक्षा करते थे, तब इस धर्माभिलाषी राजा ने अपने पुत्र को विषयो
में जोड़ते हुए उसकी धर्म से रक्षा करनी शुरू की"–इसी को

लेकिन, देवों के द्वारा पिता के इन प्रयासों की पूर्ण विडम्बना तो क
तीसरे सर्ग में निरूपित की है :–

घर में ही बाँधे गये हाथी को जैसे वनविहार की इच्छा होती है, वै

राजकुमार को भी कदाचित् नगरोद्यान में जाने की इच्छा हुई। पिता शुद्धोदन ने पुत्र के मनोरथ की पूर्ति के लिए आज्ञा दे दी। परन्तु साथ में ऐसी आज्ञा भी जारी की कि राजमार्ग पर आर्त-दुःखी-जनता को निकलना नहीं है। क्योंकि अपना पुत्र सुकुमारचित्त वाला है, और आर्त जनता को देख कर वह उद्विग्न हो सकता है (बु-३-४)।

परन्तु देवों ने मार्ग में क्रमशः जराग्रस्त एवं रोगग्रस्त मनुष्य का निर्माण करके सिद्धार्थ को उद्विग्न कर ही दिया। जैसे किसी वृषभ के समीप में ही वज्रपात होने से वह उद्विग्न हो जाता है वैसे ही कुमार भी संविग्न हो जाता है। राजा ने पुत्र के बिना विहारयात्रा किये वापस आ जाने का निमित्त जान लिया। मार्ग के शौचाधिकारियों को डाँटा और मार्ग की पुनः परीक्षा करवाके एवं रथ के सारथि को भी बदल कर, 'कदाचित् रसान्तर होगा' ऐसा सोचकर (३-५१) तीसरे दिन फिर से राजकुमार को विहार यात्रा के लिए भेजा। परन्तु उन्हीं देवों ने उनको एक मृतशरीर को उठा कर जा रहे चार आदमियों को दिखाया (३-५४)। सारथि ने भी जो बात नहीं बतानी थी, वही 'अवाच्य' बात को यानि मृत्यु के स्वरूप को–कुमार के सामने वर्णित कर दिया। पिता के सर्वविध उपाय विफल हो जाते हैं। Man proposes and God disposes —यही तो मनुष्य जीवन की शाश्वत विडम्बना है।[७] जिसको irony of fate कहते हैं। एक पिता अपने पुत्र को वैरागी देखना नहीं चाहता था, लेकिन देवों ने वही चाहा था। अतः मनुष्यों के सतर्क प्रयासों को एक क्षणार्ध में ही देवों ने विफल कर दिया।

(२) मृत शरीर को देखकर, और मृत्यु अवश्यंभावी है ऐसा जान कर कुमार घर जाना चाहता है। परन्तु रथ को पद्मषंड की ओर दौड़ा दिया। इस उद्यान में, पहले से ही अनेक वाराङ्गनाओं को लेकर पुरोहितपुत्र उदायी आया हुआ था। सभी वाराङ्गनायें राजकुमार की ओर आकृष्ट तो होती है। परन्तु कुमार के प्रभाव से न कुछ बोल सकीं, न हँस सकीं (४-७)। तब उदायी ने सभी वाराङ्गनाओं को वीतरागी ऋषिओं को भी चलायमान करने वाली स्त्रियों का स्मरण करवाया (४-१६ से २०)। और अन्त में आज्ञा दी कि राजा शुद्धोदन की राज्यलक्ष्मी पराङ्मुखिनी न हो जाय ऐसा प्रयत्न किया जाय। वाराङ्गनायें राजाज्ञा से प्रेरित हो कर और कुमार की मृदुता देख कर फिर से उत्साहित हो जाती हैं। वे पूरे मद और मदन से राजकुमार को वश में लाने के लिए उद्युक्त होती हैं। जिसका बड़ा शश्ङ्गारिक वर्णन ४-२९ से ५३ श्लोकों में दिया गया है। एक ओर वाराङ्गनाओं की निर्लज्ज शृङ्गारिक क्रीड़ायें हैं, और दूसरी ओर धैर्य से संयमित इन्द्रियों वाला सिद्धार्थ है। वह तो एक ही बात सोच रहा है कि–क्या एक दिन मरना ही है?। (मर्तव्यमिति सोद्वेगो न जहर्ष, न विव्यथे। ४-५४) यहाँ पर कवि ने दो परस्पर विरुद्ध मनोभावों को आमने-सामने रखे हैं–Juxtapose किया है–वही परिस्थिति (Irony) का विडम्बना का निर्माण कर देती है।

(३) मृच्छकटिक (अष्टम अङ्क) में शकार विविक्ति स्थान देखकर वसन्त सेना का अनुनय शुरू करता है। परन्तु वसन्तसेना शकार को तो मन से तिरस्कृत कर रही है। ऐसी स्थिति में जो दो विभिन्न मनोभावों का संनिधिकरण हुआ है, वहाँ वसन्तसेनारूप उद्दीपन-विभाव के उदासीन होने पर शृङ्गार का रसाभास निष्पन्न होता है, जो अन्ततोगत्वा हास्य का निर्माण करता है। परन्तु 'बुद्धचरित' के (स्त्रीनिवारण नामक) चतुर्थ सर्ग में वाराङ्गनाओं के सामने निश्चल खड़े सिद्धार्थ का चित्र भी विडम्बनापूर्ण Ironical–है। क्योंकि मद एवं मदन से सक्रिय बनी वाराङ्गनायें (सिद्धार्थ में) रति को तो उत्तेजित नहीं कर सकती हैं, बल्कि विरति को जन्म दे रहीं हैं। राजकुमार स्त्रियों की ओर अनुकम्पा से सोचता है कि–ये स्त्रियाँ अपने चञ्चल यौवन को जानती नहीं हैं। ये स्त्रियाँ व्याधि एवं मृत्यु से भी अनभिज्ञ हैं। निश्चित ही ये लोग अचेतन हैं। इत्यादि। इस तरह कामासक्ति के सामने विरक्ति का विडम्बनापूर्ण चित्रण कवि की रचना-गत युक्ति का एक उत्कृष्ट निदर्शन है। डॉ. राधावल्लभ त्रिपाठी जी–अश्वघोष के जिन रससांकर्य को 'दुर्लभ' कह कर प्रशंसा करते हैं, उसके मूल में यह विडम्बनापूर्ण चित्रण की कामयाबी रही है।

(४) 'महाभिनिष्क्रमण' नामक पञ्चम सर्ग में संसार से विरत हुआ सिद्धार्थ जब पिता से प्रव्रज्या की अनुज्ञा माँगता है, तब पिता शुद्धोदन उसे 'गृहस्थधर्म में प्रवृत्त होकर, वार्धक्य में ही तपोवन प्रवेश करना चाहिए' इत्यादि वचनों से सलाह देते हैं। और बाद में आज्ञा देते हैं कि "न यास्यति"–यह घर से बाहर नहीं जा सकेगा। तत्पश्चात् पिता फिर से एकबार पुत्र के रक्षण में तत्पर होते हैं और उत्तम कामोपभोग का भी इन्तजाम करते हैं।[8] रात होने पर कुमार प्रासाद पर चढ़ता है। वहाँ उत्तम अङ्गनायें भेजी जाती हैं, जो संगीत से उसे बहलाती हैं। परन्तु कुमार उसमें लिप्त नहीं होते हैं, बल्कि उसके मन में तो अभिनिश्चक्रमिषा दृढ़ हो गई थी। यहाँ पर भी, देवों ने फिर से मनुष्य पिता के प्रयत्नों की विडम्बना करते हुए प्रमदा जनों को गाढ निद्रा में डाल दिया, और उनके सुन्दर गात्रों को विकृत भी कर दिया। जिसको देख कर कुमार के मन में यह स्त्रियों के द्वारा की जाती पुरुषों की विडम्बना का पर्दाफाश हो जाता है। कुमार अब ठीक तरह से जान लेता है कि–सुन्दर वस्त्र एवं विविध आभरणों से वञ्चित होता हुआ पुरुष स्त्रियों के विषय में अनुरक्त रहता है। सिद्धार्थ विमान से नीचे उतरता है। देवों के द्वारा ही भवन का द्वार अपावृत हो जाता है। सारथि छन्दक जो कि नरेन्द्रशासन को अच्छी तरह से जानता था (कि कुमार को प्रासाद में से बाहर नहीं निकालना है) फिर भी वह अज्ञात रूप से प्रेरित होता हुआ 'कन्थकं नामक अश्व को ले आता है। कुमार को लेकर जब छन्दक नगर से बाहर निकल जाता है तो यक्ष लोग उस अश्व के खुर को अपने करकमलों मे धारण कर लेते हैं अर्थात् बिना कोई पदरव हुए कुमार नगर से बाहर निकल जाता है। पिता के दूसरी बार के प्रयत्नों का भी वैफल्य सिद्ध होता है।

पुत्र को विषयोपभोग में लिप्त करने के, एवं राजप्रासाद में ही बंद कर रखने के पिता के प्रयासों की देवों के द्वारा दो बार विडम्बना होती है।

(४) काव्य के पूर्वार्ध (१ से ६ सर्ग) में देवों के द्वारा मनुष्य के प्रयासों की विडम्बना होती दिखाई पड़ती है। परन्तु काव्य के उत्तरार्ध (७-१४ सर्ग) में, आश्चर्यकारक रूप से स्वयं वाचक ही एक भारी विडम्बना का भोग बनता है। अब तक जो सिद्धार्थ एक भोला-भाला राजकुमार था, पितृआज्ञा के अधीन रह कर जो केवल प्रासाद में ही ललिताङ्गनाओं के बीच जीवन व्यतीत करता था, जिस को नगर जीवन का भी परिचय नहीं था, वही राजकुमार दृढ़ मनोबल वाला एक तार्किक बुद्धिमान तत्त्वान्वेषक बन कर हमारे सामने खड़ा होता है। कुमार के भोलेपन से संगोपित रहा यह चरित्र, ऊपर ऊपर से ऐसा दिखाई देता है कि कर्मों के उपचय होने से देवों के द्वारा सञ्चालित हो रहा है। परन्तु कुमार जब घर से बाहर निकल कर तपोवन में चला जाता है, और वहाँ के तपस्वियों के विचारों की आलोचना (सर्ग-७ में) करता है तब मालूम पड़ता है कि यह जितना दिखाई पड़ता था इतना सुकुमार मति नहीं था। उसने रास्ते में ही बिम्बसार के सामने जो 'कामनिन्दा' (सर्ग-११ में) की है और अराड़ ऋषि के (सर्ग-१२) साथ जो शास्त्रार्थ करके उनकी तत्त्वनिष्ठा का तार्किक खण्डन किया है, उसे देख कर हम दंग रह जाते हैं। कवि ने भी अब (उत्तरार्ध में) सिद्धार्थ को 'राजकुमार' न कह कर 'बोधिसत्त्व' (९-३०) कहना शुरू कर दिया है। इस तरह 'बुद्धचरित' के उत्तरार्ध में पूरे काव्य ने करवट बदल दी है। इसी को रचना-गत विडम्बना (Structural Irony) कहते हैं। जिन लोगों ने यह रचनागत विडम्बना का अनुभव नहीं किया है, और अश्वघोष के ('सौन्दरनन्द' में आये हुए) शब्दों का उद्धरण[9] देकर ऐसा कहा है कि-"अश्वघोष ने एक मिशनरी के रूप में धर्मोपदेश करने के लिए ही 'काव्य' का माध्यम स्वीकारा है"-वह पुनर्विचारणीय है।

काव्य के उत्तरार्ध में, राजकुमार सिद्धार्थ का जो परिवर्तित परिपूर्णसत्त्व बोधिसत्त्व (९-३०) के रूप में परिवर्तन कर दिया गया है, उसके द्वारा की गई तत्त्वसमीक्षा के कतिपय विचार निम्नोक्त हैं :-

(1) पिता ने मन्त्री के मुख से कहलाया था कि-"राजलक्ष्मी की गोद में लोटते हुए गृहस्थों ने भी मोक्षधर्म प्राप्त किया है" (९-१९) इस का खण्डन करते हुए सिद्धार्थ ने कहा है कि-शमप्रधान मोक्षधर्म कहाँ, और दण्डप्रधान राजधर्म कहाँ? (इन दोनों की तुलना ही नहीं की जा सकती)। यदि शम में रति हो, तो राज्य शिथिल होगा, यदि राज्य में मति हो, तो शम में विप्लव होगा। शान्ति व तीक्ष्णता का मेल नहीं हो सकता, जैसे शीतल जल व उष्ण अग्नि की एकत्र स्थिति सम्भावित नहीं है।(९-४९)

(2) कामोपभोग की निरन्तर अतृप्ति प्रकट करते हुए सिद्धार्थ ने कहा है कि-जैसे हड्डी चबा कर भी भूखे कुत्ते कभी भी तृप्त नहीं होते हैं वैसे ही जिन्हे भोगकर भी लोग तृप्त नहीं होते है, जीर्ण अस्थिपिञ्जर के समान उन कामों में किस आत्मवान् का आनन्द होगा?''(११-२५)

(3) सिद्धार्थ विविध कामनाओं की पूर्ति को 'भोग' संज्ञा के योग्य नहीं मानता है। क्योंकि उनकी दृष्टि में 'भोग' तो वास्तव में एक तरह का 'दुःखप्रतीकार' ही है। जैसे कि तृषा के शमन के लिए ही शीतल जल होता है, क्षुधा-नाश के लिए ही अन्न भोजन होता है, और वात एवं आतप के निवारण के लिए ही घर होता है। यह वस्त्रादि द्रव्य तो दु:खप्रतीकार के उपाय हैं, उसमें भोगबुद्धि करना, या उसे 'भोग' संज्ञा उचित ही नहीं है। (११-३६,३७) इस श्लोक के शब्द द्रष्टव्य हैं :–

दुःखप्रतीकारनिमित्तभूतास्तस्मात्प्रजानां विषया न भोगाः।
'अश्नामि भोगान्' इति कोऽभ्युपेयात्प्राज्ञः प्रतीकारविधौ प्रवृत्तः।

(4) इसी तरह अराड़-मुनि के सांख्यदर्शन में रहे तर्क-दोष को भी उद्घाटित करते हुए सिद्धार्थ ने कहा है कि

गुणिनो हि गुणानां च व्यतिरेको न विद्यते।
रूपोष्णाभ्यां विरहितो न ह्यग्निरुपलभ्यते॥ (१२-७८)

सत्त्वादि तीन गुणों से रहित को मुक्त आत्मा नहीं कह सकते। क्योंकि गुण न रहे, और 'गुणी' अवशिष्ट रह जाय–ऐसा कैसे होगा? 'गुणी' (गुणवान्) संज्ञा तो तब ही सुसंगत रहेगी कि जब उस में कोई गुण रहे। जिस तरह से उष्ण गुण से रहित को कोई 'कोई 'अग्नि' ही नहीं कहेगा अतः 'निस्त्रैगुण्य' की स्थिति को 'मोक्ष' नहीं मान सकते।

क्षेत्रज्ञो विशरीरश्च ज्ञो वा स्याद् अज्ञ एव वा।
यदि ज्ञो, ज्ञेयमस्यास्ति ज्ञेये सति न मुच्यते॥१२-८०

अर्थात्–"शरीररहित क्षेत्रज्ञ 'ज्ञ' (जाननेवाला) कहने योग्य है कि 'अज्ञ' कहलाने योग्य है, यदि क्षेत्रज्ञ को 'ज्ञ' कहेंगे, तो उसके लिए 'ज्ञेय' (जानने का विषय) भी अवशिष्ट रहना चाहिए, और 'ज्ञेय' के रहने पर उसे 'मुक्त' नहीं कहा जायेगा।"

इस तरह, काव्य के पूर्वार्ध में भोला-भाला अव्युत्पन्न बाल सा व्यवहार करनेवाला सिद्धार्थ, जब काव्य के उत्तरार्ध में मन्त्री को, तपस्वियों को, बिम्बसार को और अराड़ मुनि को अपने "तत्त्वनिष्ठुर" (११-६९) वचन कहने लगता है तब इस काव्य का सहृदय वाचक एक आश्चर्यजनक विडम्बना का अवश्य अनुभव करता है। यह अनुभव बड़ा चमत्कृति-पूर्ण है, जो इस काव्य को 'महाकाव्य' बनाता है।

'बुद्धचरित' में प्रयुक्त रचनागत विडम्बना का परिचय करने के साथ-साथ, अन्य प्रकार की विडम्बनाओं का भी 'बुद्धचरित' में संनिवेश हुआ है, उसका प्रदर्शन किया जाता है:–

(१) नाट्यात्मक वक्रोक्ति (-विडम्बना) [Dramatic Irony] : संवेगोत्पत्ति होने के बाद जाम्बूवन में जब कुमार चिन्तन कर रहा था, तब एक भिक्षुवेषधारी उसके सामने उपस्थित

हुआ। उसको देखकर कुमार के चित्त में भी प्रव्रज्या की इच्छा प्रदीप्त हो जाती है। वह नगर में वापस लौट आता है। उसको आते हुए देख कर राजकन्या बोलती है। कि–

सुखिता बत निर्वृता च सा स्त्री पतिरीदृश इहायताक्ष यस्याः।
इति तं समुदीक्ष्य राजकन्या प्रविशन्तं पथि साञ्जलिर्जगाद॥५-२४

"मार्ग में प्रवेश कर रहे सिद्धार्थ को देख कर कोई राजकन्या बोली जिस स्त्री का पति ऐसा 'आयताक्ष' है, वह सुखी और संतृप्त (निवृता) ही होगी।"

राजकन्या के ऐसे शब्द सुनकर वह परम शान्ति का अनुभव करता है। कवि कहते हैं कि यहाँ 'निर्वृता' शब्द को सुनते ही सिद्धार्थ के मन में परिनिर्वाण प्राप्त करने के बुद्धि प्रकट हुई :–

अथ घोषमिमं महाभ्रघोषः परिशुश्राव शमं परं च लेभे।
श्रुतवान् स हि निवृतेति शब्दं परिनिर्वाणविधौ मतिं चकार॥ (५-२५)

यहाँ पर वक्त्री राजकन्या के पक्ष में 'निवृति' शब्द का अर्थ संतृप्ति, प्रसन्नता, सुख या आनंद अभीष्ट है।[10]परन्तु श्रोतृपक्ष में-सिद्धार्थ के लिए–उसी शब्द का अर्थ 'मुक्ति, निर्वाण' में प्रकट होता है।[11] परिणाम स्वरूप सिद्धार्थ के मन में परिनिर्वाण की इच्छा प्रदीप्त होती है।[12]कोई एक अर्थ में बोला गया शब्द, श्रोता के लिए दूसरे ही अर्थ का यदि अभिधान करता है तो वह 'नाट्यात्मक विडम्बना' का उदाहरण बनता है।

(२) इसी तरह का एक दूसरा भी उदाहरण देखिये :–

सिद्धार्थ अपने जीवन में सब से पहली बार नगरयात्रा के लिए बाहर जाता है। इस बात को सुनकर सभी पौराङ्गनायें अपने अपने प्रासादतल पर चढ़ गईं। अट्टालिकाओं के ऊपर एवं घरों की खिड़कियों में सर्वत्र मुखकमल ही दिखाई दे रहे थे। उन सभी स्त्रियों ने जब जाज्वल्यमान राजकुमार को देखा, तब बोल उठती हैं कि 'धन्यास्य भार्या' । इस राजकुमार की भार्या को धन्य है' (३-२३)। इस वाक्य के पीछे नगर-स्त्रियों के मन में ऊठी ईर्ष्या के व्यञ्जना तो हो ही रही है; परन्तु आगे चल कर, जब यही राजकुमार सोती हुई पत्नी और पुत्र को छोड़कर गृहत्याग कर देता है तब, यही वाक्य एक प्रकार से विडम्बनापूर्ण बन जाता हैं। नगर स्त्रियों कि लिए–'धन्यास्य भार्या' का अभीष्टार्थ भिन्न है; परन्तु सिद्धार्थ पत्नी यशोधरा की भावस्थिति को देखते हुए, यही वाक्य यशोधरा के पक्ष में विडम्बनापूर्ण बनकर करुण व्यंजक सिद्ध होता है।[13]

(३) संवेगोत्पत्ति के बाद, मुमुक्षु सिद्धार्थ अपने पिता से परिव्रज्या की अनुज्ञा माँगता है। तब पिता उसे कहते हैं :–"तुम अभी तरुणावस्था में हो, धर्माचरण का यह काल नहीं है। और बूढ़े पिता को छोड़कर चले जाने पर तुझे अधर्म होगा। गृहस्थ धर्म में पहले रत रहने के बाद वार्धक्य में ही तपोवन प्रवेश करना चाहिए"। (५-२५ से ३३). तब सिद्धार्थ करुणस्वर में, लेकिन बड़ी दृढता के साथ कहता है कि–

यदि मे प्रतिभूश्चतुर्षु राजन् भवसि त्वं, न तपोवनं श्रयिस्ये।
न भवेन्मरणाय जीवितं मे, विहरेत् स्वास्थमिदं च मे न रोगः।
न च यौवनमाक्षिपेज्जरा मे, न च संपत्तिमिमां हरेद्विपत्तिः॥५-३५

हे राजन्! यदि आप चार बातों में मेरे 'प्रतिभू' जमानतदार (surety, guaranter) हो सकते हो, तो मैं अवश्य वन में नहीं जाऊँगां। जैसे कि–१. मेरा जीवन मरण के लिए न हो, २. कोई रोग मेरे इस स्वास्थ्य का हरण न करे। ३. जरावस्था मेरे यौवन को नष्ट न करे, और ४. कोई विपत्ति मेरी इस संपत्ति का हरण न करे।

यहाँ पर जो विडम्बना विजृम्भित हो रही है वह इस प्रकार की है: (१) अपने पुत्र का लालन-पालन करने वाला एक पिता पुत्र को प्रव्रज्या लेने से रोक रहा है। पिता की दृष्टि में उसका पुत्र सांसारिक भावों से अनभिज्ञ एक बाल है। जबकि पुत्र संसार की क्षणिकता, अनित्यता से पूर्ण अभिज्ञ हो चुका है। और (२) एक पुत्र अपने लालन-पोषण करने वाले पिता से अपने 'प्रतिभू' जमानतदार-बनने की माँग कर रहा है। जो कभी भी संभव नहीं हैं। एवमेव, (३) कवि ने यहाँ सिद्धार्थ के मुँह से पिता शुद्धोदन को 'राजन्' ऐसा सम्बोधन करवाया है। अर्थात् यह पिता तो एक राजा भी है, परन्तु राजा होते हुए भी इन पूर्वोक्त चार बातों में वह किसी भी तरह से 'जमानतदार' नहीं हो सकता है। एक राजा की यह लाचारी-यह बेचारापन-उनके जीवन की बड़ी विडम्बना है। एक राजत्व का मिथ्यापन है, उपहास है।[14]

(४) अभिनिष्क्रमण की रात्रि में सिद्धार्थ अश्वपालक छन्दक को जगाता है और 'कन्थक' नामक अश्व को ले आने को कहता है। (५-६८) कन्थक अश्व ने एक ही रात में अनेक योजनों का अन्तर काट कर सिद्धार्थ को दूर-सुदूर के तपोवनों में पहुँचाया था। इस कन्थक अश्व के साथ अलग अलग प्रसङ्ग में सिद्धार्थ ने, यशोधरा ने एवं पिता शुद्धोदन ने बातचीत की है। ये तीनों प्रसङ्गों के वर्णन में भी कवि ने विडम्बना तत्त्व को ही कार्यान्वित किया है। जैसे कि

(क) सिद्धार्थ कन्थक को कहते हैं कि आज दिन तक तो तुमने युद्धभूमि पर शत्रुओं को परास्त करके राजा को जीत दिलाई है। परन्तु आज तुझे मुझ को अमृत पद की प्राप्ति के लिए यहाँ से ले जाना है। (५-७५)

मर्त्य पदार्थों की प्राप्ति के लिए उपयोगी होने वाला यह अश्व आज अमृतत्व की प्राप्ति के लिए उपयोग में लिया जाता है। यहाँ दो परस्पर विरुद्ध लक्ष्य का संनिधिकरण (Juxtaposition) भी एक प्रकार की Irony-विडम्बना-लगती है।

(ख) अभिनिष्क्रमण की रात्रि में जो मार्ग एक रात्रि में ही नाप लिया था, वही मार्ग पर वापस आते समय कन्थक को आठ दिन लगे! (८-२) कपिल नगर में आकर वह घोड़ा जोर से रोते हुए हिनहिनाता है: **स्वरेण पुष्टेन रुराव कन्थको जनाय दुःखं प्रतिवेदयन्निव।** (५-१७) इस ध्वनि को सुन कर पत्नी यशोधरा कहती है कि–

"यह अनार्य कर्मा आज खूब हिनहिना रहा है, मानो राजभवन को भर रहा हो। किन्तु जब मेरे प्रियतम को ले जा रहा था, तब यह अधम गूँगा हो गया था।" (५-४०)

"उस रात में यदि हिनहिना कर लोगों को जगाता या खुरों से पृथिवी पर शब्द करता, या जबड़ों से जोरों का शब्द करता तो मुझे ऐसा दुःख न होता।" (५-४१)

यहाँ पर परिवेदना करते हुए शोकग्रस्त यशोधरा ने कन्थक घोड़े के दो विरोधी वर्तनों को आमने-सामने रख कर, घोड़े के विडम्बनापूर्ण व्यवहार की निन्दा की है।

(ग) इसी तरह, अन्तःपुर विलाप' नामक अष्टम सर्ग के अन्त भाग में राजा शुद्धोदन भी अकेले वापस लौटे हुए इस घोड़े को देख कर बोलते हैं कि–

बहूनि कृत्वा समरे प्रियाणि मे, महत्त्वया कन्थक विप्रियं कृतम्।
गुणप्रियो येन वने स मे प्रियः प्रियोऽपि सन्नप्रियवत्प्रवेरितः।५-७५

अर्थात्

(१) युद्ध में अनेक बार प्रिय करने वाले कन्थक ने आज राजा का अत्यंत विप्रिय भी कर दिया। एवम्–

(२) गुणप्रिय पुत्र राजा को प्रिय होते हुए भी, इस घोड़े ने उसे एक अप्रिय के समान वन में धकेल दिया।

(३) इस श्लोक में 'यमक' अलङ्कार देखना पर्याप्त नहीं है। परन्तु इस श्लोक में केवल 'यमक' अलङ्कार देखना पर्याप्त नहीं है। परन्तु 'प्रिय करने वाला ही अप्रिय करता है' एवम् प्रिय को अप्रिय की भाँति धकेल देने की जो चेष्टा है वह बड़ी विडम्बनापूर्ण परिस्थिति का निर्माण है।

(४) सिद्धार्थ के जन्म समय में महर्षि असित तपोवन से कपिल नगर में आते हैं। वह राजा शुद्धोदन से पुत्रदर्शन की इच्छा प्रकट करते हैं। बाद में यात्री के अङ्क में सोये हुए अग्निपुत्र जैसे बालक को देखते हैं परन्तु उसकी आँखों में अश्रु बह आते हैं। राजा उनसे पूछते है कि–क्या मेरा पुत्र स्थिरायुः तो है कि नहीं? क्या यह मेरे शोक का कारण बनने तो नहीं जन्मा है? तब असित ऋषि ने अपने आने का कारण बताया :

नास्यान्यथात्वं प्रति विक्रिया मे, स्वां वञ्चनां तु प्रति विक्लवोऽस्मि।
कालो हि मे यातुम् अयं च जातो, जातिक्षयस्या सुलभस्य बोद्धा॥ (११-६५)

"इस पुत्र के अनिष्ट की आशंका से मुझे रोना नहीं आया है, मैं मेरी वंचना हो रही है ऐसा देखकर विकल हुआ हूँ। क्योंकि एक ओर यह दुर्लभ 'जन्मान्तकर' (१-४९) का जन्म हुआ है, और दूसरी ओर मेरे मृत्यु का काल नजदीक में आ गया है। (अर्थात्-पुनर्भव कैसे न हो? यह मैं

उनसे नहीं जान पाऊंगा।) जीवन की यह भी एक विडम्बना है कि ज्ञाता के होते हुए भी, बिना ज्ञान पाये आदमी मर जाय।

समग्र कृति में व्याप्त हो ऐसी एक विडम्बना यह भी है कि शुद्धोदन के विभिन्न प्रयासों की केवल देवों के द्वारा ही विडम्बना हुई है ऐसा नहीं है। उनके पुत्र सिद्धार्थ के द्वारा भी पिता की आस्थाओं का पूरा विडम्बन हुआ है। जैसा कि–पुत्रजन्म के अवसर पर शुद्धोदन ने विप्रों को धनादि का दान दिया जिसके पुण्य फलसे अपना पुत्र राजा होने के बाद वार्धक्य में ही वन में जाय; उससे पहले नहीं (१-८६)–ऐसी उसकी मान्यता थीं इसी तरह असित ऋषि की भविष्यवाणी सुनने के बाद भी राजा शुद्धोदन ने अपने पुत्र के परम कल्याण के लिए जप, होमादि मांगलिक कार्यों के साथ देवयज्ञ भी किये थे।[15] 'अन्तःपुर विलाप' नामक अष्टम सर्ग के अन्त में फिर एकबार कवि ने कहा है कि पुत्र के चले जाने के बाद राजा ने देवमंदिरों का आश्रयण किया था और जप-जाप, होम-हवनादि भी किये थे।[16]

परन्तु काव्य के उत्तरार्ध में हम देखते हैं कि शुद्धोदन के पुत्र ने ही इसी ब्राह्मण संस्कृति की आस्थाओं का खण्डन कर दिया है। जैसा कि -

यदात्थ चापीष्टफलां कुलोचितां कुरुष्व धर्माय मखक्रियामिति।
नमो मखेभ्यो न हि कामये सुखं, परस्य दुःखक्रियया यदिष्यते॥

(११-६४) "तुमने (बिम्बसार ने) जो कहा कि इष्टफल देनेवाली कुलोचित यज्ञक्रिया धर्म के लिए करो, तो यज्ञों को प्रणाम है मैं वह सुख नहीं चाहता, जो दूसरों को दुःख देकर चाहा जाता है।"

परं हि हन्तुं विवशं फलेप्सया न युक्तरूपं, करुणात्मनः सतः।
क्रतोः फलं यद्यपि शाश्वतं भवेत् तथापि कृत्वा किमु यत्क्षयात्मकम्॥

(११-६५) "जो दयावान् है उसके लिए फल पाने की इच्छा से दूसरे विवश जीव की हत्या करना ठीक नहीं। यदि यज्ञ का फल शाश्वत भी हो, तो भी वह करके क्या जो हिंसात्मक है?"

सिद्धार्थ ने बुद्धत्व की प्राप्ति से पहले ही 'तपोवन-प्रवेश' नामक सप्तम सर्ग में 'तप द्वारा स्वर्ग प्राप्ति का सुख मिलता है', उसकी ओर आघातजनक व्यंग करते हुए कहा है कि–तप द्वारा शरीर को पीड़ा देना–इसी को यदि 'धर्म' कहते हो, और शरीर को सुखोपभोग में डुबो रखना उसको यदि 'अधर्म' कहते हो, तो शरीरपीड़ा रूप धर्म से परलोक में मिलने वाल भोगविलासादि रूप सुख को क्या नाम दिया जायेगा? सिद्धार्थ का उत्तर है कि इस पृथ्वीलोक में किये गये शरीरपीड़ा रूप धर्म से (स्वर्गलोक में) अधर्म ही प्राप्त हुआ।

जिन वेदोक्त ब्राह्मण संस्कृति की आस्थाओं का एक पिता आश्रयण कर रहा है, उसी के मिथ्यात्व की घोषणा उसका ही पुत्र भविष्य में करे यह भी भाग्य की एक विडम्बना है।

(६) अश्वघोष ने 'बुद्धचरित' में अनेक स्थान पर 'यमक' अलंकार का विनियोग किया है। वैसे यमक अलंकार तो एक शब्दालंकार ही है। अतः अर्थालंकार की अपेक्षा से वह निम्न कोटि का माना जाता है। परन्तु 'बुद्धचरित' के कतिपय यमक अलंकार की महिमा दूसरी बात पर निर्भर है। यहाँ ऐसे अनेक उदाहरण है कि जिस में, प्रथम दृष्टि में यमक अलङ्कार ही दिखाई पड़ता है, परन्तु गहराई से सोचने से वहाँ पर भी एक प्रकार के विडम्बना तत्त्व का निहित होना प्रतीत होता है। यथा–

सिद्धार्थ के मन में परिनिर्वाण की इच्छा जागृत होने के बाद वह अपने घर में प्रवेश करता है :–

अथ कांचनशैलशृङ्गवर्ष्मा गजमेघर्षभबाहुनिःस्वनाक्षः।
क्षयम् अक्षयधर्मजातरागः शशिसिंहाननविक्रमः प्रपेदे॥ ५-२६

यहाँ पर '**गजमेघर्षभबाहुनिःस्वनाक्षः**' एवं '**शशिसिंहाननविक्रमः**' इन दो शब्दो में यथासङ्ख्य अलंकार का प्रयोग हुआ है। परन्तु **क्षयम् अक्षयधर्मजातरागः**' में यमक अलंकार का प्रयोग है। 'क्षय' शब्द संस्कृत में 'निवास, गृह' अर्थ का वाचक है। उसको 'अक्षय' शब्द के सांनिध्य में रख कर कवि ने 'यमक' को तो सिद्ध किया है। परन्तु 'क्षय' शब्द का एक दूसरा 'विनाश' ऐसा भी अर्थ हैं इस दूसरे अर्थ से ऐसा व्यञ्जित हो रहा है कि जिसको अक्षय धर्म में अनुराग हुआ है, वह अब कब तक इस विनाशस्थान रूप 'क्षय' (घर) में रहेगा?[17]

अश्वघोष ने 'बुद्धचरित' के त्रयोदश सर्ग में 'मारविजय' प्रसङ्ग का वर्णन किया है। पुष्पधन्वा कामदेव, जो मोक्षद्वेषी है, सद्धर्मरिपु है, उसी को 'मार' कहते हैं। बुद्धत्व की प्राप्ति के लिए, अश्वत्थवृक्ष के मूल में दृढव्रत होकर जब सिद्धार्थ बैठ जाता है तब मार बड़े भारी त्रास का अनुभव करता है। वह अपने पुत्रों, कन्याओं और पूरे सैन्य के साथ सिद्धार्थ के सामने युद्ध के लिए उद्युक्त होता है। क्योंकि वह सोचता है कि यदि यह तपस्वी मेरा अभिभव करके लोगों को अपवर्ग मार्ग बताएगा तो, इस विश्व में मुझे रहने की कोई जगह ही नहीं मिलेगी। (१३-५)

अतः मार बड़े कटाक्ष (satire) के साथ बोलता है :–

उत्तिष्ठ भोः क्षत्रिय मृत्युभीत, चर स्वधर्मः, त्यज मोक्षधर्मम्।
बाणैश्च यज्ञैश्च विनीय लोकं, लोकात्पदं प्राप्नुहि वासवस्य॥ १३-९

"अरे मौत से डरने वाले क्षत्रिय! उठो, स्वधर्म का आचरण करो और मोक्षधर्म का त्याग करो। बाणों व यज्ञों से संसार को जीतो और इस संसार से (स्वर्ग में) जाकर इन्द्र का पद प्राप्त करो।"

यहाँ 'क्षत्रिय' को 'मृत्युभीत' कह कर, दो विरुद्धधर्मों को आमने-सामने रखकर विडम्बना का मञ्च तैयार किया गया है। लेकिन, इस सर्ग के अन्त में मालूम होता है कि विश्वसमस्त को मारने वाला अपराजेय मार (मारक) कामदेव ही पराजित हो जाता है। युद्ध में 'मार' ही मारा जाय यही तो विडम्बना है।

यहाँ 'मार' यानें कामदेव ब्राह्मण संस्कृति का प्रतिनिधि हो ऐसा दिखाई दे रहा है। क्योंकि

कामस्तदग्रे समवर्तताधि मनसो रेतः प्रथमं यदासीत्।।

(ऋ० १०-१२१-४) इत्यादि वेदवचनों से ब्राह्मणसंस्कृति में 'कामदेव' की मिथ (Myth) का आरम्भ हुआ है। वह कम बोलता है कि एक क्षत्रिय को तो अपने जीवन में शत्रु विजय करके कामोपभोग का सेवन करना चाहिए। एवमेव साथ में वेदोक्त यज्ञादि क्रियाओं के द्वारा इन्द्रत्व की प्राप्ति का प्रयास करना चाहिए।" यहाँ, ऊपर ऊपर से देखा जाय तो कामदेव और बुद्धत्व प्राप्ति के लिए प्रयत्नशील सिद्धार्थ के बीच का युद्ध वर्णित किया गया है। परन्तु काव्य के अन्तस्थल में तो वेदविहित ब्राह्मण धर्म के विरोध में बुद्ध धर्म का युद्ध वर्णित करना-व्यञ्जित करना-अभिप्रेत है ऐसा विपरीत लक्षणा से प्रतीत हो रहा है। इस बात का समर्थन ऐसे हो रहा है कि ध्यानमग्न सिद्धार्थ को अविचल देखकर स्वयं कामदेव सोचने लगता है कि–

शैलेन्द्रपुत्रीं प्रति येन विद्धो देवोऽपि शम्भुश्चलितो बभूव।
न चिन्तयत्येष तमेव बाणं, किं स्यादचित्तो, न शरः स एषः।

(१३-१६) "जिस बाण के द्वारा देव शम्भु को भी शैलाधिराज कन्या पार्वती के लिए विद्ध किया गया था, इसी बाण को यह सिद्धार्थ सोचता भी नहीं है। तो क्या यह सिद्धार्थ निर्जीव है? या वह बाण वह बाण नहीं है?" अर्थात् ब्राह्मणधर्म के महादेव कामदेव से 'किञ्चत्परिलुप्त धैर्य' (**कुमारसम्भव** ३-६६) हो सकते हैं, परन्तु बौद्धधर्म के प्रवर्तक यह बोधिसत्व सदैव अपराजित ही है।[18] वेदोक्त ब्राह्मणधर्म में तो चतुर्विध पुरुषार्थ की संकल्पना है। मनुष्य के जीवन में धर्म-अर्थ काम एवं मोक्ष-इन चारों पुरुषार्थ को समान रूप से उपस्थ माना है। परन्तु भगवान् बुद्ध ने तो केवल एक ही मोक्ष पुरुषार्थ को उपास्य माना है। इस सन्दर्भ में निम्नोक्त श्लोक द्रष्टव्य है :–

त्रिवर्गसेवां नृप यत्तु कृत्स्नतः, परो मनुष्यार्थ इति त्वमात्थ माम्।
अनर्थ इत्येव ममात्र दर्शनं, क्षयी त्रिवर्गो, हि न चापि तर्पकः।। (११-५८)

"हे राजन्! पूरा पूरा त्रिवर्ग सेवन परम पुरुषार्थ है–ऐसा जो आपने मुझे कहा, इस में मैं अनर्थ ही देखता हूँ; क्योंकि त्रिवर्ग नाशवान् है और तृप्तिदायक भी नहीं है।"

यहाँ पर धर्मादि तीन पुरुषार्थ नाशवन्त माने गये हैं; और केवल मोक्षपुरुषार्थ को ही उत्कृष्ट एवं चिरस्थायी माना गया है। अतः मार (कामदेव) और सिद्धार्थ के युद्धवर्णन के ब्याज से जो वेदोक्त ब्राह्मण-धर्म विरुद्ध बौद्धधर्म का युद्ध वर्णित किया गया है, वह भी समग्र कृति में व्याप्त एक सब से बड़ी 'संगोपित विडम्बना' है।

उपसंहार : अश्वघोष-विरचित 'बुद्धचरितम्' इयन्ता में लम्बा (१-१४ सर्ग, या चीनी अनुवाद में १-२८ सर्ग) होने के कारण 'महाकाव्य' नहीं है। परवर्ती आलंकारिकों के द्वारा निर्दिष्ट महाकाव्य के सभी लक्षणों से लक्षित होने मात्र से भी बुद्धचरित महाकाव्य नहीं है। परन्तु जिन वैश्विक विडम्बना के दर्शन पर बुद्धदर्शन का उदय हुआ है, वही विडम्बना तत्त्व को काव्य की आन्तरिक

स्तर पर अनेकविध विडम्बनाओं का निरूपण किया है; अतः बुद्धचरित "महाकाव्य" है। महान् कृति है।

इस सन्दर्भ में कवि अश्वघोष की सभी कृतिओं का साहित्यशास्त्रीय मार्मिक विवेचन करने वाले अनूठे विद्वान प्रो. के डॉ विश्वनाथ भटटाचार्य (शान्ति निकेतन) ने जो कहा है कि :–

"This shows that in Aśvaghoṣa there is no place for Art for Art's sake"[19]

बुद्धचरित में कला के लिए कला का प्रदर्शन नहीं है अर्थात् अश्वघोष के द्वारा धर्मोपदेश के लिए 'काव्य' के स्वरूप का सहारा लिया गया है। तो वह विधान सही हो सकता है। परन्तु इसका मतलब ऐसा कभी नहीं करना चाहिए कि उसकी काव्यरचना में कलात्मकता का संस्पर्श नहीं है। बल्कि आधुनिक आलोचकों द्वारा जिसका बड़ा मूल्य आंका गया है, वह 'विडम्बना तत्त्व' (Irony) का एक 'रचनागत युक्ति' (structural device) के रूप में, जिसमें साद्यन्त संनिवेश किया गया है ऐसी कृति के रूप में 'बुद्धचरित' बेजोड़ है।

FOOTNOTES

1. द्रष्टव्य: संस्कृत साहित्य का अभिनव इतिहास, ले० डॉ० राधा वल्लभ त्रिपाठी, विश्वविद्यालय प्रकाशन, वाराणसी, २००१, पृ० ११३.
2. Irony: language device, either in spoken or written form (verbal irony), in which the real meaning is concealed or contradicted by the literal meanings of the words, or in a theatrical situation (dramatic Irony) in which there is an incongruity between what is expected and what occurs. Verbal irony arises from a sophisticated or resigned awareness of contrast between what is and what ought to be and expresses a controlled pathos without sentimentality. —See : *The New Encyclopaedia Britannica,* Micropaedia Ready Reference, Vol. 6, (page—390).
3. अश्वघोषकृत "बुद्धचरित" प्रथमभाग (सर्गः १.१४) सानुवाद, सं और अनु. सूर्यनारायण चौधरी, प्रका० संस्कृत भवन, कठोतिया (बिहार), तृतीय संस्करण, जनवरी १९५५, पृ० ३७.
4. किञ्चिन्मनः क्षोभकरं प्रतीपं कथं न पश्येदिति सोऽनुचिन्त्य।

    वासं नृपो व्यादिशति स्म तस्मै हर्म्योदरेष्वेव, न भूप्रचारम्।। बु (२-२८)
5. ततः स कामाश्रयपण्डिताभिः स्त्रीभिर्गृहीतो रतिकर्कशाभिः।२-३२
6. *Irony:*—is thus an art of indirection and juxtaposition, relying for its success on such techniques as understatement,, paradox, puns and other forms of wit in the expression of incongrvities.

    — See : *A Dictionary of Modern Critical Terms,* Ed. Roger Fowler, New York, reprinted, 1999. (p. 129)
7. Irony of fate: denotes the view that god, or fate, or some part of supernatural figure, is amused to manipulate human beings as a puppeteer manipulates his puppets. Thus, by an irony of fate the messenger delivers the prisoners pardon an instant too late. —See: *Dictionary of Literary of Terms*, by S.M.W. London, 1976, (p.83)

8. इति भूमिपतिर्निशम्य तस्य व्यवसायं तनयस्य निर्मुमुक्षोः।
अभिधाय 'न यास्यतीति' भूयो विदधे रक्षणमुत्तमांश्च कामान्।। (बु. ५-३९)

9. इत्येषां व्युपशान्तये, न रतये, मोक्षार्थगर्भा कृतिः
श्रोतृणां ग्रहणार्थम् अन्यमनसां काप्योपचारात् कृता।
यन्मोक्षात् कृतम् अन्यदत्र हि मया तत्काप्यधर्मात्कृतं
पातुं तिक्तमिवौषधं मधुयुतं हृद्यं कथं स्यादिति ।। (१८.६३)
–सौन्दरनन्दं महाकाव्यं; सं रमाशंकर त्रिपाठी, कृष्णदास अकादमी, वाराणसी, १९९२.

10. व्रजति निर्वृतिम् एकपदे मनः।–विक्रमोर्वशीयम्।

11. द्वारं निर्वृतिसद्मनो विजयते कृष्णेति वर्णद्वयम्। भामिनीविलासः (४.१४)

12. 'बुद्धचरित' के Edward B. Cowell कृत अंग्रेजी अनुवाद में दोनों ही श्लोक में 'निर्वृता' शब्द का 'blessed' ऐसा अनुवाद किया है। परन्तु वह पूर्वोक्त अर्थद्वैविध्य को प्रकट नहीं करता है। See : *The Buddhacarita by Aśvaghoṣa*, Ed. E. B. Cowell, (Re-edited by S. Jain, Pub. New Bharatiya Book Corp. Delhi, 2003 (p-90).

13. *Irony* refers to a situation in which reality differs from appearance. Verbal irony occurs when the actual intent of the speaker or writer is expressed in words that carry the opposite meaning..... a form of dramatic irony is tragic irony, in which characters use words that mean one thing to them and another to those who better understand the situation.—See : *The Encyclopedia Americana,* International Edition, 1970, Vol. 15, (p. 468).

14. द्रष्टव्य : इसी आलेख की पादटीप–(६), पृ. ६.

15. अकुरुत जपहोममङ्गलाद्याः परमभवाय सुतस्य देवतेज्यः।। (१-८३)

16. समाप्तजाप्यः कृतहोममङ्गलो नृपस्तु देवतायनाद् विनिर्ययौ।। (८-७२)
(बिम्बसार ने भी सिद्धार्थ को कहा था कि–'तुम यज्ञों का अनुष्ठान करो और इन्द्र की तरह स्वर्ग करो' (१०-३१))

17. इसी तरह का दूसरा उदाहरण ५-७५ में भी मिलता है।

18. कवि अश्वघोष ने ब्राह्मणसंस्कृति के रामायण-महाभारतादि में उल्लिखित पात्रों (व्यास, ऋष्यशृंग, विश्वामित्र, अगस्त्य, बृहस्पति, पराशर, वशिष्ठ, ययाति) की भी स्त्रीविषयक पराधीनता सर्ग ४ (१६-२०) एवं ७२-८० में वर्णित की है।

19. *Aśvaghoṣa : A Critical Study;* by Dr. Biswanath Bhattacharya; Pub. by Vishva-Bharati, Santiniketan, West Bangal, 1976, (p. 232).

IV.5

THE DEEP SIGNIFICANCE ENLIVENING THE STRUCTURE OF MĀGHA'S 'ŚIŚUPĀLAVADHA'

Prof. Nitin R. Desai

The poets are aptly said to be the "unacknowledged legislators of mankind" by the English poet P. B. Shelley. Wordsworth points out that the poetry is 'the breath and finer spirit of all knowledge'. Bhaṭṭa Tauta, an Indian poetician, tells that for a poet, the capacity to visualise as well as the capacity to present beautifully—both are essential.[1] These opinions unitedly the assert that every poet does have a subtle message to convey through his poem. Such a message is aptly compared to nothing else but to the uniquely touching counsel of one's beloved, arousing and empowering one's whole being, by the poetician Mammaṭa.

The epithet '*lakṣmīpateścaritakīrtanamātracāru*' embedded in the last verse of the *'Kavi-vaṁśa-varṇana'* (i.e. an introduction to the poet's lineage), almost invariably appended to the manuscripts of the *Śiśupālavadha*', points out that the sole inspiration guiding the work is to extol the mission of the Lord Kṛṣṇa. Out of the long series of events of Kṛṣṇa's life, the poet here chooses an extremely stirring event and gives a unique literary shape to it, according to his own vision. Herein, the sole purpose moving the poet is to release vividly the essence of Kṛṣṇa's personality the 'lifeblood' that would inspire one and all; the traditional epic form conforming to the attendent conventions, being merely an observance of a contemporary custom to gratify, outwardly, the contemporary self appointed literacy critics

Although, externally speaking, the seed of the poetic action is sown in the first canto, and the fruit is fully realised in the last [the 20th) canto, the five stages of a full fledged dramatic action, considered necessary in an epic, cannot be said to have been attended to by *Māgha* here so giving up our efforts in that direction, we must try to visualise as to whether there is any deep import underlining the full passage of this long poem.

Our efforts to realise the five stages (*sandhis*) in the development of the theme, here, would be futile, mainly because there is neither internal conflict, not an external one, on the part of the hero. Although, in this epic, Kṛṣṇa is not shown as a divinity, in the proceedings of the political-cum-social action in hand, nonetheless, due to his rare all-round human excellences, he is free from strife, fear or hatred. Herein, his heroism chiefly lies in his lofty self-restraint throughout the poem. He is shown fully lodged in pose and equanimity like Lord *Viṣṇu* resting in ocean, even in the midst of hot political jingoism of the enemy. This is explicitly stated by the poet at the outset of the third canto, in this brilliant epithet: '*apeta yuddhābhiniveśasaumyaḥ*' (i.e. benign due the passion for war having been subsided).

Actually, a critical reader expects Kṛṣṇa, in his capacity of a supreme statesman, in order to carry out his political mission vis-a-vis Śiśupāla, to hold diverse talks with his colleagues, to accomplish secret tasks through spies, to send emissaries to Śisupāla, in order to carry out political expedients like *Sāma* (appeasement), *Bheda* (dissension) etc., while he is on his passage to Indraprastha. A poet with high political perceptions, would surely have created such an engrossing political diversion and would have stuffed the following eight apparently passive cantos with sensational political novelties. Thus there was a great scope for what the poetician Kuntaka calls poetic creativity relating to a subsidiary episode (*prakaraṇa-vakratā*). Instead of all this, the poet, apparently, has allowed general descriptions of nature and unending series of stray erotic pictures—albeit, related with respective changing periods of time-to roll on for so many cantos, as if the poet were asleep! A conscientious reader must patiently try to find out the *raison d'etre* of such a major mischeif' on the part of such a reputed poet.

These cantos seem to have no contribution whatsoever, to the main action as the work, e.g. the description of the mount Raivataka of the fourth canto. Moreover, these eight cantos sporadically allude only generally to the Yādavas or Mādhavas or their consorts, the clanspersons of Kṛṣṇa but to no individual character by name or to the feats of specific individuals. The seventh canto narrates in general, the fond excursions in the woods by Yādavas along of course, with their lovely consorts. But *Kṛṣṇa* is shown here to be totally aloof, in the midst of this labour of love! Here is the vivid realisation of the fond remark viz. "*niraṅkuśāḥ kavayaḥ*" (i.e. the poets spurn fetters). The discerning poet Bhāsa too aludes to this speciality of poets, in a verse discribing a mountain (in his drama '*Avimāraka*'), through this telling epithet. '*kavi-mati-vicitraḥ*' (i.e. weired like a poet). This remarkable allusion is, indeed, Bhāsa's full approval of a poet's unique style of functioning.

Māgha significantly alludes, in a smile, to the lofty creative process that a poet resorts to, in the fresh hours of early morning, in Ś. 11-6.[2] Accordingly, Māgha himself can certainly be depended upon, in the matter of conscientious handling of the theme of his epic.

Following the sane advice of Virginia Wolf (the renowned woman-writer) to defer judgement upon a literatary work and in order to do full justice to the writer, to imagine one's own self in the place of the writer, here, the results of a sympathetic concentration upon the import of this renowned work are set forth.

According to William Hazlitt, the spirit of a poet is always in search of wider horizons of life. Similarly Mahima Bhaṭṭa, an Indian poetician, calls the genius of a poet the third eye of Lord Śiva, envisioning the realities of all the three times. In view of this, unexpected turns and twists in a literary work are to be welcomed in anticipation of richer poetic truth.

Due to his enlightened devotion to Kṛṣṇa, Māgha wants to sing the glory of the Lord through his artistic creation, Kṛṣṇa's deep concern and care to nourish the tender emotional world of all sentient beings is worth emulating by mankind. Māgha seems to reckon this high psychological insight of Kṛṣṇa as anthropologically significant for the evolution of mankind to saner living.

The basic theme of this epic is centered around the age old problem of incorrigible wickedness. The solution suggested by the poet is purely benevolent execution of the wicked by a master spirit, simultaneously bringing about complete purification and transformaiton of such a straying soul. The Biblical declaration viz. "God is love" is realised during the passage of this work.

The *Paurāṇika* tradition that the soul of Hiraṇyakaśipu was reincarnated as Rāvaṇa and later on as Śiśupāla is adopted by the poet. The gist of such traditions is that the cosmic devilish power (*āsurī sampad*) lifts its head in the form of terrorism from time to time. Not merely as a worldly antidote thereof, but as the immanent (*viṣṇu* i.e. pervading) matchless supereme existence transcending and transmuting the so-called evil power, a supreme being is visualised as taking variegated incarnations at appropriate junctures. Here, in the first canto, the divine messenger (*devarṣi*) Nārada brings widely benevolent (*viśvajanīna*) recommendation of Indra, the godhead, to his associate (*upendra*) Kṛṣṇa, the incarnation, to annihilate rampaging Śiśupāla.

At this juncture, the pulsating geneous of the poet plays its creative role. The dramatist Bhavabhūti, too, while fashioning his '*Uttara-rāma-carita*', the dramatic work, had similar occasion. The traditions regarding the career of Rāma enumerate among the acts of Rāma, the execution of Śaṁbūka, the low-caste ascetic and the excommunication of Sītā, in the wake of public censure. Moreover, Sītā was ultimately shown to have been taken in by the Mother Earth, in the presence of Rāma. Though Bhavabhūti admitted the said two acts of Rāma in his drama, he delineated Rāma's unfathomable agony due to them. But the consummate artist articulately dismissed the tradition regarding Sītā's unceremonieous disappearance, and created, instead, a glorious, soothing end, befitting his consummate faith in the power of love. Similarly, Māgha's keen sensibility having spontaneously rejected certain turns of events asserted by tradition in Kṛṣṇa's life, has subtly transformed its spirit, and has convincingly achieved quite humane consummation—the poetic justice.

Certain narratives about Māgha's life, as well as specific allusions in the epic establish Māgha's dynamic appreciation of Buddha's personality and teachings. This factor seems to have definitely influenced Māgha's conception of Kṛṣṇa's personality and actions, in this work. Hence Kṛṣṇa is not shown here beheading Śiśupāla during the final congregation of the *Rājasūya* sacrifice, as shown in the *Mahābhāratā*.

Nonetheless, Kṛṣṇa is shown here to be firmly saddled in his incidental political-cum-military task, and does full justice to Indra's relevant message.

The second canto undertakes Kṛṣṇa's sincere discussion with his colleagues as to how to synthesise between two simultaneous duties—that of being an associate in Yudhiṣṭhira's *Rājasūya* sacrifice and the other regarding the final execution of Śiśupāla. There, Kṛṣṇa is keen to see that ultimately Uddhava's sane perceable opinion prevails. But he so sanely manages the talk, that even ebullient Balarāma gets contended, since he has his full say.

In the course of such talks and events, it becomes crystal clear, that Kṛṣṇa's stipulation of bypassing only hundred crimes of Śiśupāla, must have been already crossed. It actually implies Kṛṣṇa's abiding love and forbearance even for a seasoned criminal, and his deep desire to explore peaceable humane solutions to crimes. Although Kṛṣṇa undertook to honour Indra's message, he followed the dictates of his own conscience. Sane and non-violent personality of luminaries like Kṛṣṇa is pithily expressed in the verse 2.109 of Uddhava's speech.[3]

On the other hand, Kṛṣṇa's firmness of mind is well-demonstrated in this stunning declaration at the outset of the sacrifice. "This disc shall not spare the head of the king, who does not co-operate in this sacrifice, like an ordinary worker." Evidently, this was a shock-therapy, meant only for Śiśupāla and his party, either to deter them or to agitate them for final encounter.

In spite of such occasional strategic harshness of speech, Kṛṣṇa demonstrates his inherent forbearance at Śiśupāla's distribe, with full mum, in Māgha's work, unlike counter-reviling Kṛṣṇa of the *Mahābhārata*.

Actually, great souls of all times and climes are always in search of harmless, benevolent remedies to problems, even while accepting the traditional ones. Kauṭilya, the celebrated dynamic political thinker and statesman, has exhibited similar tendency in tackling various topics in his '*Arthaśāstra*'. Kṛṣṇa is identified as Bodhisattva in Ś. 15.58 and is called *Jina* (i.e. Buddha) in Ś. 19.112. At the time of Śiśupāla's diatribe, even the kinsmen of Kṛṣṇa voluntarily maintain high degree of self-control with deep conviction.

Kṛṣṇa is aptly persented here as a human-being. Just for that reason, he inspires and uplifts the spirit of a conscientious reader, by exemplifying full, all-round elevation of human ethos. Kṛṣṇa inspires the commoner more due to his studied avoidance of kingship. His chief interest is people at large. It is his patent hobby to live with and uplift the lowest among the low.

He truly expoused the mission of a 'group-server' ('*gaṇa-sevaka*') instead of foisting himself as a leader-thus exemplifying Saint Vinobā's teaching. Interestingly, in Kṛṣṇa, such true humility co-habited with inherent non-affective supremacy, benignly ruling and motivating the three worlds.

Kṛṣṇa's pleasing humility is seen in the first canto, while receiving and honouring the sage Nārada. In the second canto, keeping himself mum, he gives prominence and full say to his elders during the political deliberations. The third canto demonstrates Kṛṣṇa's full involvement in all-round developement and excellence of the city of Dvārikā. By and large, the soldiers and servants too in his procceding retinue are kind and considerate to the life around.

Due to his suave fame and lovely figure, even the women-folk of hamlets and mountainous regions, experience deep mental peace, while looking at him to their hearts' content. The damsels and housewives of cities, too, are not far behind. Due to Kṛṣṇa's uniquely enlightened soft corner for them, these women find in him their alter-ego, rather than a flimsy object of lust. Māgha revels in creating a memorable series of such exquisite pictures in the thirteenth canto (verses 31 to 48).

Kṛṣṇa's love of nature is also remarkably presented in the third and the sixth cantos. Lightly dismissing any mental burden of the imminent political-cum-military task, Kṛṣṇa is said to be desirous of 'inter-course' with nature (*riransu*).

Kṛṣṇa continues his study and practice of equanimity and non-violence through the thick of hatred, censure and impending bloodshed. And yet he maintains his dignity and self-respect, by keeping himself full mum, but just hinting his sober kin Sātyaki to give a befitting reply in his own way, to Śiśupāla, through his emissary (Ś. 17 to 37). Yudhiṣṭhira and his brothers too echo Kṛṣṇa's peace and poise.

Having thus grasped the personality of Māgha's Kṛṣṇa, the solution of the above-mentioned tangle of relevance of the cantos 4th to 11th is close at hand.

Kṛṣṇa's variegated retinue consisting of his kinsmen, professional armymen and other professionals along with their consorts, seems to have espoused consummate, enlightened vision of life. Even professionals in them are not mere hired mercenaries. They are a rare flock of emotionally balanced persons attached and dedicated to Kṛṣṇa and the values and powers cherished by him out of one's personal conviction. Vigorous, stout and victorious in their assigned duties, they have aptitude to enjoy life all round, with full zest. Like their venerated master, they are free from fevrish craving for war. Normally, they are well endowed with forbearence and love.[4] Such total mental balance itself empowers them to squarely meet any adverse eventuality, without any sting of hatred and fuss.

Such a consummate flock, mainly used to city-life, is spontaneously exhilerated and enthused when it encounters the boundless beauty and graces of the Mount Raivataka. Looking at the balanced vision of life cultivated by such a self-disciplined flock, such strong love and zest for nature is not only at its proper place, but, also point to the happy augury for one and all, in the impending crises Kṛṣṇa tacitly consents to and welcomes this momentous short break in the journey, for a meaningful intercourse of his blessed retinue with nature. So, these eight cantos lavishly describe how this well-disposed multitude enjoys and relishes the infinite beauty of nature, to their heart's content, in the sweet company of the beloved. Herein, the penetrating vision of the poet revels in exhibiting endless exercises of love, rather than multifarious political -cum-military exercises! Not this poet alone, but the traditional Indian perception of life in general, testifies to the fact that the full-fledged erotic sentiment is intimately connected with and enhances the heroic sentiment.

Each man and woman here has lovely youth and boundless propensity for love. Each one gives in one's self to nature and does not lag behind in fully imbibing the elixir of love, at its best, in the heart of one's loved through lovely thought, speech and bodily actions. Hearts of connoisseurs melt at every step here. Nevertheless, one would be wondering why these cantos contain only a series of stray stanzas on love, having no organic connection with either the characters or the central theme of the work. They can be fitted at an appropriate place in any other work of similar theme. Moreover, certain situational verses hardly fit in with the time and place of the plot. Yes, it is indeed so, externally. But this due to the contemporary conventional literary techniques, imposed here, to an extent, to gratify the excessive penchant of the courtiers and the well-to-do literary upper class, for the erotic stuff. This only reflects the erosion of sanity and benignancy, among the class governing power and pelf, and the resultant erosion in the freedom and self-reliance of full-fledged poets. Māgha, nevertheless, has, like certain later classical poets, maintained sufficient high standards of poetry, least sacrificing good taste and the core of poetic freedom.

In these eight cantos, one must admit that due to the said tilt to the nagging upper class, erotic initiatives are generally shown to be with women rather than men. Even then, excellences like self-dignity, poise, self-control, forbearance, sense of social propriety etc. of these lovely women do full justice to their lofty personality. Though men are shown to be lagging behind in these matters, they are everywhere shown to be humble and moderate enough.

These shortcomings of men are, after all, benign. On the whole, these youngsters too earn lasting weal and emotional blessedness out of this love's labour. Thus, fully enriched, instead of being gripped by lingering lust, they are shown to be in the full grip of maliness, and are fully poised to deal wirth and dominate victoriously any untoward eventuality .This is strikingly expressed in the picture of Pṛthu, Kṛṣṇa's son, at the prospect of impending righteous war, gently rubbing his breast, the sandalwood paste from which had only recently been rubbed away by the heavy breast of his consort during close embraces (Ś.17.11)! Love only empowers and cleanses one's personality.

Softened and fully humanised by the graces of domestic love, these battling members of Kṛṣṇa's dedicated army, are ever ready for fully encountering and winning the imposed battles, but are themselves free from war-fever. They favour, basically, peace, love and prosperity for all.

The denouement of the plot is but natural corollary to the all-round inner enrichment achieved by Kṛṣṇa flock. Though occasionally vanquished, gradually power of Kṛṣṇa decisively wins. Māgha's poetic sensibility bypasses the *Mahābharata* conception of Kṛṣṇa as decapitating Śiśupāla in the last sacrificial session itself. Instead, he creates a fully humane hero. Kṛṣṇa's abounding grace and enlighened forbearance even on the venomous Śiśupāla, readily allown the latter's proposition for war. Himself firmly established in his inherent boundless potential for military powers, as well as in his steadfast dignity, Kṛṣṇa fondly allows full play and exhibition of both-bravery and bravado, to his opponent. Ultimately, when Śiśupāla is at his tether's end, and due to his fatally feverish hatred, starts reviling Kṛṣṇa that the latter not only helps him out of his certain suicidal consummation, by bodily decapitation with potent benevolent disposition, but also emancipates him out of his murky fundamental ignorance, goading in to myriad misdeeds. The supremacy of great souls lies in love for all, hatred for none.

The subtle proceedings during the various stages of this epic, build up the ultimate flushing soul force of Kṛṣṇa to effect a convincing solution to a personal-cum-social evil. Kṛṣṇa's full mum and his apparent passivity through the said eight cantos seem to suggest time momentous hidden action ('action in inaction' taught by the *Gītā*). Certainly Kṛṣṇa has deeply meditated in the creative recesses of both the surrounding nature and his pure heart. The humble entreaties to; Kṛṣṇa by Śrutaśravā, his paternal-aunt (*pitṛsvasā*) and mother of Śiśupāla to spare her son through his misdeeds, seem to have abided in Kṛṣṇa's heart for ever, and must have goaded him into highly potent benevolent meditation, resembling that of the sage Kaṇva in favour of Śakuntalā in Kālidāsa's *Śākuntala*. That is why no erotic encounter of Kṛṣṇa during this period is mentioned, even though his persisting sensibility and capacity for the same at that time is vouchesated by one incidental but significant reference in Ś. 20.6. Such a lovely soul willingly observes full continence during his journey, for a noble cause.

Māgha's mutli-dimensional sensibility can hardly by pass so moving a human predicament called 'war'. The poet fully appreciates the fact, that a war unfailingly brings out the most excellent human qualities, and that it has hitherto helped to an extent, to uphold human culture and values. To that extent, Māgha has fully explored and drawn upon its many aspects to fondle and enlighten the sensibilities of the reader. But he is ultimately concerned to expose the absolescence of war for genuine human culture. Verses 15.81 to 96 contain a series of touching pictures of tragic separation between newly weds due to abrupt imposition of thoroughly misconceived war. Verses 18.67 to 79, on the other hand, present heart-rending pictures of decapitated and mangled bodies of warriors as unceremonious objects of prey for carnivorous creatures. The overall treatment of war reveals the poet's unequivocal judgement about the institution of war to the sensible. Thus, the grafting of the incident of war in the theme by Māgha, while doing justice to Kṛṣṇa's personality, bestows unto the poet a precious opportunity for a fully mature treatment of a highly touching subject.

With the divine emancipation of Śiśupāla's roaming soul, Māgha seems to exemplify consciously this well-known saying of his favourite poet Bhāravi in his *'Kirātārjunīya'* : "Even opposing a great soul is more fruitful than the friendship of the mean-minded."[5]

This significant chapter in the history of mankind ably points out that the sure solution of the world-wide terrorism is only the soul-force or the power of love seasoned by self-restraint and self-purification.

This divine prowess of Kṛṣṇa, moreover, exemplifies the following celebrated assertion about God in the *Gītā* 13.23. "He observes everything in the world, allows and even nourishes it, but fundamentally ruling over all, he always has mastery over everything."[6]

Māgha has no claims that his work is an epic or this or that. (In the *'Kavivaṁśa-varṇana'* it is called merely a *'kāvya'*—a poem.) He is concerned only with offering to the world, this lovely form of the Highest Truth called 'Kṛṣṇa'. We have to live with that with pure faith, repeating in the recesses of our soul: "I do not know any truth other than Kṛṣṇa."[7]

REFERENCES

1. दर्शनाद्वर्णनाच्चाथ रूढा लोके कविश्रुतिः।
2. क्षणशयितविबुद्धाः कल्पयन्तः प्रयोगानुदधिमहति राज्ये काव्यवद्दुर्विगाहे।
   गहनमपररात्रप्राप्तबुद्धिप्रसादाः कवय इव महीपाश्चिन्तयन्त्यर्थजातम्।। Ś.11.6
3. तीक्ष्णा नारुन्तुदा बुद्धिः कर्म शान्तं प्रतापवत्।
   नोपतापि मनः सोष्म वागेका वाग्मिनः सतः।। Ś.2.109
4. अन्यदा भूषणं पुंसः क्षमा लज्जेव योषितः।
   पराक्रमः परिभवे वैयात्यं सुरतेष्विव।। Ś.2.44
5. समुन्नयन्भूतिमनार्यसङ्गमाद्वरं विरोधोऽपि समं महात्मभिः। Kirāt. I.2
6. उपद्रष्टानुमन्ता च भर्ता भोक्ता महेश्वरः। *'Bhagavad-gītā'* 13.23
7. कृष्णात्परं तत्त्वमहं न जाने।

IV.6

TWO KŪRMAŚATAKAS ATTRIBUTED TO KING BHOJADEVA

Devangana Desai

Two Prakrit *Śatakas* on *Kūrma,* the Tortoise who supports the Earth, are inscribed on a stone slab at Dhar (Dhārā) in Madhya Pradesh. These poems are attributed to the illustrious Paramāra King Bhojadeva of Mālavadeśa (c. AD 1000-55). The two *Śatakas*, each actually having 109 stanzas, are composed in the *Āryā* metre. It was in 1903 that K. K. Lele, Superintendent of Education at Dhar, discovered the stone slab bearing the inscribed poems from among the ruins of a monument that was originally *Bhoja-śālā*, a school of learning, and brought it to the notice of Prof. E. Hultzsch, the government epigraphist.[1] Prof. R. Pischel, who has edited the inscription in the *Epigraphia Indica,* Volume VIII, tells us that it consists of 83 lines and is engraved with great care. The language of the poems is Māhārāṣṭrī Prakrit.

It was late Dr. Harivallabh Bhayani who drew my attention to these two poems on *Kūrma*, because of my interest in *kūrma* symbolism in Indian art and mythology. I asked Dr. V. M. Kulkarni whether he could kindly suggest a Prakrit scholar who would translate these *Kūrma Śatakas.* To my utter delight, Dr. V. M. Kulkarni himself kindly undertook to translate the poems into English. He has also restored corrupt verses and added a select glossary. It is for the first time that these *Śatakas* are published with English translation.* I am deeply indebted to Dr. Kulkarni for this kind gesture.

---

* The article is based on my *Introduction to Kūrmaśatakadvaya,* translated with Select Glossary by V. M. Kulkarni, published by the L.D. Institute of Indology, Ahmedabad. The verses quoted in this article are from Dr. V. M. Kulkarni's translation of the *Kūrmaśatakas.*

Although these *Śatakas,* as Pischel says, are of doubtful poetical value, they are historically very important for two reasons. First, they are among the rare extant examples of inscribed poetry in India. The other known examples, also inscribed at Dhārā, are *Khaḍgaśataka, Kodaṇḍakāvya,* attributed to Bhojadeva[2], and the play *Pārijātamañjarī* composed by a preceptor of the Paramāra King Arjunavarman in about AD 1213.[3] Secondly, the *Śatakas* are significant from the viewpoint of *kūrma* symbolism. They represent the full-blown development of the idea—hitherto found only in stray, single verses—of the Tortoise (rather than the Boar or Serpent) as the support of the earth; and, analogically, of the king as the support of the earth over which he ruled. This concept must have fascinated and flattered Mahārājā Bhoja enough to have the two poems inscribed on stone.

The first *Śataka* (here called A) is entitled *"Avani-kūrmaśataka",* and its authorship is attributed to Mahārājādhirāja Bhojadeva. However, it is very likely that the actual composition of the poems and of other works which appear as authored by him was the work of his court poets. The second *Śataka* (here called B) particularly in which King Bhoja himself is praised for ably supporting the earth, surpassing even the *kūrma* in this task, could not have been composed by him.

Bhojadeva was a man of extraordinary learning and possessed wide interests. He is credited with the authorship of a large number of works, about 40, on a variety of subjects like poetics, literature, grammar, architecture, philosophy, medicine and astronomy. In inscriptions he is praised as *kavirāja* and *vidyānidhi.*[4] The two outstanding works on Alaṅkāra, the *Sarasvatī-kaṇṭhābharaṇa* and the *Śṛṅgāraprakāśa,* were composed under his inspiration. V. Raghavan says: "Bhoja's *Śṛṅgāraprakāśa,* in thirty-six chapters, running to 1908 pages in foolscap size in manuscript, is one of the biggest works in Sanskrit Literature and the biggest in the whole field of *Alaṅkāraśāstra.*"[5] Bhoja also has to his credit an encyclopedic *Vāstuśāstra* ~ entitled *Samarāṅgaṇa-sūtradhāra* that presents canons of religious and civil architecture in 83 chapters. Bhojadeva wrote a philosophical work, the *Tattvaprakāśa,* (Illumination of the Categories), a text of 76 verses, which systematizes monistic *Śaiva Siddhānta,* and also another Śaiva work called *Siddhāntasaṅgraha.* He is also credited with an astronomical work, the *Rājamṛgāṅka,* written in *c.* AD 1042.

Bhoja shifted his capital from Ujjain to Dhārā, where he established a school known as the *Bhoja-śālā* or *Sarasvatī-bhavana,* on the walls of which he got inscribed several poems.[6] The stone slab bearing the two *Kūrmaśatakas* was one of these. The Jaina writer Merutuṅga in his *Prabandhacintāmaṇi*[7] (AD 1305) talks of 104 temples built by King Bhoja, but evidence for these is not yet available. However, it is known that Bhoja founded a town called Bhojpur (which is near Bhopal), built a huge temple there, and constructed a large tank by building dams on two rivers.[8] The Kashmir historian Kalhaṇa praises King Bhoja of Malwa for his liberality and says that he was a friend of poets *(Rājataraṅgiṇī,* VII, 259). Merutuṅga says that the King gave every day an appropriate gift to learned authors. Interestingly, he also notes (p. 62) that Bhoja called representatives of all sects and asked them about the way to achieve salvation. And they all agreed: "Religion is characterized by harmlessness, and one must honour the goddess Sarasvatī. By meditation one obtains salvation."

Both the *Śatakas* begin with an invocation to Śiva. The first hails Śiva as Lord of Pārvatī, "by whose will and supreme, unequalled power, the world is supported". The second *Śataka* begins with a prayer to the *Kaṅkāla-mūrti* of Śiva:

"May god Śiva confer on you—extend to you all happiness (śivam) -that god Śiva who easily (helayā) carries the skeleton (kaṅkāla) of that very Kṛṣṇa (Kanha) who carries the (three) worlds," B, verse 1

Here Kṛṣṇa is synonymous with Viṣṇu. This form of Śiva is noticeable in the temples of South India, but is not much prevalent in the north. The South Indian *Śaivāgamas* give detailed descriptions of the *Kaṅkāla-mūrti* of Śiva.[9] Probably the poet who composed the invocatory verse for Bhoja hailed from South India. In this context we may mention that King Bhoja's kingdom extended up to the upper course of the River Godavari and he had formed an alliance with the *Cola* king of Tanjavur at the time of his invasion to the kingdom of the *Cālukya* king of Kalyāṇa and that of the *Somavaṁśī* ruler of Mukhaliṅgam in the Ganjam district.[10] It is likely that he may have brought or invited poets from South India to his capital.

From the internal evidence of the *Śatakas,* it can be said that the poems do not seem to refer to the Tortoise incarnation of Viṣṇu, as Pischel believed, but to the universal aspect of the tortoise *(ādi-kūrma)* as support of the earth.[11] The Earth Goddess, Pṛthvī, sits on *ādi-kūrma,* as distinct from *Kūrma's avatāra,* in Central Indian sculptures. It is important to remember that *kūrma* is a symbol of stability and is placed in the form of *kūrmaśilā* in the foundation of buildings.[12] It is also a mount of the river goddess Yamunā and the *lāñchana* (cognizance) of the Jina Suvrata, Jaina Yakṣas Pārśva, (Dharaṇa) and Ajita, and Mahāvidyā Gāndhārī. These aspects *of kūrma* are independent of his incarnation as Viṣṇu. Nowhere in these two *Śatakas* do we come across any reference to the myth of *Samudra-manthana* or Churning of the Milky Ocean, in which Viṣṇu, as *Kūrma*, supports Mount Mandāra (and not the earth) at the request of gods and demons. However, we may point out here that the medieval poets, for instance, Vākpatirāja in his work *Gaüḍavaho* (see below) in the 8th century and Jayadeva in his well-known *Gītagovinda* (*Aṣṭapadī*, verse 2) in the 12th century, have referred to the *dharaṇidhara* aspect of *Kūrma* when invoking the

Kūrma-avatāra of Viṣṇu. These two roles of *Kūrma*, namely, 1] as *dharaṇī-dhara,* support of the earth, and 2] as support of Mount Mandāra, which is specifically *Kūrma*'s role as incarnation of Viṣṇu in the Purāṇas, get fused here.

But it is on the word of Śiva that the Chief of tortoises *supports the earth* (A, 3), *not Mount Mandāra, in* the *Avani-kūrma-śataka.* This reference to Śiva asking the Chief Tortoise to carry the earth is not found in the Churning of the Ocean myth, in its versions in the *Mahābhārata,* the *Viṣṇu-Purāṇa,* the *Agni-Purāṇa,* and the *Bhāgavata-Purāṇa.* It is not insignificant that both the *Śatakas* invoke Śiva and not Viṣṇu. It is also worth mentioning that Bhoja's *Vāstu* text, the *Samarāṅgaṇa-sūtradhāra* (Chapter 77, verse 38ff) does not mention *Matsya* and *Kūrma* as *avatāras* of Viṣṇu, but, begins its *avatara* list with *Varāha*.

The goodness of *Kūrma* is emphasized in the *Avanikūrmaśataka.* The *Kūrma* is "solely devoted to doing good to others" (A, 11, 38, 63). This aspect is somewhat similar to references to the tortoise in the '*Śānti Parva*' (247, 4) of the *Mahābhārata,* the *Bhagavadgītā* (II, 58) and the *Mārkaṇḍeya Purāṇa* (36, 33ff), in which it is a symbol of the self-controlled man, who has control over his *indriyas* (senses). The *Kūrma* of the *Śataka* (A, 22) withdraws its limbs within its shell. He is an instance of those who are steady and firm. The tortoise alone strives without any motive.

"The tortoise is an instance (nidarśana) of those who are steady and of firm resolve. Look! In a tortoise we find that both the qualities are ever present." A, verse 24

"Look at a muni (sage) and a kacchapa (tortoise), and see their determination." A, verse 30

"Here (in this world), everyone strives to secure one's own happiness. You alone, O tortoise, strive without any such motive (or purpose). Even thinking (for a long time), O tortoise, we do not know (we can not fathom) what your motive could be." A, verse 34

The poems reveal several points of mythological significance. The second verse of the *Śataka-A* refers to *Kūrma* as the golden mountain Meru, the world mountain in the centre of the Universe, a cosmic symbolism *(Gonda,* p. 128), and also as the "bulbous root of the creeper of the old". This reminds us of the depiction of the tortoise supporting the creeper of life at Sanchi in Central India in the 2nd century BC. The reference to Dhruva, the Pole Star (A, 29, 70, 96, 97), further establishes the cosmic symbolism of the *Kūrma*, who supports the Universe. The Pole Star above the earth and *Kūrma* below the earth—all in a single line—indicate the axis. It is the Cosmic Axis, which joins the earth and the heavens.

In several stanzas (A, 65, 69, 93, 94) the feat of the *Kūrma* in supporting the earth is ranked superior to those of 1) *Varāha*, *Kiri*, (Boar, the third incarnation of Viṣṇu), 2) *Śeṣa*, the thousand-headed Cosmic Serpent, a theriomorphic form of Viṣṇu, and 3) the *dig-gajas,* eight Elephants of the Quarters. It is said that all these divine animals display their prowess and show off while supporting the earth, whereas the *Kūrma* quietly lies below the earth and hence is not even visible.

"You support, O tortoise, the earth. You save the three worlds and manifest your power in that manner! Who does not ridicule the Boar (Kiri) and others who support the earth in order that their deeds may be noticed?" A, verse 68

We may note that in the 11th century images of Khajuraho and other sites in Central India, the ṭortoise even supports *Varāha*, who holds the Earth Goddess (Pṛthvi) on his tusk. The *Matsya Purāṇa* (Chapter 260), assigned between 5th-10th centuries, and the *Vāstu* text *Aparājitapṛcchā* (Chapter 29, verse 22), datable to late 12th or early 13th century, mention that the *kūrma* supports the right foot of *Varāha.* While the *Śatakas* do not refer to this symbolism, they implicitly recognize the greatness of *kūrma* as support of the earth.

In the first *Śātaka*, the *Kūrma* is praised as 'the one and only one who bears the burden (of the earth)" (A, 106).

"You alone, O tortoise, are really born! What is the use of others who are (merely) born here on earth to no purpose, in vain? For it is you who saved the earth that was sinking down in the nether world(pātāla) by supporting it on your back!" A, verse 62

The mother of the *Kūrma* is also praised in many stanzas for giving birth to the one who bears the burden of the earth without a grumble.

"That female tortoise alone among females is indeed blessed, who gave birth to a male offspring that bore the (entire) burden of the earth, extremely difficult to bear" A, verse 6

"Blessed are you, o female tortoise, among females on this earth, who gave birth to the offspring who does not find rest (even for a second) since its birth." A, verse 12

But this picture changes in the second *Śataka*, which eulogizes King Bhoja, while minimizing the importance of *Kūrma* in upholding the earth. For, to the *paśus* (creatures), namely, Tortoise, Serpent, Boar, and the like, the earth appears to be a heavy burden, but, King Bhoja smilingly lifts her in his hand, as to him she is light, not heavy (B, 14, 16, 31). He treats her like a plaything. The references to the King mastering the qualities of *laghutva* and *gurutva* (B, 83, etc.), and his acquiring the powers of *aṇimā* and *garimā* (B, 105) point to his attaining of yogic *siddhis*. We must remember that Bhoja was a *Śaiva-siddhāntin* with the works *Tattva-prakāśa* and *Siddhāntasaṅgraha* to his credit.

The concept of royalty or regal power was linked in medieval Indian religious and court literature with the Boar, the *Varāha avatāra* of Viṣṇu, who rescues the Earth Goddess from the nether region. From the Gupta period (4th-5th century) onwards, the Boar became a political metaphor[13] and the king was compared to the Boar, the celestial consort of the Earth Goddess, thereby suggesting that the king was her terrestrial husband (*Kṣitipati*). Now, for the first time an entire poem, the *Avanikūrmaśataka,* has been written on the *Kūrma* and its silently bearing the burden of the earth. Some single verses on the tortoise bearing the burden of the earth do exist, but not full-length poems such as the one inscribed at Dhārā. For instance, the 8th century Prakrit work, the *Gaüḍavaho,* has a *gāthā on Kūrma*, which forms a part of the *maṅgalācaraṇa* (benediction). It reads:

"Victorious is the Great Tortoise lifting the (sunken) earth with its body, as with a hand, with its (outstretched) five fingers, since under the pressure (burden) of the earth, its mouth-tip and four feet happened to be pushed out."[14]

In the 11th century, however, the scholar-king Bhoja noticeably elevates the position of the Tortoise, which excels the Boar and others in the *Avanikūrmaśataka;* and then the second *Śataka* shows that he (the King himself) even surpasses the feat of the Great Tortoise in lifting the earth. We pay our homage to the *Kūrma* and the creative King Bhojadeva, who got inscribed on stone the poems on the tortoise, which have lasted the ravages of time.

FOOTNOTES

1. *Epigraphia Indica,* Volume, VIII, (1905-06), pp. 96, 241-260.
2. Trivedi H.V. "Inscriptions of the Paramāras, Chandellas, Kachchhapaghātas and Two Minor Dynasties," *Corpus Inscriptionum Indicarum*, Vol. VII, Part-I, p. 187; Also *Archaeological Survey of India, Annual Report,* 1934-35, p. 60.
3. *Epigraphia Indica,* VIII, pp. 96ff.
4. Trivedi H.V. *op cit*. Vol. VII, Part-I, p. 187.
5. Raghavan, V. *Bhoja's Śṛṅgāraprakāśa,* Volume I, Part I, Bombay, 1940, Preface.
6. Agrawala, V. S. Introduction to *Samārāṅgaṇa-sūtradhāra,* Oriental Institute, Baroda, 1966, p. xii. Also H.V. Trivedi, *op.cit.,* p. 192.
7. Eng. Tr. by C.H. Tawney, Calcutta, 1901, p. 73.
8. Mankodi, K. "Scholar-Emperor and a Funerary Temple", in *Royal Patrons and Great Temple Art,* Ed. Vidya Dehejia, Marg Publications, Bombay, 1988, pp. 101ff.

9. Rao, T. A. G. *Elements of Hindu Iconography,* II, I, 1916, p. 307. Rao quotes the *Suprabhedāgama,* which mentions that the *kaṅkāla* held by Śiva is that of Viṣṇu, and thereby he says that the Puranic story of the murder by Śiva of Viṣvakṣeṇa (doorkeeper of Viṣṇu) is accepted and followed. Also *Śiva-Kośa, S.* K. Ramachandra Rao, Bangalore, 1998, Vol. 2, pp. 288-89, and the *Kūrma Purāṇa,* II, 31, gives this story. Dr. R. Nagaswamy, Former Director, State Archaeology, Tamil Nadu, writes in a reply to my query on Kṛṣṇa's *kaṅkāla* carried by Śiva: "There is no work in *Āgama* or *Śilpa* or Tamil works that refers to Śiva carrying the skeleton of Kṛṣṇa. I have not been able to get any reference so far. But what is of interest is that the colour of the *kaṅkāla* (skeleton) is mentioned as *kṛṣṇa-varṇa* in two texts. Obviously the colour of the skeleton was to be painted black in colour. So could it be that the verse of Bhoja you cite mentions the colour as Kṛṣṇa."
10. Trivedi H. V. in *op. cit.* Vol. VII, Part-I, p. 21; Pratipal Bhatia, *The Paramāras,* New Delhi, 1970, p. 78; *The Struggle for Empire,* HCIP, second edition, Bombay, 1966, p. 66.
11. Gonda, J. *Aspects of Early Viṣṇuism,* Leiden.1954, pp. 126-29; N.P. Joshi, *Brahmanical Sculptures in the State Museum,* Lucknow, Part 2—Volume I, Lucknow, 1989, p. 138. Joshi uses the word *ādi-kūrma* for cosmic tortoise.
12. Kramrisch, Stella *The Hindu Temple,* Vol. I, 1946, pp. 110-111.
13. Desai, Devangana *The Religious Imagery of Khajuraho,* Mumbai, 1996, pp. 64-65.
14. Translation by N. G. Suru, who has edited Vākpatirāja's *Gaüḍavaho,* 1975, p. 2. I thank Dr. Kulkarni for drawing my attention to this *gāthā* by Vākpatirāja. The Prakrit *gāthā* is as under:

    जअइ धरमुध्धरंतोरभस्णीसारिअ.-मुहग्ग-चलणेण।
    णिअ-देहेन करणे व पंचगुलिणा महा-कुम्मो।।
    (जयति धरामुद्धरन् भरनिःसारितमुखाग्रचरणेन।
    निजदेहेन करेणेव पञ्चाङ्गुलिना महाकूर्मः।।) गाथा क्रमांक १७

IV.7

AHAM BRAHMA

[*Agnipurāṇa* 339.1]

M. M. Prof. Rewa Prasad Dwivedi

'*Ahaṁ Brahma*' is a famous *Mahāvākya* of all the Vedāntas. But there is an amazing *Mahāvākya* available in the *Agnipurāṇa*. That is 'ALAM BRAHMA'.

akṣaram paramam brahma sanātanamalam vibhum
vedānteṣu vadantyekam caitanyam jyotirīśvaram. [*Agnipurāṇa* 339.1]

is the source of this *Mahāvākya*. In this statement one may take Brahman as subject (*uddeśya*) having all other epithets as predicate for it. So following would be the meaning of the sentence : 'what is known as *Parama Brahman* is called by other terms like *Akṣara* = not demisable, *Sanātana* = ever present, *Alam* = sufficing or complete, *Vibhu* = omnipresent, *Caitanya* = conscious, *Jyotiṣ* = light and *Iśvara* = almighty. The terms *(caitanya* and *Jyotiṣ* can be compounded as *'Caitanya-jyoti'*.

Among these epithets for the history of Indian Aesthetics the term *Alam* is very much important. The aesthetics has been termed as *Alaṅkāraśāstra* : a discipline which is applicable to the element called *Alaṅkāra*. We know that the history of *Alaṅkāraśāstra* in India starts with the *Nāṭyaśāstra* of Bharatamuni who flourished before the famous poet and dramatist Kālidāsa who remembers Bharata and his theory of eight *Rasa* in his famous play *Vikramorvaśīyam*

muninā bharatena yaḥ prayogo
bhavatīṣvaṣṭarasāśrayo nibaddhaḥ
lalitābhinayam tamadya bhartā
marutām draṣṭumanāḥ salokapālāḥ [Vik. 2.17]

The theories of *Nāṭyaśāstra* have been followed by the first aesthetician Daṇḍin in his work known as '*Kāvyādarśa*' and also by all the later writers up to this time. I am very much sorry to announce that among all the aestheticians none has taken the above *Mahāvākya* of *Agnipurāṇa* into account. So also the modern scholars like M. M. P.V.Kane, Dr. S.K.De and Dasagupta could not pick this statement up in their books on the History of Sanskrit Poetics. M. M. Kane has given the above verse room in his work but with the variant reading '*Aja*' for the term '*Alam*'. Now the door is closed for dealing with *Alaṅkāra*. At the same time the Nirṇayasāgara edition of *Sāhityadarpaṇa* published the text of *Agnipurāṇa* with the '*Alaṁ*' in 1936 in its appendices from the same city Bombay. MM Kane was alive at that time and published his *History* of *Sanskrit Poetics* in 1951. He had worked upon *Sāhityadarpaṇa also*. But it is a matter of sorrow that this term (*alam*) did not flash to him even after fifteen years lost since the Nirṇayasāgara edition published in 1936. On the other hand, *Agnipurāṇa* dealt with the poetics and dramaturgy in detail. Therefore the reading '*Alam*' available to them must have been honoured without hasitation.

The term '*Alam*' is capable to pervade all the elements which are enumerated as the generators of '*camatkāra*' like *Guṇa*, *Lakṣaṇa*, figures of speech like *Upamā*, *Vṛtti* and Rīti.

Luckily the current of this all-pervasive meaning of '*Alam*' term has been going on repeated in the history of Sanskrit Poetics up to the 17th century of *Paṇḍitarāja* and then after till today. Abhinavagupta had explained the *Alaṅkāra* word of the *vṛtti* on the last but one verse of *Dhvanyāloka 'ityakliṣṭaraśāsrayocita-guṇālaṅkāra-śobhābhṛto*. [page 551,1940 Chaukhamba, Varanasi] like this in his *Locana* :

Iti kārikā-tadvṛtti-nirūpaṇaprakāreṇetyarthaḥ.

Akliṣṭaraśāśrayeṇa ucitā ye guṇālaṅkārās tato yā śobhā tām bibharti kāvyam.

Udyānamapyakliṣṭaḥ kālocito yo rasaḥ sekādikṛtaḥ tadāśrayaḥ,

Tatkṛto yo guṇānām saukumāryacchāyā-vattva-saugandhya Prabhṛtīnām alaṇkāraḥ paryāptatākaraṇam, tena ca yā śobhā tām bibharti'.

It is to note here that even in the intellect of Abhinavagupta the general sense : *Paryāpti* of the term *Alaṁkāra* had flashed out, even though he could not apply the same meaning to the same word '*Alaṅkāra*' in the context of *Kāvya*. How it is so is beyond the bounds of conjecture.

The history of *Alaṅkāra* term speaks in favour of the importance of *Alam* term from the time of the *Ṛgveda* wherein the term *Aram* is used recurrently in the sense of '*Paryāpti*', yet, the rhetoricians could not draw their attention towards the same. They undertook the latter half '*Kāra*' of the term '*Alaṅkāra*' for grammatical etymology and discussed its root and suffix alone. Ornamentation is the main meaning for which

Alaṅkāra word is taken in the Sanskrit poetics . On the other hand, it is undertaken by all the poeticians that to reach the stage of *Alaṁkāratva* every figure of speech invariably be capable to create *camatkāra* that is but *Ānanda*. 'My book is valuable like yours' is the statement which is bearing all the four parts of the figure of speech called *upamā* but they do not create *camatkāra*, hence are limited up to *upamātva* and not reached the stage of *upamālaṁkāratva*. But when one utters 'the face of 'Śakuntalā is as lustrous as the globe of moon of the full moon-night' the device *alaṅkāratva* is readily available due to the *camatkāra* generated from the poetic statement. What is the specialty of *Ānanda*? The final and ultimate reply on this issue is nothing else but *Ātman* that is *Brahman*. Consequently *alaṁkāra* term is also running in the direction of *Brahman* in practice. All the other specialities called *Rasa, Guṇa* etc. have also been counted by the Indian poeticians under the heading *Alaṅkāra* in the sense of characteristics which gives the rank of poetry to any lingual statement. All the figures of speech are put into three catagories by Bhoja in his *Sarasvatīkaṇṭhābharaṇam-*

'*Vakroktīśca rasoktiśca svabhāvoktiśca* vāṅmayam' [S. K. 5.8]

Of all these three, *rasokti* is regarded as the most attractive. Here the sense of *Alaṅkāra* is taken from the term *ukti*. Though the poeticians of Kashmir or of the *Dhvani* school declared *rasa* is suggested alone and they have refuted any kind of the *abhidhā* of *rasa,* yet their declaration is limited upto the sense of taste of *rasa*. At the same time the term *rasa* is used in the sense of the thing that is tasted like *pānakarasa* or *ikṣurasa*. It is only a liquid which gives the taste of our choice. When Bhoja thinks of the *ukti* of *rasa* he at once subjects the group of things called *Vibhāva, Anubhāva* etc. which are found only in the body of poetry or any kind of Art. The painting of *Mṛtyuñjaya* Śiva [preserved in Bhārata Kalā Bhavana and printed in my work *Sāhityaśārīrakam*[1]] is very much attractive. In the field of poetics it would very well be accepted as *Vibhāva* for *Śāntarasa*. At the same time one may have the idea of Bhoja's poem *Acchinnamekhalam* etc. in the field of icons as the 'ardhanārīśvara' icon. That would be the *Vibhāva* of the *rasa* called *Śṛṅgāra*. These paintings and icons are equally capable to create *Rasa* through their own specialities and the specific capacity is their own.

The term '*alam*' is taken as the synonym of '*Brahman*' in the *Agnipurāṇa* is very much significant and welcome for the students of Poetics.[2]

FOOTNOTES

1. *Sāhityaśārīrakam*, Rewa Prasad Dwivedi, pub. by S.S.University, Varanasi, 1998
2. It is to be noted that the latter half of the term *Alaṅkāra* is meant for the sense of *Alam* alone like in the term *Oṁkāra*. What is *Om* that alone is *Oṁkāra*, likewise what is *Alam* that alone is termed as *Alaṅkāra*.

SECTION-V

POETICS

V.1

काव्यनिष्पत्तिप्रक्रिया

महामहोपाध्यायः काश्यपो द्विवेदीरेवाप्रसादः सनातनः

भारतीयायां वसुमत्यां नाट्यशास्त्रस्य विधातारं भरतमुनिमारभ्य साम्प्रतं यावद् यावन्तः कालपर्ययाः परिपूर्त्तिमिताः काव्यलक्षणे तेषां या प्रतिपत्तिस्तामिमां काव्यनिष्पत्तिप्रक्रियात्मना प्रत्यभिजिज्ञासामहे। पुरुषनिष्पत्तिरिव काव्यनिष्पत्तिरपि स्वनिष्ठायां विशेष्यतायामवच्छेदकीकुरुते पूर्णत्वमेव। तथाहि सद्योजातं शिशुशरीरं 'नेत्रद्वयम्, कर्णद्वयम्, हस्तपादद्वयम्' इत्यादिकक्रमेण, पूर्णत्वावच्छिन्नमेव निष्पत्तिं लभते, न पुनरकैकमङ्गं परिहाय। सेयं पूर्णता प्राचीनैराचार्यैर्दोषाभाव इति पर्यभाषि। दोषो नामापूर्णता तदभावश्च पूर्णता। दोषाभावोऽयं गुणपदेनापि प्रतिपाद्यते भरतेन[१]। वामनेन पुनर्गुणाभावो दोषतया[२]। अनयोर्भरतो वर्धमानत्वे दत्तदृष्टिः कुहूतः प्रस्थाय पूर्णिमां प्राप्नोति यत्र कलावृद्धिश्चन्द्रबिम्बस्य। वामनः पुनः पूर्णिमामास्थाय प्रतिप्रतिष्ठते कुहूं यावलक्षयते च कलाहानिं चन्द्रबिम्बस्य। सिंहवीक्षणमेतदिति प्रतिपाद्यं भवति।[३]

तदियं काव्यनिष्पत्तेः प्रथमा भूमिः। अत्राचार्या भरतमुनिप्रभृतयः। एतत्संप्रदायेऽनुयायिनो दण्डिप्रमुखा आचार्याः। एतेषां महावाक्यं गुणाः खलु काव्यस्यात्मेति। गुणाश्च दोषविपर्य्यासात्मान इति संख्यया दशैव भरत इव दण्डिन्यपि। उद्दिश्य निदर्शिताश्चैते काव्यलृक्षणनाम्नि स्वकीये काव्यशास्त्रग्रन्थे काव्यादर्श इति प्रसिद्धे दण्डिना एवम्–

१. श्लेषः, २. प्रसादः, ३. समता, ४. माधुर्यम्, ५. सुकुमारता। ६. अर्थव्यक्तिः, ७. उदारत्वम्, ८. ओजः, ९. कान्ति, १०. समाधयः।। [१.४१] इति।

उक्तज्ञानन्तर्येण–

इति वैदर्भमार्गस्य दश प्राणा गुणाः स्मृताः।
एषां विपर्य्ययः प्रायो दृश्यते गौणवर्त्मनि।।१.४२।।-इति

सोऽयं सम्प्रदायो नाट्यशास्त्रकृतो मुनेर्भरतस्य। यदुक्तमेतेन षोडशेऽध्याये–

एते दोषास्तु नाट्यस्य/काव्यस्य मया सम्यक् प्रकीर्त्तिताः।
गुणा विपर्य्ययादेषां माधुर्यौदार्यलक्षणाः।। ना०शा० १६.८५

श्लेषः प्रसादः समता समाधिर्माधुर्यमोजः पदसौकुमार्यम्।
अर्थस्य च व्यक्तिरुदारता च कान्तिश्च काव्यस्य गुणा दशैते।। इति [**ना०शा०** १६.८६]।
अत्रेदं स्पष्टं यद् दोषाभावगतं दशसंख्यावत्त्वमेव गुणगतस्य दशसंख्यावत्त्वस्य नियामकम्।

तदिदमाद्यमधिकरणं काव्यशारीरके।

भामहोऽत्र प्रतीपायते। स हि गुणनामकं तत्त्वं स्वीकर्त्तुं विचिकित्सते, प्रस्तौति च सहसैव प्रसादो माधुर्यं चेति द्वितयमेव लक्षणोदाहरणाभ्यां भामहालङ्कारनामके 'काव्यालंकार'–नाम्ना प्रसिद्धिमापिते स्वकीये काव्यलक्षणग्रन्थे। अन्ते च 'ओजो'–पि समुद्दिशति किन्त्वलक्षयित्वाऽनुदाहृत्य च। मार्गोऽयमेतदीयो वामनेन परामृश्यते–

'नाऽसन्तः संद्वेद्यत्वात्,
न भ्रान्ताः, निष्कम्पत्वात्,
न पाठधर्माः, सर्वत्राऽदुष्टेः [**काव्यालङ्कारसूत्राणि** ३.१५, २५-२७]

प्रसादस्य माधुर्यस्य च गुणत्वाय प्रकल्पते तयोः संप्लव ओजसा। तथोक्तमेतेन 'प्रसादो द्विविधः 'गाढबन्धः शिथिलबन्धश्चे'ति। अनयोः प्रथम ओजः, द्वितीयश्च माधुर्यम्। अनयोर्दोषाभावत्वेऽपि गुणत्वं कुत इति प्रश्ने वामनस्योत्तरसूत्रम्-गुणः संप्लवात्। अत्र वृत्तिः 'गुणः प्रसादः, ओजसा सह संप्लवात्, स शुद्धस्तु दोष एवते'ति[३.१.७] संप्लवे पुनरनुभवं प्रमाणयति–'स त्वनुभवसिद्धः [३.१.८] अत्र वृत्तिः 'स तु संप्लवोऽनुभवसिद्धः तद्विदाम्, रत्नादिविशेषवत्', इति। अत्र श्लोकः

करुणप्रेक्षणीयेषु संप्लवः सुखदुःखयोः।
यथाऽनुभवतः सिद्धस्तथैवौजःप्रसादयोः।।' इति

केवलस्यौजसो गुणत्वभावोत्प्रेक्षामिमां स्फोरयति कुन्तकाचार्यो यो हि वक्रोक्तिजीविते तमेतं गुणं न गणयति। वामने पुनः प्रसादस्यापि स्वातन्त्र्येण गुणत्वे प्रश्नः। माधुर्यस्य पुनरुभयोरप्यनयोराचार्ययोः समः समादरः।

भरतसंप्रदाये यदि न्यूनत्वमप्याद्रियते तर्हि समधिकत्वमपि कल्पयितुं शक्यत एव। तदपि च राजशेखरकुन्तकयोरालोक्यते। राजशेखरः काव्यमीमांसायां गुणाँस्त्यजति। कुन्तकः पुनः सामान्य-विशेषाभ्यां गुणान् राशिद्वये विभाज्य सामान्यत्वेन १. औचित्यम्, २. सौभाग्यं चेति गुणद्वयं कल्पयति, विशेषत्वेन पुनः माधुर्यम्, प्रसादश्चेति प्राचीनौ द्वौ नवीनौ च 'लावण्यम्' आभिजात्यञ्चे-ति द्वावि'त्येव चतुरो गुणानुद्दिश्य तेषां सुकुमार-विचित्र-मध्यममार्गगतत्वेन त्रैविध्यं प्रतिपादयति। इत्थमत्र चत्वारो गुणा नितान्तं नूत्नाः। १. औचित्यम्, २. सौभाग्यम्, ३. लावण्यम्, ४. अभिजात्यञ्चेति। माधुर्यप्रसादयोरपि मार्गत्रयगतत्वेन प्रायशोऽभिनवत्वमेव। सेयं स्वैरताया अनुज्ञा। प्रभव एतस्या भामह एव।

मध्ये वामनाचार्योऽपि स्वातन्त्र्यमधिश्रयते। स हि 'श्लेषप्रसादीने'व पृथगर्थगुणत्वेन परिकल्प्य गुणानां विंशतिसंख्याकत्वमुपपादयते। आनन्दवर्धनाचार्यो' 'माधुर्यम् ओजः प्रसादश्चे'ति त्रीनेव गुणानाद्रियते, अन्येषां त्यागे मौनमाश्रयाणस्तेषामेषां नियमने रसानभिषिञ्चति। वस्तुतस्त्रयोऽपि गुणास्तन्मतेन रसनिष्ठा एव,ताननुसृत्य क्रियमाणाः शब्दार्थबन्धा अपि मधुरादिपदव्यवदेश्या इति समेषामेव ध्वनिमार्गिणां संस्कारः। काव्यप्रकाशकारः श्रीमम्मटोऽप्यभिनवगुप्त इवैवानन्दवर्धमनुसरति। मम्मटः पुनरन्येषां त्यागे हेतुत्रयमुपष्टम्भयति–

केचिदन्तर्भवन्त्येषु दोषत्यागात् परे श्रिताः।
अन्ये भजन्ति दोषत्वं कुत्रचिन्न ततो दशे॥ ति

तदिदं द्वितीयमधिकरणं काव्यशारीरके। अत्र प्रमुखं प्रतिपाद्यं गुणः। अत्राचार्या भरतमारभ्य वामनं याज्जाता मनीषिणः। एतस्मिन्नेवावधौ रुद्रटस्यापि गणना, किन्त्वसावपि राजशेखरवन्नैव स्पृशति गुणान्। एतेषां महावाक्यं भवति 'गुणाः खलु काव्यात्मे'-ति। उक्तमेव हि वामनेन-'रीतिरात्मा काव्यस्ये'-ति[१.२.६] अत्र'विशिष्टा पदरचना रीतिरिति, विशेषो गुणात्मेति' परवर्त्तिभ्यां सूत्राभ्यां गुणविशिष्टा पदरचना' रीति-रिति फलितार्थे विशेष्यतावच्छेदकपदं गुण एव सिद्धं भवतीति।

वस्तुतस्तु वामनस्य मते रसरूपं सौन्दर्यमेव काव्यात्मपदं भजते, तस्यैवैकस्य साध्यत्वात्। सति च साध्ये साधनस्यात्मत्वमुपचारैकसाध्यम्। उक्तमिदमस्माभिर्द्वाविंशत्या कारिकाभिः काव्यालङ्कारकारिका-ग्रन्थपरिशेषभूताभिः। तथाहि–

ततश्च वामनाचार्यो रीतिरात्मेति सूत्रयन्।
सौन्दर्यमात्मा काव्यस्येत्येव सूत्रयतेऽस्फुटम्॥१२॥
वामनाचार्यसिद्धान्तस्तर्कैरुक्तैस्ततो भवेत्।
'सौन्दर्यवाद'-नाम्नैव व्यवहाराय युक्तिभाक्॥१३॥

वामनाचार्यसिद्धान्ते न रीतिर् न गुणः, परम्।
सौन्दर्यमेव काव्यात्मा यद्वाऽङ्कार एव स॥२२॥ इति।

सौन्दर्यमपीदं यथावल्लक्षितमस्माभिरेव 'वस्तुनिष्ठं करणप्रत्याहारजनकत्वं सौन्दर्यम्' इति। ततश्च चित्रमूर्त्तिगीतिकाव्यार्थगता या सहृदयहृदयप्रत्याहारजनकता तदवच्छेदकत्वं सौन्दर्यमि' -ति फलितोऽर्थः प्रत्यपाद्यस्माभिः कलासमाधि'-रिति ग्रन्थे नाट्यानुशासनस्य चतुर्थाध्यायरूपे।

तदिदं द्वितीयमधिकरणं काव्यनिष्पत्तिप्रक्रियायाम्, यत्र प्राधान्यमभजद्, गुणतत्त्वमेव काव्यशरीरगतम्। अथ तृतीयमधिकरणम्।

अलंभावः–

'काव्यं ग्राह्यमलङ्कारादि'-ति वामनोक्तौ 'अलमित्येकं पदम्, 'कार' इति च द्वितीयम्। अनयोः

प्रथमम् अलेत्यजन्तमपि-'अलि'ति च हलन्तमपि भवति। प्रकृतिभूतो धातुरत्र 'अल' इति 'अलञ्' इति वा। अर्थश्चास्य भूषण-पर्याप्ति-वारणानि। एतेषु पर्याप्तिरेव प्रमुखा, भूषणवारणयोस्तत्कार्यत्वेन प्रसिद्धत्वात्। यो हि तृप्तिं भजते स खलु नाधिकं जिघृक्षति, दीयमानञ्च 'अलमलमि'-ति निवारयति, यश्च भूषितो भवति स खलु अलङ्कृत इत्युच्यते वरप्रभृतिः। कियन्मात्रं वालङ्करणं वरादीनामङ्गेष्वपेक्ष्यत इति जिज्ञासिते समीचीनमुत्तरमेकमेव 'यतोऽधिक उद्वेजको मा भूदि'-ति। तदिदं तृप्तिमूलकमेव। पर्याप्तिमूलां च पश्यामस्तृप्तिम्। एवं पर्याप्तिरेव 'अल' धातोः प्रमुखोऽर्थः। अनेनार्थेन क्रोडीकृतं समग्रमपि विश्वम्। य एषोऽस्य सर्गः, यो वा अस्य विसर्गः, यश्चापि ऋतुचक्रात्मा परिणामोऽस्य, तत् सर्वमप्यत्रार्थरूपेण गृह्यते। अत एवाग्नेये महापुराणेऽलमिति ब्रह्मेति च पर्यायतयैवोपस्थाप्यते। तथा हि वचनम्–

अक्षरं परमं ब्रह्म सनातनमलं विभुम्।
वेदान्तेषु वदन्त्येकं चैतन्यं ज्योतिरीश्वरम्॥ [अध्याय ३३८.१]

वैदिकीयं परिभाषा, तत्र 'अरम्' इति श्रुतिः। रस्य लत्वे तु 'अलमि'ति।[५] प्रसिद्ध 'अलि'ति यद्धलन्तं पदं तेन सुशकमेव अपौरुषेये माहेश्वरे वर्णसमाम्नाये यः खल्वल्प्रत्याहारस्तस्य ग्रहणम्। स च 'अइउण्' इति सूत्रत आरभ्यते समाप्यते च 'हल्' इत्यनेन सूत्रेण। सोऽयं समग्रोऽपि वर्णसमाम्नायोऽपौरुषेयः। अलेनार्थजातमिवाऽलाऽनेन सम्पूर्णमेवाक्षरजातं संकेत्यते। ताविमौ शब्दार्थौ। अलिति शब्दः, अल इति चार्थः। उभयत्राऽपि पर्याप्तिरेव भगवती परमा।

अथ यत् 'कारपदं' तस्यापि नैकधा भवति व्युत्पादनम्। यथा चैतत् तत् पाणिनेर्भगवतोऽष्टाध्याय्यास्तृतीयस्याध्यायस्य द्वितीय-पादगतैर्घञ्विधायकैः सूत्रैरवगन्तुं शक्यते। भवन्ति हि तत्र सूत्राणि यैर्विधीयते घञ्प्रत्ययः कर्त्रर्थेऽपि। कर्मण्यणि [३.२.१] ति कर्मण्युपपदे विद्यमाने करोतेः कर्त्रर्थ एव घञ् विधीयते। कुम्भकार इति चाऽत्रोदाहरणम्। प्रकृतेऽपि 'अल' पदस्य द्वितीयान्तं रूपं कर्मण्यादाय शक्यत एव व्युत्पादयितुं घञा 'कार'-शब्दः। तथा चालं पर्याप्तं करोतीत्यलङ्कार इत्यपि स्वीकर्तुं शक्यतेऽलङ्कारशब्दस्य कर्तृव्युत्पत्तिः। 'वर्णात्कार' इत्यनेनापि पथा कारपदं स्वरूपेऽर्थे शक्यस्वीकारः ततश्चालमेवालङ्कारः इति स्वीकर्त्तुं शक्योऽर्थोऽत्र। भावेऽपि घञः प्रयोगं पश्यामः। एवं चालम्भाव एवाऽत्रालङ्कारपदप्रतिपाद्यो भवेदेव। उक्तं चैतदस्माभिरेव।

अलंभावो ह्यलङ्कारः स च सौन्दर्यतत्कृतोः।
विभक्तात्मा विभुर्जीवब्रह्मणोश्चिद्घनो यथे॥ ति।

एष चालंभावः शब्दगतेष्वनुप्रासादिषु लक्ष्यते, अर्थगतेषु च रूपकोपमादिषु। य एष रस इति सर्वातिशयी धर्मः स द्विधोपलभ्यते इक्षुरस इत्यादिष्वास्वाद्यात्मतया, आस्वादतया च रसस्य तृप्तः इत्यादिषु प्रयोगेषु। काव्ये नाट्ये कलासु च सुलभ एषः। रत्याद्युपसृष्ट एष ताँस्तानभिधानविशेषानादत्ते शृङ्गार इति हास इति वीर इति करुण इति वा। योऽयमास्वादः अत्र हि विषयोपहितं प्रत्यक्चैतन्यमेव विषयः, तदेकमेव च विषयि। तच्चोच्यते 'स्वाकार इवाऽभिन्नोऽपि गोचरीकृत' इति। अयमास्वाद एव

रसः, असावेव सौन्दर्यरूपो हृदयहारी विषयगतो विशेषः। प्रत्यक्‌चैतन्यस्य ब्रह्मरूपत्वेन स्वीकृताविययमेव तृप्तिप्रसूतिः पर्याप्तिः। एवं चालंभावार्थकेनालङ्कारपदेन आब्रह्म स्तम्बान्ताः सर्वेऽपि विसीयन्ते पदार्थाः, विसीयन्ते च तत्प्रतिपादनपरायणाः सर्वेऽपि वाचकाः स्फोटरूपाश्चैतन्यमूर्तयः शब्दा अला प्रत्याह्रियमाणस्वरूपाः। उपलब्धिरियमुपस्थाप्यते काव्यालङ्कारकारिकाया द्वितीयस्य संस्करणस्योपसंहारे–

प्रत्यक्चैतन्यमाला चेद् ब्रह्माऽभेदेन रस्यते।
अलम्भावोऽप्यलङ्काररूपो ब्रह्मेति रस्यताम्॥' इति।

एवं चेयमेव काव्यनिष्पत्तेः प्रक्रिया यत् पूर्वं प्रतिभायां दोषाभावरूपा पूर्णता, ततस्तस्यां गुणा यौवनादयः, तेषां चालम्भावो रसपर्यवसानक इति।

रेवाप्रसादस्य द्विवेदिनः

सन्दर्भ :

१. एते दोषास्तु विज्ञेयाः सूरिभिर्नाट्यसंश्रयाः। एत एव विपर्यस्ता गुणाः काव्येषु कीर्त्तिताः॥ नाट्यशास्त्रे १६.९५
२. 'गुणाविपर्य्ययात्मानो दोषाः' वामनस्य काव्यालङ्कारसूत्रम्। २.९.१।
३. अपूर्णतैव दोषस्तद् दोषाभावश्च पूर्णता। काव्यालङ्कारकारिका १४८।
   या चैषा पूर्णता सैव, गुणत्वेन मुनेर्मता। गुणाभावे च दोषत्वं वामनेन निरीक्ष्यते।
   पूर्णताभूमिका रहस्यास्य तत् सिंहवीक्षणम्, राकेन्दौ दत्तदृष्टेर्नृ कुहूं यावन्निरीक्षणम्॥ –कारिका १५०
४. १.२.७, १.२.८ काव्यालङ्कारसूत्राभ्याम्।
५. ऐतरेय आरण्यके बहुशः।

V. 2

SALIENT FEATURES OF VĀMANA'S KAVIPRIYĀ ON HIS OWN KĀVYĀLAṄKĀRASŪTRĀṆI

Dr. W.K. Lele

1. In the course of the evolution of Indian poetics Vāmana[1](Vā) stands out as the first literary theorist to write in the *sūtra*-style. His important (but some what neglected) work called, *Kāvyālaṅkārasūtravṛtti*[2] (Kl) comprises 320 *sūtras* having uneven length.[3] On these *sutras* Vā has himself[4] composed a *vṛtti*. The *vṛtti* consists of prose text, about 350 illustrative passages (which include words, expressions, halves of verses and full-length stanzas) and as many as 34 summary-type *ślokas*.[5] The whole work is divided into 5 *Adhikaraṇas* which in their turn are subdivided into 12 *Adhyāyas*. The present article proposes to analyse *Kavipriyā* (KP) in order to bring out its salient features.

2.1 Headings of the *Adhikaraṇas*

The first and the most obvious constituent of KP that attracts the reader's attention is the headings of the five *Adhikaraṇas* which are *Śārīram* (Kl 1) *Doṣadarśanam* (*ibid*, 16) *Guṇavivecanam* (*ibid*., 31) *Ālaṅkārika* (*ibid*., 47) and *Prāyogika* (*ibid*, 77) respectively. These names give the readers a broad but pointed idea of the contents of the respective *Adhikaraṇa* chapters). The last name of the above headings, in particular, makes it clear that Vā is alive to the reality that the science of poerty is as much practical as it is theoretical because the art of poetry is to be practised and cultivated by intensive and extensive mental efforts.

2.2 Sub-headings of *Adhyāyas*

What is true of the headings of the *Adhikaraṇas* is equally true of the sub-headings of the *Adhyāyas*. They are quite expressive of their contents. The twelve names of the *Adhyāyas,* namely,

प्रयोजनस्थापना, अधिकारिचिन्ता रीतिनिश्चयश्च, काव्याङ्गानि काव्यविशेषाश्च, पदपदार्थदोषविभागः, वाक्यवाक्यार्थदोषविभागः, गुणालंकारविवेकः शब्दगुणविवेकश्च, अर्थगुणविवेचनम्, शब्दालंकारविचारः, उपमाविचारः, उपमाप्रपञ्चाधिकारः, काव्यसमयः and शब्दशुद्धिः respectively, go to prove that Vā writes to a plan. He has had the complete 'structure' of his entire work in his head before he has put pen to paper. The first *Adhyāya*, section, begins with the statement of the doctrine of poetic beauty, काव्यसौन्दर्य (काव्यं ग्राह्यमलंकारात्।।२।। सौन्दर्यमलंकारः।।२।। Kl 2). The last section *Śabdaśuddhi* which lays emphasis on the utmost correctness of diction, essentially contributes to the concept of beauty. Thus this aesthetic principle runs through the whole work.

This Style of expressing the contents of (the divisions of) the text in a nutshell is called *Piṇḍavyākhyā*[6].

3. *Padavyākhyā*

The next easily noticeable feature of KP is what is called पदव्याख्या[7] which has the following functional aspects: (i) to provide meaning-completers, (ii) to establish linkages between/among words used in the *sūtra*, (iii) to dissolve compounds, (iv) to offer etymology and (v) to explain the purpose of the constituents of the *sūtra*. Let us try to understand these with the help of quotations from KP.

3.1 Meaning-comleters:

The *sūtra*: न कतकं पङ्कप्रसादनाय।

The *vṛtti*: न हि कतकं पयस इव पङ्कस्य प्रसादनाय प्रभवति (Kl 4)

Here the words पयस इव and प्रभवति supplied in KP complete the meaning of the *sūtra*.

Again, *sūtra*: रीतिरात्मा काव्यस्य।

Vṛtti: रीतिर्नाम इयं आत्मा काव्यस्य। शरीरस्य इवेति वाक्यशेषः। (ibid.)

Here, the additional words, नाम इयं, शरीरस्य इवेति वाक्यशेषः enable us to understand the sense of the *sūtra* fully.

3.2 Linkages:

Sūtra: स दोषगुणालंकारहानादानाभ्याम्।।

Vṛtti: स खलु अलंकारो दोषहानात् गुणालंकारादानाच्च संपाद्यः कवेः।। (*ibid*. 2)

Here Vā has shown how to connect the words दोष, गुणालंकार, हान and आदान According, *Doṣa* is to be linked with *Hāna* and *Guṇālaṅkara* with आदानसंपाद्यः कवेः are meaning completers.

Again, *sūtra*: काव्यं सद् दृष्टादृष्टार्थम्। प्रीतिकीर्तिहेतुत्वात्।।

Vṛtti: काव्यं सच्चारु दृष्टप्रयोजनम्, प्रीतिहेतुत्वात्। अदृष्टप्रयोजनम्, कीर्तिहेतुत्वात्। (*ibid.*)

Here the *vṛtti* makes it clear that *dṛṣṭārtha* is to be connected to प्रीतिहेतुत्वात् and अदृष्टार्थ to कीर्तिहेतुत्वात्

3.3 Dissolving compounds:

Sūtra: ओजःकान्तिमती गौडीया।।

Vṛtti: ओजः कान्तिश्च विद्येते यस्यां सा ओजःकान्तिमती गौडीया। (*ibid.*, 6)

Again, *sūtra*: स्वलक्षणच्युतवृत्तं भिन्नवृत्तम्।।

Vṛtti: स्वस्माल्लक्षणाच्च्युतं वृत्तं यस्मिंस्तत्स्वलक्षणच्युतवृत्तं वाक्यं भिन्नवृत्तम्।। (*ibid.*, 22)

The dissolution of the above compounds is so clear that they need no further explanation.

3.4 Offering etymology:

Sūtra: अनुक्तौ समासोक्तिः।।

Vṛtti: संक्षेपवचनात्समासोक्तिरित्याख्या।। (*ibid.*, 63)

Here *KP* shows how the word *Samāsokti* has been derived.

Similarly, *sūtra*: किंचिदुक्तावप्रस्तुतप्रशंसा।।

Vṛtti: अप्रस्तुतस्य अर्थस्य प्रशंसनमप्रस्तुतप्रशंसा।। (*ibid.*)

3.5 Explanining the purpose of the constitutuents of the *sūtra*:

Sūtra: उपमानोपमेयस्य गुणसाम्यात्तत्त्वारोपो रूपकम्।।

Vṛtti: उपमानोपमेययोरुभयोरपि ग्रहणं लौकिक्याः कल्पितायाश्चोपमायाः प्रकृतित्वमत्र यथा विज्ञायेत इति। (*ibid.*, 64)

Here *KP* explains the reason whey both उपमेय and उपमान have been specifically mentioned in the definition of the रूपक।

Similarly, *sūtra*: उपमानाक्षेपश्चाक्षेपः।।

Vṛtti: उपमानस्याक्षेपः प्रतिषेधः उपमानाक्षेपः। तुल्यकार्यार्थस्य नैरर्थक्यविवक्षायाम्।। (*ibid*., 74)

Here *KP* clarifies how आक्षेप comes about in the words तुल्यकार्यार्थस्य etc.

The above illustrations are just representative ones. There are scores of such illustrations in *KP* but it is needless to heap them up all here. We turn to the next feauture of *KP*.

4. *Padārthavyākhyā*[8]

Explaining the meanings of the words used in the *sūtra* is called. पदार्थव्याख्या Vā, however, does not give just word-meanings.

In other words *KP* does not instance only a one-to-one correspondence. It is something more than that. The following discussion will clarify what that more is like.

4.1 *Sūtra*: काव्यं ग्राह्यमलंकारात्।।

Vṛtti: काव्यं खलु ग्राह्यमुपादेयं भवति, अलंकारात्। काव्यशब्दोऽयं गुणालंकार-संस्कृतयोः शब्दार्थयोर्वर्तते। भक्त्या तु शब्दार्थमात्रवचनोऽत्र गृह्यते।। (*ibid*., 2)

Here Vā mentions not only the मुख्यार्थ of the term काव्य but also its औपचारिक अर्थ।

4.2 *Sūtra*: माधुर्यसौकुमार्योपपन्ना पाञ्चाली।

Vṛtti: माधुर्येण सौकुमार्येण च गुणेनोपपन्ना पाञ्चाली नाम रीतिः। ओजःकान्त्य-भावादनुल्बणपदा विच्छाया च।। (*ibid*., 6)

Thus *KP* points out the two prominent attributes of the पाञ्चाली रीति thereby distinguishing it from the गौडीया रीति।

4.3 *Sūtra*: तदुपारोहादर्थगुणलेशोऽपि।।

Vṛtti: तदुपधानतः खल्वर्थलेशोऽपि स्वदते। किमङ्ग, पुनरर्थगुणसंपत्।। (*ibid*., 8)

Here besides giving the word-meanings of the *sūtra,* Vā highlights the excellence of the वैदर्भी रीति।

4.4 *Sūtra*: अभिधानकोषतः पदार्थनिश्चयः।

Vṛtti: पदं हि रचनाप्रवेशयोग्यं भावयन्संदिग्धार्थत्वेन न गृह्णीयान्नवा जह्यादिति काव्य-बन्धविघ्नः। तस्मादभिधानकोषतः पदार्थनिश्चयः कर्तव्य इति। (*ibid*., 9)

In this passage, Vā has advanced a very convincing reason for the necessity of a diligent study of the अभिधानकोष lexicon. More importantly, he has first stated the reason and then given the meanig of the *sūtra*.

4.5 *Sūtra*: काव्यबन्धोद्यमोऽभियोगः।।

Vṛtti: काव्यस्य बन्धनं रचना काव्यबन्धः। तत्रोद्यमोऽभियोगः। स हि कवित्व-प्रकर्षमवसंदधाति।। (*ibid.*, 12)

Here by putting down the फलश्रुति of the अभियोग in the words स हि etc., Vā has as though persuaded the would-be poet to try his hand at poetic compositions.

4.6 *Sūtra*: अन्यार्थनेयगूढार्थाश्लीलक्लिष्टानि च।।

Vṛtti: दुष्टं पदमिति अनुवर्तते। अर्थतश्च वचनविपरिणामः। अन्यार्थादीनि पदानि दुष्टानि इति सूत्रार्थः।। (*ibid.*, 18)

In the passage Vā shows how the present *sūtra* is to be connected with the earlier *sūtra*, दुष्टं पदमसाधु etc., (*ibid.*, 16), how to arrive at the plural form and what is the resultant meaning of the *sūtra*.

4.7 *Sūtra*: मार्गाभेदः समता।।

Vṛtti: मार्गस्याभेदो मार्गाभेदः समता। येन मार्गेणोपक्रमस्तस्यात्याग इत्यर्थः। श्लोके प्रबन्धे चेति। (*ibid.*, 34)

This is a three-tier *vṛtti*: (i) dissolution of the compound मार्गाभेद, (ii) explanation of its meaning and (iii) indication of the area of application and/or location of the समतागुण।

4.8 *Sūtra*: सादृश्याल्लक्षणा वक्रोक्तिः।।

Vṛtt: यथा 'उन्मिमील कमलं सरसीनां कैरवं च निमिमील मुहूर्तात्। अत्र नेत्रधर्मा-वुन्मीलननिमीलने सादृश्याद् विकाससंकोचौ लक्षयतः।। क (*ibid.*, 66)

To explain वक्रोक्ति अर्थालङ्कार, Vā quotes the stanzan उन्मिमील . . . etc. and then goes on to tell what the words उन्मिमील and निमिमील denote.

4.9 *Sūtra*: अतद्रूपस्यान्यथाध्यवसानमतिशयार्थमुत्प्रेक्षा।।

Vṛtti: अतद्रूपस्यातत्स्वभावस्य। अन्यथा अतत्स्वभावतया। अध्यवसानमध्यवसायः। न पुनरध्यारोपो लक्षणा वा। अतिशयार्थमिति भ्रान्तिज्ञाननिवृत्त्यर्थम्। सादृश्या-दियमुत्प्रेक्षेति।। (*ibid.*, 67)

Here, distinguishing अध्यवसानं from अध्यारोप and लक्षणा *KP* clarifies why the word अतिशयार्थं has been used in the above definition. This latter aspect resembles 3.5 discussed earlier.

4.10 *Sūtra*: न पादादौ खल्वादयः।।

Vṛtt: पादादौ खल्वादयः शब्दा न प्रयोज्याः। आदिशब्दः प्रकारार्थः।
येषामादौ प्रयोगो न श्लिष्यति ते गृह्यन्ते। न पुनर्बतहन्तप्रभृतयः। (*ibid*., 78)

In this passage Vā supplies the implied word प्रयोज्याः to make the sense of the *sūtra* complete, clarifies the 'kind' of the word आदि and also mentions the exceptions to the rule stated in the *sūtra*.

4.11 *Sūtra* : संबन्धसंबन्धेऽपि षष्ठी क्वचित्।।

Vṛtt : संबन्धेन संबन्धः संबन्धसंबन्धस्तस्मिन् षष्ठी प्रयोज्या, क्वचित्, न सर्वत्रेति। (*ibid*., 79)

The meaning 'न सर्वत्र' can easily be inferred from the word 'क्वचित्' but Vā wants to make the sense of the *sūtra* totally free of doubt and therefore appends the *vṛtti* with 'न सर्वत्र'.

In fine, the पदार्थव्याख्या in *KP* is multi-functional and therefore multi-formal.

5. *Adhikaraṇavyākhyā*

We find that *KP* treats the topics of a number of *sūtras* at length and with due illustrations, leaving nothing incomplete. Such treatment of the *sūtras* is called अधिकरणव्याख्या. Let us consider a couple of instances of this type.

5.1 *Sūtras*: तदनिबद्धं निबद्धं च।।२७।। क्रमसिद्धिस्तयोः स्रगुत्तंसवत्।।२८।।
नानिबद्धं चकास्त्येकतेजःपरमाणुवत्।।२९।।

Vṛtti: तदिदं गद्यपद्यरूपं काव्यमनिबद्धं निबद्धं च। अनयोः प्रसिद्धत्वाल्लक्षणं नोक्तम्।।२७।।

तयोरित्यनिबद्धं निबद्धं च परामृश्यते। क्रमेण सिद्धिः क्रमसिद्धिः। अनिबद्धसिद्धौ निबद्धसिद्धिः स्रगुत्तंसवत्। यथा स्रजि मालायां सिद्धायामुत्तंसः शेखरः सिध्यतीति।।२८।। केचिदनिबद्ध एव पर्यवसितास्तद्दूषणार्थमाह–न खलु अनिबद्धं काव्यं चकास्ति दीप्यते। यथैकतेजःपरमाणुरिति। अत्र श्लोकः–
'असंकलितरूपाणां काव्यानां नास्ति चारुता।
न प्रत्येकं प्रकाशन्ते तैजसाः परमाणवः।।२९।।' (*ibid*., pp 14.15)

Here all the three *sūtras* are taken together into consideration because they all relate to a single topic. At the outset *KP* makes it clear that based on अनिबद्धत्व and निबद्धत्व there are four kinds of poetic compositions, *viz*. अनिबद्ध गद्य, निबद्ध गद्य, अनिबद्ध पद्य and निबद्ध पद्य। Of these निबद्ध गद्य means कथा, आख्यायिक etc., अनिबद्धपद्य means मुक्तक, गाथा etc. and निबद्ध पद्य means खण्डकाव्य, महाकाव्य etc. But the concept of अनिबद्धगद्य remains unclear. In view of this Vā should have provided the readers with its definition. Turning to the *vṛtti* on *sūtra* 28 it needs to be mentioned that the proficiency in 'unconnected' compositions does not, as a rule, lead to the proficiency in 'connected' compositions. Lastly, both the objectors (who hold that the beauty lies only in unconnected poetry) and Vā (who asserts that there is no beauty at all in unconneted poetry) hold extreme views and therefore both deserve to be rejected.

Thus Vā has treated the above topic fully from his own view point.

5.2 The following is a very typical example of the present category.

Sūtra: आहेति भूतेऽन्यणलन्तभ्रमात् ब्रुवो लटि।

Vṛtti: 'ब्रुवः पञ्चानाम्' इत्यादिना आहेति लट् व्युत्पादितः। स भूते प्रयुक्तः। 'इत्याह भगवान् प्रभुः' इति। अन्यस्य भूतकालाभिधायिनो णलन्तस्य लिटि श्रमात्। निपुणाश्चैव प्रयुञ्जते 'आह स्म स्मितमधुमधुराक्षरां गिरम्' इति। 'अनुकरोति भगवतो नाराणस्य' इत्यत्राऽपि मन्ये 'स्म' शब्दः कविना प्रयुक्तो लेखकैस्तु प्रमादान्न लिखित इति।। (*ibid.*, 88-89).

Vā herein shows that (i) the correct past tense form of ब्रू is आह (ii) it is always to be used with स्म (iii) some people omit this स्म out of ignorance or confusion, (iv) sometimes the scribe makes a mistake in this respect through inadvertence. This *vṛtti* displays Vā's deep knowledge of the rules of Pāṇini and an insighful reading of the literary works. It is also worth nothing here that for the omission of स्म in the passage अनुकरोति etc. Vā does not hold बाणभट्ट responsible presumably out of fraternal feelings!

With this we turn to the next kind of व्याख्या–

6. *Prakaraṇavyākhyā*[10]

There are several places in *KP* where Vā first discusses a particular point or topic in detail and then observes that with the discussioin just finished another (similar) point or topic should be taken to have been discussed. At such places he generally uses the expression. 'तेन अमुकं व्याख्यातम्।' This type of वृत्ति is called प्रकरणव्याख्या।

There are as many as 15 instances of this व्याख्या in *KP*. We only take up a couple of them for discussion and list the rest at the end of this section.

6.1 After discussin अश्लील and क्लिष्टपददोष in detail Vā writes the following *sūtra* and *vṛtti* thereon.

Sūtra: अन्त्याभ्यां वाक्यं व्याख्यातम्।।

Vṛtti: अश्लीलं क्लिष्टं चेत्यन्त्ये पदे। ताभ्यां वाक्यं व्याख्यातम्। तदप्यश्लीलं क्लिष्टं च भवति।। (*ibid*., 21)

After thus saying in so many words that there are both अश्लील and क्लिष्टवाक्य, Vā meticulously illustrates these two वाक्यदोषे।

6.2 Similarly, after having considered लिङ्गभेद उपमादोष with due illustrations and exceptions, Vā says:

Sūtra: तेन वचनभेदो व्याख्यातः।।

Vṛtti: तेन लिङ्गभेदेन वचनभेदो व्याख्यातः। यथा 'पश्यामि लोचने तस्याः पुष्पं पुष्पलिहो यथा। (*ibid*., 60)

In this illustration the word पश्यामः ought to have been used instead of पश्यामि. Of course we have to understand that this दोष is to be avoided in both लौकिकी and कल्पित उपमा because what applies to the लिङ्गभेदउपमादोष also applies to the वचनभेद-दोष।

6.3 The following are the other instances of the present व्याख्या :

(i) अलंकृतिरलंकारः। करणव्युत्पत्त्या पुनरलंकारशब्दोऽयमुपमादिषु वर्तते।। (*ibid*., 2)

(ii) एवमन्यासामपि विद्यानां यथास्वमुपयोगो वर्णनीय इति। (*ibid*.,11)

(iii) 'रतिविगलितबन्धे केशपाशे सुकेश्याः' इत्यत्र सुकेश्या इत्यस्य साभिप्रायत्वं व्याख्यातम्। (*ibid*., 41)

(iv) अनया च वर्णयमकमालया पदयमकमाला व्याख्याता। (*ibid*., 5)

(v) एतेन 'कनकफलकचतुरस्रं श्रोणिबिम्बम्' इति व्याख्यातम्।। (*ibid*.,57)

(vi) एतेन 'वेश्या हि नाम....' इत्येवमादिषु एकगुणहानिकल्पना व्याख्याता। (*ibid*., 73)

(vii) तेन विपर्ययो व्याख्यातः। (*ibid*., 78). This *sūtra* follows the *sūtra* 'न कर्मधारयो बहुव्रीहिप्रतिपत्तिकरः।' (*ibid*.)

(viii) एतेन 'क्रुद्धस्य तस्याथः.....' इत्यादयः प्रयोगाः व्याख्याताः। (*ibid*., 79)

(ix) तेन कदलीकाण्डादयो व्याख्याताः। (*ibid*.,) This sentence forms a part of the *vṛtti* on the *sūtra*. संबंधसंबन्धेऽपि षष्ठी क्वचित्। (*ibid*., 81-82).

(x) एतेन वेदिभर्त्सितर्जिप्रभृतयो व्याख्याताः। (*ibid*., 87)

(xi) तैर्महीधरादयो व्याख्याताः।

(xii) एवं गङ्गाधरादयो व्याख्याताः। (*ibid*.,)

We now pass on to the next व्याख्या type.

7. *Kṛcchravyākhyā*

When a शास्त्रकार considers a point or topic very minutely and eleborately he is said to be writing a कृच्छ्रव्याख्या. There are a few interesting instances of this व्याख्या in *KP*.

7.1 Vā consideres अवधानम् to be one of the काव्याङ्गs under the head प्रकीर्ण (*ibid*.. 11). He has treated this topic elaborately as under:

Sūtras: चित्तैकाग्र्यमवधानम्।।१७।। तद्देशकालाभ्याम्।।२८।। विविक्तो देशः।। १९।। रात्रियामस्तुरीयः कालः।।२०।।

Vṛtti: चित्तस्यैकाग्र्यं बाह्यार्थनिवृत्तिः। तदवधानम्। अवहितं हि चित्तं अर्थान् पश्यति।।१७।। तदवधानं देशात्कालाच्च समुत्पद्यते।।१८।। विक्तो देशः।।१९।। रात्रेर्यामो रात्रियामः प्रहरस्तुरीयश्चतुर्थः काल इति। तद्वशाद्विषयोपरतं प्रसन्नं चित्तमवधत्ते।।२०।। (*ibid*., 13)

Here *KP* takes up the terms अवधानम्, देश and काल and explains them one by one completely.

7.2 Vā describes अर्थगुण ओजस् in the same eleborate manner:

Sūtra: अर्थस्य प्रौढिरोजः।।

Vṛtti: अर्थस्याभिधेयस्य प्रौढिः प्रौढत्वमोजः।
पदार्थे वाक्यवचने वाक्यार्थे च पदाभिधा।
प्रौढिव्याससमासौ च साभिप्रायत्वमस्य च।। (*ibid*., 39)

According to Vā, ओजस् is expressed and therefore realized in five forms, viz, पदार्थे वाक्यवचन, वाक्यार्थे पदाभिधान, व्यास, समास and साभिप्रायत्व। He quotes suitable passages to illustrate these five forms and thus completes the treatment of the अर्थगुण ओजस्.

KP discusses अर्थगुण समाधि also in the same eleborate manner.

The व्याख्या type to be considered hereafter is called फलव्याख्या

8. *Phalavyākhyā*

This type of व्याख्या has two aspects, *viz.*, (i) to reject the opponent's arguments on a disputed topic and (ii) to incorporate the opponent's view in one's own. Let us try to understand these with reference to *KP*.

8.1 Vā divides कविशिष्य into two classes, विवेकी (discriminating) and अविवेकी (indiscriminating) and firmly holds that काव्यालङ्कारशास्त्र should be taught only to the

विवेकीशिष्य and the efforts taken to teach that to अविवेकी शिष्य simply go to waste (अरोचकिनः सतृणाभ्यवहारिणश्च कवयः।।१।। पूर्वे शिष्याः विवेकित्वात्।।२।। नेतरे तद्विपर्ययात्।।३।। (*ibid.*, 3). Upon this the opponent raises a doubt saying 'ननु एवं न शास्त्रं सर्वानुग्राहि, कुतस्तदुपादीयते। (*ibid.*, 4) meaning, if that is the case then it means that the शास्त्र doesn't favour each and everyone. Why then should it be diligently studied? Vā answers this question in the following सूत्रवृत्ति :

न शास्त्रमद्रव्येष्वर्थवत्।।४।।

न खलु शास्त्रमद्रव्येष्वविवेकिष्वर्थवत्।। निदर्शनमाह–

न कतकं पङ्कप्रसादनाय।।

न हि कतकं पयस इव पङ्कस्य प्रसादनाय प्रभवति।। (*ibid*)

Vā's position is that the science is really not of any use to the indicriminate disciples. A nut is not capable of clearing mud, it can clear muddy water. In this निदर्शन Vā has compared an अविवेकी शिष्य to पङ्क mud.

8.2 Vā conceives of the बन्धगुण समाधि as अवरोह (i.e. abundance of small and loose letters) following आरोह (i.e. abundance of long and dense letters) or as आरोह following अवरोह (आरोहस्य अवरोहे सति परिहारः) अवरोहस्य वा आरोहे सतीति। *ibid.*, 34). The opponent does not subscribe to this view. He objects saying that the समाधि गुण conceived by Vā has no independent existence because आरोह is of the form of ओजस् and अवरोह is of the form of प्रसाद (न पृथक् समाधिर्गुणः। आरोहावरोहयोरोजःप्रसादरूपत्वात्। ओजोरूपश्चारोहः प्रसादरूपश्चावरोह इति। (*ibid.*, 35) But Vā refutes this objection saying that the opponent's view-point is not correct in that ओज and प्रसाद are realized in a blended form like the streams of a river (संपृक्तक्त्वात् संपृक्तौ खल्वोजःप्रसादौ नदीवेणिकावद् वहतः) (*ibid.*) Vā adds the following सूत्रवृत्ति to his above arguments.

Sūtra: ओजःप्रसादयोः क्वचिद्भागे तीव्रावस्थायां ताविति चेदभ्युपगमः।

Vṛtti: ओजःप्रसादयोः क्वचिद्भागे तीव्रावस्थायामारोहोऽवरोहश्चेत्येवं चेन्मन्यसे, अभ्युपगमः न विप्रतिपत्तिः। (*ibid.*)

Vā contends that he is in agreement with the opponent if the latter takes the stand that आरोह means the intensity of ओजस् in some part of a poetic composition and अवरोह means the intensity of प्रसाद in some part of a poetic composition.

There are at least 15 more places where the present व्याख्या type occurs in KP. With this we proceed to the next type, viz. न्यासव्याख्या)

9. It is observed that a शास्त्रकार sometimes resorts to the views expressed in a different शास्त्र, branch of knowledge, with a view to proving his own views. The व्याख्या that occurs at such places is called न्यास व्याख्या.[13] The following is a representative example of this व्याख्या type in *KP*.

Sūtra: स्तनादीनां द्वित्वाविष्टा जातिः प्रायेण।

Vṛtti: स्तनादीनां द्वित्वाविष्टा, द्वित्वाध्यासिता जातिः प्रायेण बाहुल्येनेति। यथा– 'स्तनयोस्तरुणिजनस्य' इति। प्रायेणेति वचनात्क्वचिन्न भवति। यथा–'स्त्रीणां चक्षुः' इति। अथ कथं द्वित्वाविष्टत्वं जातेः। तद्धि द्रव्ये, न जातौ। अतद्रूपत्वाज्जातेः। न दोषः। तदतद्रूपत्वाज्जातेः। कथं तदतद्रूपत्वं जातेः। तद्धि जैमिनीया जानन्ति। वयं तु लक्ष्यसिद्धौ सिद्धपरमतानुवादिनः। न चैवमतिप्रसङ्गः लक्ष्यानुसारित्वान्न्यायस्येति। एवमन्यापि व्यवस्थोह्या।। (*ibid*., 80-81)

The above सूत्रवृत्ति can be explained as follows: The limbs of human body such as the breasts, eyes, ears, hands and feet are generally spoken of in the dual number, e.g. the two breasts of young women. Sometimes they are referred to in the singular number also, e.g. the eye of women. Vā says that the breasts (and similar other limbs of human body) belong to जाति, class, possessed of duality. This position is objectionable because class and duality to not go together. In fact duality belongs to a substance and not to a class. Vā replies to this objection arguing that the जाति is both द्रव्य and अद्रव्य at one and the same time. The मीमांसक knows why and how this is possible and Vā simply follows the मीमांसक to prove his viewpoint. Thus वामन has borrowed a principle from another शास्त्र to substantiate his own line of thinking.

We now pass on to the next type of व्याख्या।

10. On some occasions a शास्त्रकार intensely feels a need to explain the purpose or secret of the use of certain words or expressions in a *sūtra*. The *vyākhyā* he composes on such occasions is known as प्रयोजनव्याख्या[14] There are about ten instance of this type of व्याख्या. Let us discuss three important ones and only refer to the rest.

10.1 *Sūtra*: शास्त्रतस्ते।

Vṛtti: ते दोषगुणालंकारहानादाने शास्त्रादस्मात्। शास्त्रतो हि ज्ञात्वा दोषाञ्जह्यात् गुणालंकारांश्चाददीत। (*ibid*., 2)

Vā advises the would-be poets to learn the काव्यालङ्कारशास्त्र to be able to understand the nature of दोषs and गुणालङ्कारs, the former to be avoided and the latter to be adopted. Vā, however, extends this piece of advice to great poets, saying.

तस्मात्कीर्तिमुपादातुमकीर्तिं तु निबर्हितुम्।
काव्यालंकारशास्त्रार्थः प्रसाद्यः कविपुंगवैः॥ (*ibid.*, 3)

i.e. It is for the purpose of gaining name and fame and shunning disrepute that the great poets should seek the favour of the काव्यालङ्कारशास्त्र. In other words, the great poets should diligently study the science of poetics. Thus Vā explains the purpose of studying the काव्यालङ्कारशास्त्र both by the would-be poets as also by the great poets. It is intersting to note that the above piece of advice is immediately followed by the discussion on who are entitled to learn the above *śāstra*. Thus Vā has established a link between the preceding and the immediately following topics.

10.2 *Sūtra*: काव्यं गद्यं पद्यं च॥

Vṛtti: गद्यस्य पूर्वं निर्देशो दुर्लक्ष्यविषयत्वेन दुर्बन्धत्वात्। यथाहुः-'गद्यं कवीनां निकषं वदन्ति'। (*ibid.*, 13)

Here Vā assigns reason for his mentioning prose first. According to him, the subjects of prose compositions are noticeable with difficulty and the prose difficult to write. There is a saying that the prose is the touchstone of poets. It is because of these reasons that he has mentioned गद्य and पद्य in that order.

10.3 *Sūtra*: सादृश्याल्लक्षणा वक्रोक्तिः।

Vṛtti: बहूनि हि निबन्धनानि लक्षणायाम्। तत्र सादृश्याल्लक्षणा वक्रोक्तिरसाविति। यथा.........इत्येवमादिषु लक्षणार्थो निरूप्यत इति। लक्षणायां च झटित्यर्थप्रतिपत्ति-क्षमत्वं रहस्यमाचक्षत इति। (*ibid.*, 66)

The last sentence in this *vṛtti* is important in that it speaks of the 'secret' of लक्षणा-indication, namely, that it helps us to understand the sense of the poetic passage quickly.

10.4 The rest of the instances of this type of व्याख्या can be jotted down as under:

(i) शब्दस्मृतेर्व्याकरणाच्छब्दानां शुद्धिः साधुत्वनिश्चयः कर्तव्यः। शुद्धानि हि पदानि निःशङ्कैः कविभिः प्रयुज्यन्ते (*ibid.*, 9)

(ii) पदं हि रचनाप्रवेशयोग्यं भावयन्संदिग्धार्थत्वेन न गृह्णीयान्न वा जह्यादिति काव्यबन्धविघ्नः। तस्मादभिधानकोषतः पदार्थनिश्चयः कर्तव्य इति। (*ibid.*,)

(iii) काव्याभ्यासादवृत्तसंक्रातिर्भवत्येव। किं तु मात्रावृत्तादिषु क्वचित्संशयः स्यात्। अतो वृत्त-संशयच्छेदश्छन्दोविचितेर्विधेय इति। (*ibid.*, 10)

(iv) कामोपचारस्य संवित्कामशास्त्रतः इति। कामोपचारबहुलं हि वस्तु काव्यस्येति। (*ibid*., 11)

(v) दण्डनीतेरर्थशास्त्रान्नयस्यापनयस्य च संविदिति। ....नहि तावविज्ञाय नायकप्रतिनायकयोर्वृत्तं शक्यं काव्ये निबद्धुमिति। (*ibid*.,)

(vi) काव्यशरीरे स्थापिते काव्यसौंदर्याक्षेपहेतवस्त्यागाय दोषा विज्ञातव्या इति दोषदर्शनं नाम अधिकरणं आरभ्यते। (*ibid*., 16)

(vii) गुणस्वरूपनिरूपणात्तेषां दोषाणामर्थादवगमोऽर्थसिद्धिः। किमर्थं ते पृथक् प्रपञ्च्यन्त इत्याह–सौकर्यार्थं प्रपञ्चो विस्तारो दोषाणाम्। उद्दिष्टलक्षणा हि दोषाः सुज्ञाता भवन्ति। (*ibid*.,)

(viii) एते च अलंकाराः शुद्धा मिश्राश्च प्रयोक्तव्या इति विशिष्टानामलंकाराणां मिश्रत्वं संसृष्टिरित्याह (*ibid*., 75)

With this we pass on to the next व्याख्या type.

11. *Anulomavyākhyā*

When a शास्त्रकार is found to be discussing various points or topics in the same order in which they are mentioned in the *sūtras,* then, he is said to be writing an अनुलोमव्याख्या. Vā is a very disciplined शास्त्रकार. Never does he disturb the serial order of the mention of items in their actual treatment. Like all other शास्त्रकारs he first mentions the items to be discussed in brief (this brief mention of items is called उद्देश[१६]) and thereafter considers them all one by one in the same order. For example:

11.1 *Sūtra*: लोको विद्या प्रकीर्णं च काव्याङ्गानि।।

Vṛtti: उद्देशक्रमेणैतद्व्याचष्टे (*ibid*., 9)

11.2 *Sūtra*: दुष्टं पदमसाधु कष्टं ग्राम्यमप्रतीतमनर्थकं च।।

Vṛtti: क्रमेण व्याख्यातुमाह (*ibid*., 16)

Similar expressions are found as under:

एषां क्रमेण लक्षणान्याह–(*ibid*,. 18) क्रमेण व्याचष्टे (*ibid*., 22) क्रमेण व्याख्यातुमाह (*ibid*., 25) तान् क्रमेण व्याख्यातुमाह (*ibid*., 57).

11.3 As stated at 2-2 above, Vā has conceived the serial order of all the topics and subjects in the head before actually discussing them in so many words. Accordingly he finishes the consideration of the सन्देह अर्थालङ्कार then says:

संदेहवद् विरोधोऽपि प्राप्तावसर: इत्याह–(*ibid.* 68)

In short, *KP* is a fine illustration of अनुलोमव्याख्या.

We new take up the next व्याख्या type for discussion.

12. In the case of *KP* the सूत्रकार and the वृत्तिकार are same. But when the वृत्तिकार is someone else than the सूत्रकार the former sometimes chooses to heigher the purport of the *sūtra*, brings its importance to the fore and throws light on the सूत्रार्थ from all angles. Such a *vṛtti* is called ध्वजव्याख्या *KP* has at least five noteworthy instance of this व्याख्या।

12.1 Vā mentions three रीतिs, वैदर्भी, गौडीया and पाञ्चाली (*ibid.*, 4). He has all praise for the first one and devotes as many as eight *sūtras* to describe it approvingly. The contents of these *sūtras* and the *vṛtti* thereon can be summarized as under:

Of the three रीतिs mentioned above वैदर्भी is the most enjoyable because it has all the ten *guṇas* in it. If anybody wants to gain proficiency in it, he/she should try to cultivate it. To practise गौडीया and पाञ्चाली in order to get command of वैदर्भी is indeed an exercise in futility. You can never acquire the skill in weaving a silken garment by trying to weave a gunnybag cloth. That form of वैदर्भी which is devoid of compounds is called शुद्धवैदर्भी. Even the slightest meaning expressed through the वैदर्भीरीति becomes enjoyable. The rich quantity of meaning expressed in वैदर्भी is also named वैदर्भी in a secondary sense (*ibid.*, pp. 4.9).

12.2 Vā does consider एकार्थ, repetition to be a वाक्यदोष. But holds at the same time that when the speaker or writer desires to express some special meaning, एकार्थ ceases to be a दोष (न, विशेषश्चेत्) (*ibid.*, 25). These exceptions are six in number, namely, (i) प्रतिपत्ति:, (ii) सन्निधि:, (iii) शुद्धि:, (iv) उत्कर्ष:, (v) ताद्रूप्यं and (vi) विशेषणम (*ibid.*, 26-27). Let us consider a couple of them. (iii) शुद्धि: In the expression मुक्ताहार the word मुक्ता is redundant because its meaning already stands expressed by the word मुक्ताहार (= a neclace of pearls). But the poet who uses both the above words intends to convey the idea that the neckhace is studded with the purest and unmixed pearls. In view of this intention, the use of the word मुक्ता does not become repetivtive.

(iv) उत्कर्ष:–In the compound पुष्पमाला, the word पुष्प may appear to be superfluous because the word माला itself means a garland of flowers. But the speaker or writer wants to convey that only the excellent flowers are strung together to make the garland. This motive saves the word पुष्प from becoming redundant. Vā's discussion of the above six exceptions to the एकार्थ has lent fullness to the topic besides rendering it readable and interesting.

12.3 *KP* on the undernoted *sūtras* also shines out as commendable instances of वैदर्भीरीति

(i) संदर्भेषु दशरूपकं श्रेय:। (*ibid.*, 15)

(ii) काव्यशोभाया: कर्तारो धर्मा गुणा:। (*ibid.*, 31)

(iii) भङ्गादुत्कर्ष:। (*ibid.*, 50)

We now take into account the next type of व्याख्या:

13. Instructive and Demonstrative

The notion that the art of poetry is to be practised and cultivated is always there in Vā's mind while he writes the *vṛtti*. He, therefore, guides the would-be poets as well as the readers in respect of certain काव्यधर्मs. His *vṛtti* at such places is noticeably instructive and demonstrative. For example:

13.1 After having defined and illustrated (with the श्लोकार्ध अस्त्युत्तरस्यां etc.,) the बन्धगुण श्लेष, Vā demonstrates how to bring out this poetic quality in the passages which lack it, as under:

	Absence of मसृणत्व (=श्लेष)	Transformation to achieve मसृणत्व (=श्लेष)
(i)	सूत्रं ब्राह्मं उर:स्थले	ब्राह्मं सूत्रं उर:स्थले
(ii)	भ्रमरीवल्गुगीतय:	भ्रमरी मञ्जुगीतय:
(iii)	तडित्कलिलमाकाशम्	तडिज्जटिलमाकाशम् (*ibid.*, 34)

13.2 Vā adopts the same procedure while dealing with समता अर्थगुण। After quoting the verse च्युतसुमनस्य: कुन्दा....etc. he observes ऋतुसन्धिप्रतिपादनपरेऽत्र द्वितीये पादे क्रमभेदो मलयमारुतामसाधारणत्वात्। and suggests in the following *vṛtti* the remedial measure:

एवं तु द्वितीयः पाठः पठितव्यः। मनसि च गिरं बध्नन्तीमे किरन्ति न कोकिलाः इति। (*ibid.*, 42)

13.3 While discussing समता शब्दगुण he quotes the passage अस्त्युत्तरस्यां.....etc. and immediately thereafter he reproduces the verse प्रसीद चण्डि etc. to show what is contrary to समता (*ibid.*, 34).

He adopts the same style in the consideration of the माधुर्य (*ibid.*, 36), सौकुमार्य (ibid.,37) उदारता (*ibid*) and the शब्दगुण-अर्थगुण उदारता (ibid., 45). With respect to अर्थगुण प्रसाद he quotes the विपर्ययरूप line : उपास्तां हस्तो मे विमलमणिकाञ्चीपदमिदम्। (*ibid.*, 41) and points out that since the word काञ्चीपदम् denotes नितम्ब, the adjective विमलमणि is अप्रयोजक, redundant.

13.4 Vā quotes the stanza 'दृष्ट्वैकासनसंगते प्रियतमे....' etc. from the अमरुशतक to illustrate अर्थगुणशेष and then notes शूद्रकादिरचितेषु प्रबन्धेष्वस्य भूयान्प्रपञ्चो दृश्यते। (*ibid.*, 41) for the information of the curious readers. This also throws light on his critical reading of the classical literature.

13.5 While discussing the *sūtra* 'लिङ्गाध्याहारौ।।' (*ibid.*, 79) he quotes the stanza 'मा भवन्तमनल....' etc. and comments अत्र हि धाक्षीदित्यादीनामध्याहारोऽन्वय-प्रयुक्तः। (*ibid.*, 80). Here Vā instructs the readers to supply the implied words in the given passage, wherever necessary and then to appreciate its poetic beauty.

13.6 *KP* on the *sūtra* क्षतदृढोरसः इति न कप्। तदन्तविधिप्रतिषेधात्। (*ibid.*, 93) guides the reader through the dissolution of the compound क्षतदृढोरसः [वाक्यं त्वेवं कर्तव्यम् क्षतं दृढोरो येषामिति। (*ibid.*,)].

Thus Vā acts in a way as the caretaker of the readers.

We now turn to the last व्याख्या type.

14. Clarification of distinctions between various काव्यधर्म.

14.1 Vā discusses as many as 29 अर्थालङ्कारs in the third अध्याय called उपमाप्रपञ्चाधिकारः of the fourth अधिकरण named आलङ्कारिक. The said अध्याय is remarkable in that it draws distinctions between various pairs of अर्थालङ्कारs thereby facilitating their understanding by the readers. He introduces the very first अर्थालंकार, प्रतिवस्तु, saying: वाक्यार्थोपमायाः प्रतिवस्तुनो भेदं दर्शयितुमाह–(*ibid.*, 62)

Here he differentiates प्रतिवस्तु (उपमा) from वाक्यार्थोपमा which has been discussed earlier (*ibid.*, 55). We find similar expressions at the beginning of almost every अर्थालङ्कार. For example:

(i) प्रतिवस्तुनः समासोक्तेर्भेदं दर्शयितुमाह–अनुक्तौ समासोक्तिः। (*ibid.*, 63)

(ii) समासोक्तेरप्रस्तुतप्रशंसाया भेदं दर्शयितुमाह-किंचिदुक्तावप्रस्तुतप्रशंसा। (*ibid*)

(iii) अपह्नुतिरपि ततो भिन्नेति दर्शयितुमाह-समेन वस्तुनान्यापलापोऽपह्नुतिः। (*ibid.*, 63.64)

(vi) रूपकाच्छ्लेषस्य भेदं दर्शयितुमाह-स धर्मेषु तन्त्रप्रयोगे श्लेषः। (*ibid.*, 64.65)

(v) रूपकवक्रोक्तिभ्यामुत्प्रेक्षाया भेदं दर्शयितुमाह-अतद्रूपस्यान्यथाध्यवसानमतिशयार्थ-मुत्प्रेक्षा। (*ibid.*, 67)

(vi) विरोधाद् विभावनायाः भेदं दर्शयितुमाह-क्रियाप्रतिषेधे प्रसिद्धतत्फलव्यक्तिर्विभावना। (*ibid.*, 69)

(vii) उपमेयोपमायाः क्रमो भिन्न इति दर्शयितुमाह-उपमेयोपमानानां क्रमसम्बन्धः, क्रमः। (*ibid.*,70)

Similarly he has drawn distinctions between व्यतिरेक and विशेषोक्ति (*ibid.*, 72), व्यतिरेक, विशेषोक्ति and व्याजस्तुति (*ibid.*, 73) व्याजस्तुति and व्याजोक्ति (*ibid.*,) व्याजस्तुति and तुल्ययोगिता (*ibid.*,74) and तुल्ययोगिता and सहोक्ति (*ibid.*,) In respect of the last pair he makes it pointedly clear that in सहोक्ति there is no inferiority and speciality of meaning whereas these features are found in तुल्ययोगिता।

14.2 There seems to be some difference of opinion about naming certain अर्थालङ्कारs Vā deals with this topic assertively and negates the opponent's claims. For example

(i) In अपह्नुति the identity is between the meanings of two sentences whereas in रूपक the indentity is between two things. In view of this अपह्नुति cannot be called रूपक, argues Vā (*ibid.*, 64).

(ii) In the compound मुखचन्द्र and the like, there is उपमा and not रूपक (समासान्न च चन्द्रादीनां रूपकत्वं युक्तमिति।) (*ibid.*)

(iii) Some शास्त्रकारs feel that निदर्शन is अर्थान्तरन्यास. Vā does not subscribe to this views. He says इदं च नार्थान्तरन्यासः। स ह्यन्यथाभूतः। तमाह (*ibid.*,71)

14.3 He points out the similarity between उत्प्रेक्षा and सन्देह that while उत्प्रेक्षा is of the nature of भ्रान्तिज्ञान, सन्देह is of the nature of संशयज्ञान (यथा भ्रान्ति-ज्ञानस्वरूपोत्प्रेक्षा तथा संशयज्ञानस्वरूप: संदेहोऽपीति दर्शयितुमाह–(*ibid.*, 68)

Thus Vā wants to make it clear to his readers that although उपमा is at the root of all अर्थालङ्कारs there are certain subtle and positive differences between the various pairs of them. He makes these differences clear and sharper by dealing with each individual pair separately for the benefit of his readers. He is also very careful in showing similiarities between different pairs of अलङ्कारs where they occur. In fine, he tries to make his व्याख्या complete in itself and also helpful to his reader.

To sum up

Vā's KP is a trim and tidy piece of scientific writing. It is generally commendably brief but does not deny to be elaborate on demand. In it there is 'not a word more, not a shade less.' It leaves no word, no statement or no concept unexplained and unclear. It is a neat, brilliant, scholarly and instructive exposition of Vā's views and specially the theory of *rīti*. Remarkably, it guides both the budding poets and also the curious readers. It encloses Vā's views ably, fully and firmly.

REFERENCES AND NOTES

1. c. 800 AD vide P.V. Kane, *History of Sanskrit Poetics*, third revised edition, Delhi, Motilal Banarsidass, 1961, pp. 146-47.
2. पण्डितवरश्रीवामनविरचिता काव्यालंकारसूत्रवृत्ति: (कामधेनुटिप्पणीसहिता), ed. Narayan Nathaji Kulkarni, Poona, Oriental Book Agency, 1927.
3. The two shortest *sūtras* are कलाशास्त्रेभ्य: (Kl. p. 10) and अरूढार्थत्वात् (*ibid.*, 21) and the longest one is ओज: प्रसाद श्लेषसमतासमाधिमाधुर्यसौकुमार्योदारताऽर्थव्यक्तिकान्तयो बन्धगुणा:। (*ibid.*, 32).
4. प्रणम्य परमं ज्योतिर्वामनेन कविप्रिया।
काव्यालंकारसूत्राणां स्वेषां वृत्तिर्विधीयते।। (*ibid.*, 1)
5. The summary type श्लोकs appear on pages 2, 3, 5, 6, 12, 15, 20, 32, 33, 37-38, 47, 51-52 of Kl.
6. 'सङ्क्षेपतया सूत्ररूपेण अध्यायादीनां व्याख्या।' vide Vaidyanatha Neelamegha, *Tantrayuktivichara*, ed. N.E. Muthuswami, second revisd edition, Trivandrum, Government of Kerala, 1976, p. XIII.
7. 'यत्पदानां छेदं कृत्वा उच्चारणम्।' (*ibid.*,)
8. 'पदार्थव्याख्या नाम-तेषामेव पदानां विवरणम्।' (*ibid.*,)
9. 'यद्वस्तुकृतमारभ्य तदनुषङ्गेण व्याख्यानमारभ्यते।' (*ibid.*)
10. 'यस्मिन्नर्थे सूत्रे वा प्रकृतेनाप्रकृतं साध्यते।' (*ibid.*, p. XIV)
11. 'यत्र लेशत उक्तानामविस्पष्टानां प्रकरणे सूत्रे वा अर्थानां यत्नत: उद्भावनं क्रियते। (ibid.)

12. 'यत्र वस्तुनि बहुषु अनिश्चितार्थेषु एकीयमतेषु प्रस्तुतेषु वस्तुसारभूतं स्वमतं स्वमर्थमुपनिक्षिप्य एकीयमतानि तस्मिन्नेव स्वमतेऽन्तर्भावं नयति। (*ibid.*)
13. 'यस्मिन्नधिकारे वर्तमाने तेनाधिकरणार्थेन सहितं सम्बन्धमभिवीक्ष्यान्यस्यार्थो विनिक्षेप्यते।। (*ibid.*)
14. 'यत्सूत्रमभिधीयमानं स्वार्थस्य निष्पत्तौ निमित्तभावमुपैति। (*ibid.*, XV)
15. 'यत्क्रमात् सूत्रं आरब्धं तत्क्रमेण पुनस्तथा।
    अभिधा सा अनुलोमाख्या व्याख्या पूर्वैरुदीरिता।।' (*ibid.*, viii)
16. 'उद्देशो नाम यत्रार्थानां शब्दमात्रेणैव कीर्तनमुद्देश:।' (*ibid.*, II)
17. 'उन्नतत्वं महत्त्वं च ध्वजशब्दात् प्रतीयते।
    सर्वप्रकाशनं यत्र ध्वजव्याख्या हि सा स्मृता।। (*ibid.*, viii)

V.3

"सरस्वत्यास्तत्त्वं कविसहृदयाख्यं विजयते।"

CONTRIBUTION OF HEMACANDRA WITH SPECIAL REFERENCE TO SOME ART-FORMS DISCUSSED IN THE KĀVYĀNUŚĀSANA (KS)

Tapasvi Nandi

Ācārya Hemacandra (H) was a great grammarian, philosopher, poet, a writer on literary criticism and aesthetics, and above all a great *yogī*.

We will concern ourselves here only with his contribution, and through him with the contribution of Gujarat, in the field of aesthetics, particularly with reference to the art-forms presented on the stage. It may be noted that a number of writers took interest in this branch, concerning themselves both with the theory as well as practice of drama in general and minor art-forms in particular, thereby enriching the contribution of Gujarat. We will limit our interest for the present to only H., particularly the minor art-forms only as discussed by him in his *Kāvyānuśāsana* (K.S.). All our references to this excellent work on poetics will be drawn from (i) Śrī Mahāvīra Jain Vidyālaya, Bombay 64 (second Edn.) publication of the Ks., with editors Prof. R. C. Parikh and Prof. Dr. V. M. Kullkarni., and (ii) Ācārya H.'s KS.-edn. Dr. Tapasvi Nandi, pub. The L.D. Institute of Indology, Ahd. 2000 A.D.

It may be noted that H., in his KS. VIII discusses various art-forms when he gives the classification of poetry. Over and above discussing the various literary forms, he takes up dramatic forms as well. We will later see the logic behing this. But, it may be noted, that while dealing with the dramatic forms consisting primarily of the ten types of drama, he picks up minor-art forms, the *upa-rūpakas* also and goes into a greater analysis and discussion about the same in his *'Viveka'*, a very learned commentary written by him, on his own KS. At the outset it has to be made clear that he inherited a rich heritage from his earlier masters such as Bharata, Abhinavagupta and his predecessors such as Kohala and the like, Dhanañjaya and Dhanika and especially Bhoja, the last three from Mālavā, the rest representatives of the Kashmir school of thought. As rightly observed by Śrī Kireet Joshi, Gujarat is a land of harmony and H. has successfully tried to strike a balance between the Kashmir school of thought and what we designate as the Mālavā school of thought, even in the field of literary criticism and art-criticism, in short, aesthetics in general.

We will now turn to H. In his KS. VIII i, H. divides *Kāvya,* first into *Prekṣya* and *Śravya*. The former is *'Abhineya'* and the latter is *'an-abhineya. Prekṣya* is further subdivided (K.S. VIII.2) into *'Pāṭhya'* and *'Geya'. Pāṭhya* (KS. VIII. 3.) consists of the ten major types of *rūpakas* such as *Nāṭaka*, *Prakaraṇa,* etc., to which are added *Nāṭikā* and *Saṭṭaka.* The definitions read in H. are accepted from Bharata. But for *Saṭṭaka,* not read in Bharata, H. relies on the ŚṛPra. (i.e. *Śṛṅgāra-prakāśa*) of Bhoja (ch XI. Śr. pra.) We will not discuss the classical art-forms such as the ten or twelve major varieties of *rūpaka* here, but we will concern ourselves here only with what are termed the *upa-rūpakas* or minor art-forms which perhaps had the same antiquity with popular base. This means that these art-forms were as old as the classical major art-forms and were parallel in their origin, but had a regional, popular, folk-based colouring about them. We may call them folk-art forms as against the classical art-forms. These were many and through various sources they are counted as many as 45+, if we take them separately by their names. May be, at times, different authorities give different names to one and the same art-form, or, in other case, same name is given to virtually different art-forms also. So, H. at K.S. VIII. 4 further classifies the *'geya'* i.e. *upa-rūpaka* into twelve art-forms, which are all basically *'prekṣya'*, i.e. to be viewed on the stage, *the varieties of performing art in general.* The basic difference between the ten major classical forms of drama and these *upa-rūpakas* is that the former have *'abhinaya' or* 'acting' as their soul, while the latter have a lot of dance and music or primarily dance as their soul. Thus, at KS. VIII.4., H. enumerates (i) *ḍombikā* (ii) *bhāṇa* (iii) *prasthāna* (iv) śiṅgaka (v) *bhāṇikā* (vi) preraṇa (vii) rāmākrīḍa (viii) hallīsaka (ix) rāsaka (x) goṣṭhī (xi) śrīgadita and (xii) *rāgakāvya.*

For the definitions of *goṣṭhī, kāvya* and *śrīgadita* H. seems to have derived inspiration from Bhoja, and for the rest H. accepts the definitions as given by the "*cirantanas*" i.e. the ancients as quoted in the *Abhinavabhāratī* (A.bh., pp. 179, vol. I. gos. Edn. NS. ch. IV; Edn. K. Krishnamoorthy, '92, Vadodara, 0.I.) Before we examine these definitions of various art-forms, it may be noted that H., accepting

Bhoja's terminology, calls them "*padārthābhinaya-svabhāvāni*". H. (KS. VIII, 4, pp. 445, *ibid*) takes up "*ḍombikā*" first for treatment. Bhoja bearly mentions "*ḍombalikā*" and treats it very briefly under *Śabdālaṃkāra prekṣya*" (ch. X. Śr.pra. pp. 381, Edn Josyer).

KS. VIII. 4 talks of the '*geya*" art-forms such as—

"*geyaṃ ḍombikā-bhāṇa-prasthāna-śirigaka-bhāṇikā-preraṇa-rāmākrīḍa-hallīsaka-rāsaka-goṣṭhi-śrīgadita-kāvyādi.*" (pp. 445, *ibid.*)

H. Observes: "*Padārthābhinaya-svabhāvāni ḍombikādīni geyāni rūpakāṇi cirantanair uktāni. tad yathā-*

59. "*channānurāga-garbhābhir*
uktibhir yatra bhupateḥ
āvarjyate manaḥ sā tu
masṛṇā ḍombikā matā"

60. *nṛsiṃha-sūkarādīnāṃ*
varṇanaṃ jalpayed yataḥ,
nartakī tena bhāṇaḥ syād
uddhatāṅga-pravartitaḥ,

61. *gajādīnāṃ gatiṃ tulyāṃ*
kṛtvā pravasanaṃ tathā,
alpāviddhaṃ su-masṛṇaṃ
tat prasthānam pracakṣate.

62. *sakhyāḥ samakṣaṃ patyuryad*
uddhataṃ vṛttam ucyate,
masṛṇaṃ ca kvacid dhūrta-
caritaṃ śiṅgakastu saḥ.

63. *bālakrīḍā-niyuddhādi*
tathā sūkarasiṃhajā,
dhavalādi-kṛtā krīḍā
yatra sā bhāṇikā matā

64. *hāsyaprāyaṃ preraṇaṃ tu*
syāt prahelikayā'nvitam,

65. *ṛtu-varṇana-saṃyuktaṃ*
rāmākrīḍam tu bhāṣyate

66 *maṇḍalena tu yan nṛttam*
hallīsakam iti smṛtam,
ekas tatra tu netā syād
gopa-strīṇām yathā hariḥ

67 *aneka-nartakī-yojyaṃ*
citra-tālalayāśrayam,
ā catuḥṣaṣṭi-yugalād
rāsakaṃ masṛṇoddhatam.

68. *goṣṭhe yatra viharataś*
ceṣṭitam iha kaiṭabhadviṣaḥ kiñcit
riṣṭāsūra-mathana-prabhṛti
tad icchanti goṣṭhīti.

69 *yasmin kulāṅganā patyuḥ*
sakhyagre varṇayed guṇān
upālaṃbhaṃ ca kurute
geye śrīgaditaṃ tu tat.

70. *layāntara-prayogeṇa*
rāgaiścāpi vicitritam,
nānā-rasaṃ sunirvāhya-
kathaṃ kāvyam iti smṛtam.

[11/8 *ādi-grahaṇāt śampā-cchalita-dvipadyādi-parigrahaḥ prapañcas tu brahma-bharata-kohalādi-śāstrebhyaḥ avagantavyaḥ* (pp. 449, *ibid.*).]

Thus H. knows śampā, *chalita* and *dvipadī* from other sources going with the authorship of Brahma-bharata, Kohala and the rest.

He must have known all other minor art forms known through A.bh., Ś.pra, *Daśa-rūpaka-avaloka* (DR-A), etc. But he chooses to concentrate more on the twelve as noted above perhaps because they were more popular in the region of Gujarat in his days.

In his *Viveka*, H. further elaborates on the nature of these *uparūpakas* which are primarily defined after, as noted above., the '*cirantanas' as quoted in the A.bh.,* and also after Bhoja. While elaborating on the nature of these in his *Viveka,* H. follows the lead of the A.bh. H. has accepted Abhinavagupta's observations which are read at different places, but, H. has woven together and created a clean statement. We feel that the editor of the A. bh. (Vol. I. ch. IV. Dr. Krishnamoorthy) should have looked into H.'s *Viveka* carefully. Even Dr. K. Krishnamoorthy has not done it to our satisfaction. Our *gurus* Dr. Kulkarni and Prof. Parikh have also left the task of critically comparing the relevant portions from the A.bh. and *Viveka*, to posterity. We promise to do it on some other occasion. But for the present we will proceed with H., on *ḍombikā* and other art-forms as read in his *Viveka*. One thing for sure is that at least Dr. Raghavan has certainly not looked into H. and his *Viveka* carefully. When Dr. Raghavan observes that Ṣidgaka of Abhinavagupta could be

Śrīgadita of Bhoja, he seems to be quite off the mark. Actually Ṣiḍgaka of the A.bh. is read as *Śiṅgaka* or *Śiṅgaṭaka* by H. (pp. 446, *ibid*). This Ṣiḍgaka of A.bh. is the same as Śiṅgaka or Śiṅgaṭaka of H. and is certainly not the *Śrīgadita* of Bhoja as Dr. Raghavan observes (pp. 569, Bhoja's Śr:pra. by Raghavan). The picture that emerges clearly is that Dr. Raghavan has not paid due attention to H. like both Dr. Kane and Dr. De., and this is very very very sad. In his *Viveka,* of course, accepting the lead of the *A. bh.,* H. has accepted quite often words, phrases and sentences from the great Abhinavatupta, but H. has managed to evolve a much clearer design, not seen in the A. bh. clearly.

H. explains as follows:— The province of *geya-kāvya* is threefold such as the *masṛṇa* or graceful, the *uddhata* or forceful and *miśra* or mixed. In the artform such as the *ḍombikās* which are primarily promoted to flatter a king, the form is graceful. In *bhāṇakas* such as in the description of the behaviour of Nṛsiṃha, etc., the form is only forceful. That even in pure graceful, there is some element of forceful, is appropriate. Here, the difference is based on the proportion of forceful or graceful pattern. There is a higher or lower degree of either in the artistic mixture. The first type, i.e. that in which the *masṛṇa* is seen in higher degree as compared to the forceful, is seen in *Śiṅgaṭaka*. When forceful is predominant and the graceful is mixed in a lower degree, we get *bhāṇikā*. The other varieties of *geya-kāvya* such as *preraṇa*, rāmākīḍa, *rāsaka, hallīsaka,* etc. are graced with the mixture of these two in a higher or lower degree.

A *prima facie* view is now considered. The objection is that in cases of *ḍombikā, Śiṅgaṭaka,* etc., the statements or utterances are found not to be relevant with one another. Now, in this case, how can these art forms be pleasing to the taste? The answer is, 'No.' H. says that in prayers to the deities which are conceived either as males or females, *Śṛṅgāra* is said to be delineated every where. But we do not find any contradiction here. Same is the case with these art-forms which carry only apparent contradiction. We may observe here that words read in the *Viveka* are from the A.bh (pp. 171, Ns. IV. GOS, *ibid.*) H. quotes directly from the A. bh. and observes that the description in male or female form depends on the prayer to the diety concerned. It is, therefore, that in *Cūḍāmaṇi-ḍombikā* we read, "*he devi ḍombi*," etc.

In such art forms as *rāga-kāvyas* e.g. the *Rāghava-vijaya*, there is a message of the fourfold aims of life i.e. *caturvargopadeśa*. Actually, H. defined '*Kāvya'* but there the term used is '*rāga-kāvya*' as read in the A.bh. After A.bh., again, H. suggests that in *ḍombikā* and the rest the prominent emotion is that of clandestine love. Once again, H., quoting from the A.bh. (pp. 172, *ibid*), observes that in case of such art-forms as *Bhāṇa, Preraṇa, Bhāṇikā*, etc., the theme in the nature of parables and fables, *anyāpadeśa arthāntaranyāsa,* and *nidarśanā* (in the A.bh., we read *dṛṣṭānta* for *nidarśanā),* including advice to men through description of the acts of wild animals, and all this-is something like a bit of the *Pañca-tantra*, cast in a semi-dramatic form. We may observe that H. chooses to follow Abhinavagupta in suggesting the nature of *bhāṇa* to be didactic as against Bhoja's *bhāṇa,* which is devotional and it extols gods.

After this observation, H. discusses the difference between *pāṭhya-rūpaka* and *geya* (*upa-rūpaka).* He suggests that in '*pāṭhya'* variety, (i.e. in the major ten *rūpakas*), both '*aṅga*' i.e. movement of limbs and '*gīta*' are not fixed or certain. This means that in these drama-forms, to dance with movement of limbs is not obligatory. '*Kara*', '*karaṇa*', '*cārī*', '*maṇḍala*', etc. which are useful for '*aṅga*', are uncertain in nature because of irregualr rhythm, in case of *rūpakas*. These are practised with the dominance of *rasa* in focus, and hence this uncertainty in *rūpakas*. But, observes H., in *geya* (*upa-rūpakas*) movement of limbs i.e. *aṅga* and *gīta* i.e.song, are of fixed nature in themselves. This means that as in case of a '*mantra*' or charm, there is no change of letters, similarly here, in case of these minor art-forms, the pattern of *laya* (rhythm), *yati* (stop), etc. is fixed as per the special type of art-form concerned. Of course, at times, *aṅga* (or movement of limbs) is predominant as in '*prasthāna',* or at times *vāda*/speech is central as in *bhāṇaka*¸ when there is practice of *bhagna-tāla* or *parikramaṇa*. Or, as in case of *Śiṅgaṭaka*, we have predominance of the narration which is presented through song (*gīyamāna-rūpakābhidheya-prādhānyam)*. At times, the *nṛtta* (i.e. dance form with limb-movement as principal and not an emotion), is chief, as in case of *ḍombilikā* presentation. Because of this variety, such performance is termed '*Valli-mārga* i.e. a street-performance with variety, in common parlance. But with all this, one point emerges and that is that '*geya*' is qualified chiefly by the playing of instruments along with songs. In case of *Rāga-kāvyas* the presentation is mainly through song alone. For example, '*Rāghava-vijaya'* (which is a *rāga-kāvya*) is sung only *in ḍhakkā-rāga'* alone, and '*Mārīca-vadha*' in the *grāma-rāga* called '*kakubha*'. Here it may be noted that H. has overlooked one remark from the A. bh. wherein it is stated that though the *rasas* and situations differ, the tune or rhythm and the time-measure (*laya/tāla*) do not change in a *rāga-kāvya* as in drama proper.

In *Pāṭhya* i.e. drama proper, observes H. for bringing about a feeling of direct experience, the fixation of the use of language or dialect, with reference to a given character, the use of metre and figures of speech, etc., are fixed. Now that which is sung (=*gīyamāna*) (as in the *upa-rūpaka*) is not always presented through acting, for fear of non-congruousness. But here (in *uparūpakas*) some *sāttvika* form of acting, which is meant for conveying this or that meaning along with a certain tune/

rhythm and time-measure, is interwoven, in view of the predominant *rasa*. The intended object is filled in with the help of *'dhruvā-gīta'* here. As the cooks add required ingredients in the item under preparation, so in *geya* form also some such element (of acting) is added. But in such art-forms as *ḍombikā* and the rest, there is no presentation as in case of an actor of *rūpa, i.e.* of the form of character such as Rāma, Duṣyanta etc. which is of an extra-ordinary nature.

In *ḍombikā* and the rest, the beauty of letters seen in the use of special letters, is principal, and there is no possibility at all of acting here, as it is primarily of the form of *nṛtta* or limb-movements. In *ḍombikā,* the lady dancer speaks some sentence of common usage, and when her speech is presented in form of a song, how can there be an experience of direct-feeling (*kaḥ sā*kṣātkāra-*kalpārthaḥ*? pp 448, *ibid*). On the other hand, an experience such as direct, is the main object in *pāṭhya* variety. So, what happens in *ḍombikā* or *kāvya (i.e. rāga-kāvya)* art-forms is like a local dance or song performance that carries away the heart of people through the device of giving an advice indirectly, or by suggesting an idea through some means.

In illustrations such as "*heṭṭhe viḍombī,*" etc. there is an effort to please a king in a *ḍombikā-prayoga,* through a song or playing of instrument, or dance, to convey such meaning that is cherished by the king. There is, in between, a type of presentation of the activity of a paramour, or an expert messenger etc., which pleases the mind of a prince. In the end, the performance of *ḍombikā* ends after the lady dancer making suggestive gestures to a king or prince, as if he is somebody else, cleverly acts for extracting money from him. This is seen as in *Guṇamālā ḍombikā*. All this, H. seems to accept from the A.bh. (pp. 175, *ibid.*) In *Guṇamālā*, the dancing artist gets involved in pleasing songs, suggesting, "I say this to you," etc., and tries to convey the secret love for the prince, in her own heart, and she dances in co-ordination of rhythm and time-factor (*tāla/laya*). The outward form is of course of popular dance. The dancer also exhibits such physical gestures as raising of eye-brows, horripilation, casting of glances, etc., to show that the theme of her song enters into the king's heart. Thus by principally providing entertainment through song, and presenting physical gestures that go with the same, the dancer, catching the heart of the king through dance, renders the song subservient, and presents body-movements in keeping with the emotion concerned. This *ḍombikā* art-form is not of the type of direct experience as in case of a drama. For, in this art-form, there is no concealment of the dancer's own self (i.e. *rūpaṇa,* as in case of the actor) through the medium of *āhārya abhinaya,* i.e. costumes, set-up, etc. Thus, the presentation does not carry an effect of direct experience, but the dancer presents a dance-theme, with some acting, to a near similar effect. So, there is no manifestation, as in case of a *rūpaka,* (i.e. a major type of drama) of an extra-ordinary form here. In '*geya*' variety, there is no attempt to impart advice or information (i.e. *vyutpattyanusandhānam*), but in '*pāṭhya*' variety, i.e. major *rūpaka,* proficiency is a principal goal. This is so ordained by Bharata Muni with reference to the *pāṭhya*. Here ends H.'s discussion.

H. thus discusses elaborately the different impressions created from artistic point of view, between *pāṭhya rūpakas* and *geya upa-rūpakas*. On one hand, such types as *nāṭaka* and the rest are of the form of direct exprience (=*sākṣatkārakalpa*), white *ḍombikā* and the rest do not have this strength, but through the element of dance and music, there is a chance of suggesting the inner feelings of heart, of course, to some extent only. The *Ācārya* draws from the A.bh., but makes the presentation clearer and to the point, which is not seen in Bhoja and the rest. Of course, in the DR. and the *Avaloka,* we get an idea of the difference in the arts of *nṛtya* or dance, *nṛtta* or rhythmic bodily movements and *nāṭya* or drama proper, *Nṛtta* is an art-form dependent solely on *tāla* and *laya* i.e. rhythm and time-measure, which could be compared to modern dance patterns in the west, with horizontal and vertical bodily thrusts in principal. This can be placed with 'break' or 'twist' art-forms of dance. *Nṛtya* is a classical dance-form with emotive content, such as the *Bharata-nāṭyam* and the rest. *Nāṭya* is *rasa*—oriented drama proper. It may be noted that when H. enumerates '*saṭṭakādi*' as forms of *rūpakas,* which were taken only as *upa-rūpakas* by ancients such as Kohala and the like, it is clear that these art-forms must be involving a lot of the element of acting-*abhinaya*-proper, and therefore, these must be capable of the dramatic effect. A close examination of the A.bh. suggests that the limits of *rūpakas* and *upa-rūpakas* were not water-tight, but H. has specified the basic difference in these two art-forms more clearly and candidly. One thing emerges clearly that these *up a rūpakas* were perhaps evolved as forms of folk-art and the difference in their types and their number expanded with the passage of time. That H. has accepted *ḍombikā, bhāṇa, prasthāna, śiṅgaka, bhāṇikā, preraṇa, rāmākrīḍā, hallīsaka, and rāsaka from* A.bh. and the ancients, and three-art-forms such as *goṣṭhī, śrīgadita,* and *kāvya* from Bhoja, is clear. This is true so far as the question of defining and explaining these art forms theoretically is concerned. But the fact remains that these art-forms and also perhaps some others were a living tradition so far as folk-art was concerned in Gujarat of H.'s times. Not only poets wrote such scripts but artists of performing arts presented them on stage before spectators. Bhoja also derived inspiration from both Abhinavagupta and also ancients like Kohala. An interaction beween Mālavā and Gujarat also can be imagined in the field of folk-art. Bhoja mentions twelve *uparūpakas* such as *śrīgadita, durmilikā, prasthāna, kāvya* (i.e. *citra-kāvya*), *bhāṇa* (which is three-fold; *śuddha, citra* and *saṅkīrṇa*), *bhāṇikā, goṣṭhī, hallīsaka, nartanaka, preṅkhaṇaka, rāsaka* and *nāṭya-rāsaka* (also called '*carcarī*').

If we accept difference in an art-form going by difference in name given to the same, though of course in a single name also we come across difference in definition and concept by different authorities, we can count in H. such art-forms as additional ones e.g. *ḍombikā, śiṅgaka, preraṇa, rāmākrīda* and *(rāga) kāvya,* as compared to Bhoja. Bhoja's *durmalikā,* (*citra*) *kāvya, nartanaka, prekṣaṇaka,* and *nāṭya-rāsaka* are missing in H. *Durmilikā* seems to be a vulgar art-form, not read in A.bh., but also read later in the N.D. (=*Nāṭyadarpaṇa* of Rāmacandra and Guṇacandra, H's. pupils), and Śāradātanaya's *(Śa.) Bhāva-prakāśana* (B.P.) As '*prasthāna*' is noted in the A.bh., we read it in H. also and this art-form is true to its name because in it a lover underatkes a journey. The N.D. later, accepts the definition from Śr. fra. or Śā., *'prasthāna'* is not identical conceptually with that of either Abhinavagupta or Bhoja. We have no clue for the source of his concept.

The concept of (*citra*) *kāvya* in Bhoja is not clear and it has contents of magic. We read notations of *rāga, tāla* and choreography, but the meaning is not clear to us. In *upa-rūpaka* called '*kāvya'* there is one *rāga,* in *citra-kāvya,* however, there are many *rāgas*. Bhoja has an elaborate discussion on *Bhāṇa*, which is accepted by Śā. who places it in *anuṣṭubh* verses. For him, as in *Bhāṇa,* so also in *Bhāṇikā, lāsyāṅgas* are presented. For Bhoja, '*nartanaka*' is four-fold such as *śamyā, lāsya, chalika* and *dvipadī*. Bhoja, while discussing *śabdālaṃkāras*, mentions six-fold *prekṣyālaṅkāra* such as *tāṇḍava, lāsya, chalika, sampā (=śamyā), hallīsaka* and *rāsa*.

Bhoja has '*prekṣaṇa*' also, which is missing in the A.bh., and H. Śā. presents it in a clumsy way. *Nāṭya-rāsaka* is also not read in H. but is seen in Bhoja, the N.D., and Śā. Thus, so far as minor art-forms i.e. *upa-rūpakas* go, H. mainly accepts the lead of A.bh., and then Bhoja. Whatever it may be but a vast storehouse of literature and a rich heritage of performaing arts are both reflected in the works of Bhoja and H., who suggest and discuss theoretically the pleasing aspects of the living tradition of folk-art as prevelant in those days in Mālavā and Gujarat, suggesting of course, a harmonious blending of traditions, an interaction of regional culture.

V.4

RASA AND ITS INFINITE TYPES —A MODERN PERSPECTIVE

Dr. R. S. Betai

We look before and after
And pine for what is not,
Our sincerest laughter
With some pain is fraught;
Our sweetest songs are those
that tell of saddest thought.
—Shelley (To a skylark)

Background-Indian Perspective :

When Ānandavardhana lays down the different types of *Dhvani,* it is clear from the whole treatment that to him *Rasadhvani* is *Dhvani* par excellence. He calls it *Asaṅlakṣyakramavyaṅgya Dhvani* because, as Abhinavagupta clarifies, the order of evolution of *Rasa* is there[1] but it is not clearly deciphered "at the time of the actual *Rasa*-experience that leads to instantaneous supreme delight.[2] The process of *Pratyāyana*-communication—is so swift and with the attention, interest and indulgence of the connoisseur by heart, the emotional experience evolves so fast that he is not conscious of the stages of evolution of *Rasa* in his heart; actually he is not expected to become conscious of it. Once the enlightened reader comes to the stage of becoming conscious of the process, he ceases to be a *Sahṛdaya* (who tastes of the nectar of *Rasa*) he becomes a critic. We can even say that this too is a *Camatkāra* of the taste of *Rasa* and the *Ānanda* born thereof that poetry yields.[2] Abhinavagupta is specific in his statement.

"Again, *Rasādidhvani* is fully systematic (in evolution); there is no *Kāvya* devoid of it. Though *Rasa* is the very life of all *Kāvya,* still, even though *Rasa* is full of *Camatkāra* itself, when just a part of it becomes inducer (of *Rasa*), the *Camatkāra* gets enhanced."[3]

Now this *Rasa* has endless types and therefore, in the enumeration of the types, it is considered to be just one. Ānanda states-

"The sub-divisions of its parts and its own sub-divisions become endless indeed if one were to take into account their mutual permutations and combinations also.[4]

In the *Vṛtti* that follows, Ānanda shows that the nine *Rasas*, their *sthāyibhāvas*, *Vibhāvas, Anubhāvas* and *Vyabhicāribhāvas* and combination of these will be the first step to know that *Rasa* can have endless types. *Rasa* is again eightfold, *Aṣṭ-amūrti* like Lord Śiva and here again countless types step in through their combinations and the permutations and combinations of their subsidiaries and so on.

Ānanda further elaborates this endlessness when he states—

"Now if the endless sub-divisions of these figures and the divisions of its intrinsic soul, viz., sentiments, abiding emotion, the semblance and cessation of these which once again become endless by contact with different *stimuli* of setting, response, and passing moods—and all the mutual relationship possible between each other amongst them be added up and reckoned, it would be clear that the entire varieties of even a single sentiment will baffle all counting not to mention the impossibility of counting all varieties of all the sentiments."[5]

One can very well guess that Ānanda and Abhinava base their concept of these types on the infinite variety of moods, situations, and so on. It is needless to count arithmatically the types as some Hindi writers do; the number of the types does not end there also. The infinite variety of human temperament with their infinite situations that lead to infinite variety of moods, conflicts and consequent emotional experience of human beings as humans have their deep impact on the evolution of *Rasa* in poetry as the subtlest of all arts. Abhinava and Ānanda know so well that *Rasa* and beauty of poetry and the consequent aesthetic experience and aesthetic delight are based in the emotional experiences of human beings. That is the reason why our critics accept that poetry is primarily based on the deep and acute emotional experiences of man and woman as human beings in life and that is the reason why the erotic, the pathetic and the heroic are the three *Rasas* that dominate much of poetry.[6] That is again the reason why Ānanda takes the erotic as the most dominant sentiment in poetry. He states—

"The poet should be very attentive in regard to that sentiment as it is more delicate than every other sentiment. As the Erotic sentiment is invariably within the experience of all persons, it is not only the most charming but also the most important sentiment.[7]

Emotional experience in human life and human relations and emotional experience of poetry that has attained the status of *Rasa*, primarily differ in one point. In poetry, at least three hearts are identified in one common experience of emotion-the reader, the character and the poet. That later on evolves as objective or universal as westerners concede, and that evolves in the connoisseur's heart as a uniquely sweet and tasty drink as Abhinava states.[8] That is the reason why Tauta states-

"In (drama and poetry, real aesthetic delight evolves through) the common emotional experience of the hero, the poet and the reader."[9]

The *Rasatva* of *Rasa*, its *Camatkāra* lies in this and it proves the truth of the famous Upaniṣadic statement—

"He is *Rasa* (incarnate). He experiences that *Rasa* and becomes completely identified in the delight that it yields to him."[10]

A Modern Perspective

As we come to the modern perspective of *Rasa* and its infinite types, we should first understand the precise meaning of the word "modern". It means that literature and those writers who are influenced by the modern philosophy, trends and the changed outlook. There can thus be poets who belong to the modern age but might not be modern, as, there could be, in rare cases, poets of old who were modern.

It is rightly opined that the seeds of modernisation were sown, for the first time almost, with the industrial revolution that at a certain stage brought in what we can call the industrial culture. As time passed, this culture became so very complex, and constantly changing that it gave birth to modern philosophy as also modern poetry.

Let us now interpret *Rasa* and its endlessness of the types in modern terminology and in modern interpretation. This will further elaborate and strengthen the views of Ānanda and Abhinava in particular and of Sanskrit poetics in general. It will bring us still nearer to the truth and secret of *Rasa* in poetry, the beauty pictured thereof and its real *camatkāra*.

It has been stated now and again that realities of life and the human experience of emotions born thereof, have a direct bearing on poetry. This is true irrespective of the constantly changing forms of poetry, the isms that evolve, the changing expectations of the readers from poetry, even the changing interest in poetry. No ism, be it idealism, realism, surrealism, existentialism, naturalism, absurd or any, can claim to be completely free from the stark realities of the life and society of the poet and their bearing on the mind of the poet and the reader. The complexity, subtelty of modern life and philosophy brought in its train complexity in poetry. Poetry becomes more confounding and difficult to grasp; much less to enjoy. Perhaps that led Virginia Woolf to state that, in modernism "all human relations have shifted-those between masters and servants, husbands and wives, parents and children. And when human relations change, there is at the same time a change in religion, conduct, poetics and literature."

Darwin and Marx had a deep impact on this fast change. As time passed, new outlook brought in new perspective of reality and it gave shocks to all. Individualism asserted itself and individualistic culture evolved. It also led to a visible, marked trend of individual's alienation from conventions.

The definitions of surrealism and absurd are a proof of this. Any ism in poetry comes from some philosophy of life current in some society or other. If we were to state that the impact of this on human mind and human emotions is reflected in the poetry of the currency of that ism, we will be very near to the truth.

In the last 200 years, the last fifty in particular, human life has moved and changed at rocket speed. The constructive and destructive effects of the inventions of atomic devices, the gigantic speed with which science and technology take strides, mechanication, the wars, the new inventions in all spheres of life, the consequent fast development of social sciences, the gigantic efforts at economic and social uplift of masses, the new education and consciousness of women, these and so many other factors have deeply influenced human values, human relations, human emotions and so on. Just like the facilities and widened knowledge of the modern days, tensions and strifes of modern life are far more acute than those experienced by our ancestors and forefathers. This has a deep influence on human emotions, and consequently the poetry that the modern man writes. As a result, the nine *Rasas* adopted by our critics of old, their *sthāyibhāvas* and also the *Vibhāvas, Anubhāvas* and *Vyabhicāribhāvas* etc. would not be enough. Even these have inherently changed and may be, they require to be newly defined. Man's nature to experience emotions and experience these deeply and acutely remains the same, but, their expressions have adopted many more types and so the *Rasa* experience has widened.

The complexity of modern life has in its strain brought complexity in poetry and in *Rasa* and its depiction. Relation between man and woman, between man and man has almost revolutionised; women have become more assertive; concept of heroism has changed; concept of pathetic is no more the old one. Again, moral values and concepts have basically revolutionised. Great, indescribable unrest has overtaken man. Shelly stated "I bleed" in the nineteenth century. But the mental and emotional strains and tensions that have overtaken, shall we say, overshadowed and overpowered man today show that Shelly was more fortunate and happier than the modern man to-day for whose experience 'bleed' would be a very mild word indeed and the modern man struggles to shake off his strains and tensions, he tries to carve out a new path and that often brings in new strains and tensions also. Science deprived man of faith in god, faith in the working of the supreme power. Man tries, struggles to shape his own destiny. All this has a deep impact on his life, his philosophy, his arts, his poetry, and consequently the *Rasa* or emotional depiction and experience objectivised and universalised, that is the very core of poetic beauty. Under these circumstances, the eight main forms of *Rasa*—रस, भाव, रसाभास, भावाभास, भावोदय, भावशान्ति, भावशबलत्व etc. will also be fully useful to the modern lover of poetry and literature.

All this has again a deep impact on the relation between the poet and the connoiseur (*Sahṛdaya*). What Bhaṭṭa Tauta stated in the ancient days —"When the relation of the hero of the *Kāvya*, the poet and the connoisseur becomes identified—" will now have to be redefined. The modern poet can no more take his reader for granted, or, even when he follows in his composition, the taste of his reader, he cannot grasp it easily. Very often the poet of to-day claims, as did say Jayadeva in his "*Gītagovinda,*" that he writes for the delight of his heart—*svāntaḥ sukhāya-;* but the modern reader may not cultivate his taste following the poet. This explains the constant complaint of so many enlightened readers that modern poetry is difficult to understand, the meaning intended to be conveyed does not find smooth and easy communication and therefore interests far less of readers and so on. All this naturally affects our very concept of *Rasa*, its number, its infinite types and so on. Man's life, learning, relations, outlook, realities of life, realities of human relations, everything has become so very complex that his poetry is also bound to get complex, complicated, abstruse and difficult to grasp.

Symbols and symbolism worked wonders in the realm of western poetry as also partially Sanskrit poetry. Symbols and Symbolism have the capacity to give beautiful poetic shape to man's emotions and so to *Rasa*. Grasp the symbol and you grasp the emotion of *Kāvya*. This is the impact of symbols in poetry. They are meant to intensify the effect of suggestion-*Vyañjanā* in poetry and bring it nearer and easily too to the intended effect. But symbols bring in conventionalism too in poetry and in a slow but sure process, symbols change; old symbols give place to new ones, while some very effective ones persist for long. To-day with the fast change in life, change in symbols has grown faster, and, at least in western poetry its speed of change is unique.[11]

This is a challenge to the poet as also to the reader, more so because to-day symbols have become more abstruse. Sanskrit *Rasa*-poetry used rather few symbols and the very effective ones lasted for long. The function therefore of symbols in *Rasa*-poetry now needs to be reconsidered.

Sanskrit poets had before them the ideal of instantaneous, unique, other-worldly delight through the experience and taste of *Rasa* as Mammaṭa stated in brief but very effective words. The critics went a step further and stated that the delight yielded by *Kāvya* through the *Rasa*-experience should attain to the status of identity with Brahma experienced by the liberated soul. This had of course placed a veil of mystery round *Rasa*-experience and the consequent delight that it yielded. Then followed a line of critics that did not agree and scholars like Rāmacandra-Guṇacandra came to the conclusion that *Rasa* yields happiness and sorrow both-सुखदुःखात्मको रसः. But the last word of Sanskrit poetics in the matter came from Viśvanātha when he very rightly and tersely stated—

"The fact that even from *Karuṇa* etc., poetry yields indescribable delight to the connoisseur (need not be challenged because) the experience of modern, enlightened (poets and readers) is the only proof in the matter."[12]

Even to-day the view persists. Poets, at least the best of them, write for delight, which may often even be a momentary escape from the horrifying realities of modern life. The modern life takes its toll, through even to-day, atleast in the best modern poetry, emotional experience is the basis and so, nobody can state that *Rasa* can be banished or outlawed from modern poetry. Even the reader in the midst of his very fast life full of stresses, strains, and tensions, seeks delight from poetry, in some cases momentarily to forget tensions of life, but very often to drink deeper of the wine of life. Pessimism, sorrow, tensions, pathos, is not the only tune in which the modern poet writes or sings. This would widen far and wide and bring to endless variety and infinity the types of emotional experience and therefore types of *Rasa*.

All this will convince us that the endlessness of the types of *Rasa* in poetry, as propounded by Ānandavardhana, Abhinavagupta and others following them, remains the truth of poetry to-day, but its boundaries have gone far wider and far deeper with the vast change in the life of modern man resulting in a very deep impact and glaring change in his conception of art and poetry, the purpose of poetic composition, the emotional experience that it is expected to yield and its impact on the reader and so on.

It should, however, be asserted in no uncertain terms that *Vyañjanā* and *Dhvani* have become more dominant and more pronounced in modern poetry. The incessant play of suggestion is there in modern poetry, and it is no poetry if suggestion does not dominate. But suggestion has spread its net far and wide, and so has *Rasa* some emotional experiences that man has, or that he desires. But it must also be conceded that in modern poetry, in any of its isms, *Vyañjanā* and *Dhvani* and *Rasa* have also been deeply influenced and changed. If we try to understand the truth of this new perspective in a mental and emotional world of man and literature, we will be convinced that they are full with new vigour and new life.

FOOT-NOTES

1. Vide : *'Locanaṭikā'* सम्यक् न लक्षयितुं क्रमो यस्य, तादृशः। Dhv. 2.2.52.
2. *Kāvya Prakāśa,* 1-3.
3. Vide : Dhv. 2.3. 52.
   स च रसादिध्वनिर्व्यवस्थित एव; न हि तच्छून्यं काव्यं किञ्चिदस्ति। यद्यपि रसेनैव जीवति सर्वं काव्यं तथापि च रसस्यैकघनचमत्कारात्मनोऽपि कृतश्चिदंशात्प्रयोजकीभूतादधिकोऽसौ चमत्कारो भवति।
4. तस्याङ्गानां प्रभेदा ये प्रभेदा स्वगताश्च ये।
5. ये प्रभेदा निरवधयो ये च स्वगतास्तस्याङ्गिनोऽर्थस्य, रसभावतदाभासतत्प्रसशमलक्षणा विभावानुभावव्यभिचारि-प्रतिपादनसहिता, अनन्तास्वाश्रयापेक्षया निःसीमानो विशेषाः तेषामन्योन्यसम्बन्धपरिकल्पने क्रियमाणे रसस्य प्रकाशः परिसंख्यातुं न शक्यते किमुत सर्वेषाम्। 2.21.52 वृत्ति
6. Vide: Dhv. 2.8.
7. शृङ्गारे विप्रलम्भाख्ये करुणे च प्रकर्षवत्। माधुर्यमार्द्रतां याति यतस्तत्राधिकं मनः।
   And the *Locanaṭikā* thereon
   'सम्भोगशृङ्गारान्मधुरतरां विप्रलम्भः ततोऽपि मधुरतम करुण इति तदभिव्यञ्जनकौशलं शब्दार्थयोर्मधुरत्वं मधुरतमत्वं चेत्याभिप्रायेणाह।
   शृङ्गाररसो हि संसारिणां नियमेनानुभवविषयत्वात्सर्वरसेभ्यः कमनीयतया प्रधानभूतः।
8. The word used by Abhinava as he describes his अभिव्यक्तिवाद is पानकरसन्यायेन.
   Mammaṭa also says—
   पानकरसेन चर्व्यमाणः, पुरः इव परिस्फुरन् हृदयमिव प्रविशन् etc.
9. नायकस्य कवेः श्रोतुः समानोऽनुभवस्ततः।
10. रसो वै सः। रसं ह्येवायं लब्ध्वाऽऽनन्दी भवति।
11. From the lecture delivered by 'Mr. Bennet and Mrs. Brown' under the title in 1924.
12. विश्वनाथ in साहित्यदर्पण; 3.35

V.5

THE CONCEPT OF "ALAUKIKA" IN THE RASA THEORY

S.S. Antarkar

(I) Introduction :

One of the most important questions on which the classical Indian aestheticians are sharply divided is whether *Rasa*-aesthetic experience—is *laukika* or *alaukika*. Prof. V. M. Kulkarni observes "The total range of meanings conveyed by the word '*alaukika*' cannot be expressed through any one English expression. Different expressions such as '*sui generis*', 'autonomous', 'extra worldly,' 'non-worldly,' 'other—worldly', 'supra normal', 'transcendental', etc. have been used by critics in different contexts for the term '*alaukika*.'[1] It may be added to Prof. Kulkarni's observation that the Sanskrit expression "*alaukika*" itself is used in the Sanskrit intellectual tradition in different senses in different contexts. For example, The Nyāya System talks of '*alaukika*' perception of three types —*Sāmānyalakṣaṇa, jñānalakṣaṇa* and *yogaja* and distinguishes it from *laukika* perception"; '*alaukika*' is also used in the sense of '*pāralaukika*', '*pāramārthika*', *atīndriya* and so on.

Instead of trying to find an appropriate expression in English for the Sanskrit word '*alaukika*', this paper proposes to inquire whether and in what respects, if any, is aesthetic experience, aesthetic enjoyment, aesthetic perception qualitatively different from non-aesthetic experience, non-aesthetic enjoyment, non-aesthetic perception. The paper does not propose to discuss the controversy whether aesthetic experience is cognitive or non-cognitive for two reasons: (i) Whether aesthetic experience is construed as cognition or affection; the basic question whether the aesthetic cognition or affection is qualitatively different from the non-aesthetic one remains unanswered; and (ii) Secondly as Gilbert Ryle says,[2] "At least in this field, the partitions are down between the Faculties of cognition, conation and feeling". The question whether aesthetic experience is cognitive or non-cognitive, therefore, may not be proper. The inseparability of the cognitive, conative and affective aspects of aesthetic experience may constitute its *sui generis* character.

The paper does not propose to discuss the issue historically by dividing the aestheticians into two sharp groups of *laukikatāvādins* and *alaukikatāvādins*. This is because even an ordinary person would find the experience of watching a funeral procession in drama different from that of watching a real funeral procession. Every aesthetician—whether he subscribes to *laukikatāvāda* or *alaukikatāvāda* has to account for this difference. The two schools would map this difference in different ways—either as a difference in degree or as a qualitative difference. But this being a philosophical controversy and not a factual disagreement, it is, in principle, not resolvable in the light of certain theory-neutral facts accepted by both the parties.

The paper proposes to examine this controversy with special reference to Prof. R.B. Patankar's critique of *alaukikatāvāda*. The next section, therefore, begins with the discussion of the methodological issue about the conceptual tools to be used in discussing this controversy. The third section will discuss Prof. Patankar's approach to the *Rasa* theory. Having argued that the Rasa *theory* is both intelligible and relevant even today, the fourth section discusses whether *alaukikatva* is identical with Kant's autonomy. The fifth and concluding section argues for the necessity of distinguishing between three categories—(a) Kantian autonomy possible only in Free beauty (b) *alaukika* and (c) *laukika* experience in what Kant called 'dependent beauty'.

(II) Methodological Issue

Dr. R.B.Patankar, a renowned aesthetician, while discussing *Rasa* theory in his '*magnum opus*' in Marathi—'*Saundarya Mīmāṁsā*' (1974) suggests that it is better to discuss the *Rasa* theory by keeping aside the traditional Indian concepts such as '*brahmāsvādasahodara*', '*ānanda*', '*jīvātmā*', '*paramātmā*', '*samādhi*', etc. This is because firstly "the use of such terms, instead of bringing clarity to the discussion, creates pleasant smoky atmosphere of obscurity and misunderstanding". He sarcastically remarks, "While talking of 'aesthetic relish', Bharata himself used the analogy of relishing food. But after Bhaṭṭanāyaka, it seems to have been felt that such ordinary examples are insufficient and the terms like '*parabrahmāsvādasavidha*', '*brahmāsvādasahodara ānanda*' came to be freely used. This creates an illusion that during the period from Bhaṭṭanāyaka to Viśvanātha, spiritual bliss had become as familiar to people as the relishing of food at Bharata's time. This does not seem to be probable. At least now it is for the good of all that we don't use language of spiritual bliss."

Prof. Patankar's observation and suggestion raise two questions about methodology to be adopted in understanding the classical Indian aesthetic theory. Firstly, granting that the use of religio-spiritual and metaphysical concepts has given rise to obscurity, the proper solution is not to ban that terminology but to bring clarity into it by removing the clouds of misunderstanding by proper logico-linguistic or conceptual analysis. Secondly, the conceptual tools that we use today to understand the classical Indian aesthetic theories should not be alien to the basic classical Indian conceptual framework. Umashankar Joshi's warning that in understanding the terms of the classical Indian aesthetics—like *aucitya*, *sthāyibhāva*, *sahṛdaya*, *dhvani*, and the most enigmatic of them all '*rasa*' along with '*rasānubhava*' '*rasāsvāda,*' if we use ideas and technical terms rooted in different cultural milieus, we have to be careful not to be misled by superficial similarities."[4] In this context, Prof. V.Y. Kantak's observations seem to be very pertinent. He observes, "the conceptual tools we use today are themselves derived from the Western tradition of thought largely initiated by Plato and Aristotle"[5]. They are treated as universally valid and are used as yardstick to evaluate to what extent the Indian concepts conform to those norms and to what extent they are aberrations from those norms." Prof. Kantak very ably shows the radical difference between the Western ideas of drama, imitation, action, hero, plot etc. and the corresponding classical Indian ideas of *nāṭya*, *anukṛti* or *anukaraṇa*, *rasa*, *nāyaka* etc., and argues that the Western mode of thinking is unsuited to the understanding of the classical Indian arts like dance, drama and music. Prof. Kantak emphasises the following differences between the Western conceptual framework and the *Nāṭyaśāstra's* conceptual framework.(i) "*Rasa* refers at once to the totality of elements that compose the 'organic' unity of the artefact and the aesthetic experience aroused in the appreciator. A play is '*rasotpatti*' and '*rasāsvādana*' both at the same time—thus joining the act of artistic production with the act of enjoyment." He adds, "In Western criticism, it has been observed, there is no such term which indicates both at once—the term 'artistic' having basic reference to source, and the term 'aesthetic' to response". (ii) The *rasa* theory lays special emphasis on the distancing of the aesthetic experience from life-emotions with their practical pressures which incidentally would seem to discount any form of 'realism' as such, (iii) Thirdly and more importantly, the *Rasa* experience is always marked by a rare unparalleled Serenity. All *Rasas* are tasted in a state of perfect tranquility, which owes to the withdrawal of the ego from its practical behests. Prof. Kantak concludes, "The great premise behind all this is the poised state of the soul conceived of as central to all art activity. The consciousness gains a composure, a repose, a *saṁvidviśrānti*, freed from the grossness of appetite and agitation (*kāma* and *krodha*)[6]". All these notions make the classical Indian dramaturgy qualitatively different from the Western one. Prof. Kantak says, "We do these plays (classical Indian plays) wrong to judge them as though it were the same.[7]" There are controversies among the classical Indian aestheticians on many points. But they share in common the basic conceptual framework provided by Bharata's *Nāṣyaśāstra*. Prof. Patwardhan rightly says, "In fact the *rasa*-doctrine and the supreme importance of the portrayal of *rasa* in drama as propounded by Bharata has been accepted *in toto* by all writers on poetics and the portrayal of human emotions has been regarded, by them as the essence of poetry and drama[8]".

(III) Prof. Patankar on Rasa Theory

Within the autonomy of the Classical Indian framework, we may discuss the controversy whether *rasa* is *laukika* or *alaukika*. However, modern aestheticians like Dr. Patankar, who have come to the classical Indian aesthetic theories

(i) by first getting initiated into and then mastering Western aesthetic tradition beginning with Plato and Aristotle through Kant, Hegel, Marx, Croce upto Langer, Wittgenstein and others; and

(ii) by assuming "that there is a universal human mind which responds to similar situations in similar ways, irrespective of age and country[9]"

find that the *Rasa* theory contains:

(a) parts which are completely unintelligible to us—e.g. Bharata's lists of *Sthāyibhāvas* and *Vyabhicāribhāvas* because we are unable to understand the principles of classification that Bharata used;

(b) other parts which possess only historical significance or interest- e.g. The problem regarding the number of *rasas*; and

(c) a part which is not restricted in like manner to a particular age- e.g. the concept of *sādhāraṇīkaraṇa* (universalization) and the concept of 'autonomy[10]'.

We may begin by questioning the assumption that the universal human mind responds to similar situations in similar ways. No doubt natural responses of human species to similarsituations would be similar, in so far as they have the same physiological and biological structure. But the essential nature of man consists in 'cultural freedom', i.e. freedom to construct and use language as a system of conventional symbols; to develop religion, art, literature, culture and so on. In these matters there is diversity. Different communities have developed different languages, food-habits, dresses, different types of music, dance, drama and literature, different systems of rituals and forms of worship, different conceptual frameworks and so on. This cultural pluralism exemplifies different styles of living. There isn't one and only one correct way of living. This is an expression of the essential freedom of human spirit, which makes us preserve and respect the identity of each culture. Any attempt to reduce this cultural plurality to an abstract uniformity is detrimental to the identity and autonomy of each culture.

I want to suggest that the universal human mind perceives and responds to situations in a variety of ways. The problem is not to accept one of them as valid at the cost of others nor to judge them by some abstract, universal extra-cultural yardstick; because such a yardstick is not available, but to understand and appreciate similarities and differences among various cultures. Different cultural responses have, to use Wittgenstein's expression, 'family resemblances,' but not essential identity or uniformity. The ways in which the classical Indian aesthetics understands art-forms like dance, drama and poetry and the classical Indian *darśanas* understand epistemology, metaphysics and goals of life, the ways in which they understand psychology, morality, rationality, aesthetics, religion and spirituality have their distinctive unique nature. The approaches of Patañjali, Buddha, Mahāvīra, the Upaniṣads to the human mind and consciousness have a fundamental unity. Their concern is how to elevate, transform the ordinary normal human mind which is disturbed, distracted and deluded (*kṣipta*, *vikṣipta*, and *mūḍha*) into the mind which has stability, concentration and tranquility (*ekāgra niruddha*). This approach differs fundamentally and qualitatively from the approaches of modern scientific psychology, philosophical psychology of Ryle, and also from clinical psychology. The classical Indian thinkers are not concerned with the description of normal mental functioning nor again with understanding and curing aberrations and abnormalities but with elevating the normal mind to the highest level of purity, sanity and serenity, which level is variously called *samādhi*, *jīvanmukti* (liberated from passions), *sthitaprajña* (steadfast wisdom), *buddha* (the enlightened one). It is a development from the level of passions through the rational level to the spiritual level. In the language of Vedānta from *manomaya kośa* through *vijñānamaya kośa* to *ānandamaya kośa*. This metaphysics, this epistemology, the *yoga* psychology and the theory of *puruṣārthas* provide the larger or overall conceptual framework within which theories of ethics, aesthetics have to be understood. The normal human mind is to be spiritually elevated through reflection on *Ātman* in philosophy, through penance, various types of meditation and other spiritual practices in religion, through self-control and practising various *vratas* and virtues in ethics and by sublimating natural emotions and attitudes (*sthāyibhāvas*) through arts like dance, drama, music etc. The highest spiritual level is called '*ādhyātmika* level.' Art activity is a way for elevating human psyche from sensuous pleasures and pains, psychological stress and sorrows to, what Prof. Kantak calls, "the poised state of the soul conceived as central to all art activity.[11]"

Once this central point of the role and function of art according to the Classical Indian Aesthetics is grasped, the completely unintelligible aspect of the *Rasa* theory starts becoming intelligible. Bharata's list of *sthāyibhāvas—rati*, *hāsya*, *śoka*, *krodha*, *bhaya* etc. are natural tendencies and emotions which are regarded as obstructions to inner peace and outer social harmony. They are to be sublimated through art activities like dance, drama and music. Thus the list of *sthāyibhāvas*, though not exhaustive, can be shown to have some spiritual significance. Many of the *sthāyibhāvas* like *rati* (*kāma, love*), hāsa (laughter), *śoka* (sorrow), *krodha* (anger), *utsāha* (enthusiasm), *bhaya* (fear), *jugupsā* (disgust) are natural dispositions which are regarded as 'passions' (*vikāras* or *kaṣāyas*) to be controlled. This is seen from the list of spiritual virtues, which are their opposites -e.g. *virati, aśoka, akrodha, abhaya*. *Rati* or *kāma* is sublimated by aesthetically enjoying, say, *Rāsalīlā* of Kṛṣṇa and Gopīs. This enjoyment is *śṛṅgāra rasa*. Our anger against unjust and vicious actions and persons is sublimated when we witness how the hero defeats and punishes the villain in a drama. This is *raudra rasa*. Our natural tendency to laugh and ridicule any act of foolishness, inconsistency is elevated by enjoying comic scenes in a drama. Our sorrow gets elevated in *karuṇa rasa* and so on.

The problem regarding the number of *rasas* need not have only historical interest though it is a problem of details and need not detain us. Some aestheticians have already added *śānta* rasa and *bhakti rasa* to the list of *rasas*. But if the concept of *rasa* is necessarily connected with the concept of *sthāyibhāva* then the theorist will have to mention *sthāyibhāvas* corresponding to the additional *rasas*. I am, however, not inclined to accept Prof. Patankar's hypothesis that Bharata arrived at the list of eight or nine *rasas* on the basis of his study of the dramatic compositions available to him. The number seems to be based on the psychological findings about the nature of human mind from the spiritualist point of view.

Prof. Patankar approaches the controversy whether *Rasa* (aesthetic experience) is *laukika* or *alaukika* in the classical Indian aesthetic tradition by interpreting *alaukika* to mean what Kant means by 'autonomous'. Kant postulates Taste as a distinct faculty different from and independent of both, (a) theoretical reason- i.e. sensibility and understanding which give us scientific knowledge of the self and the world and (b) practical reason which gives knowledge of morality. Kant, therefore, defines beauty as "that which, apart from concept, is represented as the object of universal disinterested, and necessary delight.[12]" Thus the universe of beauty is autonomous and totally independent of all other theoretical and practical concerns. Such an autonomy of beauty and aesthetic delight can be realized only in pure formal art which has no content. In such a beauty the sole foundation of the judgment of taste is the Form and consideration of any interest-theoretical or practical- is regarded as vitiating the purity of the judgment.

Kant, however, does not restrict the scope of aesthetics or beauty only to the pure judgement of taste. He, therefore says, "Aesthetic, just like theoretical (logical) judgments, are divisible into empirical and pure.[13]" Kant, therefore, is led to recognize and distinguish two kinds of beauty: 'free beauty' and 'dependent beauty.' Kant says "The first presupposes no concept of what the object should be; the second does presuppose such a concept and with it, an answering perfection of the object.[14]"

The former "pure judgment of taste is entirely independent of the concept of perfection, while the latter presupposes 'an objective finality i.e. the reference of the object to a definite end.[15]" This end may be either external i.e. utility or internal i.e. the perfection of the object. Kant warns that the aesthetic delight in an object should not be confused with its utility and even with its perfection. Kant asserts that if the judgment of taste in respect of the delight in the beautiful is made dependent upon the end involved in the delight in perfection (the internal end) as a judgment of reason, and is thus placed under a restriction, then it is no longer a free and pure judgment of taste[16]. For example, the beauty of a person, the beauty of a horse or of a building such as a church or a palace, "presupposes a concept of the end that defines what the thing has to be and consequently a concept of its perfection; and is therefore merely attendant beauty[17]". Though this combination of the good with beauty mars the purity of aesthetic judgment, Taste also "stands to gain by the combination of intellectual delight with the aesthetic." What governs human person inwardly is the idea of a rational and morally good person, which includes many intellectual and moral virtues (benevolence, purity, strength, or equanimity etc). The ideal of beauty makes these perfections "visible in bodily manifestations;" it embodies the inner perfection in visible expressions. Such an embodiment "involves a union of pure ideas of reason and great imaginative power in one who would even form an estimate of it. Such an ideal of beauty does not permit any sensuous charm to mingle with the delight in its object in which it still allows us to take a great interest. "An estimate formed according to such a standard can never be purely aesthetic and that one formed according to an ideal of beauty cannot be a simple judgment of taste[18]."

The classical Indian aestheticians were dealing not with pure formal beauty, which, in the Kantian terminology, is called 'Free beauty;' but with the 'ideal of beauty' which in the Kantian scheme is 'dependent beauty'. As Prof. Patankar rightly points out, Kant's autonomism is limited only to 'Free beauty'. The ideal of beauty is not possible in 'Free beauty' because in 'Free beauty' neither categories of understanding nor ideas of reason are involved.

With this understanding of (i) Kant's distinction between 'free beauty' and 'dependent beauty', (ii) his view that beauty of a human person involves the idea of inner perfection visible in bodily manifestation, and hence (iii) it belongs to 'dependent beauty' or 'ideal of beauty', we find that the Kantian concept of 'autonomy' of beauty or aesthetic experience is misplaced or totally out of place in the whole discourse of *Rasa* theory. The controversy between *laukikatāvāda* and *alaukikatāvāda* is only valid within the field of dependent beauty and it is a 'category mistake' to understand '*alaukika*' in terms of Kant's 'autonomy' as Prof. Patankar does.

Prof. V. M. Kulkarni in his article "Abhinavagupta on the Alaukika Nature of Rasa" states Kant's autonomist position in Prof. Patankar's words and referring to the condition that art experience is not mediated by any concepts, says "no Sanskrit aesthetician has thought it necessary to say that art experience is not mediated by any concepts. Śaṅkuka has deontologised the art object. But no Sanskritist deconceptualised art experience." Prof. Kulkarni claims that Abhinavagupta, as a champion of *alaukikatāvāda* can be justifiably described as "autonomist in the popular and wider sense of that word" and adds, "to call him an autonomist in the restricted sense in which Kant uses the term, would be a highly misleading and inexcusable error". He further says "it would be better to coin a new appropriate term (other than autonomy) in English to express Abhinavagupta's concept of '*alaukikatva*' and a new suitable term (other than *alaukikatva*) in modern Indian languages like Marathi, Gujarati, Hindi etc., to express Kant's concept of autonomy. If this suggestion is followed a lot of confusion in the minds of scholars reading books on Abhinavagupta and his *alaukikatva* in English and modern Indian languages would be avoided[19]".

Prof. Patankar has used the term '*svāyatta*' for 'free beauty' and '*parāyatta*' for 'dependent beauty' and has even pointed out that the whole discussion of aesthetic experience not involving concepts is valid only in the context of 'free beauty' and that "the concepts have important place in the latter (dependent beauty)[20]" If Prof. Patankar is so clear about this distinction between 'free beauty' and dependent beauty and if concepts have an important place in the latter, why does he demand or expect *Rasānubhava* to be "free from concepts" for being characterised as '*alaukika*'? Why does he hold that Śaṅkuka was laying foundation for an autonomist theory of art when he propounded the theory of *citraturagapratīti*' and that the autonomist stand also needs "the deconceptualisation of the aesthetic experience as Kant has maintained"[21]? Is he tacitly identifying '*alaukikatva*' with 'Kantian autonomy'? Is such identification not a part of confusion in the minds of scholars as feared by Prof. Kulkarni? Let us see whether these questions can be answered by considering Prof. Patankar' s criticism of *alaukikatāvāda* and his response to the distinction between *laukika* and *alaukika*. If my arguments are right, it is necessary to distinguish between three categories :- firstly, free beauty (*svāyatta*) and Dependent beauty (*parāyatta*) and then the latter to be subdivided into *alaukika* and *laukika*. The Classical Indian Aestheticians did not discuss pure formal beauty—what Kant calls 'free beauty' which is absolutely autonomous. They were mainly interested in arts like drama, dance and poetry in so far as they express inner perfection through linguistic and bodily manifestation. One of the central questions discussed by the

Classical Indian Aestheticians was, whether the aesthetic experience is *laukika* or *alaukika*. It is important to see how Prof. Patankar responds to the distinction between *laukika* and *alaukika*.

(a) Prof. Patankar begins by distinguishing various senses of pleasure with a view to finding out which pleasure is *laukika* and which is *alaukika*. But he *a priori* rules out any talk of or reference to spiritual experience or spiritual joy (*ātmānanda*, *brahmānanda*, *samādhi*) which the *alaukikatāvadins* have alluded to. Not only this, he further rules out even qualitative distinction among pleasures in one sentence 'dogmatically' by saying "pleasurable sensations abstracted from objects of desire may differ in quantity but cannot differ in quality *a la* Bentham. I said 'dogmatically' because the controversy whether pleasures differ only in quantity or also in quality does not end with Bentham. But Prof. Patankar seems to think that Bentham's view is final and indubitable. It is a perennial issue like many other philosophical issues and is still an open question. Moreover, in the classical Indian tradition qualitative distinction among pleasures (i) on the basis of the Sāṅkhya *guṇas-sattva*, *rajas*, and *tamas* and also (ii) on the basis of bodily, mental, intellectual and spiritual levels, seems to have been accepted by both the *laukikatāvādins* and *alauakikatāvādins*- the controversy being to which category does the aesthetic experience belong?

(b) If aesthetic delight is to be distinguished from other pleasures and joys, then, says Prof. Patankar, "We must follow Kant. For Kant, aesthetic delight is disinterested in the sense that one does not bother about the ontological status or reality of object of enjoyment. Thus Kant is able to distinguish aesthetic delight from sensuous pleasures on the one hand and moral joy on the other. But such aesthetic delight is possible only in 'free beauty'. The delight one derives from 'dependent beauty' is reducible either to sensuous pleasure, or satisfaction of human urges or to moral joy. The disinterested and *alaukika* joy is possible only from pure formal art. Here, Prof. Patankar uses the term '*alaukika*' for 'delight from free beauty[22]. Prof. Patnakar does not tell us why to follow Kant and not Śaṅkuka and Abhinavagupta?

(c) The delight one gets from music produced by mere arrangement of musical notes is '*alaukika*', because, here only formal structure of musical notes is important and relevant; and no concepts of understanding such as cause-effect are used. This is not a sensuous pleasure, it is a pleasure arising from pure formal structure of musical notes and therefore *alaukika*. This will be accepted by Kant also.[23]" But it will not be accepted by Śaṅkuka, Abhinavagupta or any *alaukikatāvādin*.

These and similar quotations show that Prof. Patankar identifies '*alaukika*' with Kant's autonomous joy. But this identification won't be accepted either by Kant or by the *alaukikatāvādins*. This is an example of getting misled by superficial similarities between two technical terms rooted in two different cultures. While autonomous joy is possible only in pure formal structural beauty, even according to Kant, the aesthetic delight from art-forms like drama, poetry and dance which are art-forms with content belong to, what Kant calls,' dependent beauty'. Therefore, Kant's criterion of autonomous beauty is not, in principle, applicable to the aesthetic delight of dependent beauty. The *alaukikātāvādin* distinguishes aesthetic experience from pleasant sensations and from the satisfaction of human urges by saying that they are impersonalized, generalized emotions; they are educated and learned tastes, they are devoid of practical interest, they are spiritualized emotions and so on. Thus personal sorrow (*śoka*) disturbs one's mind, but, when it is impersonalized and regarded as representative of human sorrow and expressed through a poem or dance or a drama, the sorrow as a natural emotion is transformed into 'human compassion' (*karuṇa-rasa*) which helps the person to transcend his disturbed mental state. This experience of *karuṇa-rasa* is, therefore, regarded as '*alaukika*' by the *alaukikatāvādins*. Art, therefore, functions as 'a blasphemy against human nature.'

A person's suffering becomes less when it is compared to the suffering of other persons because the person realises that he is not the only person to suffer; that there are many other persons who have similar suffering; personal sorrow becomes even lesser when he sees greater sufferings of other persons. But when the same suffering is universalized and expressed aesthetically through poetry, dance or drama, it no more remains 'my' or 'your' suffering. It achieves the universal, impersonal level of 'human suffering' from which neither the artist nor the art-appreciator (*rasika*) wants to run away or escape; because in a way it is no one's suffering. In a personal sorrow,, there is a state of disturbance and movement to escape from that disturbance. When an individual becomes one with universal human suffering, his personal passion is transformed into passion for all. 'Passion for all' says Krishnamurti, "is compassion." *Alaukikatāvāda* holds that art transforms or elevates natural emotions (*sthāyibhāva*) to a higher, spiritual level; *śoka* transforms into *karuṇa rasa*; sexual urge (*rati*) transforms into erotic love (*śṛṅgāra rasa*) and so on. The word '*alaukika*' here refers to the *ātmika* or *ādhyātmika* or spiritual level. Art is regarded neither as craft nor as an entertainment, nor as wish-fulfillment but as educative, elevating the mind to the semi-spiritual level by purifying or sublimating natural emotions. *Rasānubhava* i.e. aesthetic experience is, therefore, compared not with natural likes and tastes but with spiritual delight and is called '*alaukika*' in general or *brahmānandasahodara* in particular by the *Vedāntins*.

(V) Conclusion

Whether aesthetic experience differs from non-aesthetic experiences qualitatively or quantitatively, whether the difference between them is qualitative or a matter of degrees is a perennial controversy in Indian aesthetics, because it rests on one's philosophical perspective. But '*alaukika*' was throughout understood as akin to *ādhyātmika* or as qualitatively similar to spiritual experience. Prof. Patankar, however, outright dismisses this meaning of '*alaukika*'and attempts to refute *alaukikatāvāda* by (i) first interpreting '*alaukika*' in the Kantian sense of autonomy and having done so, (ii) by arguing that since concepts are used in aesthetic experience, it cannot stand the test of *alaukika* in the sense of Kantian autonomy. No doubt the traditional *alaukikatāvādin* also insists on autonomy and distinctive character of art experience. He maintains art experience to be qualitatively different from (i) cognitive experience; (ii) practical experience, including moral experience; (iii) experience of sensory pleasure, entertainment etc. He also holds that (iv) the art object does not have ontological status that objects of the real world have, (v) But he does not deny the role of concepts in art experience. Kant also does not deny the role of concepts in the case of 'dependent beauty'—literature, drama, dance etc. what follows from this is that autonomy necessary and sufficient for *alaukikatva* in arts with content is different from Kantian autonomy. Instead, Prof. Patankar denies *alaukikatva* on the ground of (v) above. The *Alaukikatāvādin* would make distinction between (a) Kantian autonomy of 'free beauty' to be found only in pure formal art (b) *Alaukikatva* accepting qualitative difference between art experience and other real life experiences and defining autonomy in the wider sense excluding (v) above and (c) *Laukikatva*—accepting continuity and only difference of degree between art experience and other real life experience. It seems to me that Prof. Patankar has done injustice to the traditional *alaukikatāvāda* (a) by defining *alaukikatva* in terms of Kantian autonomy, which, even according to Kant, is not applicable to arts with content, arts dealing with human beings and human affairs; arts which are not purely formal; (b) by *a priori* ruling out comparison of aesthetic experience with spiritual experience, and (c) by claiming to have refuted *alaukikatāvāda* by arguing that it fails to stand to the test of Kantian criterion of autonomy.

Bibliography :

(1) Daya Krishna (Ed) *India's Intellectual Traditions* (1987, Motilal Banarasidass, Delhi) [IIT]

(2) Kant. Immanuel *The Critique of Judgment* (tr. by James Creed Meredith) (1911, Clarendon Press, Oxford) [CJ]

(3) Kulkarni V. M. (Ed) *Some Aspects of Rasa Theory* (1986. B. L.Institute of lndology, Delhi) [RT]

(4) Patankar R. B. : *Saundarya Mīmāṁsā* (In Marathi, 1974. Mouj Prakashan, Mumbai) [SM]

(5) Ryle Gilbert, "On forgetting the Difference between Right and Wrong" in A. I. Meldon, (Ed) *Essays in Moral Philosophy* 1958, University of Washington Press, Seattle.

REFERENCES

1. [RT] p.28
2. Ryle p. 152
3. [SM] p.256, 257
4. [RT]p. 102
5. [IIT] p. 128-129
6. [IIT] p. 143
7. [IIT] p. 143
8. [RT] p. 6
9. [RT] p. 110
10. [RT] p. 110, 111
11. [IIT] p. 143
12. [CJ] p. 50 & 85
13. [CJ] p. 13
14. [CJ] p. 13
15. [CJ] p. 69
16. [CJ] p. 73
17. [CJ] p. 73
18. [CJ] p. 80
19. [RT] p. 42
20. [SM] p. 92
21. [RT] p. 118
22. [SM] p. 242, 243
23. [SM] p. 240

V.6

ON TRANSCENDING MEANING AND METAPHOR

Prof. Dr. (Mrs.) Shubhada Joshi

The paper is developed in the following way :

(i) what is meaning is explained with the help of a distinction between cognitive and non-cognitive in the first part.

(ii) The second part discusses 'metaphor' and 'meaning' with a cognitive standpoint especially of Davidson in his famous article. It is this article which brings in the forefront the problem of meaning of a metaphor when meaning is completely equated with the cognitive.

(iii) The third part tries to evaluate the account of *Dhvani* as given by *Dhvanyāloka* of Ānandavardhana as well as *Locana* of Abhinavagupta.

(iv) The fourth is a conclusion, which also discusses the possibility of extension of *Dhvani* in understanding the performing arts, i.e the *Lalitakalās*. It can assign meaning to mysticism. What is suggested is at this stage the metaphor and the meaning, both are transcended as that which is known through *Dhvani,* is really unspeakable (*avācya*) indescribable (*anirvacanīya*), without words (*aśabda*), beyond description (*avarṇanīya*). extra ordinary *(alaukika)* and silence (*śānta*).

I

According to the empiricists only that which is known through perception or observation and which can be described as either true or false is meaningful. It is the cognitive, which makes it meaningful. That which is not cognitive, which can't be known empirically, is meaningless. Such utterances may have psychological impact but if they don't have any cognitive content then it is meaningless. It also can be said that it is the picture theory of language as put forth by Wittgenstein in *Tractatus* which equates meaning with the cognitive. Similar position is taken by Nyāya—Navya Nyāya school in the Indian tradition while dealing with the problem of meaning. According to Nyāya there is a relation between *Pada* (term) and *Padārtha* (object) i.e. the cognitive content or meaning of a word which is revealed and in a sentence. The *Padas* i.e. the individual terms (of a sentence) are related to one another by way of *ākāṅkṣā*, *yogyatā*, *sannidhi & tātparya*. It is through this relationship the meaning is revealed. Kumārila also supported this view of *abhihitānvaya* which takes a stand that words independently express separate meanings which are subsequently combined into a sentence expressing one connected idea.

As against this, Prabhākara and his followers believed in *anvitābhidhānavāda* i.e. the words denote things only as revealed by the factors of injunction. According to Mīmāṁsā, letters are direct cause of verbal cognition and are eternally related to its meaning[1].

For both Nyāya and Mīmāṁsā, words and meanings are known through their relation either by convention or by eternal relation, but it is basically literal (*vācya*) which is known through the power of *abhidhā* and like congnitivists, the Nyāya theory is supporting *Pada-Padārthasaṁbandha*. Kumārilabhaṭṭa accepts *abhihitānvaya,* but, he doesn't agree with cognitive aspect of Nyāya because Mīmāṁsā supports the view that words are meaningful in the context of injunctions or prescriptions[2], for Mīmāṁsā holds extreme prescriptive or even neo naturalist position, a position close to Nowellsmith. According to this school, descriptive sentences are meaningful only in the context of prescriptions (*Vidhi*). By themselves observation sentences are meaningless as the utterance doesn't lead to any *action* (*Kriyā*). All descriptive sentences are *arthavāda*, of three types: first contrary to observation which is to be understood metaphorically; second as per the observation which is redundant as it has no purpose and third which is not known empirically. In this paper, I don't intend to discuss Mīmāṁsā position. Instead, I will discuss the doctrine of *dhvani* which is discussed byĀnandavardhana.

The claim that only the cognitive content makes the utterance meaningful is challenged by the emotivists and the post-emotivists. According to these non-cognitivists, the meaning is not exclusively determined by the cognitive content. The non-cognitive is also equally meaningful. The function theory of language as put forth by Wittgenstein in the *Philosophical Investigations* has made room for the meaning of the non cognitive. According to this theory, language is multifunctional and to understand the meaning is to understand the function performed by the language. So non-cognitivists deny that meaning is necessarily cognitive, as according to the function theory, not all words necessarily denote some quality of an object as is held by the descriptionists. Again the function performed by the language is not just one single and that of description but there are very many other functions such as command, questions, criticism, sorrow, grief, insistence, prescription etc. The multifunctionalism suggests that other uses of language also are to be respected, (e.g. Nowellsmith on Jenus principle or A—D and G words.)[3] while talking about metaphors, philosophers either reject it as meaningless and futile or support as effective mode of communicating in a suggestive way. Philosophers like positivists and supporters of picture theory in the Western tradition belong to the first category and supporters of function theory of language uphold the second position. In Indian tradition also Nyāya thinkers believe that words only have literal meaning. Their position resembles with the picture theory and they reject any possibility of suggested meaning communicated by metaphors. However, it is very interesting that they accept *upamāna*, (comparison) as a valid source of knowledge, which shares some characteristics of a metaphor.

Meaninglessness of 'Metaphors' is argued at length by the supporters of cognitive theory of meaning. According to this theory, meaning is connected with facts and has the truth value. It is the outcome of theory of Wittgenstein. According to this theory all linguistic utterances which are non-cognitive are not meaningful, though such usages may have many good emotive impacts or may have a pragmatic value. The supporters of this position such as empiricists, logical positivists, deny any meaning to metaphor. They argue on the ground that there is no cognitive content in the metaphor. Hence they reject the view that metaphor has any other meaning in addition to its literal sense or meaning or conveys another sense or meaning.

II

The function of a Metaphor is not to communicate the literal meaning but to convey the implied or rather the suggested meaning. The problem is that the suggested meaning is different from the literal meaning hence cognitive theories find it difficult to account for metaphors.

Davidson writes, "I agree with a view that metaphors can't be paraphrased but I think this is not because metaphors say something too novel for literal expression but because there is nothing there to paraphrase."[4]

Davidson further says that the central mistake against which he will be inveighing is the idea that a metaphor has, in addition to its literal sense or meaning another sense or meaning.[5]

He finds that, this idea is common to many who have written about metaphors. It is found in the works of literary critics like Richards, Empson and Winters, Philosophers from Aristotle to Max Black, Psychologists from Freud to Skinner and linguists from Plato to Uriel Weinreich and George Lakott.[6]

While examining Max Black's supports for metaphorical meaning, he says "According to Black's interaction theory a metaphor makes us apply a "system of common places" associated with the metaphorical word to the subject of the metaphor: in "Man is a wolf" we apply common place attributes (stereotypes) of the wolf to man. The metaphor, Black says, thus 'selects, emphasizes, suppresses and organizes features of the principal subject by implying statements about it that normally apply to the subsidiary subject.'[7]

If paraphrase fails according to Black, it is not because the metaphor does not have a special cognitive content but because the paraphrase "will not have the same power to inform and enlighten as the original.... it fails to be a translation because it fails to give the insight that the metaphor did"[8]

The problem for Black is 1) inadequacy of the literal to express the suggestive 2) equalizing meaning with the cognitive and thereby equating meaning with the literal. Davidson states this equation still more emphatically. He writes, "There is then a tension in the usual view of metaphor to hold that a metaphor does something no plain prose can possibly do and on the other hand it wants to explain what a metaphor does by appealing to a cognitive content just the sort of thing plain prose is designed to express."[9] Here also Davidson finds that on cognitive criteria of meaning, it is very difficult to justify metaphor even though he agrees that it is an effective tool.

He writes, "Metaphor is a legitimate device not only in literature but in science, philosophy and the law. It is effective in praise and abuse, prayer and promotion, description and prescription. For the most part I don't disagree with Max Black, Paul Henel, Nelson Goodma, Monroe Beardslely and the rest in their accounts of what metaphor accomplishes, except that I think it accomplishes more and that what is additional is different in kind. My disagreement is with the explanation of how metaphor works its wonders.[10]

"I have quarrel with these descriptions of the effects of metaphor only with the associated views as to how metaphor is supposed to produce them (the effects)."[11] On the cognitive, descriptive grounds, it is very difficult to justify the claim of metaphorical meaning. It can be justified only on non-cognitive, emotive, suggestive grounds.

III

Paraphrasing of a metaphor—"Many of us need help if we are to see what the author of a metaphor wanted us to see and what more sensitive or educated reader grasps. The legitimate function of so-called paraphrase is to make the lazy or the ignorant reader have a vision like that of the skilled critic."[12] The critic is so to speak a *Sahṛdaya*.

The metaphorical meaning is called *dhvani* in Indian Tradition. It is interesting to note the similarities between the opponents of *dhvani* in the Indian Tradition and the cognitivists opposing the meaningfulness of a metaphor in the western tradition, as well as the supporters of a *dhvani* or suggestive, metaphorical meaning and the non-cognitivists in the western tradition.

The supporter of congnitivist position in the Indian Tradition is Nyāya School and has raised many objections in order to reject the claim of suggestive meaning, whearas the *dhvanivādins* have emphasised the limitations of literal meaning and have argued for the need of the metaphorical or the suggestive meaning.

It is this metaphorical meaning '*dhvani*' which is the essence of poetry but some say it is non—existent (*abhāva*), others call it *lakṣaṇā* i.e. implied meaning and some others say that *dhvani* can't be expressed in appropriate words. Even those who deny *dhvani* are of three types.[13]

According to the first type, the meaning of a word is possible only by way of conventional meaning i.e. *saṅketa*. According to Nyāya, the conventional meaning or *saṅketa* of every word is determined by God. It is *vācyārtha* i.e. the literal meaning. There is nothing like *dhvani* or metaphorical meaning. According to the second, the literal meaning is inadequate to explain, hence, it is the implied meaning i.e. *lakṣyārtha* that explains the meaning, hence no *dhvani* is required. According to the third type, *dhvani* cannot be described in words in an appropriate manner, hence there is nothing like *dhvani*.

Ruyyaka's '*Alaṁkāra-sarvasva*' mentions twelve different positions rejecting *dhvani*. The important ones are as follows:[14]

According to Bhāṭṭa Mīmāṁsākas, *dhvani* should be included in *tātparya* i.e. intention. This implies a type of cognitivism. The Prābhākaras equate it with *abhidhā* i.e. the literal meaning. This is also a congnitive position. *Dhvani* functions in the way of two types of implied meanings i.e. *lakṣaṇā*. viz—*upādāna lakṣaṇā* and *lakṣaṇā*. Hence there is no need to accept any further type of meaning as *dhvani*. According to Nyāya, suggestive meaning i.e. *Vyaṅgyārtha* is known by two types of inferences (*anumāna*) . viz. *Svārtha* and *Parārtha*. According to some, the suggestive meaning is known by a valid source of knowledge called *Arthāpatti*.

Dhvani explained :—

Vastudhvani—The suggested meaning is expressed in words while explaining the suggested meaning of the metaphor. That metaphor is *vastudhvani*. The first verse of *Uddyota* illustrates the doctrine of *vastudhvani*. The verse is "May the nails of Viṣṇu who took the form of lion due to his own will[15]............" in this verse it is suggested that even though in this verse the nails are like the instruments for killing the demons, they are the part and parcel of the body, hence the "first case" i.e. *prathamā vibhakti* is used for nails to suggest that they are not mere instruments as indicated by the "third case" i.e. *tṛtīyā vibhakti,* but they are the *kartā*, hence *prathamā* and have very special power of destruction of the demons and protection of the devotees. This is the example of *Vastudhvani*. Further, it is suggested that Divinity does not require any external instruments for killing the demons.

The nails of Narasiṁha are used to kill Hiraṇyakaśipu who is pain incarṇate. Hence the nails destroy the pains and sufferings of the devotee, and suggest the benevolence of the Divine. The adjectives such as *svaccha*, *mṛdu*, etc. suggest that the nails are even better than the crescent moon (*Indu*). Looking at the purity and the curvatures of the nails, the moon repents in her mind as the similarity ends only at this point. The nails are effective in removing sufferings and pains of the devotees who have surrendered at the feet of the Divinity. This is *Alaṁkāradhvani*. The *alaṁkāra* is *vyatireka* as the *upameya,* viz, nails, is superior to *upamāna* i.e. the moon & the superiority of the nails is also suggestive and not expressed in a straightforward way. *Dhvani*, as it is an imagination of the mind of moon which is suggested & emotions like grief & sorrow are superimposed on her. It is also *Apanhuti alaṁkāra* because nails are not nails but are called the moon in a suggestive way.

The moon thinks that earlier she was the only one desired by the people because of purity and beauty, but, now the nails compete her and are ten in number and also qualitatively superior. Thinking this way the moon is lamenting in her innermost mind, this is *utprekṣā* and *apanhuti alaṁkāradhvani*. All the three types of *dhvanis,* viz. *vastu.*, *alaṁkāra* and *rasa* are illustrated in this verse.

Dhvani or implied meaning is explained in *Dhvanyāloka* as the implict i.e. *pratīyamāna* which shines supreme in the expressions of the first- rate poets and towers above the beauty of the striking external constituents like the charm of a beautiful lady.[16] (Udyota 1 verse 4).

The inner or suggested is different from the perceived. Just as the beauty or the charm of a lady exceeds the beauty of all the individual limbs observed separately and delights like ambrosia the eye of the admirer in a most unique fashion, so also does this implicit (i.e. *pratīyamāna*) meaning. There are various types of implicit meanings (*Pratīyamāna*). One type of *pratīyamāna*, is where explicit meaning is recommendatory (*vidhi*), but, the implict or the suggested meaning is of prohibitory (*niṣedha*) nature, e.g. the verse which says,[17] 'Ramble (wander) freely O pious man. That dog today is killed by the fierce lion that dwells in the forest on the river Godā.' The verse is commented upon by '*Locana*' saying,[18] Wander or Ramble is in the imperative form, which suggests that the permission is granted and the time for wandering is also appropriate. What is stated is that now the dog is dead so there is no reason for unnecessary fear. But what is further suggested is the fierce lion is there and now is the time for the lion to come out on the banks and if you were worried of the dog earlier you can't even think of or even dream of wandering on the banks of *Godā*. This is uttered by the beloved (*abhisārīkā*) who secretly wants to meet her lover at the dells of river Godā and doesn't want that sage to disturb them.

The point in favour of *vyaṅgya* is that 'wander' etc. literally is of the nature of *vidhi* i.e. of the nature of recommendation and the suggested meaning is of *niṣedha* i.e. of prohibition which can't be attributed to *vācya* i.e. the literary meaning as it will lead to contradiction. So *niṣedha* i.e. prohibition has to be suggestive.

Then the objection is raised by the opponents of *dhvani* saying that *tātparyaśakti* doesn't stop at the literal sense. It goes even beyond it and covers the implicit e.g. all the other words (*padas*) of the above mentioned are not in conformity with the verb 'wander'. So *mukhyārtha* i.e. the prime meaning becomes *bādhita* i.e. the primary meaning becomes incompatible. Bhāṭṭa Mīmāṁsakas advocate the theory of *abhihitānvayavāda,* which holds that literal meaning of each individual term is made explicitly clear by *tātparya* i.e. the conclusion. It means not only the literal meaning of each term but also relation between the terms is important which is known by *tātparyaśakti*. The 'wander' etc. sentence is based on *Virodha sambandha*. Hence *tātparya* tells us about the *niṣedha* and not *vidhi*. Even in day-to-day functioning of the language, it is never said that this is implied by his utterance', but, it is impressed as 'this is uttered.' Hence there is no *vyañjanāśakti*.

To this the reply given by the *dhvani-vādins* is that the *vyañjanā-śakti* is there. There are three powers 1. *abhidhā* 2. *lakṣaṇā* and 3. vyañjanā. Literal meaning is *abhidhā* and is determined by *saṅketa*. (1st time conventional meaning decided by God) and *saṅketa* is on the class (*jāti*) and not on individuals i.e. *vyakti*. If particulars (*vyakti*) are taken for *saṅketa* then it will lead to infinity (*ānantya)*. It also implies *vyabhicāra* as it violates the rule that only that should be communicated on which there was *saṅketa*.

Further objection raised by the *dhvanivādins*. is *vyavahāra* i.e. common day-to-day function is possible only with the help of *vyakti* then how Mīmāṁsā position says that *saṅketa* is on *jātī*. It cannot be acceptable. To this the answer is that *vyakti* is understood by *ākṣepa* i.e. *arthāpatti* e.g. *gotva* i.e. cowness cannot exist without *govyakti* hence *'go' śabda* indicates *govyakti* i.e. an individual cow which is known by *arthāpatti*.

The supporters of *dhvani* also argue saying that again in the example 'wander etc' *mukhyārthabādha* i.e. sublation of primary meaning does not take place as in the case of *Gaṅgāyāṁ ghoṣaḥ* or *siṁho baṭuḥ*. In these two sentences the expectancy (*yogyatā*) is absent in the (*padas*) words or the terms of the sentence hence the primary meaning is sublated and secondary meaning takes place. As *mukhyārthabādha* is not possible in case of 'wander ....' meaning is not revealed by *lakṣaṇā* but is revealed by *vyaṅgya* or the suggested meaning.

In the example 'wandering' .... the suggested meaning is to protect the site of secret meeting of the two lovers and it is *vastudhvani* and the function of the suggestion is of the prohibition (*niṣedha*) so it is called *niṣedha-vyaṅgya*. It is not *lakṣaṇā* as complete rejection of *vācyārtha* i.e. literal meaning is discarded and 'bank' is understood instead of Gaṅgā.

Prayojana is the intention of the speaker, who while saying '*Gaṅgāyāṁ ghoṣaḥ* does not directly say that *ghoṣaḥ* is on the banks of Gaṅgā but puts it as in the midst of Gaṅgā. The purpose of speaker is not revealed by *vācyārtha* i.e. the literal meaning (as words are absent). The qualities of Gaṅgā and *ghoṣaḥ* are equated and only suggested by *vyaṅgyārtha*. Coolness and purity (*Śītalatva*, *Pāvitrya*) are there in Gaṅgā, but not in the banks of Gaṅgā, that is why *Gaṅgāyaṁ ghoṣaḥ*. In case of '*Siṁho baṭuḥ' anumāna* (inference) is not possible as *vyāptijñana* is absent. The boy is very brave and is understood by *vyañjānā śaktī* alone.

This knowledge is not possible by memory either, because in memory there is certainty of remembering the past experience. But in case of *simho baṭuḥ,* which of the characteristics of *siṁha* (lion) are recalled is not certain. It is to be understood by suggestion only.

Again *abhihitānvaya* has accepted *vyañjanāvyāpāra*. According to this theory it is believed that *saṅketa* is the accompanying reason of *abhidhā* and *ākānkāṅkṣā*, *yogyatā*, *sannidhī* are the factors accompanying *tātparya*. So the accompanying factors of *vyañjanā* are different hence it is *vyañjanāvyāpāra*.

The *Anvitābhidhāna* (Prabhākara) believes that meaning of a term (*pada*) as well as meaning of its relation to other terms in the sentence are not known by two separate reasons such as *abhidhā* and *tātparyaśakti*. But, it is known only through *abhidhā*. All the functions are the functions of *abhidhā* and they go on extending. The objection is how it can be one function as the *viṣaya*.[19] The different meanings are known through the different functions and if the extended function is not one, but combination of many, then what is the problem in accepting *vyañjanāvyāpāra?*

The examples of *Dhvanyāloka* illustrate multifunctional use of language. It is literal and yet it is more meaningful when it is suggestive. Same words in different context are understood differently.

IV

It is the doctrine of *Dhvani* or the metaphorical suggestive meaning which is not only the essence of poetry (*Kāvyasya ātmā dhvaniḥ*) but also the essence of fine arts and performing arts. It is *Rasadhvani*, which is the essence of entire aesthetic endeavour. It is different from *vastu-dhvani* and *alaṁkāra dhvani*. It is unspeakable i.e. *avācya*. It cannot be paraphrased. It is irreducible. (*Na hi rasādṛte kaścidarthaḥ pravartate*). According to the supporters of *Dhvani* the treatise on Indian aesthetics can be prepared with the help of the doctrine of *Dhvani*.[20] It is *Dhvani* or the suggestive, prescriptive, non-cognitive which can also be extended for *manovyāpāra* i.e. all linguistic utterances for mental conduct. The mental conduct concepts are to be understood metaphorically and not literally. Abhinavagupta, the commentator of *Dhvanyāloka* of Ānandavardhana and ardent scholar of Kashmir Śaivism, supports *Dhvani* because the Final or the Ātman or Divine can neither be talked of nor understood literally, hence, is to be understood suggestively. It is prescriptive, and it is far more important than the literal, as literal is only the body, and suggestive is the self. The literal is required as that is the only available mode of communication and that is necessary but it is not sufficient. The cognitive content in it is important but a stage comes when even the cognitive content also is dropped and what remains is only the irreducible 'silence' (*Śānti*).

REFERENCES

1. औत्पत्तिकस्तु शब्दस्यार्थेन संबंधः। पू. मी. १.१.५.
2. Mīmāṁsā view supporting the *vidhivākyas*.
3. Nowellsmith, P. H.—*Ethics*.

4. Davidson, Donald 'What metaphors mean', p. 439.
   (A.P. Martinich (Ed)).—*The Philosophy of Language.*
5. *Ibid.*, p. 438.
6. *Ibid.*, p. 437.
7. *Ibid.*, p. 446.
8. *Ibid.*, p. 446.
9. *Ibid.*, p. 447.
10. *Ibid.*, p. 439.
11. *Ibid.*, p. 447.
12. *Ibid.*, p. 447.
13. Virkar P. N. ध्वन्यालोक with 'लोचन', p. 18. (Ed) Maharashtra Rājya Sāhitya Sanskriti Maṇḍaḷ Mumbai 1983.
14. *Ibid.*, p. 21.
15. स्वेच्छाकेसरिण: स्वच्छस्वच्छायायासितेन्दव:।
    त्रायन्तां वो मधुरिपो: प्रपन्नार्तिच्छिदो नखा:।। ध्वन्यालोक उद्योत १श्लोक १.
16. प्रतीयमानं पुनरन्यदेव वस्त्वस्ति वाणीषु महाकवीनाम्।
    यत्तत्प्रसिद्धावयवातिरिक्तं विभाति लावण्यमिवाङ्गनासु।। ध्वन्यालोक उद्योत १श्लोक ४.
17. भ्रम धार्मिक विस्त्रब्ध: स शुनकोऽद्य मारितस्तेन।
    गोदानदीकूललतागहनवासिना दृप्तसिंहेन।। ध्वन्यालोक, p. 77.
18. *Ibid.*, pp. 82 to 86.
19. *Ibid.*, p. 99.
20. *Ibid.*, p. 27.

V.7

THE NOTION OF TIME AND IT'S APPLICATION IN POETICS—A FEW OBSERVATIONS

Dr. Uma Vaidya

The notion of 'Time' is an important topic which is discussed at length by all Indian and Western philosophical systems. This article is restricted to the Sanskrit Grammatical concept of Time and its application in Sanskrit poetics. Pāṇini, Patañjali and Bhartṛhari are the three important grammarians who have thought over the notion of Time and have treated it as an important component in the grammatical explanations of the words. These three have different methods of word-explanations though they have a common goal to explain the words of day-to-day language. Pāṇini's aim was not to write the philosophy of grammar, but,was to arrive at the correct formation of words in practice and therefore, no explanation of the concept of Time is separately found in Pāṇinian *Aṣṭādhyāyī* except a few rules which employ the word '*Kāla*' as a *śabdarūpa* and there is no implication of the concept of Time as a philosophical entity.

However, in the '*Pāṇinīyaśikṣā*' some references are found to '*Kāla*' in the context of pronunciation. *Pāṇinīyaśikṣā* is a small treatise which is also called as '*uccāraṇa*-śāstra'[1] . In this process of articulation, the 'Time' is an important factor because the classification of vowels as short, long and prolated is based on the unit of Time which is required for the articulation of a single vowel.[2] *Mātrā* is the measure of Time and the *ekamātrika* is called *hrasva, dvimātrika* is called *dīrgha* and the *trimātrika* is called *pluta*.[3] This *hrasva* and *dīrgha* in grammar is called *laghu* and *guru* in rhetorics. The science of poetry, especially the science of prosody has used this time-measure very cleverly. *Geyatā* or the musical quality of the words is an important attribute of any good poetry. This musical quality totally depends upon the *Tāla* and *Laya* which is inherent in the words. The poet selects a particular word from it's synonyms on two criteria—The first is the shade of meaning that is presented by that particular word and the second important criterion is the order of short and long vowels in that word. That is to say the time required for the utterance of that word as to be fitted, in the prosodial arrangement. The *Vṛttaśāstra* is based upon this foundation of *laghutva* and *gurutva* of the syllables and therefore, the *Mātrā-vṛtta*-s and even the *akṣaragaṇa vṛtta*-s depend upon the *mātrā*—which is the measure of Time.

The Late Prof. H. D. Velankar has observed[4] that there are three types of *Vṛttas*.

"In ancient India three different kinds of music are found to be underlying a metrical composition.

(1) music of voice-modulation or the *svara-saṅgīta*.

(2) music of sound-variation or *varṇaṅgīta*.

(3) music of time-regulated accent or the *Tāla-saṅgīta*.

This third variety is produced neither by skilful modulation of voice nor by the fixed succession of short and long sounds but by means of stressing the voice or sound after the lapse of a definite period measured by time-moments called the *mātrā*-s i.e. *kāla-mātrā*s. This music is produced out of strokes upon a time-keeping instrument like a hand-drum. The Sanskrit name for these strokes is *Tāla*, derived from the root *taḍ*—to strike. This variety of music is essentially based on the well-regulated lime-element.

An important feature of *varṇa-vṛtta* is the *Yati* or the metrical pause introduced in the middle of the line. This is regularly admitted at specific places as against the irregular pause which is noticed in the case of Vedic-metres. It's origin has of course to be traced to the ease of recitation but gradually it first became conventional and then compulsory. It is interesting to note that introduction of *Yati* in the metrical lines helped the formation and fossilization of many different metrimusical units of different length."

This idea of *Yati* or a pause in the *vṛtta-s* reflects on the *Vyavasthita-kāla* i.e. the disciplined (time)—pause to be used by the reciter. It shows that the seed of *Mātrā-baddha-kāla* which is seen in the *Pāṇinīyaśikṣā* is not only developed in poetics but its blossom is seen in the science of prosody. It is interesting to note that Pāṇini was also aware of the changes made by the poeticians in the *hrasva-dīrghatva* of vowels. He knows well that a composite syllable which follows a short vowel, transforms that short vowel into a long one and therefore, he restricts some grammatical operations to such long vowels. For example, the Pāṇinian rule '*ato halāderlaghoḥ*' P.A. 7.2.7 prescribes optional *vṛddhi* to the vowel 'a' which is originally *hrasva* and is followed by a simple consonant (and not by a conjunct-consonant) and therefore, the root *Rakṣ* and *Takṣ* where the 'a' of the root becomes prosodially long because of the following conjunct-consonant, will not have optional *vṛddhi*, and the single forms as *arakṣīt* and *atakṣīt* are to be used. Therefore, the time required for the utterance of a particular word is an important point for consideration in poetics. Pāṇini has not shown any concern with 'Time' as an abstract philosophical principle but,has stressed on its practical application and the same is found in poetics in an elevated status.

However, from Patañjali onwards the picture started changing. He started incorporating the philosophical notions in grammar. His famous theory of eternality of words, of their meaning and their relation to each other was presented through the phrase '*siddhe śabdārtha-saṁbandhe*'. Patañjali hereby proclaims that the words are eternal, their meaning is also eternal. This very idea of eternality between the two is the base of '*Sāhitya*' or literature. The word *Sāhitya* itself is defined as '*śabdārthayoḥ sahitatvam sāhityam*' i.e. togetherness of word and its meaning is called *sāhitya*. The notion of togetherness presupposes the *kālasannidhi* and *sthalasannidhi* i.e. the nearness of time and place. This uninterrupted relation of the words with their meaning, that is sāhitya with reference to the Time, is an essential factor of literature. The concept of eternality reflects on the past, present and future time. Continuous existence of a particular quality in a particular object is called 'eternality'. The word 'continuity' again throws light on the attribute of Time. According to the grammarians the Time is one and indivisible. In this way eternality (*Nityatā*) and continuity (*Sātatya*) have the bearing on Time and therefore, any *Sāhitya* will invariably be thought only in the light of the Notion of Time.

The *kālasannidhi* is not only an attribute of *Sāhitya* but it is an essential factor in the whole process of understanding the meaning of words. The poeticians along with the Mīmāṁsaka-s unanimously agree to the point that the meaning of the sentence is understood only if there exist *ākāṅkṣā, yogyatā* and *sannidhi*,[5] that is, expectancy (of the words for each other), capability (of being in relation with each other) and the togetherness of words in a particular sentence. This togetherness is of two types : *kālasannidhi* and *sthalasannidhi*, and all the words in a sentence should be uttered at one and the same place and at the same time. The gap or passage of Time in the utterance of words will make the words non-cognisable and therefore, Time is an essential factor in the process of knowledge.

Moreover, the appreciation of the poetry depends upon the instantness of cognition of words. The *Rasa* is produced as soon as the word is understood and the word is understood as soon as it is uttered. If there is a gap of time between the utterance of the word and cognition of the word then the '*Rasaniṣpatti*' is harmed and the sole objective of poetry that is '*sadyaḥparanivṛti*' is lost. Mammaṭa has enlisted[6] the six objectives of poetry as '*kāvyam yaśase*' etc. and there he says that, 'instant highest satisfaction to the mind' is the most important objective; in Mammaṭa's words, it is '*sakalaprayojanamaulībhūtam*'. In achieving this goal, through poetry, the 'Time' plays an important role which is suggested by the word '*sadyaḥ*'. If this time of utterance and time of cognition is not properly calculated by the poet, reciter or the reader it will not allow the sentiment to be produced. The idiom '*kālaḥ pibati tadrasam*' can also be explained in this context thus. That is why, a slow speaker is never an effective speaker. The speaker must plan the pause in the words and sentences. He should not be too slow or too fast and thus the time-management is an important quality of a good speaker and of a good poetry too.

Here are some observations on the *Sphoṭa*—theory (in relation with the notion of Time) as this theory is commonly accepted by the grammarians and the poeticians too. Traditionally the *Sphoṭa*—theory is to the credit of Sphoṭāyana who is a pre-pāṇinian scholar of Grammar, but, this theory is discussed thoroughly by Bhartṛhari in his *Vākyapadīya* and it is supposed to be the by-product of Patañjali's theory of '*siddhe śabdārtha-saṁbandhe*'. As stated earlier, the relation between word and meaning is eternal. This *nityatā* is of two types[7]—*kūṭasthanityatā* and *pravāhanityatā*. That which has no origin and which always remains unchanged is called *kūṭasthanitya* i.e. absolute eternal and the words are coming under this category. The other type is *pravāhanityatā* or continuity. Something which is present in different substrata but docs not perish with the substrata is also eternal and that is *pravāhanityatā*. When one cognises a word in its thousands of utterances, it is eternal in the sense of continuity—Mammaṭa explains it in following words—'*Bālavṛddhaśukādyudīriteṣu ḍitthādi -śabdeṣvityanye*'[8]

The *Vākyapadīya*, however, emphasises the eternity of meaning in the sense of continuity and seeks support from the *Mahābhāṣya*. Yāska also says[9]—'Eternal indeed is the relation of the meaningfuls with their meanings.' The fact that 'the meaning invariably comes to the mind whether an object corresponding to it is present or not' is taken as a proof to prove that the relation between the word and the meaning is eternal. According to Bhaṛtrhari, the meaning of a sentence which resides in the mind of the speaker is one, eternal and indivisible and he names it as *Sphoṭa*. This *Sphoṭa* which Bhartṛhari considers as the word-principle i.e.

Śabdatattva') is manifested through words and thus that which is called the *Śabdatattva*' on philosophical level, is called .as 'the *sphoṭa*' on the practical level. It means the word-principle and the eternal meaning of the words are manifested through words. Thus, the concept of *sphoṭa* as is envisaged by Bhartṛhari serves as the medium to form the relation between the word-principle and the word and that relation may be titled as Micro-macro-relation. When Patañjali says that the word i.e. *śabda* is of two kinds i.e. eternal one and the transitory one, Bhartṛhari clarifies by saying that the eternal one should be understood as either the universal (or *Jāti*) or the *sphoṭa* and that the transitory one should be understood as either the particular (*vyakti*) or the sound (*dhvani*).

This *sphoṭa*-theory is also made use of by the poeticians to serve their purpose. Mammaṭa while explaining the *dhvani-kāvya* says[10], '*sphoṭarūpasya vyaṅgyavyañjakasya*' etc. The word *sphoṭarūpa* is a qualified and the word *vyaṅgyavyañjakasya* is a qualifier. According to Mammaṭa. the inherent meaning (*vyaṅgya*) is manifested through the words (*vyañjaka*) which are in the form of *sphoṭa* (i.e., the *sphoṭarūpa*). Here, the shade of the meaning of the word *sphoṭa*, seems to be changed. The word '*sphoṭa*' is taken here as the utterance of words through which the inherent meaning is manifested and this explanation is corresponding to what Patanjali has said about the *sphoṭa* as *dhvani*, the second type of word.

The tradition explains the word *sphoṭa* in two different ways.

(1) *sphuṭyate vyajyate vā varṇaiḥ (saḥ antarnihitaḥ arthaḥ sphoṭaḥ*)'- it is in this sense that Bhartṛhari uses the word *Sphoṭa.*[11]

(2) *sphuṭyante yajyante vā varṇaḥ yasmin (saḥ sphoṭaḥ nāma prakriyā yasyām varṇāḥ uccāryante*)'—Mammaṭa accepts this sense of *sphoṭa*. Therefore, *sphoṭa* according to Mammaṭa. is a process which is the real cause of the manifestation of meaning. If the *sphoṭa* is a process then it will have *pravāhanityatā* because any action or *kriyā* is always *sāvayava,* but, *akhaṇḍa*. In Mammaṭa's words it is *pūrvāparībhūta.*[12] This *pūrvāparībhūtatva* of an action which is accepted by the poeticians in the explanation of the *dhvanikāvya* is expressed by the ingenious idea of tenses in Pāṇini. *Abhavat, Bhavati* and *Bhaviṣyati* are the three parts of the same *Bhavana-kriyā*. As they are mentioned in past, present and future tense, they make a continuous process of *Bhavana*. In fact,the Time is one and indivisible, but, this division as tenses etc. is imposed upon it for the practical convenience.[13]

According to Bhartṛhari, the 'Time' is responsible for the temporal sequence in which all phenomena take place and all objects appear. He singles out the *Kālaśakti* (power of Time) which is in fact the most important one among the many powers of *śabdatattva*. It is the creative power (*kartṛ-śakti*) which is also called *svātantrya-* i.e., power of complete freedom. Every effect has its own cause, special, material or otherwise, but, all the special causes depend upon Time, thus, it is an auxiliary cause (*sahakārikāraṇam*) of everything. *Uccāraṇa*, *dhārana*, *arthajñāna* and *vināśa* are the four functions of the phonemes and when they are performed in the temporal sequence govern the whole process of cognising the meaning of a word. This cognition is possible because of the two powers of Time, which are named as *abhyanujñā-* granting permission and *pratibandha-* prevention.[14] Origin of the things (it is the pronunciation of words in the context of poetics) is due to the *abhyanujñā* function of Time. Unless the Time permits, the words will not come from the speaker and unless the time permits they will not be cognised by the listener. The words which have got existence, have to continue till they serve their purpose. This continuity is also due to the *abhyañujṅā* function only. The *pratibandha* is another power of Time which prevents the things from existence either before their time or after their time. The phonemes get perished after the word-meaning is cognised. It is due to the power called *pratibandha*. Therefore, the existence of words, their cognition and creation of *Rasa* are all depending on the two powers of *Kāla*. The *Rasa* is the soul of poetry,[15] but, is produced and relished only because of the powers of Time.

As a conclusion, it may be said that this article presents a few observations on the notion of Time as presented by the grammarians and as used by the poeticians. The observations are as follows :—

(1) The musical quality of a poem and the science of prosody thereby, mainly depend upon the disciplined use of Time.

(2) The most important objective of poetry that is '*sadyaḥparanirvṛti*' can be achieved only with the help of Time.

(3) The role that is played by the notions of Time in cognising the words is very important and the word-cognition is possible only with the help of *kālasannidhi*, *abhyanujñā* and *pratibandha*.

(4) According to the poeticians (as is seen from Mammaṭa), the *sphoṭa* is a process of producing sounds which manifests the inherent meaning. Any process cannot be thought without the important role of Time in it because the process is *sāvayava* and *akhaṇḍa*. It is interwoven in past, present and future which are actually the attributes of *Kāla*. In this way, the two

important grammatical concepts that is Time and *Sphoṭa* are applied by the poeticians to explain their own theories.

(5) Lastly, the word '*Sāhitya*' i.e. literature which is the major topic for study in poetics also reflects on *kālasānnidhya* of *Śabda* and '*Artha*'.

REFERENCES :

1. Mahato Damodar, *'Pāṇinīyaśikṣā'*, Motilal Banarasidas, New Delhi, 1999, p. 3, stanza—2.
2. *Ibid.*, p. 17, stanza—11.
3. *Ibid.*, p. 17, stanza—11.
4. Velankar, H. D., (An Article) ' 'Ancient Indian Metres', published in *Ramkrishna Mission Journal*, p. 1.
5. Hatvalane and Hatvalane, ' *Kāvyaprakāśa,* Sahitya Seva Prakashana, Satara, p. 8.
6. *Ibid,* p. 2.
7. Ayer K.A.S. *'Bhartṛhari',* Deccan College, Poona, 1969, p.74.
8. Ref. 5, p. 12.
9. Varma, S. K., '*Vākyapadīyam*'(*Brahmakāṇḍam*), Munshiram Manoharlal Publishers, p. 21, stanza—23.
   'नित्यो हि अर्थवतामर्थैरभिसम्बन्धः'।
10. Ref. 5, p. 6.
   'प्रधानभूतस्फोटकरूपव्यङ्ग्यव्यञ्जकस्य शब्दस्य ध्वनिरिति व्यवहारः कृतः'।
11. Ref. 7, p. 159.
12. Ref. 5, p. 10.
13. Bhartṛhari, '*Vākyūpadīyam'*, Abhyankar-Limaye, University of Poona, Sanskrit-Prakrit Series, Vol.11, Poona, 1965, p. 100, stanza-32.
14. *Ibid*, p. 98, stanza 4-5,
15. Viśvanātha, '*Sāhityadarpaṇa,*' Editor P. V. Kane, Mumbai, 1923, p.5, stanza 3.
   वाक्यं रसात्मकं काव्यम्।

V.8

BHOJA'S THEORY OF *AHAM-ŚṚṄGĀRA*-SYNTHESIS

Dr. Rajendra I. Nanavati (Vadodara)

(1)

Nearly a millenium before, Bhoja was sitting in the ancient city of Dhārā, was most probably aware and very conscious that nearly a millenium still before him, the great legendary king Vikramāditya was sitting on the throne of Ujjayinī and ruling the same region which he was ruling now; and therefore was perhaps vying with that king of yore consciously or unconsciously by trying to be just, benevolent and by being a patron to and repository of our great tradition of learning and wisdom in nearly all its aspects. Such sincere efforts to bring together and consolidate all the knowledge and wisdom of Hindu traditional culture was once witnessed in the centuries around the beginning of the first millenium when our epics (particularly the *Mahābhārata)*, our fable literature *(Pañcatantra)*, our knowledge of literary and performing arts (the *Nātya-śāstra)*, our traditions of socio-religious practice (e.g. the *Manusmṛti)* etc. were being formed into great compendia of traditional wisdom. One would like to believe that Vikramāditya, the great of the Paramāra Dynasty in the Ujjayinī of yore, with the help of his traditionally famous nine intellectual gems, had tried to consolidate or at least strongly initiate the process of consolidating the Brahmanic Hindu wisdom of traditional lore to counter the fears of the sweeping influence of Śramaṇic religions—particularly Buddhism—growing out of all proportions and of the in-thrusts and onslaughts of the invaders like Hūṇas, Śakas and Yavanas. Almost after a millenium of Vikramāditya, King Bhoja of Dhārā was foreseeing a similar menace to Hindu cultural traditions from the violent Muslims-and even perhaps from the surreptitious Christians—spotted around the corner and attempting to influence the traditional Hindu society. The popular tradition has somehow been juxtaposing these two monarchs—King Vikramāditya and King Bhoja—through the tales of the thirtytwo dolls—of the legendary throne of the great king Vikramāditya. Popular memory may not be accurate, but it often conceals great truths. Both the we are great, both were ruling the same area almost in the middle of this vast subcontinent, historically they were around the beginnings of the first and the second millenia and both were aware of the dangers threatening the traditional Hindu cultural values. Both seem to have adopted a similar approach to counter the alien (and even indigenous) dangers against the Hindu society—that of consolidating its lore of traditional wisdom in all its possible aspects. Bhoja's works and their comprehensive character can be better explained from this point of view. The older king is reputed to have had the traditionally famous nine intellectual gems in his court as mentioned in that famous verse:

धन्वन्तरिः क्षपणकामरसिंह-शङ्कु-वेतालभट्ट-घटकर्पर-कालिदासाः।
ख्यातो वराहमिहिरो नृपतेः सभायां रत्नानि वै वररुचिर्नव विक्रमस्य॥

The latter one also is known to be a great patron of learning and learned scholars though any verse mentioning the gems of his court is not known. With the help of this team of scholars, as also because he himself was a great scholar, Bhoja aimed at synthesizing the conflicting trends in various disciplines. He seems to chalk out the basic design of his works of which then the details might have been worked out and filled in by his court-scholars under his continuous observation. His must have been a great mind organising a number of traits into a harmonious whole. At least, so far as his contribution to Classical Sanskrit Poetics is concetned, we can certainly say that he offers a great synthesis of a grand tradition.

(2)

The distinctive feature of Bhoja's aesthetic theory is his concept of *Rasa*. It is unique in the history of Indian Aesthetics. In propounding this theory, Bhoja appears to adopt a monistic as well as a pluralistic approach simultaneously.

Bhoja seems to take his cue from the following verse of Daṇḍin who in it is explaining the *rasa*-based *alaṁkāras*. The verse is :

प्रेयः प्रियतराख्यानं रसवद् रसपेशलम्।
ऊर्जस्वि रूढाहङ्कारं युक्तोत्कर्षं च तत्त्रयम्॥[१]

Bhoja, in the first place, endorses the view that *rasas* also are *alaṁkāras*. He says, *preyaḥ, rasavad* and *ūrjasvi* are *rasas* when they are *yuktotkarṣa*— 'heightened'; otherwise, they are merely *guṇas* called *preyaḥ, bhāvikatva* and *aurjitya*. The *preyaḥ, rasavad* and *ūrjasvi* are a higher type of *alaṁkāras* since they are related to *bhāvas*. Bhoja explains through them his own concept of the three-level *rasa*.

According to Bhoja, the first state of *rasa* is *rūḍhāhaṁkāra;* this is the basic or fundamental stage of *rasa*. *Rasa* in this state is of the form of *ahaṁkāra* and exists in every soul as a result of the experiences of past lives. This *abhimāna* which is 'Self-consciousness' can also be looked upon as *Śṛṅgāra* or 'Self-love' in a highly philosophical sense. In Bhoja's own words:

रसोऽभिमानोऽहङ्कारः शृङ्गार इति गीयते।
योऽर्थः, तस्यान्वयात् काव्यं कमनीयत्वमश्नुते॥
विशिष्टादृष्टजन्मायं जन्मिनामन्तरात्मसु।
आत्मसम्यग्गुणोद्भूतेरेको हेतुः प्रकाशते॥[2]

This *abhimāna-ahaṁkāra-śṛṅgāra* develops into *Māna*—'dignity, self-respect' or consciousness; it is the 'I', the 'ego' which is at the root of, is the most primary cause of, all experiences as their experiencer. This stage is also called *parā koṭi*.

The second stage, *madhyamāvasthā,* occurs when the one basic *ahaṁkāra-rasa* manifests itself as *abhi-māna* 'Self-assertion, consciousness of Self, revealed in attaching itself to desires, to several outward objects with which it comes into contact. The one basic *rasa* thus manifests itself in multiplicity of forms. All the eight *rasas* described by Bharata, or the twelve given by Bhoja, or even all the fortynine *bhāvas* (including *vyabhicārins* and *sāttvikas)* can develop to the state of *rasa* in this stage. In fact, even when fully developed to the state of *rasa,* in this stage, they will be called *bhāvas* only.

आलम्बनविभावेभ्यः स्वेभ्यः स्वेभ्यः समुन्मिषन्।
रसो रत्यादिरूपेण भाव इत्यभिधीयते॥[3]

Thus, in this stage, the several *bhāvas* which have arisen out of the one *ahaṁkāra* are attended by their respective *vibhāvas* etc. and develop to the state of their climax. Though developed to the state of climax, really speaking, they are *bhāvas* only, they can be called *rasas* only secondarily, because the real *rasa* is only one, the *ahaṁkāra-rasa,* and it is only when *ahaṁkāra* is present as *abhimāna,* as the experiencer, that the different *rasas* can be relished. (In the terminology of Abhinava, *ātman* is neither *viśeṣata ullikhita,* nor *atyantatiraskṛta)*.[4]

. The third and final stage, also called *uttarā koṭī,* occurs when all the several *bhāvas* reaching their individual climax become transformed into one unitary *rasa* which is now called *Preman*. The climax of individual *bhāvas* itself is only *preman*.

The *bhāvas* which were several in the second stage now reach their highest intensity and are synthesized into the one *rasa* which is *preman.* The entire process of this *rasa* is very well expressed in these words of Dr. Raghavan : "Thus *ahaṁkāra* or *abhimāna* of the first stage becomes *abhimāna* for various outward objects and becomes the manifold *bhāvas* of *rati* etc., and those *bhāvas* themselves develop into respective *rasas* and culminate in Love or *preman* through which they again pass into the first fundamental *rasa* of *ahaṁkāra*[4a].

In this way, in the first and third stages, in the *parā koṭi* and *uttarā koṭi,* the *rasa* is only one. "We are there in a *monistic-pāramika* stage." Only in the middle stage, the *vyāvahārika* stage, *rasa*-pluralism has some scope. Again, in the third stage, the several manifestations of the *bhāvas* of the middle stage return to the original one *rasa.* The several *vikṛtis,* as it were, return to their *prakṛti.* "This third stage is therefore only the involution of the evolved."[4a]

(3)

The above brief statement of the *rasa*-theory of Bhoja reminds us of and draws our attention to the numerous parallels of thoughts and ideas strewn across the millenia of the development of Indian thought.

The very idea of reducing the various *rasas* to one in their ultimate state of relish can be traced back to the famous Upaniṣadic statement: *raso val saḥ/*[5] Similarly Bhoja's idea of synthesizing all *rasas* and *bhāvas* into *preyas* or *preman*[6] as seen in his words *rasāṇstviha premānam eva āmananti*[7] can be traced to that famous Upanisadic passage wherein Yājñavalkya preaches Maitreyī: *na vā are sarvasya kāmāya sarvam priyam bhavati, ātmanas tu kāmāya sarvam priyam bhavati/*[8]

Again, when Bhoja identifies *rasa* with *Śṛṅgāra* on the one hand and with *ahaṁkāra-abhimāna* on the other, he is admitting two senses of *Śṛṅgāra* : one at the *vyāvahārika* stage where it is the *prakarṣa-yukta* state of *rati,* and another in the sense of *abhimāna* - soul's attachment towards outward objects. Prof. K C. Pandey brings out this second connotation of *Śṛṅgāra* clearly; "... the word *Śṛṅgāra* is used by Bhoja in the Śr.Pra. in the context of his theory that *Śṛṅgāra* is the only *rasa,* not in the ordinary sense of the word as an aesthetic configuration, the central fact of which is love, but, in the sense of self-feeling of a particular type, which is due to the pure religious deeds of those in whom the quality of *sattva* predominates and arises from or is strengthened by the residual traces of the experiences of the past births and takes a man to the highest cultural level. (*yena śṛṅgam ucchrayo rīyate/* Śr.Pra. p. 420)"[9] In this aspect of the theory, the implication of the Sāṅkhya school of thought is too patent. It is the *ahaṁkāra* in the Sāṅkhya system which makes all worldly experiences of pleasure and pain possible for the *Puruṣa*. Similarly, it is the *ahaṁkāra* of the *Rasika* which makes all the *rasānubhavas* possible for him. A slight diversion will immediately be noticed. In the philosophical system, the experiences can be either pleasurable or painful, in the *kāvya,* all the experiences ultimately transform into *preman* only.

Prof. K. C. Pandey points out a slight discrepancy in Bhoja's proposition from the philosophical point of view. "... very often Bhoja identifies *Śṛṅgāra* with *ahaṁkāra,* 'ego-feeling' or *abhimāna,* but that is due to ignoring the distinction between the quality and its possessor."[10]

(4)

Bhoja's indebtedness to his predecessors in the field of Sanskrit Poetics is too obvious. The very concept of *Rasa*-synthesis in *Śṛṇgāra* is already found in the *Agni-purāṇa* before him :

अक्षरं ब्रह्म परमं सनातनमजं विभुम्।
वेदान्तेषु वदन्त्येकं चैतन्यं ज्योतिरीश्वरम्॥
आनन्दः सहजस्तस्य व्यज्यते स कदाचन।
व्यक्तिः सा तस्य चैतन्य-चमत्कार-रसाह्वया॥
आद्यस्तस्य विकारो यः सोऽहङ्कार इति स्मृतः।
ततोऽभिमानस्तत्रेदं समाप्तं भुवनत्रयम्॥
अभिमानाद् रतिः सा च परिपोषमुपेयुषी।
व्यभिचार्यादिसामान्याच्छृङ्गार इति गीयते॥
तद्भेदाः काममितरे हास्याद्या अप्यनेकशः॥[११]

Even the concept of all *rasas* evolving from a single *rasa* and involving into it is found in the text of the *Śānta-rasa-prakaraṇa* in the *Rasādhyāya* of the *Nāṭya-śāstra* of Bharata. Vide:

भावविकारा रत्याद्याः शान्तस्तु प्रकृतिर्मतः।
विकारः प्रकृतेर्जातः पुनस्तत्रैव लीयते॥
स्वं स्वं निमित्तमासाद्य शान्ताद् भावः प्रवर्तते।
पुनर्निमित्तापाये च शान्त एवोपलीयते॥[१२]

Bhoja takes the concept of *Śānta*-synthesis from *Nāṭya-śāstra* as well as Abhinavagupta and puts *Śṛṅgāra* in the place of *Śānta* following the enunciation of *Agni-purāṇa*. He, of course, adds a clarity in the concept by introducing the detail of the three stages and his *Śṛṅgāra*-synthesis is more in keeping with the relishable nature of *Kāvyāsvāda* rather than the peaceful characeristic of *Śānta*. This difference in the approaches to the poetical problem of *Rasa*-synthesis may very well be attributed to the fact of the difference of the social status of their authors—the *Sāttvika* ascetic finding a solution in the *Śānta*-synthesis, the *Rājasika* king in the *Śṛṅgāra*-synthesis.

(5)

Dr.Raghavan raises some doubts about Bhoja's theory. According to Bhoja, all *bhāvas,* when nourished, attain to the state of *rasa*. This also includes the *sāttvika bhāvas* like *stambha* etc. Bhoja says: **अयं च स्तम्भः पुष्टोऽपि सात्त्विकत्वात् सदैव अन्यानुयायीति नानुभावादिभिरनुबध्यते। अस्यापि (रोमाञ्चस्य) सात्त्विकत्वाद् अन्यानुबन्धादयो न जायन्ते॥**[१३]

Dr. Raghavan's objection is : "How can an unattended thing be considered *pusṭa* or developed? If it is still looking upto something to render itself understood *anya-mukha-prekṣin,* how is it leading? A mere description of *stambha* cannot make an instance of *stambha-rasa*. The concept of *rasa* means (1) an emotional state and (2) an emotional state which is *pradhāna*. This *pradhānatva* is not a mere question of a poet nourishing a *bhāva*. It means that the *bhāva* is, by nature, a major mood, within which occur a number of secondary emotional states... There cannot be *viśrānti* in a minor or fleeting feeling."[14]

The main point, however, appears to be something else. Can *stambha* not be the subject of a single verse? Can it not be poetic? And if it can, then should the relish of it not be called *rasa* ? Mainly, it is the question of the poeticity of stray verses to which Bhoja and other theoreticians like him appear to be addressing themselves in all such cases. *Viśrānti* is required from the *Bhāvaka's* point of view, but we know that Lollaṭa is representing the poet's point of view, and from the poet's viewpoint, even a single state/situation can become the subject of a poetic composition and the source of poetic delight. Many verses in Amaruka's *centum* are the evidences in point. If, then, we accept Lollaṭa's view of *rasa* as being *kāvya-niṣṭha* 'residing in the poem', then anything depicted in an isolated verse, in a *muktaka,* in a *subhāṣita,* will be *rasa*. This view which was observed to be in a rather primitive state in poeticians like Rudraṭa etc. is observed to be carried to its logical extremity in Bhoja. It was to answer this problem of the poeticity of the individual verses that, in the end, Jagannātha, though he adhered to the principles of *Rasa* and *Dhvani,* yet has propounded the theory of *ramaṇīyatā* in order to explain the poetic delight of the single verses.

REFERENCE

1. *Kāvyādarśa*, II. 275.
2. भोज सरस्वतीकण्ठाभरणम्. 5. 1-2.
3. *Ibid*. 5.13.
4. *Nāṭyaśāstra* GOS Edn. Vol. I, p. 273.
5. तैत्तिरीयोपनिषद् 2-7.
6. Cf. "Hāsya is love for Hāsa; Vīra is love for Utsāha and so on." *The Number of Rasas,* Raghavan V., pp. 133-4fn.
7. शृङ्गारप्रकाश: Ch. XI, p. 431.
8. बृहदारण्यकोपनिषद्. 4-6.
9. His *Indian Aesthetics,* I, p. 198.
10. *Ibid*., pp. 197-8.
11. अग्निपुराणम् 338. 1-5, as noted by P.V. Kane in his *History of Sanskrit Poetics,* p. 9.
12. भरतनाट्यशास्त्र, GOS, Vol. I, pp. 328-9.
13. सरस्वतीकण्ठाभरणम्, p. 498.
14. *Op. Cit*., pp. 139-40.
15. See above fn. no. 3 (=and) 13.

SECTION-VI

PHILOSOPHY AND RELIGION

VI.1
KHYĀTI-VĀDA IN PRATYABHIJÑĀDARŚANA

Prof. Dr. G.V. Tagare

0.1 What is प्रत्यभिज्ञा (*Pratyabhijñā*)

(Pratyabhijñā) प्रत्यभिज्ञा *(PB)* is 'recognition'; recognition that every individual soul is no other than the Supreme Soul or *Parama Śiva* himself.' This philosophy is the development of *Īśvarādvayavāda* —an Agamic philosophy developed (promulgated?) by Vasugupta (A.D. 825), a Śaiva teacher in Kashmir. Though Agamic, this philosophy is not anti-Vedic. Apparently it looks like the *Advaita-darśana* of Ādi Śaṅkarācārya. But their fundamental concepts being different, they developed independently and differently. *Para Śiva* and the *Para Brahman* are different fundamental concepts.

01.1 Difference in the concepts :

Para Śiva of Kashmir Śaivas (Vasugupta) and

Para Brahman of Śāṅkarādvaita

The confusion is due to similarities in the implication of the terms *Advaya* and *Advaita*.

0.1.1.1 The concept of *Para Śiva* :

The concept *Paraśiva* is regarded as being endowed with *Prakāśa* or Absolute Knowledge and *Vimarśa*—the Willpower capable of doing anything—even the creation, sustenance and destruction of the universe. This power is essential, as bereft of it, Śiva will be powerless or lifeless or inert like a stone[1] It is a fundamental concept that *Śakti* is inseparable from Śiva. Such a separation is never held by Śaivas[2].

0.1.1.2 The Concept of *Para Brahman*

The *Para Brahman* in *Śāṅkara Vedānta* is only *Prakāśa* or knowledge. He has not the capacity to do anything. The creation of the universe takes place when the *Para Brahman* is associated with *Māyā* or *Avidyā*. So according to Śaṅkara, the world is an illusion (*Māyika*), not real. The *Brahman* is the reality.

The concept of *Māyā,* led to two different levels of reality or *Satya* : (1) *Vyāvahārika Satya* and (ii) *Pāramārthika Satya*. It is *Bhrānti* (misapprehension) that one regards a piece of string as a serpent or a mother of pearls as silver.

Introduction or belief in the concept of *Māyā* has given rise to the above complication. But with Kashmir Śaivas, *Para Śiva* is the only reality. There is no scope to misapprehension. Śiva being all-pervasive, both the string and the serpent are real, there is no need to believe that one is a *Pāramārthika Satya* and the other is *Vyāvahārika Satya*. The world is Śiva and is real.[3] Śiva is immanent and transcendent to the universe.

Q. 2. Why *Pratyabhijñā*?

Vasugupta was not an easy-chair philosopher. In fact, in ancient India, philosophy was a pathway to *Nirvāṇa,* or *Mokṣa,* the end of the cycle of births and deaths, the highest goal (*Puruṣārtha*) in life. Vasugupta prescribed three courses to such a situation :

(1) *Śāmbhava Upāya*
(2) *Śakta Upāya,* Not related to *Śakti* cult
(3) *Āṇava Upāya*

Excellent as these Paths were, they involved some Yogic practices and were difficult for common men to follow or practise. Vasugupta's disciple, Somānanda—(A.D. 850-900) studied the ancient Śaiva Āgamas and promulgated *Pratyabhijñā* as a new path.[4] Monier Williams in his *Sanskrit English Dictionary* defines it. : 'Regaining knowledge or recognition (or the identity of the Supreme and the individual soul') p. 765 b.) The individual soul or the *Ātman* is originally and essentially the Supreme Śiva. But he was led to believe in his identity with his psycho-physical mechanism called his 'body'. 'The recognition or realization' 'I am Īśvara and none else' is *Pratyabhijñā*. According to MM Vasudeo Shastri Abhyankara'[5] *Pratyabhijñā*. is different from memory. In memory, there is no necessity of the presence or existence of the person or thing remembered. When I remember my friend who is dead or far away or in another country, it is memory.

But in *Pratyabhijñā*, the presence of the person is essential. I saw a person some time in the past. I meet him again and it occurs to me that *this is* the same person whom I met some years ago. This is a sort of the identification of the present with the past. When I experience again my original real nature as Maheśvara which was forgotten, it is *Pratyabhijñā*.

Q. 3. What is *Khyāti*

The term *Khyāti* from *Khyā:* To tell. It means 'That which has been told, opinion, *Bhrama* declaration, preception. This view can be about:

1. The *Ātman — Ātmakhyāti* the apprehension about or of the Soul.
2. *Asat-khyāti*—the apprehension of *Asat* (non-being)
3. *Akhyāti*—Non-apprehension (of anything)
4. *Anyathākhyāti :* Apprehension of another thing or a thing as otherwise.
5. अनिर्वचनीयख्याति—The apprehension of another thing or a thing as otherwise.

Examples of the above :

(1) आत्मख्याति or स्वख्याति. Even विज्ञानवादिन्s are accommodated in this ख्याति

(2) असत्ख्याति–According to स्याद्वादरत्नाकर (p. 125) in shell-silver illusion, the silver that is perceived is really non-existent.

(3) अख्याति-चार्वाक-शिवागम (?): प्राभाकर मीमांसा is different from शैव अख्याति

(4) अन्यथाख्याति-न्याय, भाट्टमीमांसा

(5) अनिर्वचनीयख्याति-शांकर अद्वैत

In Śāṅkara philosophy, reality is two-staged—पारमार्थिक and व्यावहारिक. Due to माया, विवर्त false apprehension (भ्रान्त ज्ञान) is caused. माया is अनिर्वचनीय. But in प्रत्यभिज्ञा or शिवाद्वैत there is no scope to विवर्त or भ्रम. In शुक्ति-रजत or रज्जु सर्प as both were Śivas there is no scope for any भ्रम. There is no मिथ्याभ्यास.

0.4 Conclusion :

Silver and mother-of-pearls are Śiva and there is no scope for भ्रम or ख्याति. Here ख्याति is used in the sense of ज्ञान. We may, however, concede to call it संकुचित ख्याति if some stamp of ख्याति is desired.

FOOTNOTE :

(1) यदि (शिव:) निर्विमर्श: स्यात्, अनीश्वरो जडश्च प्रसज्येत। क्षेमराज's पराप्रवेशिका २

(2) न शिव: शक्तिरहित:, न शक्तिर्व्यतिरेकिणी।
शक्ति-शक्तिमतोर्भेद: शैवे जातु न वर्ज्यते।। –सोमानन्द in शिवदृष्टि 3.2.3

(3) श्रीमत् परमशिवस्य पुन: विश्वोत्तीर्ण-विश्वात्मक-परमानन्दमय-प्रकाशैकघनस्य एवं विश्वमेव शिवादि-धरण्यन्तमखिलमभेदेनैव स्फुरति, न तु वस्तुत: अन्यत्तु किचिद् ग्राह्यं वा ग्राहकं वा।
–क्षेमराज:–प्रत्यभिज्ञाहृदयसूत्र ३, p. 34.

(4) सुघट एष मार्गो नव:। –उत्पल in ईश्वरप्रत्यभिज्ञाविमर्श IV.1.15

(5) अहमीश्वर एव नान्य इत्येवं य: साक्षात्कार: स प्रत्यभिज्ञेत्युच्यते।
दर्शनाङ्कुरटीका on सर्वदर्शनसङ्ग्रह IV.1.16.
अभिनवगुप्त defines: प्रतीपम् आत्माभिमुख्येन ज्ञानं प्रकाश: प्रत्यभिज्ञा।

VI.2

CONCEPT OF 'ĀNANDA' IN KEVALĀDVAITA VEDĀNTA

Prof. Esther A. Solomon

Brahman is defined as '*Ānandam Brahma*' (*Brh. Up*. 3.9.28), '*Satyam jñānam anantam Brahma*' (*Taitt*. Up. 2.1.1), '*Vijñānam ānandam Brahma* (*Brh. Up*. 3.9.28). We can make a general statement that Śaṅkarācārya is not very enthusiastic about explaining the word '*ānanda*'. The reason perhaps is that '*ānanda*' is regarded as a synonym of '*sukha*', pleasure, which is at the cost of something and is based on duality. As a result, an impression is created that Śaṅkarācārya understands by '*ānanda*' '*duḥkhābhāva*' absence of pain. Maṇḍana Miśra, on the other hand, very forcefully and at length proves that '*ānanda*' which is the very nature of *Brahman* or the Self (*Ātman*) is positive in character. But we have some passages in the works of Śaṅkarācārya which help to clean this misunderstanding. A passage from Śaṅkarācārya's commentary on the *Bṛhadāraṇyaka Up*. is an instance in point.

Daniel Ingalls has made a comparative study of the commentaries of Śaṅkarācārya on the *Bṛhadāraṇyaka Up*. and the *Brahma-sūtra*. He has felt that there is more originality in the *Bhāṣya* on the *Brh. Up*. than in the *Bhāṣya* on the *Brahma-sūtra,* because he gets a free hand in the former and indulges in comments that are not bound down by tradition, while in the *Bhāṣya* on the *Brahma-sūtra,* he has taken great care to see that he does not stray from the traditional interpretation. (See 'The Study of 'Śaṅkarācārya'—*Annals of the Bhandarkar Oriental Institute*, 33, 1952). Nevertheless, Śaṅkarācārya has given his own interpretation many a time, e.g. in the '*Ānandamayādhikaraṇa*' (*Brahma Sū. Bhāṣya*, I.1.19), and also as regards *jīvan-mukti* (liberation after death) and so also as regards the part played by *kriyā* (religious rites) and *jñāna* (knowledge) in the attainment of self-realisation.

Śaṅkarācārya's interpretation of the *Bṛh. Up.* passage, '*Vijñānam ānandam Brahma*' (3.9.28) is given here in support of what has been said above. Śaṅkarācārya says that in popular usage '*ānanda*' is regarded as a synonym of '*sukha',* and in the Upaniṣads, *'ānanda'* along with '*Vijñāna*' is found as an attribute or qualifier of *Brahman*. *Brahman* is of the nature of *ānanda* and is also *vijñāna.* Can it be said that *Brahman* experiences its own *ānanda,* and liberated souls who have attained the nature of *Brahman* also experience this *ānanda* ? According to the Vaiśeṣikas and the Sāṁkhyas, there is nothing like *sukha* (pleasure) in the state of liberation, while others hold that there is extreme Self, shining *sukha* in the state of liberation. Śaṅkarācārya says that body and sense-organs are required for knowledge or experience, but, these are not there in the state of liberation. And if *Brahman* could have its own knowledge, its oneness would be contradicted. It is not that *Brahman* knows itself as *ānanda;* it is of the nature of *ānanda*. But this *ānanda* is not something, that can be experienced or known; it is not an object of knowledge. If the knowledge of *ānanda* is eternal, it is the very nature of *Brahman* and it is meaningless to say that *Brahman* knows its own nature. This can be said only when the experience of *ānanda* is occasional. Thus, it is clear that Śaṅkarācārya regards *ānanda* as the very nature of *Brahman* and his stress is on distinguishing it from the conception of *sukha* which can be known, can be experienced. Śaṅkarācārya discussess his conception of *Ānanda* again in his *Bhāṣya* on *Bṛh. Up*. 4.4.6 *('Natasya prāṇā utkrāmanti, brahmaiva san brahmāpyeti*—its vital organs do not go out; being *Brahman*, it merges into *Brahman*). This one free from worldly desires merges on death into *Brahman* because it was always *Brahman*. If liberation is regarded as a change of state brought about by death, the *Kūṭasthatva* (absolute changelessness) and *ekatva* (oneness) of the Self would be set at nought, and *mukti* (liberation) would be something brought about by *kriyā* (action) and would not be eternal. In reality, liberation is eternal and so the very nature of the self (*Ātman*) as light-heat is the very nature of fire. Liberation cannot like bondage-breaking be regarded as the production of the negation, of something. There is nothing except *Brahman*, so there is no bondage which has to be torn off. Liberation means the destruction of *avidyā* (false knowledge, nescience), as when the false knowledge of a serpent in a rope is set aside, the serpent goes away because it was never there (*Bṛh*. *Up*. *Bhāṣya*, pp.333-384—*Works of Śaṅkarācāya,* Vol.2, Ashtekar and Co., Poona, 1918).

Some say that in the state of Liberation, such *vijñāna-ānanda* are manifested as different from the *vijñāna -ānanda* experienced in the world state. Śaṅkarācārya refutes this view. What is meant by saying that *vijñāna-ānanda* is manifested ? If it is the very nature of the Self, it is meaningless to say that it is manifested in the state of liberation, because it is eternally shining. If it is said that it is the nature of the self, but because of the covering of the *Upādhis*, (adjuncts) it shines forth only occasionally, then it could never shine forth, because something else would be required to bring this about. If *vijñāna-ānanda* are the attributes of the Self, their experience would not be possible, because one's own attributes cannot be experienced. *Śāstra* and teaching are useful for getting rid of *ajñāna* (ignorance). *Avidyā* does not affect the self in any way, so the self (*Ātman*) remains what it is, whether it is the state of bondage or of liberation. Self is the witness (*sākṣin*) of '*ajñāna*' (—'I do not know'—), but one cannot be a witness of one's own natural attribute, so *ajñāna* cannot be a natural attribute of the self. And one who knows himself as a subject to error or ignorance is not such.

Maṇḍana Miśra has thrown profuse light on the concept of *ānanda* in his *Brahmasiddhi*. Maṇḍana Miśra was a senior contemporary of Śaṅkarācārya and was converted to *Kevalādvaita* as a result of a debate with the latter, but, still had independent views of his own. The *Brahmasiddhi* has this verse at the outset:

"Ānandam ekam amṛtam ajam vijñānam akṣaram /
asarvam sarvam abhayam namasyāmaḥ prajāpatim //

Discussing the term '*Ānandam*', Maṇḍaṇa Miśra says that according to some, '*ānanda*' signifies '*duḥkha-atikrama'*, transcendence of all pain. If '*ānanda*' were to signify bliss as the nature of *Brahman*, the activity of a person seeking liberation would be motivated by a passion (*rāga*) for bliss, and such an activity could only lead to *saṁsāra*. Now, the *Bṛh. Up*. 4.4.23 says that it is the pacified and controlled one who sees the Self. Therefore, the scriptural passages describing bliss (*ānanda*) refer to the transcendence of all frustration or pain (*duḥkhātikrama*). In ordinary life we see that the word '*sukha'* (pleasure) is used when one transcends the pain of hunger, etc. Others say that pleasure is this cessation *(Dṛṣṭo hi kṣud-duḥkhādi-nivṛttau sukha-śabdaḥ. Saiva ca sukham ityanye. (Brahmasiddhi, Brahma-kāṇḍa,* p.1). It cannot be said that in that case a stone would be blissful, because, pleasure is an inner fluctuation or mode *(pratyag-vṛtti)* that is experienced, or it is the apprehension of the self as qualified by that *pratyag-vṛtti* by the cessation of frustration.

The answer to this is that bliss (or pleasure) is not merely the cessation of *duḥkha*. We see that a person up to his waist in a cool pond has *sukha* in the lower part of his body and *duḥkha* from the heat of the day in the upper part, and yet it is said that there is *sukha* because of the former. Moreover, if *sukha* were merely absence of *duḥkha,* the denizens of one hell would have *sukha* from the absence of the *duḥkhas* of other hells. And one suffering from pain due to the contact with the object of one sense-organ may have the absence of pain due to the contact with the objects of other sense-organs. And one who is free from pain may have pleasure from contact with certain sense-objects. Also, there is a difference in pleasures, but, not in the cessation of pain (or frustration) (*duḥkha*).

It may be argued that pleasure is produced by the removal of desire which if unfulfilled is of the nature of *duḥkha*. The answer to this is that we observe that people indifferent to a thing enjoy it when it is experienced. And it cannot be said that enjoyment produces desire and then produces pleasure by the extinction of desire, for enjoyment does not always extinguish desire. And the removal of desire by taking into consideration the faults of the objects does not produce pleasure. It cannot be said that the difference of degree in pleasures can be explained by the difference of degree of the previous desires, because, it is the things that come undesired and without effort that produce greater pleasure. Moreover, we do not consider that the state before the awakening of desire and after enjoyment and the cessation of desire is pleasurable. In any case, if an object produces desire when it is experienced, its enjoyment cannot extinguish desire. Moreover, sometimes the enjoyment of objects one has a great craving for produces not pleasure (*sukha*) but frustration (*duḥkha*). It is always the previous experience of something as pleasurable that produces desires. Sometimes people are frustrated by the cessation of desire, for example, if they are suffering from certain ailments like jaundice, and this is because they cannot experience certain pleasures. It is not proper to deny such a thing as positive pleasure which is experienced by each and every one. It seems that it is taught that pleasure is absence of *duḥkha* only as a good piece of advice to those attached to pleasure. The primary meaning of the word '*ānanda*' (bliss) (with reference to *Brahman*) is pleasure (*sukha*), something other than the cessation of pain or frustration (*duḥkha*) because something for which the Vedic word (*śabda*) is the only *pramāṇa* should be understood in accordance with the word.

All wishing (*icchā*) is not *rāga*, and so activity for the bliss of *Brahman* is not based on *rāga* (passion). *Rāga* is an obsession for non-existent qualities (*guṇas*) projected by *Avidyā*. But the wishing, the complacancy of the mind *(cetasaḥ prasādaḥ)* and the inclination (*abhiruci*) towards the truth that results from the clarity in seeing the truth are not rage. If the activity of trying to be free from the suffering of *saṁsāra* and reaching the bliss of *Brahman* were *rāga,* no one could escape from *saṁsāra*. If all activity were forbidden by the scripture, no activity, not even the activity for liberation, would be possible.

An objection may be raised that if bliss can be experienced in *Brahman*, there would be the duality of agent (*kartṛ*) and object (*karman*) of action, and so also of action (*kriyā*) and means (*karaṇa*). But it is not experienceable, it is as good as non-existent, and cannot be a *puruṣārtha* (end aim of man).

The answer to this is that the fruit of a *pramāṇa*, viz. *pramā,* valid knowledge, itself is not non-experienceable, because the possibility of anything's being experienced is dependent on its being experienced. Nor is it an object of experience in the same way as the thing known is, because *pramāṇa* has only one fruit. It is experienceable as being self-luminous (*sva-prakāśa*). So also the agent of knowledge is experienceable as being self-luminous, because if it is not knovn, the reflective consciousness *(anusandhāna)* between the agent, object and fruit of *pramāṇa* would not be possible, and so there would be no difference between what is known by oneself and what is known by someone else. Nor is it experienceable as the thing known (*karman*), because then it would be different from itself, and would not be itself. Like the fruit and the agent of *pramāṇa,* the blissful nature of *Brahman* is experienced as it is self-luminous, and not experienceable as it is not an object of experience.

Again, an objection may be raised that attributes (*dharmas*) are of two types, positive (*bhāvarūpa*) and negative (*abhāvarūpa*). If bliss were a positive attribute of *Brahman*, it would be a different entity from the *Vijñāna* (consciousness) of *Brahman*, so that one of the two would be the substrate (*dharmin*) and the other the attribute (*dharma*), and there would be duality. Therefore, the word 'bliss' (*ānanda*) in reference to *Brahman* means only 'absence of pain' (*duḥkhābhāva*), just as *Śruti* describes, *Brahman* as *'asthūlam anaṇvahrasvam* ...' (not coarse, not fine, not short ....) (*Brh. Up*. 3.3.3.).

The answer to this is that in *Brahman*, Bliss and Consciousness are identical, just as in the case of the moon 'light' (*prakāśa*) identical with 'joy' (*āhlāda*) is communicated by two words (joyful and light), or in the case of the sentence 'The sun is an exalted light', the form of light and exaltation are not different from each other. The supremacy of *Brahman*'s bliss is not merely the absence from it of suffering in the form of dependence on means (*sādhana*), or of perishableness, for in things the knowledge of which depends on *śabda* (scriptural word) we must follow that only. Only if *Brahman* is positive Bliss, can worldly bliss be a portion (*mātrā*) of it as the *Śruti* says. This is so by the limitation (*avaccheda*) of its Bliss. The self is Bliss also because it is the object of the highest love (*preman*)—every creature desires its own existence as the scripture says. Bliss is experienced in deep sleep as we know from the reflection (*parāmarśa*) on waking that we slept well and from scripture. (See *Brahmasiddhi* pp. l-5 of Maṇḍaṇa Miśra, edited by Kuppusvami Sastri, 1937—Madras Govt. Oriental Manuscript Series, No.4).

A better example can be given, though only an example, to give some idea of the state of liberation as no words can describe it. Suppose you are sitting on a chair and reading an engrossing story or play. As you proceed in your reading, you are more and more engrossed and start forgetting the world around you, and even yourself to some extent. A stage comes (lasting for some time) when the book drops on your lap, the sense-organs stop operating (—the eyes may be open or shut—) the mind is at rest, there is not even a flutter of the intellect, everything is still, tranquil. You are at peace with yourself. You are just yourself—Existence, Consciousness, Bliss -*Sat—Cit—Ānanda*.

VI.3

A BRIEF ACCOUNT OF ŚRĪ ĀDI ŚAṄKARA'S LIFE AND HIS PRINCIPAL DISCIPLES

Dr. W.R. Antarkar

Men like Śrī Ādi Śaṅkārацārya are accidents of centuries and not every- day occurrences. The great American thinker Emerson once said, "When Nature has work to be done, she creates a genius for it." Such people come for certain special purposes particularly spiritual geniuses and for some work or with a divine mission and in the process, leave behind an undying and a glorious tradition, which keeps the light of their work burning and enlightening numberless persons for centuries. Their personalities and their work lie beyond the reach of ordinary human understanding and man's imagination staggers to think about and evaluate them.

Persons like Śrī Ādi Śaṅkarācārya are really saints and mystics in the true sense of these words and they are nothing but the Divine form, come down to the earth with a special mission. The ordinary persons are able to comprehend only their outer form and thereby they bear out the statement of Lord Kṛṣṇa अवजानन्ति मां मूढाः मानुषीं तनुमाश्रितम्। परं भावमजानन्तो मम भूतमहेश्वरम्।। (*Gītā*: 9:11). Many of their deeds, which are called miracles, are beyond the reach of the human mind, though for them, they are just normal deeds.

There are about 17 or 18 biographical accounts which can be compositely called *Śaṅkaravijayas*, purporting to give his life account. The *Śaṅkaravijayas* are the real and main sources of his life and though they do not necessarily agree among themselves even on important topics, they serve to give us (only) an outline idea of the main incidents in his life.

The 17 or 18 biographies or *Śaṅkaravijayas* belong to different periods of time, ranging from his own time upto about the 19th century A.D. Added to this is a vast literature critical and/or otherwise, written in different languages like English, Marathi, Hindi, Gujarati etc. The earliest of these biographies is generally supposed to be *Bṛhat Śaṅkaravijaya*, attributed by tradition, to his close contemporary Citsukha for 25 continuous years. He was originally from Gokarna and was called Viṣnu Śarman, was his co-disciple at Kālaḍi in the *Gurukula* and later his disciple also.

The second important work is *Prācīnaśaṅkaravijaya*, attributed to one Ānandagiri alias Ānanda Jñana, which is much shorter than *Bṛhat Śaṅkaravijaya* but is supposed to follow it closely. Unfortunately, none of these two works, even like some others which could have thrown important light on the life of Śaṅkara, has come to light so far, though a number of stanzas and quotations come across in works like *Suṣamā* (a commentary on गुरुरत्नमालिका—containing the *Guruparamparā* of the Kāñci Kāmā Koti Mutt) and the book, *the Age of Śaṅkara* (Part I only) by the late Mr. T. S. Narayana Śāstry who had with him the 2nd part called शंकराचार्य सत्पथ in 170 chapters in ms. form only containing the details of Śaṅkara's life.

According to all the *Śaṅkaravijayas* (and some other works also) Śaṅkara was born as a result of great and severe penance to Vṛṣādrinātha, the deity of the place by his parents Śivaguru and Āryāmbā, at a sufficiently advanced stage of life. He was named Śaṅkara after Vṛṣādrinātha, the deity worshipped by his parents. His father performed his thread ceremony in his 5th year and sent him to a *Gurukula* nearby but himself expired shortly thereafter. Śaṅkara performed his obsequies and then his studies continued. According to Citsukha, his co-disciple at the *Gurukula*, Śaṅkara was an extraordinarily brilliant student and he is reputed to have written at the age of 6yrs. a small tract called बालवेधग्रह (a copy of which is available in the Saraswati Mahal Library, Tanjavur).

After he completed his studies at the *Gurukula*, he came home and then instead of becoming a house-holder as per his mother's desire, he wanted to become a *Sannyāsī*. At that time, Śri Gopāla Kṛṣṇa, the deity, which was till then being worshipped by his mother and whose temple stood (and stands even today) on the bank of Cūrmī or Periyar river, flowing by the side of Śaṅkara's house, directed him in a dream to go to one Śrī Govinda Muni on the bank of the Narmadā river for regular inititation into *Sannyāsa*. After giving a promise to his mother to be present by her side whenever she remembered him and also to perform her obsequies himself after her death, he set out for the north and was joined at Gokarṇa on the way by his *Gurukula* co-disciple Viṣṇu Śarmā (later to become Cit.) and when he reached Govinda Muni, he found that he was also waiting for him, being directed by Śri Kṛṣṇa in a dream to initimate him into *Sannyāsa*. Govinda Muni then initiated him into *Kramasannyāsa* and taught him for two years the Śāstras, particularly the *Vedāntaśāstra*, available then and then at his instance only, he took him to Badrikāśrama where Govinda Muni's Guru Gauḍapāda was living in eternal *Brahmaniṣṭhā* at 120yrs. Gauḍapāda gladly received him and taught him for 4 years and then with his permission Śaṅkara wrote an extensive commentary on Gauḍapada's *Kārikās* on the *Māṇḍūkya-Upaniṣad*. Overjoyed to see his commentary, he asked him to write *Bhāṣyas* on the *Prasthānatraya*, which Śaṅkara did. He wrote 16 in all, including the one on the *Kārikās*, by the time he was 16 years old only. Then, one day, he took him to Kailāsa, where Lord Śiva manifested there as Dakṣiṇāmūrti, initiated him into *Adhyātmasannyāsa* and then asked him to spread the doctroine of *Advaita* which he had propounded in the *Bhāṣyas*.

When Śaṅkara came back to the Badrikāśrama, he made Viṣṇu Śarmā at his request a *Sannyāsin*, who thus became his first disciple and named him Citsukha. Then, he brought out the image of Lord Nārāyaṇa from the Alakanandā river and established it there. Just at that time, a person called Agni Śarmā came from his mother, who had by now become very old and desired to see Śaṅkara. Immediatly, Śaṅkara went with Citsukha to Kālaḍy where one day, she was on her death bed and then at her instance, Śaṅkara composed a very beautiful hymn (श्रीकृष्णाष्टक)–श्रियाऽश्लिष्टो विष्णुः स्थिरचरवपुर्वेदविषयो. . . शरण्यो लोकेशस्तव भवतु कृष्णोऽक्षिविषयः॥ etc., in praise of Lord Kṛṣṇa who, as a result, appeared before her in bodily form. Overjoyed to see the Divine form of Lord Kṛṣṇa, she blessed her son and passed away peacefully.

As promised earlier, Śaṅkara performed her funeral rites in the backyard of the house (a *Samādhi- mandira* still stands at the place) and while he was making ready to leave the place, a young person named Sanandana came there from Govinda Muni, who was then counting his last days on the bank of the Narmadā river and wanted to see him before he left the world. Śaṅkara immediately started along with Sanandana and reached the place where Govinda Muni was lying half- conscious but on hearing Śaṅkara's voice, opened his eyes, then gave him a parting advice and asking his disciples to follow him, he also closed his eyes and passed away peacefully. Due to the last word Om on his lips at the time of death, a *Samādhi* was erected at the place by Śri Harṣa Vikramāditya, the then king of Ujjain and his son by his Vaiśya wife and that is the famous Omkāreśvara *Mandira*, now regarded as one of the twelve famous *Jyotirliṅgas*. (At present, there is no *Liṅgam* there, which is said to be '*Gupta*' (concealed).

Thereafter, Śaṅkara initiated Sanandana into *Sannyāsa* at his instance only, who thus became the second of his principal disciples.

Thereafter, Śaṅkara started propagating his philosophy of *Ādvaita* to persons who came to him for the same and also initiating some of them into *sannyāsa*, as and when he thought fit. Generally, his chief disciples are known to be four but it seems that the actual number of such disciples was six. There are two stone-sculptures in Kāñcī, one inside the compound of the Goddess Kāmākṣī temple, showing six standing disciples in a row below a stone-stature of Śrī Śaṅkarācāya, whose *samādhi* it is supposed to be. But even the great *Parācārya* told me personally that he did not insist that it was the actual burial place of Śaṅkara. The second sculpture inside Kāñcī Kāmakoṭi Mutt today in Śiva Kāñcī consisting of a stone image of Śaṅkara with three disciples standing on each of his two sides. I have personally seen both the sculptures. The six disciples are.

(1) Citsukha (Viṣṇu Śarmā) :

How this Citsukha as Viṣṇu Śarmā came into contact with Śaṅkara right from *Gurukula* and the later account of his life upto his initiation by Śaṅkara into *Sannyāsa* and renaming him as Citsukha has been seen already. He is said to have written an extensive eye-witness account of Śaṅkarācāya's life and is called *Bṛhat Śaṅkaravijaya* or *Guruvijaya* which, according to Mr. T.S.N. Śāstry, consisted of three parts *viz.* (i) पूर्वाचार्य-सत्पथ (an account of *Ś*aṅkara's predecessors in 30 Chs *(ii)* शंकराचार्य-सत्पथ in 170 chapters, containing the life account proper of Śaṅkara and *(iii)* सुरेश्वराचार्य-सत्पथ in 24 chs., containing an account of Sureśvaracārya. Mr. Śāstry tells us that he had obtained a mutilated copy of the second part only. Neither this part nor the other two parts have become available so far even after a very intensive search for them throughout India. According to the Dwārakā *Śaṅkaramaṭhaparamparā*, this Citsukha became the second *Pīṭhādhipati* of the said mutt and died at the ripe old age of 80 yrs or (90yrs?) Citsukha was obviously the first disciple/ *Sannyāsī* of Śaṅkara.

(2) Sanandana or Padmapāda :

He was the second disciple / *Sannyāsī* of Śaṅkara. He was already a married person when he came to see Śaṅkara on the bank of the Narmadā river, having been married to the daughter of his own maternal uncle Divākarādhvarin, a staunch follower of Prabhākara Bhaṭṭa, one of the three outstanding Pūrva Mīmāṁsakas of the time, the other two being Kumārila Bhaṭṭa and Maṇḍana Miśra. Somehow, he had become fed up with his married life and having heard about Śaṅkara, had come to see him for spiritual guidance. He was, however, required to go to Kālaḍy to convey the message of Govinda Muni, who was almost on his death bed, to Śaṅkara, who had gone there already to see his mother, who was reported to be in the last stage of her life. This was how he came into Śaṅkara's contact, who first attended to his dying Guru after going to him on the bank of the Narmadā river and after his passing away and at the instance of Sanandana, initiated him into *Sannyāsa*. Later, he is said to have written a gloss on Śaṅkara's *Bramhasūtrabhāṣya* but somehow, except the portion thereof on the first five *Pādas* (quarters) of the *Bhāṣya*, the remainning part of the gloss is reported to have been destroyed and hence, has not come down to us. The five *Pādas,* which are available to us today are well-known as *Pañcapādikā*.

The other disciples had noticed that Śaṅkara treated him with greater favour than the rest and hence to show to them why he did so, when one day Śaṅkara was standing on a bank of river Ganges, called Sanandana who was standing on the opposite bank and asked him to come to him. Sanandana felt that if his *Guru* could take him across the ocean of life (भवसागर), he could certainly help him across over to the opposite bank of the river on the surface of the river-water. He then started walking on the river-water and it is said that a lotus appeared under every step he took thereupon and thus he came to Śaṅkara. This proved to the other disciples why Śaṅkara favoured him more and henceforth, he also came to be called Padmapāda (पादे पादे पद्मं यस्य सः।) This incident shows what real and/ or extreme faith is and can do. Later on, Śaṅkara appointed him as the first head of the Govardhana Mutt, which he established at Jagannātha Purī on the east coast of India.

(3) Toṭakācārya or Giri :

His original name was Kalānātha and though he used to attend Śaṅkara's discourses, he was considered to be only an ordinary disciple, looking after Śaṅkara's physical needs like washing his clothes, cleaning his utensils and so on. One day. Śaṅkara was about to start his discourse but waited because Giri (the other name of Kalānātha) had not arrived. Seeing this, Padmapāda suggested to Śaṅkara that he should begin his discourse as there was no difference between Giri's hearing and the wall's hearing it. Śaṅkara did not like this and just as Giri came there, he cast at him a glance of (spiritual) grace. To the surprise of all the disciples including Padmapāda., Giri immediately burst forth into a hymn of eight stanzas in the Toṭaka metre, praising Śaṅkara and imploring his Divine Grace. The first stanza of the hymn is: विदिता न मया विशदैककला। न च किंचन काञ्चनमस्ति गुरो। द्रुतमेव विधेहि कृपां सहजाम्। भव शङ्करदेशिक मे शरणम्।। (This was a case of *Śaktipāta*-transfer of spiritual energy—to dispel the egoism of the disciples). On account of the Toṭakā metre of the eight stanzas (अष्टक), he became known as Toṭakācārya and he was later placed by Śaṅkara in charge of the Jyotirmaṭha in the Himalayas when he established it there.

(4) Sureśvarācārya :

In Śaṅkara's time, Kumārila Bhaṭṭa was the most prominent Pūrva Mīmāṁsaka (exponent of the religion of Vedic sacrificial rituals) and opponent of the *Jñānamārga* or *Advaita* Philosophy. Naturally, Śaṅkara wanted to win him over to his own view of the supemacy of spiritual knowledge over the mere performance of the Vedic sacrifical ritual. But by the time he went to him in a village called Ruddhapur, he was found immolating himself in a chaff-fire (*Tuṣāgni*) and half—burnt, trying to atone for his *Gurudroha* in respect of a Jain Sādhu (Vardhamāna Mahāvīra. according to Citsukha) and denial of God in an attempt to establish the supremacy of the way of the Vedic religion of sacrificial rituals. When Śaṅkara expressed to him his own desire, Kumārila (Bhaṭṭa) pleaded his own inability but directed him to his own disciple Maṇḍana Miśra at Māhiṣmatī. Śaṅkara accordingly went to him and had a debate with him for some days and convinced him about the supremacy of (Spiritual) knowledge (*Jñana*) over mere ritualistic action, which was only a means to qualify oneself for it, when performed completely selflessly and then in keeping with the vow, agreed upon by both that the vanquished was to adopt the *āśrama* of the victor, Śaṅkara initiated Maṇḍana into *Sannyāsa* and named him Sureśvara. Śaṅkara appeares to have had great respect for him and desired that he should write *Vārtikas* on his *Bramhasūtrabhaṣya* but when he asked him to do so, some disciples expressed a doubt about his bringing out the true import of Śaṅkara's writing, having been an exponent of the Vedic *Karmakāṇḍa* all his life, Śaṅkara asked him to write an independent work which would show his real inner conversion, Sureśvara wrote नैष्कर्म्यसिद्धि and then also wrote *Vārtikas* on the *Bhāṣyas* of Śaṅkara on the छान्दोग्य-बृहदारण्यकउपनिषद्s. When Śaṅkara established the different mutts, he did not make him the head of any mutt but entrusted him with the work of supervising the working of the same and seeing that they were carrying on properly the work of propagating the pure Vedic Religion and the philosophy of *Advaita* he had tried to proclaim through his various *Bhāṣyas* and to propagate personally throughout the country and for which only he had established the mutts in the difrent parts of the country, from the North to the South and from the East to the West.

(5) Udaṅkācārya :

When Śaṅkara was staying for some time in Biharipur near Prayāga, after the completion of the morning duties, he used to expound his *Bhāṣyas* in the morning to his disciples and hold discussions in the afternoon, when he cleared their doubts and difficulties, if any. Sometimes, he used to take them round for a stroll. One day, he took them to the well-known Akṣayavaṭa, where he saw a young man whose body was affected with leprosy from head to foot and who was trying to commit suicide. Just then, he happened to see Śaṅkara and struck by his face beaming with spiritual brilliance, he came to him and bowed down before him. When Śaṅkara asked him the reason for his attempt to commit suicide, he showed to him the marks of leprosy all over the body and said that being young, he felt hungry but due to his disease, could neither beg for food nor could he do any work to earn a living and hence was trying to end his life, which he could bear no longer. He then, prayed for his mercy. Śaṅkara took pity on him and put his hand of grace on his head and to the astonishment of all the disciples as well as himself, he became completely free from all the marks of leprosy (*Aṅka*). All the disciples spontaneously uttered in a chorus 'उदङ्क, उदङ्क' (उद्गतः अङ्कः यस्य सः)—one whose marks of leprosy had disappeared (उद्गत) and thereafter, he came to be known by that name only i.e. उदङ्क/उदङ्काचार्य. Seeing this power of Śaṅkara he now fell at his feet and implored him to enlighten him spiritually. And then followed between them, a small conversation in the form of questions by Śaṅkara and answers by Udaṅka and they have been put into one beautiful stanza, which later came to be called, एकश्लोकी. It runs thus :

किं ज्योतिस्तव, भानुमानहनि मे रात्रौ प्रदीपादिकम्।
स्यादेतत् रविदीपदर्शनविधौ किं ज्योतिराख्याहि मे।
चक्षुः, तस्य निमीलनादिसमये किं, धीः, धियो दर्शने।
किं तत्राऽहं, मतो भवान् परमकं ज्योतिः, तदस्मि प्रभो॥

Meaning :

Śaṅkara : Which is your light (for seeing objects) ?

Udaṅka : For me, the Sun by day and Lamp etc. by night.

Śaṅkara : This may be (so) (but) tell me which is your light for seeing the sun, lamp (etc.)?

Udaṅka : The eye (or eyes).

Śaṅkara : Which (is your light) when the eyes are closed (etc.)?

Udaṅka : Intellect (is the light).

Śaṅkara : Which is your light for perception of the intellect?

Udaṅka : There, I am (the light).

Śaṅkara : Hence, you are the supreme light.

Udaṅka : O Lord, I am the light (my self).

Citsukha tells us that the last words viz. ज्योतिस्तदस्मि प्रभो imply that he became a self-realised person there and then.

Śaṅkara's curing Udaṅka represents the employment by Śaṅkara of his divine power or transference of spiritual energy while Udaṅka's self-realisation or spiritual transformation may be said to represent what in the language of Psychology of Religion is called 'Sudden conversion'. Udaṅka must have been a near -perfect person spiritually and was just waiting for the final touch which was supplied by Śaṅkara. He was an instance of a spiritual genius. Persons like Śaṅkara come for the final lift and then such persons like Udaṅka do not need to go through the process of rigorous penance and the like. As Śrī Ramaṇa Maharshi said 'gun-powder catches fire in an instant'. They only need an ignition, which is provided by persons like Śaṅkara only.

(6) Hastāmalakācārya :

Prabhākara Bhaṭṭa was one of the three stalwart *Pandits* of the Pūrva Mīmāṁsā school in Śaṅkara's time and his doctrine was known as the *Guru-mata* (गुरुमत) while the doctrine of Kumārila Bhaṭṭa was known as the *Bhāṭṭa Mata* (भाट्टमत). Prabhākara Bhāṭṭa stayed at a village then known as Śrī Vallī Agrahāra (अग्रहार=colony) and modern Zanśī (झांशी). The entire *Agrahāra*, which consisted of 2000 families, was his follower. When he heard about Śaṅkara and his victory over Maṇḍana Miśra, he came out to meet him and convert him to his own view when Śaṅkara happened to visit his village but Citsukha tells us that within two or three hours only, Śaṅkara convinced him about the superiority of *Jñana* to mere *Karma-Mārga* and that the Vedic rituals when performed without any desire for fruit and by surrendering them all at the feet of God, (in the words of the *Gītā Bhāṣya* (ईश्वरार्पणबुद्ध्या), all of which ultimately culminated into *Parābhakti* the higest spiritual attainment by making him fit for attaining the highest knowledge (ज्ञाननिष्ठयोग्यता—again *Gītā Bhāṣya*) leads one to realisation of the Divine in direct experience. Prabhākara was so much impressed by the discussion and convinced about Śaṅkara's spiritual eminence that he now fell at his feet and told him that he had a son (called पृथ्वीधर or पृथ्वीधव) about 12 or 13 yrs. old, who had suddenly stoppẹd talking or doing any wordly activities and had not changed inspite of all his efforts, temporal and otherwise, like performing his thread-ceremony (व्रतबन्धन) and now entreated Śaṅkara to do something to cure him. Śaṅkara asked Prabhākara Bhāṭṭa to bring the boy to him and when Prabhākara Bhāṭṭa brought him to Śaṅkara and when the boy sat in front of him, Śaṅkara immediately realised that he was born *Siddha* and then putting his hand on his head, he asked him who he was

(कस्त्वम्). Once again, to the surprise of all gathered there, he burst forth into a philosophical poem, the burthen of which was स नित्योपलब्धिस्वरूपोऽहमात्मा (I am the undying, eternal and everpresent *Ātman*), who is the real and the ultimate or final cause of the universe and everything that takes place therein. The poem consists of 12 Stanzas which begin with the following stanza: निमित्तं मनश्चक्षुरादिप्रवृत्तौ। निरस्ताखिलोपाधिराकारकल्पः . . . रविर्लोकचेष्टानिमित्तं यथा सः। स नित्योपलब्धि. . . .मात्मा।

(He is the ultimate cause of the activities of the mind, eyes etc. even as the Sun is the original source of all the activities of the world). Prabhākara Bhāṭṭa was astonished to hear this and when Śaṅkara said to him that the boy was likely to be of on use to him and asked him to hand him over to him, Prabhākara Bhāṭṭa did so and then initiating him into *Sannyāsa*, Śaṅkara named him Hastāmalaka (हस्ते आमलक इव आत्मज्ञानं यस्य–who has self-realisation like an *Āmalaka* in the hand) and finally placed him in charge of the (Kūḍali) Śṛṅgerī mutt which Śaṅkara later established at the confluence of the Tungā and Bhadrā rivers as its first पीठाधिपति. Then, as directed by Dakṣiṇāmūrti, he travelled throughout India, encountering followers of various sects and creeds like Śiva, Gaṇapati, Viṣṇu, Sūrya, Kumāra, claiming them as the highest deities and even some sects like the Bhairavas and the Kāpālins with some undesirable practices also. He had to argue with the leaders of these sects and was assisted in his work particularly by his chief disciples like Sureśvarācārya and Padmapāda and perhaps by Citsukha also. He refuted their doctrines in so far as they were against the doctrines of *Advaita* and did not demolish them completely and at the same time, purified their religious practices, where necesasary, so as to bring them under the one banner of the Vedic religion and within the fold of *Advaita*. Thus he helped in a way to unify the Indian people in one fold, with some internal diffrences, like Saura, Gāṇapatya, Vaiśṇava and so on but none as the independent Ultimate Reality but only as forms of manifestations of one Supreme Reality, which he called *Brahman* in terms of the Upaniṣads in particular and this was his doctrine of *Advaita* he preached in his *Bhāṣyas* and during the various discussions. Most probably, it was for this reason that later on, he came to be called षण्मतस्थापनाचार्य but there is no direct evidence for this concept, as applicable to him, in the 17 or 18 *Śaṅkara-vijayas*, the main source of his life account . He has, however, been called षोडशभाष्यकार on account of his 16 *Bhāṣyas* on the प्रस्थानत्रय, सनत्सुजातीय, विष्णुसहस्रनाम, नृसिंहपूर्वतापनीय and श्वेताश्वतर उपनिषद्A

As said earlier, the different *Śaṅkaravijayas* are not in agreement even with regard to important events in his life and there have been a number of controversies in regard to them. Particularly, the exact venue of सर्वज्ञपीठारोहण (in Kāśmīr or

Kāñcī), the exact occasion of his परकायाप्रवेश,the establishment of a 5th mutt at Kāñcī and lastly, the place where he actually laid down his body (in Kāñcī in the south or some-where in the Himalayan regions in the north). Even his authorship of the *Gitābhāṣya* has been challenged. The most important is,of course, his date in history. I have written detailed articles in responsible Journals like the *Journal of the Asiatic Society*, Bombay, *Bhāratīyā Vidyā* of Bhāratīyā Vidyā Bhavan, Bombay, *Oriental Thought*, Poona (1961) and an independent book on *Kañci Kāma. Mutt* (B. O.R.I. Poona Publication).

I have tried to show in my articles in *Bhāratīya Vidyā* that Śaṅkara is more likely to have ascended the *Sarvajñapīṭha* in Kāñcī only, it being reserved for Abhinava Śaṅkara to ascend it Kāśmir (T.S.N. Śāstry) and that the incident of *Parakāyāpraveśa* must have taken place on this occassion only and not after Śaṅkara-Maṇḍana discussion. I am quite sure about Śaṅkara's authorship of the *Gītā Bhāṣya* (my article in *Oriental Thought*) and his establishment of a Mutt at Kāñcī of which he became the first head, on account of which and for no other reason, it came to be called *Gurumaṭha*, while the other 4 mutts came to be called *Śiṣyamaṭhas*, because their first heads were the direct disciples of Śaṅkara. His asking Sureśvarācārya, who was appointed by Śaṅkara to supervise the working of all the Mutts including the one at Kāñcī was, it seems, later misinterpreted to mean that the Kāñcī Mutt was made by Śaṅkara a permanent supervisory authority with regard to the other 4 mutts.

Regarding Śaṅkara's date, it fluctuates between 509 B.C. to 477 B.C. (Citsukha's *Bṛhat Śaṅkara- vijaya, Prācīna Śaṅkaravijaya* according to Mr. T.S.N. Śāstry in his book *Age of Śaṅkara* pt.I and even *Śaṅkarendravilāsa* by Vākpati Bhaṭṭa quoted in Suṣamā—a commentary on *Gururatnamālikā*—a succession list of Kāñcī Mutt heads and 788 A.D. to 840A.D. (Mr. K.B.Pathak and Western scholars like Max Muller *-Ind. Anti.*) and about 650 AD. to 683 AD (Prof. R.M. Umesh and Mr. R. G. Sharma). The gap between the two dates is very wide and unless and until works like *Bṛhat Śaṅkaravijaya*, *Prācīna-Śaṅkaravijaya* and *Śaṅkarendravilāsa* by Vakpati Bhaṭṭa (the last has been claimed to be a biography of Abhinava Śaṅkara, said to have been the 36th or 38th head of the Kāñcī Kāmakoṭi Mutt, which is said to give the span of his life as 788 AD to 840 A.D. and many of the incidents in whose life are said to have been grafted on to those in Ādi Śaṅkara's life) come to light and unless and until the objections raised by Mr. R.G. Sharma, Prof. Umesh and the like against the pre-Christian date for Ādi Śaṅkara have been answered satisfactorily, scholars will continue to hold that Śaṅkara must have flourished sometime between the latter part of the 7th (not earlier than 650 A.D.—Prof. Umesh) and / or earlier part of the 8th Century A. D.

Lastly, in my humble opinion, Śaṅkara must have passed the last days of his life at Kāñcī only, where he establisahed the 5th mutt, may be residential only, for himself and of which he became the first head, thereby starting a *Guruparamparā* which continues today also even actively and it was here, perhaps in front (of the idol) of Śrī Kāmākṣī Goddess, as said by Anantānandagiri in his *Śaṅkaravijaya*,that he laid down his body though the traces of the exact place where his body was interred and where, perhaps, even some kind of a *Samādhi*—like structure was erected,have been "lost in the careless flow of time."

Śrī Ādi Śaṅkara's passing away only shows that what appears must disappear one day or the other sooner or later, however great it may be and only proves the dictum quoted by Dr. S. Radhākrishnan, i.e "time spins fast,life fleets and all is change. Everything flows, nothing is." The only solace for the thinking mortals is that though such persons no more belong to the finite world,their benign spiritual presence always abides for the welfare of the mundane people. As said by Śrī Rāmadāsa Swāmī (Shivaji's *Guru*) to his weeping disciples at the time of his laying down his body, "Though it is true that my (material) body is gone (i.e. no more) I am there in the form of the Universe" माझी काया गेली खरें। परी मी आहें जगदाकारे।।)

Such is the life account of Śrī Ādi Śaṅkarācārya in short and a brief account of his principal disciples.

[A major part of this article is based on Mr. T.S.N. Śāstry's book '*Age of Śaṅkara* -Pt.1. 1916 A.D.]

VI.4
YOGA IN A WIDER WORLD

Prof. Krishna S. Arjunwadkar

[Paper in its original version was read at the *Indic Health Conference,* held on September 20-21, 2002, in the University of Cambridge (DHIIR, Faculty of Divinity), UK. It is renamed and revised later for Indian readers.

Abbreviations used in this article :

ĀV = *Āyurveda*; BG = *Bhagavad-gītā*; GS = *Gorakṣaśataka*; HY = Haṭha-yoga; HYP = *Haṭha-yoga-pradīpikā*; RY = *Rāja-yoga*; Upa. =Upaniṣads; YS = Yoga-sūtra]

Spread of Yoga in UK :

Yoga, along with *Āyur-veda* (ĀV), has been spreading in the world progressively during the last few decades, so that it is difficult today to find an educated man in a civilised country whom the word *Yoga*, and perhaps ĀV, is unknown. The recent history of the *Yoga* movement in Britain, now more than a quarter of a century old, has on record the condition for government support that its interest would be limited to the physical aspect of the discipline, keeping off the philosophical and or spiritual aspect. This outlook has given rise to the concept of *Modern Yoga,* as distinguished from the Classical *Yoga* of Patañjali. A separate, self-supporting body called *The British Wheel of Yoga* was created to train and certify teachers in *Yoga*. The number of teachers trained and certified by this body has, on the basis of its own statement, now crossed 4000. Besides, there is the Iyengar Institute of *Yoga* in London which has trained another 2000 *Yoga* teachers. (Figures are indicative, and not meant to be accurate.) A number of *Yoga* schools spreading all over UK are run by private individuals belonging mostly to the community of teachers created by the two official bodies mentioned earlier.

This history goes further back to Victorian times if even the limited world of admirers of *Yoga* is taken note of. It is on record that a spiritual teacher named Shivapuri Baba (1826-1963! One hundred and thirty-seven years!!), also known as Swami Govindananda Bharati, came to England when he was fifty (1876), and 'transplanted' *Yoga* on this land. His disciples and friends included Queen Victoria herself who called him a friend. 'He had no fewer than eighteen audiences with Queen Victoria,' says an informed author on *Yoga*.[1]

The term *Yoga* conveys a range of meanings

The concept of *Modern Yoga* need not surprise an informed Sanskritist. The term *Yoga* has changed its meaning by way of expansion and or limitation since ancient times. History of this word shows that as early as when the *Bhagavad-gītā* (BG) assumed its present form (400 B.C.-400 A.D.), the scope of the term *Yoga* was widened so as to include in its span such spiritual practices as action (duty, *karman),* devotion *(bhakti),* renunciation *(sannyāsa)* and knowledge *(jñāna)* not aimed at worldly ends, besides meditation *(dhyāna)* in which sense the term was already established. This range is not unrelated to the goal of *Yoga*, viz. liberation. What the BG offers is a ladder towards this goal for those who cannot follow the rigorous full time course of *Yoga* as conceived by Patañjali, or that of renunciation as conceived by the Upaniṣads (Upa.). The BG may thus be regarded a supplement to the courses of spiritual life as outlined in the Upa. and Patañjali's work, *Yoga-sūtra* (YS), emphasising progressive elimination of mental involvement rather than physical action. At the same time, this text offers in its singular style philosophical thought at the highest level, reconciling apparently conflicting terminology of different schools. The Buddhist tradition has its own scheme of *Yoga* and its terminology. And yet it is closer to Patañjali's *Yoga* to the extent that some scholars would deem Buddhism as a branch of the *Yoga* system.[2]

Modern *Yoga*

Yoga in the phrase '*Modern Yoga*' has undergone change in the other direction, being limited only to a part of what it is conceived by Patañjali to be, if we ignore the inclusion of ĀV in its objective. (In fact, a not very old Sanskrit text entitled '*Āyurveda-sūtra*' has already made an attempt to combine *Yoga* with ĀV.) In Patañjali's scheme, *Yoga* primarily means control of the mind (YS 1.2), implying meditation, and secondarily, the aids to its control. It is among these aids that *Modern Yoga* occupies, statistically, about one-fourth of the total room, being limited to postures and breath-training. This, too, can be said from a wider outlook as far as the scope of postures in Patañjali's work is concerned, for any one reading the contents of this work can discover that posture is limited in Patañjali's scheme to what would provide a stable and comfortable physical position suitable for meditation (YS 11.46), and not as a means to promote sound health. Vyāsa, the commentator, however, enlists about a dozen basic postures in this context, implying that they are relevant to the subject. In its widest scope, the concept of postures comprises—say the authors of some books on *Haṭha-yoga* (HY),—as many varieties as there are species in the whole world,—8.4 million according to the *Gorakṣa-śataka*.[3] (GS, verse 6) and *Gheraṇḍa-saṃhitā*[4] (II. 1). The number of postures considered as notable in the latter work is 84, of which 16 are stated to be in actual practice. The GS reduces the number 16 further to 2 only!

Haṭha-yoga and *Rāja-yoga*

This brings us to the topic of the HY or the *Yoga* of Force vis-a-vis the *Rāja-yoga* (RY), or the *Royal Yoga*, of Patañjali, on the points of their philosophy and practice. Although there are traces of the HY concepts in the *Kaṭha Upa*. (VI. 16) and the *Śvetāśvatara Upa*. (11.12), systematic works on this subject are not as old as Patañjali. Of the few works on this subject, the *Haṭha-yoga-pradīpikā*[5] (HYP) of Svātmārāma is by far the only work with a logical planning, elegant style and exposition worth the name of a treatise. Although the author gives everything in the system faithfully, he opens by saying that he is expounding HY only as a means of access to RY (1.2), discussed by him by employing a special terminology (IV). In the opening verses of his work, he has no doubt given a long list of leading HY masters, who, by 'cheating' death, still move about freely in the three worlds (1.5-9). This is achieved through imprisoning the breath in the body by practising *prāṇāyāma,* for death means escape of the breath from the body (II.3). The motif of cheating death occurs frequently in the work (e.g. III.3). The topic of miraculous powers *(siddhis)* in Patañjali's YS (III. 16-48) comes closer to this HY concept; but, Patañjali warns (III.37) practitioners of *Yoga* to avoid the temptation to get lost in them and consequently miss the main object of *Yoga*, viz. liberation.

In contrast to Patañjali's scheme of eight aids of *Yoga* in which posture and breath-training (or breath-restraint) are in the third and the fourth places, the HYP mentions them as the first and the second steps of HY (1.17, II. 1). Corpulent persons are advised to practise 'Six Operations' *(ṣaṭ-karmans)* before turning to *prāṇāyāma* (II.36). The second item *(basti)* in the list of the 'Six Operations' is the precursor of the modern enema method of cleaning the intestines. Next comes the topic of ten *Mudrās* (III) intended to awaken the Kuṇḍali or Kuṇḍalinī ('serpent power' that blocks the Suṣumnā passage) which is central to the entire system. It is in this section that the most controversial physiological concepts in the system and some of the most obnoxious *(vajrolī* III.83), and self-torturing *(khecarī* III.32...)

practices occur. The warning that this doctrine is a guarded secret, and must be obtained from an authoritative teacher, recurs in this text almost as a refrain. What *Modern Yoga* has chosen from the complex system of HY is only the multiplicity of postures and, presumably, breath-training.

A probe into the claims of the *Haṭha-yoga*

The difficulty in the understanding of the HY theory is that we have no means to verify its claims. That HY masters like Matsyendra and others have become immortal by retaining their body is no more than a matter of belief. No practitioner of HY is available who can convincingly vouch that he has cheated death. What we actually see in our own lifetime is that all those who make a claim to Yogin-hood in the HY sense of the term are as mortal as other men. The elaborate scheme of 72,000 veins in the body with the queenly Suṣumnā nerve-centre *(nāḍī)* brought under control with *the prāṇāyāma* practice is more imaginative than real. Imprisonment of the breath in the body (implying voluntary stopping of breathing) leading to immortality is simplistic logic which cannot explain free movement of the HY masters in the whole world without breathing, as the HY tradition believes. What needs to be seriously investigated, as Basham observes, is the ability of a practitioner of HY to stop pulsation and suspend associated functions of the body, at will.

One wonders how the practice *of vajrolī* (meaning, briefly, re-absorption of the spilt semen through the male organ) makes men stronger and immortal. HYP recommends *sahajolī* (besmearing body with the ashes of cow dung after *vajrolī)* and *amarolī* (drinking of one's own urine,— *'śivāmbu* therapy' as it is popularly known. The word *'śivāmbu'* occurs in this sense in the commentary by Brahmānanda on HYP 11.96.) Finally, how all this is related to the ultimate goal of the RY of isolating oneself from worldly bonds, as the author of HYP claims and elaborately details in the last chapter of his work, is a mystery. In contrast to this work, the GS is more logical and consistent, as it does not talk of 'cheating death' and making the body immortal. Although it talks of 8.4 million as the maximum number of postures, it reduces this number to two *(siddhāsana* and *padmāsana,* GS verse 7), implying their utility in meditation. The GS may thus be considered a more reasonable attempt to combine HY and RY, avoiding logical inconsistencies incurred by HYP. The absence in GS of obnoxious and self-torturing practices in HY pointed out earlier supports this conclusion. When such questions remain unanswered, it is misleading to use the term HY to signify only a part of the system, viz. postures and breath training, as some *Yoga* fans do. The newly invented term '*Modern Yoga*' is a safe way to avoid such inconsistencies.

Some more shades of the meaning of *Yoga*

In works like the *Yoga-vāsiṣtha* (Y V, a 12th c. work in my view) and the *Yoga-yājñavalkya-saṃhitā* definitely post-YV work),—two works in a class by themselves in their outlook towards life and their perspective of philosophy,—we find the concept of *Yoga* much more diluted so as to enable even a person of reasonably moderate outlook and habits to make a claim to the honorific designation, '*Yogin*'! If one can think of a popular form of *Yoga* (one can call it *Family Yoga*), here it is. For consideration of the space at my disposal, I have to resist the temptation to go into the otherwise amusing details of these texts.

What the contemporary man expects of *Yoga*

The most obvious way out of this wide and perplexing usage of the term *Yoga* is to disown Patañjali and others, as far as their main thrust is concerned, if the interest of the contemporary society is limited to the specified heads of *Yoga*, viz. postures and breath-training. This is no doubt a practical approach. After all, what does an average student of *Yoga* wish to gain by it? Of course, the sound functioning of the body and a healthy life, reasonably free from ailments. I have been for years a reasonably regular practitioner of physical exercises. These included some items practised during my young age, like 'wrestling' with the wrestler's post *(malla-khāmb)* as well as with a live companion, of course in Indian style, and some *Yogic* postures too; and I don't remember to have been seriously ill during the last more than three decades. This has undoubtedly enabled me to maintain competence in my intellectual and creative pursuits too. In addition, I can claim a certain amount of a serious study of this subject in recent years through a direct access to its first sources on the strength of my life-long specialised Sanskritic study and equipment, an unusual combination of the old Sanskritic, and the modern university, systems.

Sweet are the uses of philosophy

At this point, I feel I must pause and ask myself: what role do my life-long study and teaching of Indian philosophy play in my reasonably sound physical and mental faculties in the mid-seventies of my life? What is the secret of my ability throughout my career as a scholar and an author to take up ever new challenges and handle new subjects, work on them with concentration and make original contribution to their study? The simplest reply is: it is a natural gift. But it is not the full reply. My study of Indian philosophy, particularly of Śaṅkara, has given my mind, I confess, a certain amount of equanimity which has promoted my sound health, both physical and intellectual. What I read, teach and write on does shape my mental attitude in an imperceptible but substantial way; and no one can deny that a sound mind does not fail to tone one's health in the long run. Given enough scope, philosophy has the potential to develop an outlook in an individual to look at oneself objectively, which enables one to face peacefully any unpleasant events in everyday life. If I am thinking in the right direction, it would be injudicious to deprive a student of *Yoga* of its deeper concerns. The area of research of DHIIR[8] is: 'health, medicine and well-being'; and well-being is as much concerned with mind as with body. Would anyone believe that even Kauṭilya (3rd c. B.C.), a die-hard diplomat and the author of the celebrated Sanskrit work on state craft and administration, recommends philosophy as a subject of study for a prince? He argues that its study polishes the process of thinking, speech and action and maintains mental balance in calamity and prosperity (*Artha-śāstra* 1.2). Likewise, an ĀV authority, Vāgbhaṭa (*Aṣṭāṅgahṛdaya*, AH, *Sūtra*. 1.26), recommends philosophy as a cure for mental disorders rooted in the excess of anger, grief, fear, jealousy, greed etc (Suśruta.[9] *Sūtra*. 1.25). It is interesting to note that ĀV authorities prescribe a righteous, philanthropic way of life as a general scheme of maintaining mental health (AH Sūtra. 11.20-30).

Insights of Patañjali and Vyāsa

And there is more to it, as far as Patañjali's exposition is concerned. *Yoga* is control of the mind; and for controlling it, it is necessary to know what it is. Explaining mind and its attributes, P and Vyāsa, the commentator, show insights into the subject that cannot but engage a serious reader's attention. As everyone has a mind, it is as much important to know its functioning, may be broadly, as to know that of one's body. It is interesting to note that Vyāsa describes the mind (YS II.13) as a fisherman's net with innumerable knots which correspond to latent impressions *(vāsanās)* of memories. The image surprisingly fits the organisation of the Hard Disk (HD) of a PC which is nothing but a store house of memories at various levels—of applications, programmes and data. Every experience as a rule leaves an impression on the mind that has the ability to be stimulated by an appropriate situation or context. All education including even that of *Yoga* is, in fact, the process of deepening impressions of information of a lasting value. Indeed, Patañjali does talk of deepening impressions of control as against those of worldly life (1.50, III.9). Like all specialised education, *Yoga* is channelling of mental faculties towards a willed goal. Though introduced as a background for the study of *Yoga*, Patañjali's analysis of mind into five broad states *(vṛttis,* 1.5-6)—right knowledge, erroneous knowledge, verbal knowledge, (deep) sleep and memory (which includes dream)—is the oldest comprehensive effort to probe into the working of the mind. Although geared to the exposition of *Yoga*, it is significant even from a non-Yogic viewpoint. Sleep as a state of mind is germane to the concept of the soul in Upaniṣadic as well as *Yoga* philosophy which does not conform to the popular view that there is no consciousness in deep sleep. Consciousness in deep sleep, being pure as awareness of the Self, is shorn of all worldly identities; and the popular mind cannot think of consciousness that has no practical identity.

Science and philosophy

If even a diplomat like Kauṭilya and a physician like Vāgbhaṭa argue in favour of and recommend the study of philosophy, there is no reason why those interested in the well-being of the common man should shun it. It is wrong to think that philosophy worth its name is a matter of faith or a mere figment of imagination. The philosopher follows the same methodology as does a scientist in the pursuit of his search. The only difference is that while the scientist focuses his search on the objective world, the philosopher focuses on the inner, the subjective one. Observation, conclusion, logic, proof, hypothesis in the absence of a direct proof, range of verification, reasoning,—these are the trodden paths of research whether for a scientist or for a philosopher so far as metaphysics and psychology are concerned. Ethics, though in Western convention included in philosophy (it is not, as far as Upaniṣadic tradition is concerned), differs from the other two divisions, as it is founded on the consideration of human ideals and not of higher reality. Ethics thinks in terms of 'should' and 'should not', that is, something in human power to decide, while the other two do so in terms of 'is' or 'is not', that is, something beyond the human power to decide. So when I compare science and philosophy to find out the methodology they share, I exclude ethics.

The area of philosophical search

It would be worthwhile to discuss how philosophy helps the human mind to build up a wider and balanced outlook. Philosophical search in Indian tradition, broadly, arrived at the conclusion, millennia ago, that the soul in its purest nature is nothing but consciousness. All other adjuncts which define its worldly identity (race, nationality, caste, class, sex, colour, age, profession and so on) are superimposed on the soul through an erroneous knowledge of itself persisting through lives after lives. Even a superficial, casual thought is enough to convince one that some of these adjuncts are merely conventional and are subject to change, and hence not an essential part of the soul. Aspects of identity which are determined by birth and stay for life can also be shown to be extraneous to the nature of the soul, as the soul can exist untouched by them during the state of deep sleep characterised by pure consciousness. The actor playing the role of Hamlet on stage does not carry his identity as Hamlet into real life, once the play is over, obviously because that identity is assumed for artistic purposes and is, hence, superimposed. Adjuncts of the soul as illustrated above are similarly superimposed. The only difference between these two types of super-impositions is that the first (of Hamlet on the actor) is conscious, the second (of worldly adjuncts on the soul) is not. This fact places the first type in a separate, hitherto unrecognised epistemological category of cognition which, in the absence of an established name, I have named 'willed cognition' in an article on this subject. The entire range of what is called culture is covered by this 'willed cognition'. The second type of super-imposition is on a par with the experience in the state of dream, both being rooted in ignorance or erroneous knowledge. Shakespeare's poetic image in 'All the world's a stage' comes nearer the philosophical outlook than that of the stage, as 'actors' on this vast stage of the world are not aware that they are playing roles. An awareness of this fact develops a tolerant outlook towards life.

Ideological inbreeding

I admit that absence of a philosophical outlook is not the sole factor that breeds intolerance and, let me add, mass mania; but it is the root factor. Another factor is ideological inbreeding, that is, lack of, or resistance to, exposure to other ideologies. This happens in water-tight sects or groups in which the constant hammering of set principles or doctrines conditions the thinking process of the members of the group to the extent that they willingly believe in imaginary ideas as truths and make real-life decisions under their influence even at the cost of their lives. Horrifying consequences of such conditioning are not lacking in human history; they perpetuate even to our own times. A professor of physics at the university level teaching science in a country answering to this description observes that he has to supplement his statements such as 'oxygen unites with hydrogen to produce water' with the provision, 'at the will of God'. It is time to ask: is the civilised world really interested in curing this disease by going to the roots? If it is, the only cure is: exposure, education, and a wider outlook rooted in an acquaintance with philosophical brain storming. But it is doubtful whether the intense lust for power prevailing in world power centres would permit them to reconcile with such a view.

An alternative to philosophical exercise

We cannot ignore the case of those who lack intellectual equipment for or are not temperamentally inclined to wrestle with philosophical problems. In consideration of such cases, BG (XII.3.., XVIII.62...) recommends the path of total devotion to God. This path is founded on the faith that the world is a manifestation of God (VII. 19), and that love for it is no less than the worship of God. This path is different from that of devotion for worldly gains (BG VII.20-23). (Compare this latter attitude with the practice of *Yoga* for *siddhis* in Patañjali's scheme, or immortality in the HY scheme.) If one can thus surrender oneself to God, one is relieved of all mental stress; and this attitude contributes greatly to sound physical health. No one, least of all, a man of the medical profession, can deny that mental peace is a major contributing factor to the maintenance of health. What is called 'Faith Cure' is part of this attitude. While discussing surrender to God, we have to remember that the concept of God in this attitude is what we find in BG, and not the one in Patañjali's *Yoga* system. In the latter, God has no more than a nominal place, comparable to that of the constitutional head of the state in a satisfactorily operating democratic set-up.

Back to the philosophy of Yoga

All this discussion should point in the direction of not ignoring the philosophical contents of Patañjali's *Yoga* while focussing on postures and breath training. Even a general acquaintance with philosophy on the intellectual level, and alternatively, devotion to God in a selfless spirit, promises to make individual and group life smoother and more comfortable. An awareness of the highest goal keeps men striving for higher ideals, following the motto, 'Excelsior!' To stop at postures and breath training is to have a PC hardware without any software installed on it. Let us not re-exemplify the old story of an Arab silk merchant who wanted to send his merchandise to a far-off market. As the story goes, when the wooden boxes were filled with silk rolls and were ready to be mounted on camels, the merchant sharply instructed his servants: 'Be careful. In case it rains during the journey, see that no drop of water touches the boxes.' They nodded obediently, and left with the caravan. As their master predicted, they had to face heavy rain on their way. Faithful to the master's warning, they promptly opened up the boxes, pulled out the costly silk and covered the boxes with it; and, literally, no drop of showers touched the boxes!

FOOTNOTES :

1. Feuerstein Georg, 'The last Teachings of Yoga', *Yoga and Health* (A British Magazine devoted to Yoga), January, 2003, p. 22.
2. For Buddhist scheme of Yoga, see "Some Notable Similarities and Differences in the Buddhist and the Orthodox Yoga Systems, M.G. Dhadphale; *Parisamvāda* 1, Sampurnananda Sanskrit Vishva-vidyalaya, Varanasi.
3. *Gorakṣa-śataka,* critical edition published in the *Yoga-Mīmāṁsā Magazine*, March 1958, Kaivalya-dhama, Lonavla (India)
4. *Gheraṇḍa-saṃhitā,* published by Munshiram Manoharlal Publishers Pvt. Ltd., New Delhi (India), 1996.
5. *Haṭhayoga-pradīpikā* of Svātmārāma; with the commentary *Jyotsnā* by Brahmānanda and English translation: published by The Adyar Library and Research Centre, Madras (India), 1994.

6. *Yoga-vāsiṣṭha,* published by the Nirnaya Sagara Press, Mumbai, 1911. For my views on this text, see my article "Yoga-vāsiṣṭha : A frank appraisal" Published in the *Annals of the Bhandarkar Oriental Research Institute*, Pune, 2002 issue)
7. *Yoga-yājñavalkya-saṃhitā,* translated by T. K. V. Desikachar and published by Krishnamacharya Yoga Mandiram, Chennai (India), 2000.
8. DHIIR—Dharam Hinduja Institute of Indic Research, a part of Centre for Advanced and Theological Studies, Faculty of Divinity, University of Cambridge, UK. This Institute was established in January 1995 through a generous benefaction from the Hinduja Foundation (UK) in memory of Dharam Hinduja (1969-1992), the son of Mr. S.P. Hinduja, Chairman of the Foundation.
9. Suśruta is the oldest author (6th c. AD?) on ĀV who has systematically treated the topic of surgery at a time when anaesthesia was unknown, which reveals his insights and resourcefulness in the subject. He describes about a hundred steel instruments for use in surgical operations, and recommends the use of a magnet to pull out iron particles in eyes. He knew plastic surgery as he has given a detailed account of the restorative operation of an earlobe.

VI.5

THE HINDU APPROACH TO OTHER RELIGIONS

Prof. Leela Arjunwadkar

[Paper read at the Inter-religious Meeting organized in Pune by the Papal Seminary, on August 21, 1993.]

Before going to the subject, I must clarify a few points :

(i) Because of the vastness and complexity of the subject, I have limited myself to only the broad features.

(ii) Hinduism has proliferated into so many sects and sub-sects and at so many levels that it is virtually impossible to make any statement that will be applicable to all Hinduism.

(iii) Therefore, what I have said relates and refers to the more cultured and refined form of Hinduism.

(iv) It is a universal fact that no religion is, on the practical plane, what it theoretically claims to be, though the gaps between these two may be different in width.

(v) My treatment of the subject is very broad and general.

In the very beginning we have to face the difficulty of defining Hindu religion. It is not, like several other religions, a mono-prophetic religion. Naturally enough, its history does not begin with any particular person, date or year. Equally naturally, it has not sprung from or chained down to particular space-time constraints. So, to quote Radhakrishnan, 'it is a movement, not a position; a process, not a result; a growing tradition, not a fixed revelation.' What goes by the name of Hinduism has had a long history and tradition. During this long vista of time, peoples of different races and cultures have been pouring into India. And yet, Hinduism has maintained its identity, while accommodating in its fold different Ur-Indian cults, practices and foreign religions. It has squarely faced proselytising activities of other religions backed by political power, and still a large majority of Indians have remained Hindu.

To many, the term 'Hindu' is just a name without any content. It is very difficult to pinpoint the essential qualifications for being a Hindu. Neither any specific concept of God nor any particular system of theology, neither any one philosophical ideology nor any particular ritualistic dogma,—there is nothing that this vast mass of Hindus has in common. And still, as Vincent Smith puts it, 'India, beyond all doubt, possesses a deep underlying fundamental unity, far more profound than that produced either by geographical isolation or by political superiority. The unity transcends the innumerable diversities of blood, colour, language, dress, manner and sect.' Behind the facade of multifarious beliefs, creedal practices, sectarian dogmas, ritualistic do's and don'ts, we find (—and this is what puzzles foreigners most, as has been mentioned by Sir Edmond Hillary in '*From Ocean to the Skies*') that all Hindus believe in only one God or principle as the Supreme Reality. A Hindu, howsoever monotheistic his inclinations, generally tends to uphold monism of one sort or other.

In its long history Hinduism has gathered around itself a vast mass of concepts, beliefs, deities, cults, customs and practices. That is why Louis Fischer describes it as 'a sponge-religion'. If because of this plurality Hinduism has never had the rigid, institutionalised compactness of a mono-prophetic religion, it is precisely because of this that Hinduism has got an inbuilt catholicity of outlook, tolerance and respect for others' ways of life and thought. 'While fixed intellectual beliefs mark off one religion from another, Hinduism sets itself no such limits. Intellect is subordinated to intuition, dogma to experience, outward expression to inward realisation.'

There is an interesting anecdote of how the first ancestors of the Parsees, because of their religious persecution in Persia, left their homeland and came to the Gujarat coast. They wanted to anchor their ships there. They asked for the king's permission. A sagacious person that he was, he sent them a jar of milk. The leader of the Parsees was an equally wise man. He responded by adding sugar to that milk. The Gujarat king appreciated this gesture and gave them permission to land. Just as the Parsees suggested by their action that they won't curdle and spoil the milk, but would sweeten it, it was also imaginative on the part of the king to offer them milk which is the symbol of succour, nourishment, purity and honesty.

For a Hindu, since Vedic times, a guest is veritably a god *(atithi-devo bhava)* and as a householder, it is his duty *(dharma)* to offer him food, shelter and hospitality. This has been equally true on a wider Indian level. Hindus in different provinces have welcomed such guests from olden times. These guests were of two types: their own brethren like the Jainas, the Buddhists, and Sikhs in later times. All these, though professing different faiths, were first cousins as it were. The other guests were outsiders like the invading Greco-Bactrians (before the Christian era), Scythians and Huns, Syrian Christians (nearly from the beginning of the Christian era), Jews, Parsees and Muslims in different periods of history.

Generally speaking, their influences on Hinduism were marginal, superficial. Except for the acceptance of some deities worshipped locally and local practices, no important influence can be traced. The most significant influence would be the acceptance of Gautama Buddha as the ninth incarnation of Viṣṇu. It was, however, during the last two centuries that different organisations like the Prārthanā-samāj, Brāhmo-samāj, Ārya-samāj with specific influences from Christianity or Islam (may be by way of inspiration or of reaction) appeared. The roots of Sikhism go back to the 15th century.

Another very important feature of the long history of Hinduism is that it is almost free of any religious persecution. The only worth mentioning exception would, perhaps, be the Śaiva-Vaiṣṇava feuds. But they were definitely not as gory as some 'modern' scholars would like to think. 'Religious fanaticism and persecution is a characteristic of later centuries.'

Moreover, Hinduism was never a proselytising religion. It never had any missionary activity as the very concept of conversion was unknown to it. This is yet another piece of evidence to show that Hinduism aims at the betterment of the individual through his heart. Buddhism and Jainism were monastic religions proclaiming *ahiṃsā,* and their missionary activities were never vehement and coercive. Besides, they were essentially Indian religions nurtured by and for the people of this soil. Moreover, they shared with Hinduism cardinal beliefs like rebirth and *karma-vipāka.* They had a well-defined ethical code of conduct which was not essentially different from the Hindu one—whatever their differences in the metaphysical field.

One very striking feature of Hinduism was the freedom to oppose: to doubt was never denied to any one. Right from Ṛgvedic times (cf. *yo asyādhyakṣaḥ parame vyoman so aṅga veda yadi vā na veda //*), we have evidence for this freedom of thought. The Upaniṣadic seers also welcomed sincere doubts and queries. In fact, I might mention, it is an established practice in traditional Indian dialectics that you first take heed of the point of view and arguments of your opponent., refute them and then consolidate your position. (Texts like *Śāṅkara-bhāṣya. Pañcadaśī, Sarva-darśana-saṃgraha*, even the Buddhist *Milinda-pañha*, are good illustrations of this.) In the *paṇḍita-sabhās,* Hindu, Jaina, Bauddha scholars came together, wrangled, raised objections and doubts, argued and discussed important philosophical, metaphysical points. This is true *paṇḍita-vāda. Rāja-vāda* seeks to silence the opposition through its might. The *pundits*, on the other hand, never came to blows. In fact, it is to the credit of the Indian scholars in general and Hindu scholars in particular, that they cherished and kept alive an atmosphere of freedom of thought and religious democracy. Cārvāka's views came to us because of this attitude only.

This went on for centuries, while the life of the masses went smoothly and peacefully in their own ways and emperors like Aśoka, Harṣa-vardhana, Śivājī gave large grants to all religions practised in their territory. In the Islamic tradition, such a liberal and eclectic attitude, I must mention, is seen in Emperor Akbar's conception *of Dīne Ilāhī* and again in the development of Sufism.

It is to the credit of such a mental build that we never find in the long history of Hinduism any Socrates being given poison, any Galileo being imprisoned or any Joan being burnt at the stake. 'Heresy-hunting, the favourite game of many religions, is singularly absent from Hinduism.' This is so because Hindism has always believed in two things:

(1) That all religions are vertical pathways leading to the same summit as is succinctly observed in the following verse:

yaṃ śaivāḥ samupāsate śiva iti brahmeti vedāntino
bauddha Buddha iti pramāṇa-paṭavaḥ karteti naiyāyikāḥ /
arhann ity atha jaina-śāstra-niratāḥ karmeti mīmāṃsakāḥ
So'yaṃ vo vidadhātu vāñchita-phalaṃ trailokya-nātho hariḥ //

The main note of Hinduism is one of respect and good will for other creeds. 'It is neither fair to God nor man to believe that one particular religion or people are the chosen of God'; that those who won't come to that fold will forever languish in hell. To quote Radhakrishnan: 'While Hinduism hates the compulsory conscription of men into the house of truth, it insists on the development of one's intellectual conscience and sensibility to truth.... Those who love their sects more than truth end by loving themselves more than their sects.'

(2) That religion is not a mere intellectual luxury or just a correct intellectual conviction. It is, above all, right conduct. Rather than what you think, what you become is important. All education is useless as chaff if it does not flower into actual experience, into the purification and integration of the human being.

Hinduism extends nearly unlimited freedom in speculation, but, paradoxically enough, insists on strict conformity to practice. As a consequence, the closely knit social order which it posits, has in many ways become unjust and outdated also. But with all that, Hinduism is essentially a mystic-personal religion that aims at the chastening, purification and ennoblement of man's personality. This makes Hinduism in its infrastructure essentially a 'secular[1] religion, that is not averse to or in conflict with other religions or modernity. Indeed, it has been aptly remarked that 'Hinduism has evolved as Religion and, not as a particular religion.' In this context I am reminded of the words of a Polish professor whom I met some years ago: 'As I have been brought up in the best Christian tradition,' he had said, 'I am a perfect Hindu.'

This state prevailed for a long time. But when adherents of entirely different religious ideologies came on the scene, especially those with an inbuilt aggressiveness and often backed by military prowess and political power, things came to be settled in an entirely different way. There was very little of academic, intellectual give-and-take. Matters of religion came to be decided with the point of sword. Again the high, liberalised aspect of Hinduism did not percolate to the Hindu masses who were caught in the meshes of petty, smaller and yet smaller do's and don'ts. So it was easy for coercive conversion to spread its tentacles.

The upper echelons of Hindu intellectuals remained passive and tolerant to the extent of being completely nonchalant. The victims of conversion accepted this *as fait accompli* and were lost to the main stream, perhaps with some bitterness. It is a sad paradox that those who could spread their wings wide enough to shelter aliens shut them down on their own kin. Liberal on the outer side, inner insulation was very rigid.

The tragedy has worsened tremendously because people are becoming more and more touchy about trash, about worthless details, rather than paying any attention to the real spirit of religion. Religious fundamentalism has greatly darkened the minds of the people. Indeed, it has been well said: 'People will do anything, even die for religion, but practice religion.' It is with regard to such conditions that Swift has said: 'We have enough religion to hate one another, but not enough to love one another.'

That means: it is high time we revamp our attitudes to religion in general. Rather than parading religiosity, we should learn to be sincerely religious, whatever the religion of our faith. We have to humanise religion that has been over-deified on the one hand, and debased on the other. In this context, as thinkers like Radhakrishnan advocate, Hinduism will have a lot to give. I do by no means mean that everything is alright with Hinduism. It has its own abuses. But its history of tolerance and catholicity, its approach to other religions as being equally worthy of respect, its inbuilt secular nucleus and intensely personal character will go a long way to help the world to get out of the welter it is in.

It would be a fitting end to quote the two beautiful prayers *(śānti-mantras)* for universal well-being and peace:

sarvepi sukhinaḥ santu sarve santu nirāmayāḥ /
sarve bhadrāṇi paṣyantu mā kaścid duḥkha-bhāg bhavet //
asato mā sad gamaya /
tamaso mā jyotir gamaya //
mṛtyor mā amṛtaṃ gamaya //
om śāntiḥ śāntiḥ śāntiḥ //

REFERENCES :

1. Radhakrishnan S. : *The Hindu View of Life.*
2. Dandekar, R.N. : *Insights into Hinduism.*
3. Dandekar, R.N. : *Some aspects of the History of Hinduism.*
4. Joshi Mahadeva-shastri (Editor): *Bhāratīya Saṃskṛti Kośa.*

VI.6

SAUTRĀNTIKA BUDDHIST THEORY OF WORD-MEANING

Nagin J. Shah

Buddhist philosophy is very vast, deep, sharp and thought-provoking. It has enriched Indian philosophy by building up various systems in its fold. Its *Sautrāntika* system of critical realism has given us formidable logic. A system of *Vijñānavāda* idealism has developed its own logic. A system of *Śūnyavāda* is a consistent and sustained dialectic, embodying a staggering critique of Reason. Buddhist philosophy served as the strongest rival *(pradhāna-malla)* to other systems of Indian philosophy. Buddhist criticism, very difficult to refute, compelled rival thinkers to defend their theories strongly and to make them more logical, cogent and consistent, and even to revise them introducing new concepts. Buddhist thinkers have considerably influenced other thinkers. Gauḍapāda and Āc. Śaṅkara were influenced by the *Vijñānavāda* logic to such an extent that among *Purāṇic* thinkers a view was current that *māyāvāda* is Buddhist *Vijñānavāda* in disguise.[1] Kumārila was constrained under the pressure of *Vijñānavāda* to formulate his theory of *jñātatā*. Jayanta in his *Nyāyamañjarī* writes : *aho bata ime kebhyo bibhyataḥ śrotriyāḥ paraṁ kim api vaiklavyam upagatāḥ /... viṣayagrahaṇakāle vijñānāgrahaṇamātrakeṇa bāhyārthanihnavavādinaḥ Śākyāḥ śakyāḥ śamayitum/*[2] Prabhākara has accepted some views under the Buddhist influence. Praśastapāda has been compelled by the Buddhist thinkers to revolutionise the entire system of Kaṇāda. For instance, he introduces altogether a novel concept *avibhakta ālocana* in the *Vaiśeṣika* categories *(padārthas)* against the Buddhist attack. *Nyāya* system has developed under the impact of Buddhist logic. Its progress and maturity are due to the constant healthy struggle and confrontation with lively dynamic Buddhist logicians.[3] An eminent scholar of Indian logic observes : A comparative study of Diṅnāga and Gaṅgeśa, the founder of sub-school of *Neo-Nyāya*, will reveal that

Gaṅgeśa's much-vaunted innovations are a tiny fraction—in many cases they are bodily the same—of those introduced in the school of Diṅnāga.

Even now by studying Buddhist philosophy one is provoked to think and ponder over the problems of philosophy that have permanent value. In what follows, I present, as an instance, *Sautrāntika* realist theory of word meaning.

The *Nyāya-Vaiśeṣika* thinkers contend that the convention as to the meaning of a word is fixed by God. But the Buddhist logician being atheist maintained the correct position that the convention as to the meaning of a word is fixed by human beings.[4] And he agrees with *Nyāya* logician on the point that this convention one learns from the usage of elders *(vṛddha-vyavahāra)* But the question as to what it is that a word means is vital. Does it mean a real thing? According to the *Nyāya* position, a word expresses a universal, which, for him, is a real entity. The Buddhist vehemently criticises the *Nyāya* position that a universal is a real entity and establishes that it is a mental construction. So, he criticises the view that a word expresses a real independent universal. He contends that a word expresses 'exclusion of the opposite'. For instance, the word cow expresses the 'exclusion of non-cow'. He points out that we use words so that the hearer may proceed towards things efficient to generate a purposive action after having avoided all other things that are inefficient to generate that purposive action.[5]

It might be contended that the words express the universals in order that the efficient individuals might be indicated through it as it is not possible for words to express individuals themselves. This view, says the Buddhist, is absurd . How can one direct one's activity towards that which, though related to the expressed, is not itself expressed? Nobody cuts the staff-bearer when he is asked to cut the staff. It might be said that though words express the universals, we direct our activity towards individuals because the performance of an action is not possible with reference to the universals. On this argument, the Buddhist points out, the speaker should always become incoherent in his speech because he does not actually express that with reference to which he wants the hearer to perform the relevant function.[6]

To find a way out, one might suggest that let words express the individual qualified by the universal as it is capable of generating purposive action . But the Buddhist asks as to why words do not express individuals directly? If it is useful or fruitful to employ words for the sake of expressing individuals, then why are they not employed to express individuals directly? What is the use of the intermediary, the universal? If it is said that words are not employed to express individuals directly because the latter being infinite the formation of convention with respect to them all is not possible, then this difficulty would persist even in the view that words express individuals qualified by their respective universals. It is so because even through mediation of universal, nothing else but individuals are to be expressed by words. And it is a rule that words can never express that in connection with which the convention is not formed. Hence it is incumbent on the upholders of the present view to form convention with regard to individuals. But this is not possible as they themselves have shown. Moreover, it is never observed that a particular word conventionally connected with one thing can become automatically connected with another thing simply because these two things are related with one another. The upholder of the present view might urge that even the Buddhists themselves are of the opinion that convention is formed in connection with the universal—which according to them is of the form of the exclusion of the opposite—inspite of a full knowledge that their position would involve all the contingencies that are there in the view under consideration. Certainly, the theory that words express the 'exclusion of the opposite' is on par with the theory that words express individuals qualified by the universal, because even according to the Buddhist theory, words express the excluded qualified by the exclusion. There is nothing special in the theory of the 'exclusion of the opposite' in as much as the exclusion it speaks of is but a substitute for the universal and the 'individual qualified by exclusion' a substitute for the individual qualified by the universal.[7]

The Buddhist answer to this is strongly worded : Let those contingencies that arise in connection with the theory of *Tadvat* equally vitiate our theory of *Apoha,* but, let the universal be not an independent entity. Even those who believe in an independent entity called universal should accept the fact-hood of the exclusion of the opposite. If there were no exclusion of the thing from its opposite, then even the realist *Nyāyavaiśeṣika's* universal would lose its *raison d'etre*. This exclusion from the opposite constitutes the identity of the given things; hence let the individual things qualified by the exclusion of the opposite be grasped by us through words. That is, the view that words express individuals qualified by the exclusion of the opposite is the most sensible. Of course, it is not that this view is absolutely free from all defects. It is humanly impossible to evolve a theory which is absolutely faultless. But there is no need of positing an independent entity called universal. The function assigned to the universal can very well be performed by the 'exclusion of the opposite'. And this exclusion is indispensable in both the theories. Moreover, we use a word in order that the hearer may act to achieve an intended object avoiding all others. Now, if the word were not to exclude the intended object from other objects, then how will it be possible for the hearer to act with reference to that intended object?Again if a word were not to express the 'exclusion of opposite', then activity and prevention of activity both being equally allowed with reference to any object—injunctions, positive and negative-would be useless and consequently the use of words would become a mockery. So, words should invariably express the 'exclusion of things from their opposite.' This exclusion is common to all the excluded things. Thus, the exclusion of the opposite has even the characteristic of the realist *Naiyāyika*'s universal, namely 'remaining one while residing in many'. Hence it becomes clear that one who, having abandoned the exclusion, posits an independent entity called universal betrays his attachment to fiction or unreality.[8]

The *Nyāya* logician might urge that on the view that without knowing non-A we cannot know A, the knowledge of A would depend on the knowledge of non-A and *vice versa* with the result that the non-cognition of one (A or non-A) would mean the non-cognition of both (A and non-A) and this in turn, would lead to the impossibility of convention or language. Let us explain the point. On the view that A means exclusion of non-A, A can never be grasped as such i.e. excluded from non-A without the grasping of non-A; and even non-A can never be grasped without the grasping of the non-A's nature, namely, its exclusion from A and this exclusion cannot be possible without the knowledge of A. This being the case, it would not be possible for us to form convention as no convention can be formed with regard to things that are not determinately known. In short, to connect a particular type of thing with the word 'A' we should first exclude them from non-A, but how can this be possible before our knowing those former things as A?[9]

The Buddhist asks the *Nyāya* logician as to whether or not he excludes from the universal A, the universal of the form of non-A when he fixes convention even with regard to the universal A. If yes, then here also a question would arise as to how he can grasp something as non-A before knowing A. Thus, the difficulty that vitiates the Buddhist view of exclusion of the opposite vitiates even the Nyāya view of the universal. Even if the difficulties be common to both the positions in question, the Buddhist position is less objectionable because it dose not posit a hypothetical entity like 'universal'.

According to the Buddhist logician, the words express the exclusion of the opposite only. When there are many things having a common effect, a person desirous of conveying all these things uses one word which invariably excludes those things not producing that effect. He does not use the word to express the thing itself.[11]

Things, though discrete, produce one common effect just as visual sense-organ, colour, light, etc., though different from one another, generate one common effect, viz. visual perception. Things (say, individual cows), differing from one another by their very nature, generate, in a person who observes them, one common effect, viz. a conceptual cognition or a mental concept (say 'COW') and it is this concept (*vikalpa*) that serves as the basis of our applying one name to many things that generate this concept.[12] Words have nothing to do with things. They are connected with concepts which are mental constructions. And further it is said that concepts give rise to words and words, in turn, give rise to concepts. *vikalpayonayaḥ śabdāḥ vikalpāḥ śabdayonayaḥ.*

The Buddhist is right when he tells us that what is common to all the members of a class is not an eternal indpendent entity called universal, but, not when he argues that what is thus common is nothing positive but a negative feature of the form of exclusion of the opposite (*anyāpoha* or *atadvyāvṛtti*). There is no denying that what is common to the members of a class excludes them from things not belonging to this class, but, that is no ground for denying that these members share any positive features in common. He himself does not hesitate to declare that 'performing the same function' is one positive feature comon to all the members of a class, but, he prefers negative mode of describing this feature under the misconceived hope that that will enable him to assert that those members share nothing in common (an 'exclusion of the opposite' being mere absence is after all nothing) and the object grasped by thought (verbal cognition) is something fictitious (being of the form of 'exclusion' this object is after all fictitious).

Really, the root-error of the Buddhist lies in his insistence that real things being of the nature of unique particular, share no features in common and his insistence that thought (or verbal cognition), since it cognises not a unique particular, but, features common to the members of a class, cognises something fictitious.

The Buddhist repeats that a word expresses nothing positive but simply the exclusion of one kind of things from things not of that kind. But, one might ask him if it is not by virtue of possessing certain positive features in common that the things in question are excluded from the other things. If yes, then there seems to be no sense in insisting that a word expresses nothing positive. As a matter of fact, the Buddhist did not mean to deny to words a positive import. He is even correct in refuting the *Nyāya* position that a word expresses an eternally existing universal. He is equally correct in pointing out that one type of things differs from another type not because these two types are possessed of two different universals, but, because they are possessed of two different causal capacities. It is, therefore, not very difficult for the Buddhist to maintain that a word means a particular type of things because these things, all of them, possess a particular causal capacity; nay, this is actually what he maintained though he preferred to formulate his position in the form: 'a word means a particular type of things because these things are excluded (different) from those not possessing a particular causal capacity which they possess.'

REFERENCES

1. *Māyāvādam asac chāstraṁ pracchannaṁ bauddham eva tu*
—*Padmapurāṇa*
2. *Nyāyamañjarī (Prathama Āhnika)* with Gujarati translation, L.D. Institute of Indology, Ahmedabad, p. 37.
3. *Kutārkikājñānanivṛttihetuḥ .../ Nyāyavārtika,* p. 1
Yadyapi bhāṣyakṛtā kṛtavyutpādanam etat tathāpi Diṅnāgaprabhṛtibhiḥ arvācīnaiḥ kuhetusantamasasamutthāpanenācchāditaṁ śāstram.../ Nyāyavārtikatātparyaṭīkā, p. 1.
Icchāmi kim api puṇyaṁ dustarakunibandhapaṅkamagnānām/ Udyotakaragavīnām atijaratīnāṁ samuddharaṇāt// Nyāyavārtikatātparyaṭīkā, p. 1.
4. *Arthajñāpanahetur hi saṅketaḥ puruṣāśrayaḥ/ Svopajñavṛttisahita-Pramāṇavārtika-Svārthānumānapariccheda, (SPS),* Ed. Pt. Dalsukh Malvania, B.H.U., Banaras, p. 75.
5. *Api pravarteta pumān vijñāyārthakriyākṣamān/ Tatsādhanāyetyartheṣu saṁyojyante'bhidhāyakāḥ//95// SPS,* p. 30.
6. *Vyakter aśakyacodanatvāt lakṣitalakṣaṇārthaṁ jāticodaneti cet/ aśabdacodite saty api sambandhe kathaṁ pravarteta? Na hi kaścid daṇḍam chindhītyukte daṇḍinaṁ chinatti/ Nāpyasambhavād vyaktau pravṛttiḥ/ Evam hyasambaddhapralāpī syāṭ/ SPS,* p. 30.
7. ... ... *tadvān alaṁ sa ca/ sākṣān na yojyate kasmād ānantyācced idaṁ samam//96// Tatkāriṇām atatkāribhedasāmye na kiṁ kṛtaḥ/ tadvaddoṣasya sāmyāc cet ... ... //97// SPS,* pp. 30-31.
8. ... ... *astu jātir alaṁ parā//tadanyaparihāreṇa pravarteteti ca dhvaniḥ/ Ucyate tena tebhyo'syāvyavacchede kathaṁ ca saḥ//98//* One may study the *Svopajñavṛtti* on this *Kārikā.* SPS, p. 31.
9. *Avṛkṣavyatirekeṇa vṛkṣārthagrahaṇe dvayam/ Anyonyāśrayam ityekagrahābhāve dvayāgrahaḥ//116//*
10. *Teṣām avṛkṣāḥ saṅkete vyavacchinnā na vā yadi//117// Vyavacchinnāḥ kathaṁ jñātā prākvṛkṣagrahaṇād ṛte./ Anirākaraṇe teṣāṁ saṅkete vyavahāriṇām//118// Na syāt tatparihāreṇa pravṛttir vṛkṣabhedavat/* SPs. p. 38.
11. *Ekakāryeṣu bhedeṣu tatkāryaparicodane//139// Gauravāśaktivaiphalyād bhedākhyāyāḥ samā śrutiḥ/ Kṛtā vṛddhair atatkāryavyāvṛttinibandhanā//140// Na bhāve sarvabhāvānāṁ svasvabhāvavyavasthiteḥ/ Yad rūpam śābaleyasya bāhuleyasya nāsti tat //141// Atatkāryaparāvṛttir dvayorapi ca vidyate/ Arthābhedena ca vinā śabdābhedo na yujyate//142// SPS,* p. 43.
12. *Kārikās* 121-124 with *Svopajñavṛtti,* SPS, p. 39.

VI.7

THE THEFT OF LOTUS-STALKS AND THE VARIOUS TABOOS

Dr. (Mrs.) Sindhu S. Dange

There occur two tales of theft of lotus-stalks or that of lotus (or lotuses) in the *Anuśāsanaparvan* of the *Mahābhārata* (*Mbh.*). The first tale is regarding the theft of lotus-stalks (*bisastainya—'bisa'* taken here to mean not the 'lotus-fibres' but the lotus-stalks, which are used for eating). This occurs in the 93rd chapter of the *Anuśāsanaparvan* of the *Mbh*. The sages viz. Kaśyapa, Atri, Vasiṣṭha, Bharadvāja, Gautama, Viśvāmitra, Jamadagni, Arundhatī, their maid-servant Gaṇḍā and her husband Paśusakha (a *śūdra*—the couple being *śūdra*?) in the times of a great drought, being tormented by hunger while wandering from place to place, came to king Vṛṣādarbhi's kingdom. The king wished to offer them several things in their bad days, which they strongly rejected, as for a *brāhmaṇa*, accepting anything (other than *dakṣiṇā*) —'*pratigraha*'—was a sin. The king got annoyed for this repudiation of his offer from them (which he might not have expected). In order to teach them a lesson, he created a '*kṛtyā*' (a female evil spirit) having offered an oblation accompanied with *mantra*-s and placed her as a guardian of a lake full of lotuses. He asked her to get the names of all of them (including the servant-couple) known to her and kill all of them by playing black magic on them:[1] All of them told the *kṛtyā* their respective names, each of them giving the etymological explanation of his name. And to all of them she gave permission to enter the lake. When Śunaḥsakha, who was Indra in disguise and had come there to test the integrity of the sages, told his name giving explanation of it, she asked him to tell it again,for she could not catch the exact import of it. Śunaḥsakha became angry and struck the *kṛtyā* at her head with his staff (*Brahmadaṇḍa*), thus reducing her to ashes. The sages together with Arundhatī and the servant-couple, entered the lake and gave offerings with water. They gathered lotus-stalks from that lotus-lake and kept them on the bank. But when they came out of the lake, the lotus-stalks collected by them were not there on the bank, for, they were taken away by somebody. They felt sure that the person committing that theft of the lotus-stalks was one of them and so they decided to swear (Mbh. Anu. 93 . 20-112)

Here we have a long list of taboos[2] (prohibited actions or deeds), the sin of committing which was to befall the person, who stole the lotus-stalks. Atri mentions touching a cow with foot; urinating while facing the sun ; undertaking the daily Vedic study on the days and occasions, when it is not to be undertaken (*Ibid*. 113). Vasiṣṭha states studying on the *anadhyāya*-days (prohibited days);[3] dragging a dog; though a mendicant having licentious behaviour; killing a person who has surrendered;[4] subsisting on the income gained through a daughter[5] and desiring money from a niggard (*Ibid*. 114-115). Kaśyapa warns of speaking everything at all places ; destroying a thing kept as deposit[6] giving false testimony while standing as a witness[7]; having flesh which is not intended for gods or manes (*pitṛ*-s); giving gift which may be revoked or is not made good if promised ; approaching a woman (for copulation) at day-time (*Ibid*. 116-117). Bharadvāja speaks of discarding one's duties towards women, kinsmen and cows ; scoring victory over a *brāhmaṇa* ; by repudiating a preceptor and on one's own, studying *ṛk-s* and *yajuṣ* (i.e. *Ṛgveda* and *Yajurveda*); offering oblations in the fire, which is in dry wood or grass (*Ibid*. 118-119). Jamadagni points out releasing excreta in waters; killing a cow and hating her; approaching one's wife on the prohibited days; earning one's livelihood through one's wife; becoming a guest of each other[8] (*Ibid*. 120- 121). Gautama mentions discarding the Vedas, having first studied them; not maintaining the three fires; selling Soma; residing in a village swept by flood near a *brāhmaṇa*, who has married a *śūdra* woman[9] (*Ibid*. 122-123).

Viśvāmitra tells the sin accruing to a person, whose elderly persons and servants are maintained by others in spite of he being alive, that of a person having many sons but not having any means of livelihood;[10] that of being a thoroughly learned but impure *brāhmaṇa*, as well as arrogant due to amassing wealth, moreover squeezing (money) and jealous by nature, that of a '*varṣācara*' (according to Monier Williams, this word is of obscure meaning) hired servant, that of an officiating priest of a king (?) and that of a person acting as a priest at the place of a person, who is not entitled to perform a sacrifice (*Ibid*. 124-126). The sins pointed out by Arundhatī, Gaṇḍā and Paśusakha are more on the side of the rules of morality, except the point of '*śulka* (taking which the girl is given to the bridegroom in marriage)[11] in the mouth of Gaṇḍā (*Ibid*. 127-131). Then speaks Śunaḥsakha (who is Indra in disguise) that a person who takes away the lotus-stalks may give his daughter in marriage to an offering priest (Adhvaryu priest)[12] or to a person well-versed in the Vedic studies and has observed the vow of celibacy *(brahmacarya)* or to a person, who having studied the *Atharvaveda* takes the final bath as a mark of the completion of his studies (*Ibid.* 132). Now this swearing was perfectly in favour of the sages and so it was revealed that Śunaḥsakha (i. e. Indra) himself had committed the theft of lotus-talks to test the integrity of the sages (*Ibid.* 134-135).

Another tale which occurs in the 94th chapter, of the *Anuśāsanaparvan* of the Mbh. is regarding the theft of Agastya's lotus (or lotuses—here the word is 'puṣkara', sing. no., but it can be taken to denote plu. no. as per the maxim '*jātau ekavacanam*'), when the sages Bhṛgu, Vasiṣṭha etc. and the kings Śibi, Dilīpa etc. come there, visiting various holy places. As Agastya's lotus is not seen, obviously stolen by somebody, he casts aspersions on these personalities, who in turn swear, each of them pointing out the sin accruing to a person stealing the lotus of Agastya as equal to that for the various types of wrong doings. Many of these are common to what we have already noted in the context of the tale from the 93rd chap. Dragging a dog for livelihood seems to be a serious matter and hence tabooed (*Mbh. Anu.* 94. 17, 20, 34c). Manu mentions a *śvakrīḍī* (one who keeps dogs for pleasure) as a '*paṅktivigarhita*' i. e. a person in whose company or with whom meals are not to be partaken of (*Manusmṛti* 111 .164). The *Bhāgavata Purāṇa* states that those who are the masters of dog or donkey are pierced by the servants of Yama with arrows (V. 26. 24). To treat ailing persons also seems to be a taboo[13] (*Mbh. Anu* 94. 22a). Approaching a woman (for union) by day-time is regarded a taboo (*Ibid.* 24b, 27ab). Striking a cow with foot, urinating while facing the sun and abandoning a person who has surrendered are regarded as serious sins and they are tabooed (*Ibid.* 32). Again giving a daughter in marriage by taking *śulka* is tabooed (*Ibid.* 31c). To entertain a person from the family as a guest is tabooed (*Ibid.* 28a). According to the rule of the Dharmaśāstra, a guest (*atithi*) is always an unknown person. Going by a vehicle dragged by a donkey is tabooed for a respectable person (*Ibid.* 34ab). The sin of many of the lapses which a person is said to commit, if he steals Agastya's lotus, fall in line with the rules of prohibition prescribed in the Dhannaśāstra texts. Such lapses mentioned are—having greed for the deposit kept; giving false testimony while standing as a witness (*Ibid.* 18bc); speaking false, always opposing the righteous persons (*Ibid.* 31ab); knowing the rules of righteous conduct, but, not following them (*Ibid.* 39c).

The three verses coming at the end of each of the two chapters (*Anu* 93rd and 94th) clearly serve as 'charter', telling us the various types of gain to be obtained by a person, on reciting or studying these two tales, bringing out the aetiological purpose of the tales.

It is interesting to see that such taboos are prescribed by the *Śatapatha Brāhmaṇa* in the context of the Pravargya rite, for which the reason forwarded is that he who either teaches or partakes of this Pravargya, enters that life or that light. It is said that he should not cover himself with a garment, while the sun shines, lest he should be concealed from the sun. He should not spit while the sun shines, lest he should spit on the sun. He should not discharge urine while the sun shines, lest he discharge it upon him (*Śat. Br.* XIV. 1.2.33). It has to be pointed out that the taboos or the prohibited things stated here come under the day-to-day beliefs and practices, while those mentioned in the two tales of the *Mbh.* definitely aim at teaching the moral code.

The practice of taking an oath or swearing dates back from the *Ṛgveda*. Vasiṣṭha says that if he is '*anṛtadeva*' ('whose gods are false' i.e. defunct) or if he approaches the gods in vain, Agni should injure him (RV VII. 104. 14ab and Sāyaṇa on it). Vasiṣṭha on this very occasion swears that he would die that very day if he is really a sorcerer and he who calls him (i.e.to Vasiṣṭha) a sorcerer, would be separated permanently from his ten heroic sons (i.e. his sons will die). Sāyaṇa says that this is also in the form of a '*śapatha*' (swearing or taking an oath).[14]

In the very word '*śapatha*' the root is / *śap*—'to speak', from which we have the word '*śabda*' (a word) as also the word *śāpa'* (curse). But the efficacy of the spoken word was no doubt preceded by the efficacy of the emotion of the inarticulate wish or will. The essence of cursing and swearing was thus in existence before the human speech was developed.[15] But as seen above, the punishing power of a word is particularly conspicuous in the case of an oath and its contagious character resembles that which is attributed to tabooed persons and things, and it acts mechanically.[16] While taking into account the serious note struck in the swearing by the sages or by other personalities in the two tales, which are being discussed, we can take into account the definition stated by Westermarck. An oath is essentially a conditional self-imprecation, a curse by which a person calls down upon himself some evil in the event of what he says not being true. The efficacy of the oath is originally entirely magical; it is due to the magic power inherent in the cursing words.[17]

We have already noted that the two tales from the *Mbh.* (*Anu. parvan*) mention a series of taboos, which are customary abstinences or negative rites as they may be called. Taboo (or 'tabu') stands for the whole mass of fear-inspired inhibitions in so far as they proceed directly from the religious emotion, as it regulates the social tradition. The prohibited deeds or actions spoken of in the two tales serve a double purpose, in that they reflect the fear-inspired beliefs prevalent in the society of that time or those beliefs which might have travelled from a hoary past upto that time and might have been still maintained by the then society. Secondly they are pressed into service here to serve as a code of moral conduct, which is full of several 'dos' and 'don'ts', both being equally important.

It has to be noted that the two tales from the *Mbh.* discussed above, dealing with the theft of lotus-stalks or lotus, are based on a *gāthā* which occurs in the *Aitareya Brāhmaṇa*. The *Ait. Br*. deals at great length with the problem of the exact time of the morning Agnihotra, whether the morning offerings are to be given before sunrise or after the sun has actually arisen, and comes to the conclusion that the morning offerings are to be given in the fire after the rise of the sun (*Ait. Br*. V. 29-31 = 25. 4-6). While enjoining the evening offerings in the fire after the setting of the sun (when the darkness sets in), the *Ait. Br*. quotes a *gāthā*, which is in the form of swearing on the part of a certain person (Ibid. V. 30 = 25. 5). Sāyaṇa while commenting on the *gāthā*, refers to an old account of the seven sages, when one of them charged with the theft of lotus-stalks swore before them. The *gāthā* points out that a person stealing the lotus-stalks would get a series of sins viz. the sin which accrues to a person, who makes a false charge against a sinless person; the sin which a sinful person accepts; the sin which a person commits, while turning away a guest arrived at the evening time. The person, when swearing, is determined to face the consequences of these sins, if he has committed the theft of lotus-stalks. The account preserved in the *gāthā* was certainly of olden times. The *gāthā* itself came from the secular tradition and it was used by the *Ait. Br.* as an *arthavāda* to support the *vidhi* of giving offerings in the fire in the evening time. Actually these offerings are for the sun and thus it is evening Agnihotra. (as we have noted the morning Agnihotra, in which offerings are given in the fire when the sun has risen). The Ait. Br. says that the sun is *'eka-atithiḥ'*, (i.e. 'an excellent guest', like '*ekavīraḥ*' meaning 'unparallelled warrior', though Sāyaṇa takes this word to mean 'one living in a foreign land, without any relatives'), who resides among the sacrificers offering oblations. He being a guest is to be given hospitality and is not to be turned away, as is pointed out by the *gāthā*.

The *Ait. Br.* states as *arthavāda* several *gāthās* and even *yajñagāthās*, on some occasions. Though *yajñagāthās* were a contribution of the ritualist- circles, the *gāthās* definitely came from the popular or secular circles. It was the tradition of the *sūta*-s which preserved this popular or secular literature, at times making additions or omissions and (may be !) on some occasions having their own compositions.[18] According to Winternitz, the credit of composing the two great epics goes to the tradition of the *sūtas.*[19] He says that there was an inexhaustible store of prose and verse narratives—*Ākhyānas*, *Itihāsas, Purāṇas* and *Gāthās*—forming as it were literary public property[20], which was drawn upon by the Buddhists and the Jains, as well as by the epic poets.

It seems that in the floating mass of literature, preserved in the secular tradition, there was current a mythical tale of a certain unknown person, who had committed a theft of lotus-stalks or lotuses, as is recorded in the *gāthā* from the *Ait. Br*. The *Mbh*. used it for imparting moral instructions and laying down various taboos, by coining the two tales, woven round the names of sages and personalities, who were illustrious. However, we have to admit that these two tales serve as a window for us to have a glimpse of the ancient Indian moral code.

NOTES AND REFERENCES :

1. Hastings, J., *Encyclopaedia ol Religion and Ethics* (= *ERE*), Vol. IX, p. 135a. The name of a person stands as his very soul—his 'name-soul'. Hence the practice of keeping the real name secret and giving another name to the boy for daily use to save him from being conjured with magic and thus being harmed.
2. The word 'Taboo' was introduced into English by Captain Cook. He first met with the word in 1777 in Tonga. (Cook, J. and King, J., *A Voyage to the Pacific Ocean*, London, 1776-1780. Vols. I & II by Cook, J. and Vol. III by King, J.). In general, the word 'Taboo' signifies that 'a thing is forbidden[3], and it is applied to all cases, where things are not to be touched. See *ERE*, Vol. XII, p. 181. The word 'Tabu' ('Taboo') stands for the whole mass of fear-inspired inhibitions in so far as they proceed directly from the religious emotion. see *Ibid*. p. 183a.
3. For the days of *anadhyāya* ('no-study' of Vedic-texts) for the students, there were regular holidays (New-moon day, Aṣṭakā etc.) and also casual holidays for the death of a relative, teacher, king etc., also for the occurrence of natural phenomena like earth-quake, solar or lunar eclipse, rain-bow, fierce gale, rain, thunder etc. See Ram Gopal, *India of Vedic Kalpasūtras*, Delhi, 1959, pp. 344-345.
4. *Manu.Sm*. VII. 90-98 for *'yodhadharma'* (rules to be followed by a *kṣatriya* when he is fighting on the battlefield). see *Ibid*. 91, for 'not to kill a person, who has surrendered'.
5. *Ibid*. III. 52: Manu says that those who subsist on the wealth of wife, daughter or women in the house, being sinful, go to wretched condition in the other world.
6. For the rules regarding *'nikṣepa'* (deposit) and *'upanidhi'* (a sealed deposit, the exact idea of its value not being given to the person with whom the deposit is kept), see *Ibid*. VIII. 179-196.
7. Manu says that a statement given by a person, standing as a witness, out of greed,

infatuation, fear, friendship, passion, wrath, ignorance, childlike behaviour i. e. inadvertence, is regarded as false, see *Ibid.* VIII.118. Manu prescribes punishment (*daṇḍa*) for this. see *Ibid.* 120-122.

8. The idea that a person arriving as an '*atithi*' (guest) has to be practically a stranger to the householder is maintained in the *Dharmaśāstra* tradition and hence a person, who belongs to the same village or who is a friend or a fellow-student is not an '*atithi*'. *Gautama Dh.S.* V. 36; *Manu Sm.* III.103; *Yājn.Sm.* 1, 107, 111, for details, also see (Mrs) Dange, S. S., "*Atithi* : A Probe in Concept", *Studies in Indology (Prof. Mukund Madhav Sharma Fel. Vol.),* Sri Sadguru Pubns., Delhi, 1996, pp. 119-122.
9. The son of such a *brāhmaṇa* (who has married a *śūdra* woman) is called 'pāraśava' ('*as* good as a corpse'). see *Manu Sm.* IX. 178.
10. cf. *Nirukta* 11. 8—the interpretation of *Ṛgveda* I. 164. 32d given by the *Parivrājakas*, that a person (obviously a poor person), having many children, goes to wretched condition.
11. A girl given for money is said to be '*śulkadeyā*'. see *Mānava Gṛ. S.* 8. 1-11; *Kāṭhaka Gṛ. S.* 15. 1-5; *Ibid.* 16. 1-5. also *Manu Sm.* III. 31, where Manu calls this practice to be a feature of the 'Āsura' form of marriage, also *Ibid.* III.51—The father should not take any '*śulka*', for he will be deemed an '*apatyavikrayī*' (i. e. seller of his child, here daughter).
12. *Ibid.* III. 28-Manu mentions 'Daiva' form of marriage, in which a girl, decked with ornaments etc. is given to a priest, who duly officiates at a sacrifice, during the course of its performance.
13. The twin-gods Aśvins were not entitled to the share of Soma, as they moved among people as physicians. *Jaiminīya Brāhmaṇa* III. 124—aśvinau—*bhiṣajyantāv* '*idam carato' napisomau* / for the whole account of their getting that share, see *Ibid.* III. 120-128; also *Śatapatha Br.* IV. 1. 5. 1-15.
14. Manu refers to swearing undertaken by the great seers and gods, also by Vasiṣṭha before Sudāsa Paijavana. see *Manu Sm.* VIII. 110. Manu deals with the topic of '*śapatha*'. *Ibid.,* VIII. 111-116.
15. *ERE* Vol. IX., p. 430a & b.
16. *Ibid.* 431a.
17. *Ibid.* 430a.
18. (Mrs) Dange, S. S., "Sūta—The Paurāṇika" *Purāṇa*, Varanasi, Vol. XL, No. 2, July 1998, pp. 83-91.
19. Wintemitz, M., *History of Indian Literature*, Vol. I (Intrn., Veda, National Epics, Purāṇas and Tantras), Munshiram Manoharlal, New Delhi, 2nd ed. 1972 (Uni. of Calcutta 1927), p. 315.
20. *Ibid*, p. 314.

VI.8

A GLIMPSE INTO HUMAN RIGHTS IN ANCIENT INDIA

Dr. Alka Bakre

Human Rights otherwise known as Fundamental Rights are traditionally known as natural rights.[1] The concept of human rights is of central importance in the development of the modern world. The expression, 'Human Rights' used in the sense of 'Rights of man' goes back to the last decades of the 18th century. However, the idea of law, defining and protecting the natural rights of the members of society is much older. The Spanish theologian, lawyer Franscisco de Victoria (1480 A.D.-1546 A.D) was the first one to use legal reasoning, moral principle and political courage to consider human rights in relation to international law.[2]

The event of issuing universal declaration of Human Rights in 1948 by the Human Rights Commission of the United Nations indicated an awareness of the importance of this concept especially in the modern age. In fact, it was a landmark in the history of the world.

Contemporary norms regarding human rights in India are the outcome of the process of modernisation. This process is always seen to be going hand in hand with that of westernisation. This twin process takes cognisance of various principles such as liberty, rational reasoning, non- discrimination of any kind, non-subjection to torture or punishment, non- arbitrariness in arrest, detention or exile, the right to be presumed innocent until proved guilty, the right to own property in an arbitrary way, the right to freedom of thought, conscience and religion, the right to equal access, the right to service, and the like. The same principles have been stated in the 'Preamble', 'Universal Declaration of Human Rights' adopted by the General Assembly of the United Nations.[3] The concept of human rights is definitely a product of modern ideology. Still, the inner dynamics pertaining to it could be examined in a unique socio-cultural, socio-religious and socio-historical framework of ancient India on the basis of ancient Sanskrit Texts.

This concept encompasses a vast area, each having many sub areas. However, here the attempt will be to focus only on one area, viz. the area of human rights and social stratification, with two sub-areas, viz. (i) Human rights and hierarchical gradation due to *varṇa* differences and (ii) Human Rights and gradation due to sex—difference.

Human Rights and Stratification caused by Varṇa Differences

Every great institution has its own extremes of good and evil. *Varṇa* system in India which is an institution in itself was not exceptional. The *Ṛgveda* which is the oldest of all the Vedas reflects unstratified society. It is doubtful whether the reference to the four orders of society, viz. *Brāhmaṇa, Kṣatriya, Vaiśya* and *Śūdra* originating from the sacrifice of the First Being and arising out of his mouth, arms, thighs and feet respectively indicated their status-difference leading to hierarchical social gradation. At the same time, it is important to take note of the subtle hints indicated through the request to Aśvins to encourage *Vipra-s* and *Kṣatriya-s* for their excellent deeds (Ṛv.VIII. 35. 16-17) or through the reference to Indra who was believed to be having an utter dislike for Soma juice that was pressed by people who hated brahmins. Equally important are the statements in the (Av) such as, 'Insult inflicted upon brahmin women leads to unwanted occurrences such as miscarriage, untimely death, violent massacres' (Av.V17), or The nation where brahmin women are insulted cannot prosper, cannot have abundance of cattle' (Av.17. 16-17) or 'A person destroying a brahmin is hated by all. Nobody should destroy a brahmin who is as respectable as Agni. The kings who carried away brahmins' cows were defeated' (Av.XVIII. 5-6, 10). 'Kṣatriya kings who insulted brahmins and killed them were besmeared with blood. They met with their own destruction' (Av.V.19.3).

Sacrificial Texts

What is hinted at with subtle suggestions is clearly stated in the Brahmanical Texts which reflect a stratified society with the brahmins at the top. Thus, according to the Tait. Br. *Brāhmaṇa varṇa* was divine and *Śūdra varṇa* was *asurya varṇa*.[4] This was against the principle of equality, one of the important human rights.

In the Ṛgvedic age, the functions of the four *varṇas* were not precisely demarcated. However, the post—Vedic period, especially that of the works on Dharma-śāstra was characterised by such demarcation. *(Manu S.* IX. 1. 88- 90, *Yāj.S.* I. 118-119, *Hārīta S.* 1.12, II.2-3, *Viṣṇu Dh.S* 1.10-15, also *Gaut. Dh.S.* IX. 1-3,

7.50). To cite a few more examples, according to *Manu S*. (IV. 147), a *brāhmaṇa,* should study the Veda. This is his highest *dharma.* According to *Yāj.S.* (1.198), the creator created *Brāhmaṇa-s* in order to preserve the Vedas, to satisfy gods and forefathers and to safeguard *dharma.* According to all the works on Dharmaśāstra,[5] and the *Mbh.,*[6] service to the twice-born ones was the exclusive duty of the *Śūdras*. The *Śūdras* were prohibited from accumulating wealth *(Gaut.Dh.S.* X. 64-65). Such statements were against the principles of non-discrimination.

The works on Dharmaśāstra abound in statements which again reflect a definite attempt to eulogise the *Brāhmaṇas*, to bestow the highest honour on them and to degrade the *Śūdras.* Thus, the *Viṣṇu Dh.S.* (XIV.20-22) states that the gods are invisible deities, but the brahmins are the visible ones. Manu *(Manu S.* 1.100) stated that the entire wealth on the earth belongs to *Brāhmaṇas*. They deserve everything on account of the priority of birth and mastery of the entire world *(Manu S.* 1.95). *Gaut.* S. stated that the king could rule over everybody except the brahmins. Even according to the *Tait. S. (Tait. S.* II.6.10.1-2), threatening or striking a *Brāhmaṇa* was a punishable deed.

Discriminatory attitude

Brāhmaṇas enjoyed special privileges. Ancient Indian Texts reflected discriminatory attitude in terms of special favour to *brahmins* and an inclination to adopt severity towards persons belonging to lower *varṇas.* Thus, according to the *Śat.Br.* XIII. 6.2.18, *Manu S.* VII.133, Āp. Dh.S. 11.10.26, brahmins were not to be taxed *(akarāḥ śrotriyāḥ). Vas. Dh.S.* (III.26) expected a king to collect 1/6th part of wealth from persons other than brahmins. *Gaut. Dh.* S.(VIII.12-13) prohibited kings from beating brahmins, putting fetters around them, fine them, drive them out, censure or abandon them. *Mitākṣarā* is also liberal while laying down punishments for brahmins.[8] Even Kauṭilya held that corporal punishment is never to be inflicted upon brahmins *(Kauṭ. Arth.* V.11.12).

The points stressed in the statements such as, The *dvijas* only can study the sacred texts' *(Manu S.* 11.165), The *Śūdra*s are not to be initiated. No sacred rite is to be performed upon them' (*Ibid.* X. 126) are too well known to be further commented upon. They have violated the basic principles of human rights of non-subjection to and arbitrariness with respect to fair treatment. The religious norms preventing the *Śūdra*s from consecrating sacred fires and performing sacrifices *(Jaimini* 1.3.25 ff), expecting them to perform every religious rite without the accompaniment of the recitation of the sacred *mantras (Manu S.* X.127) and content themselves with listening to the *Itihāsas* and *Purāṇas* show that the *Śūdra*s were deprived of the right to religion.

Bhakṣyābhakṣyavicāra

Brāhmaṇas were allowed to have food at the residences of persons belonging to the three higher *varṇas*. The Mbh. expected a *brāhmaṇa* to be served by a *Śūdra* from a distance.[9] The Purāṇa-s expressed similar thoughts. Thus, according to the *Kūr.P., a Brāhmaṇa* should not eat food offered by a *Śūdra*. This *Purāṇa* declared that a *Brāhmaṇa* violating this norm will be born as a *Śūdra (Kūr.P.*II. *17.1).*

The Concept of Pollution and Outcasts –

The *Saṁhitās* do not reflect an idea of pollution. However, in the course of time, intensification of *varṇa* differences led to hierarchical gradation. This in turn culminated into the ideas of purity and impurity and gave rise to the concept of pollution. Manu regarded persons belonging to a *Brāhmaṇa varṇa* to be superior to others and expected *Cāṇḍālas* to stay at the cemetery *(Manu S.* X.36.51). The statements preventing *Brāhmaṇa*-s from staying in the company of outcasts (Manu.S.IV.79ff, Āp.*Dh.*S.II. 1.2.8-9), those mentioning the need for getting rid of impurities caused by physical contact with the *Cāṇḍālas* or by merely looking at the Cāṇḍālas through plunging into water *(Āp.Dh.S.* 1.1.2.8-9), those stating that, the roads trodden by the Cāṇḍālas are impure (Yāj. S.I. 194, 197) hint at inhuman treatment meted out to a certain section of society which is always against the basic principles of human rights.

Puranic Age

Purāṇic statements such as, 'A person who is in constant contact with outcasts incurs sin. One receiving favours from them would become an insect. A *dvija* accepting a valuable thing from them would become an insect or will be born as an ass and a person performing a sacrifice for an outcast would become a worm' *(Mārk.P.* 14.83-84), indicate that the composers of the Purāṇa-s also had thrown to the winds the basic principles of human rights.

Even in the Purāṇic age, the members of the *Brāhmaṇa-varṇa* were held in high esteem.[10] Persons belonging to different *varṇas* were expected to follow their respective duties.[11] However, at times, the composers of the Purāṇas are seen to be cherishing liberal ideology through statements such as, There is nothing like a *Brāhmaṇajāti*'[12], 'Brahminhood is determined by one's own behaviour'[13], 'Even a Śūdra endowed with good qualities can become a *Brāhmaṇa*'[14], 'Hence, there is no difference between a *Brāhmaṇa* and a *Śūdra*[15], The *Brāhmaṇas* are not as bright as the rays of the moon. The colour of the *Kṣatriyas* is not like that of a *kiṁśuka* flower, that of the *Vaiṣyas* is not like that of turmeric and that of *Śudras* is not like that of coal.[16] Since, the father of all *prajās* is the same, there is no difference in the types of births.[17] However, it must be noted that the attempt to spread liberal ideology was not prompted by an awareness of the importance of the principle of equality. The composers of the Purāṇas had realised that the ritualistic *(karmakāṇḍātmaka)* and the philosophical *(jñānakāṇḍātmaka)* aspects of the Vedic religion could not be pursued by the masses, who in turn were likely to be fascinated by the rise and popularity of Buddhism and Jainism. In order to wean these people away from them, the composers of the Purāṇas had shrewdly stressed the principle of equality of status.

Social Gradation due to Sex-difference

The Vedic period reflects both bright as also dark aspects with respect to the world of women. The Ṛv.(X.27.12) refers to a beautiful girl who selected a suitable match for herself. In the Ṛgvedic age, brides enjoyed good status in their families. They were blessed to be the queens in their respective families.[18] Both husband and wife were considered to be the joint owners of the house *(Rv.* III. 53.4). The wife was regarded as the ornament of the house (Ṛv.1.66.3). There were educated women like Lopāmudrā, Viśvavārā, Sikatā, Apālā or Ghoṣā, who enjoyed high status. The Upaniṣads refer to a *Brahmavādinī* like Maitreyī, who was interested in indulging in philosophical discussions and achieving the highest knowledge *(Br. Up.* 11.4). At the same time, there were charms and rituals in order to ensure the birth of a male issue in preference to that of a female one *(Av.* III. 23, VI. 110) or the statements such as, 'The son is the source of joy and the daughter that of trouble[19]. The *Śat.Br.* glorified women stating that a man who is just 'the half' becomes complete when he has a wife and when he begets children'.[20]

On the one hand, the *Mbh. (Śānti* p. 144.4) praises a wife stating that 'the house of a householder without wife would be void. A wife is an excellent medicine with which all sorts of sorrow can be destroyed' *(Ibid.* III.58.29). *Aśv. Śr.S.* (1.11) indicates that women had the same status as that of men in performing religious activities. *Āp. Dh.S.* considers the status of the husband and wife to be the same in performing activities and reaping the fruits.[21] *Harita Dh. S.* indicates that the girls were getting initiated and hence were also being educated.[22]

According to *Nār. S.*, 'Women have been created to enable men to have issues. Woman is a field in which men sow the seed.[23] However, in the course of time, the status of women went on deteriorating. The expectations of a wife stated in several texts have been against the principles of equality and freedom. Thus, Jaimini (V.1.24) stated that a wife is never comparable to husband, as the husband is a man and that he is learned, while the wife is a woman and she is *avidya.*[24] The *Mbh.* has elsewhere considered the husband to be the wife's god, the highest destination.[25] Manu idealised the dependence of women on some male member or the other throughout their lives *(Manu* S. IX.2-4). He stated that the creator created passion, anger, wickedness, dishonesty, misbehavior and an interest in beautification in women *(Manu.S.* IX. 17). He expected the wife to respect, honour and wait upon her husband even though the latter may be self-willed and vicious.[26] Later texts expected the change in the role that a woman had to play. They subordinated her position to that of her husband. They expected her to be in harmony with her husband, to worship her in-laws, other elderly persons and guests. They prohibited her from visiting others' residences, from standing at the doors or windows, from carrying out activities independently, from performing sacrifices by herself and expected her even to wait upon her husband *(Viṣṇu S.* XXV. 2 ff). According to the norms laid down by *Vyā. S.,* she should follow her husband not only like a shadow or a friend, but even like a maidservant *(Vyā. S.* ll.27)and should regard her husband to be the highest deity *(Ibid. 36).* Even according to *Yāj.S.* (1.76), the wife should obey the order of her husband and should have pleasing speech. *Aṅgira* S.(69) considered a woman disobeying her husband's order to be of free will and deeds *(kāmacāriṇī). Atri S.* declared that a woman drinking water poured on her husband's feet would reach the highest abode of either Śiva or Viṣṇu *(Atri S.* 137). *Kātyāyana S.* (XIX. 12) assured that a woman waiting upon her husband would reach all the worlds. *Dakṣa S.* expected a woman to be favourable, devoid of harsh, unpleasing speech, skillful, expert, of good nature, devoted to her husband and glorified such a woman stating that with these excellent qualities, she is Śrī (Beauty, Grace, Wealth or the Goddess of Wealth) and not *strī.*[27] Even the *Rām.* considered the husband to be the support and shelter of the wife and expected her to wait upon him.[28] Smṛti writers like Manu considered marriage to be a means with which the husband's supremacy over the wife was established *(Ibid.* V. 152). The Brahmanical Texts allowed even a widower to perform Vedic sacrifices.[29] However, Smṛti writers like Manu expected a bereaved husband to get married immediately after the death of his wife. *(Manu S.* V.160). Manu allowed the husband to discard his wife if she was found to be disagreeable to him.[30] However, he expected the wife to be faithful to him even after the latter's death *(Ibid.*V.160). Due to the permission to marry again, men became irresponsible in discharging their duties towards their first wives who became helpless. Discontinuation of *upanayana* in the case of women brought them on par with the *Śūdra*-s. Manu (IV.205) prohibited brahmins from even attending sacrificial sessions performed by women. No wonder, therefore, that women were bracketed with the *Śūdras*.[31]

The Purāṇas laid down more or less similar norms and stressed the same values. They expected a woman to consider her husband to be her highest destination, to adore him like a god and even wait upon him.[32] To inculcate this value, The *Mārk.P.* stated that a woman doing so can fulfil all her desires. *(Mārk P.* 16.57). The Purāṇas even expected her to work hard like a slave and fulfil the sexual desire of her husband *(Pad.P.* 7.11.29). The *Bh.P.* prohibited women from wearing many ornaments and stepping out of their residences when their husbands and in-laws were away, *(Bh.P.* I. 3.2) thus, restricting their freedom. The *Br. V.P.* considered a woman getting up early in the morning, cleaning the courtyard, carrying out and completing the domestic work wholeheartedly and welcoming the guests to be righteous *(Br V.P.* 84. 15-17) and regarded a woman devoted to her husband to be the best *(uttamā) (Ibid.* 84.87). Following the norms laid down by the works on Dharmaśāstra, the Purāṇas also stressed the concept of the adoration and deification of the husband by the wife. Quoting Manu's verse *verbatim* (Manu S. IX.3), even the Pad. P. (1.52.23) has stated that a woman is protected by her father, husband and the son and that she should never be independent. *Bh. P.* (1.13.2) prohibited women from wearing many ornaments and from stepping out of the residence when the husband and in-laws are away.) The *Var. P.* considered a woman who got up before her husband did, who slept after her husband did, who observed mum when her husband was silent, who kept standing when her husband was standing, to be an ideal woman *(Var.P.* 209.4-5). The *Ska. P.* (III.2.14) expected the wife not to shout even when she is being dragged by her husband forcibly and be in a happy mood even when she is beaten by him. *Vyā.S.* expected a widow to ascend on to the same fire enkindled for performing the funeral rites of her husband.[33] The *Ska. P.* also glorified such a woman stating that she will achieve the merits acquired by a person who performs Aśvamedha sacrifice *(Ska. P.* 3.2 53). The same Purāṇa expected widows to sleep on the ground and prohibited them from using fragrant substances or fragrances *(Ibid.* 4.1.4.49-50).

In conclusion it can be stated that social stratification, discernible in both the sub-areas, viz. that caused by *varṇa* differences and that caused by sex-difference indicates that -

(i) No attempt was undertaken to value the basic principles of human rights such as equal status, freedom of movement, freedom of expression and the like.

(ii) As regards stratification caused by the *varṇa* differences, it can be stated that the composers of the Purāṇas realised that the ritualistic *(karmakāṇḍātmaka)* portion of the early Vedism was difficult to follow (due to its rigidity and complexity). The philosopshical *(jñānakāṇḍātmaka)* portion of the same was difficult to pursue because of its incomprehensible nature.

The existence of Hinduism, therefore, was threatened by the rise and popularity of Jainism and Buddhism. In order to wean these people away from them, some Purāṇas intentionally scattered the statements stressing the importance of the principles of equality, freedom and the like. They tried to bridge the wide gaps between different *varṇas* and enhance the status of *Śūdras*. This was done by them only at the superficial level, as is clear from the repeated statements made by them to establish the supremacy of the persons belonging to the *Brāhmaṇa-varṇa*. However, no such attempt even at the superficial level was undertaken by them to enhance the status of women.

(iii) At the same time, it must be noted that like *Śūdras*, single women were deprived of the right to religion. By laying down various types of *vratas* which could be performed by them without being accompanied by their husbands, the composers of the Purāṇas provided them with an opportunity to participate in the religious matters.

(iv) Ancient Indian people have been cherishing certain values regarding women. Killing a woman was considered to be an offence.[34] Women always had full or partial control over *strīdhana*. Different Smṛti writers held different views about it. Yājñavalkya held that a woman is entitled to get 1/3 of her husband's property (Yāj.S. 1.76). According to *Gaut.Dh.S.(28.19),* a widow is an heir along with *sapiṇḍa-s* or *sagotras*. As pointed out by A.S. Altekar, "This history of *strīdhana* is undoubtedly a proud and glorious chapter in the history of Hindu civilisation."[35]

(v) As shown above, many works on Dharmaśāstra depicted the dependence of women on some male member or the other. At the same time, they have also presented statements such as, 'Women need to be protected or are protected by some male member or the other, especially by their close relatives such as the father, the husband or the son'.[36] Though this statement upfront implies the ideal concept of dependence of women, it could also, albeit debatably, reflect the concern shown for women in general and female members of one's own family in particular—it may imply that a woman was always thought to be 'cared for'.

(vi) Although, society was patriarchal, the mother was loved, respected and even apotheosized. Motherhood was a highly cherished value even in ancient India *(Vas.Dh.S.* 13.47, *Baudh.Dh.S.* II.2.48, *Atri* S.151, *Mbh. Śānti P.* 267.31, 343.18, *Vana P.* 313.60). Hence, ancient Indian people also cherished the tendency of adoring women. Consequently, in ancient

India, the status of women was superior to that of the *Śūdras*. For the same reason, social gradation caused by sex-differences was not as sharp and as condemnable as that caused by *varṇa* differences.

A LIST OF ABBREVIATIONS

Ādi P.	*ĀdiParva, Mahābhārata*
Agn.P,	*Agni Purāṇa*
Ait Br.	*Aitareya Brāhmaṇa*
Aṅgira S.	*Aṅgirasmṛti*
Anu.P.	*Anuśāsana Parva, Mahābhārata*
Āp. Dh.S.	*Āpastamba Dharmasūtra*
Āp.Gr.S.	*Āpastamba Gṛhyasūtra*
Āśv.Sr.S.	*Āśvalāyana Śrautasūtra*
Atri S.	*Atrismṛti*
Av.	*Atharvaveda*
Baudh.Dh. S.	*Baudhāyana Dharmasūtra*
Bh.P.	*Bhaviṣya Purāṇa*
B. O. R. I.	Bhandarkar Oriental Research Institute
Br.P.	*Brahma Purāṇa*
Br.Up.	*Bṛhadāraṇyaka Upaniṣad*
Br.V.P.	*Brahmavaivarta Purāṇa*
Dakṣa S.	*Dakṣasmṛti*
Gaut. Dh. S.	*Gautama Dharmasūtra*
Gaut. S.	*Gautamasmṛti*
Hārīta Dh.S.	*Hārīta Dharmasūtra*
Hārīta S.	*Hārītasmṛti*
Kat. S.	*Kātyāyanasmṛti*
Kauṭ. Arth.	*Kauṭilīya Arthaśāstra*
Kūr.P.	*Kūrma Purāṇa*
Manu S.	*Manusmṛti*
Mārk. P.	*Mārkaṇḍeya Purāṇa*
Mbh.	*Mahābhārata*
Nār.P.	*Nārada Purāṇa*
Pad. P.	*Padma Purāṇa*

Ram.	*Rāmāyaṇa*
Rv.	*Ṛgveda*
Śānti P.	*Śanti Parva*
Śat.Br.	*Śatapatha Brāhmaṇa*
Ska. P.	*Skanda Purāṇa*
Tait.Br.	*Taittirīya Brāhmaṇa*
Tait.S.	*Taittirīya Saṁhitā*
Vām.P.	*Vāmana Purāṇa*
Van.P.	*Vana Parva, Mahābhārata*
Var.P.	*Varāha Purāṇa*
Vas.Dh.S.	*Vasiṣṭha Dharmasūtra*
Viṣṇu Dh. S.	*Viṣṇu Dharmasūtra.*
Viṣṇu S.	*Viṣṇusmṛti*
Vyā.S.	*Vyāsasmṛti*
Yāj. S.	*Yājñavalkyasmṛti*

REFERENCES :

1. Gains Ezejiofor, *Protection of Human Rights under the Law,* Butter North & Co. Ltd., London, 1964, p. 3
2. Egon Schwelb, *International Encyclopaedia of Social Sciences,* Vol.6, ed. by David Sills, The Macmillan Co. & Free Press Inc., 1968, pp. 540-541
3. Annex A, Preamble, 'Universal Declaration of Human Rights' adopted by the General Assembly of the United Nations, Institutions for the Protection of Human Rights, Paris, 1965
4. *Tait. Br* I.2.6.
   दैव्यो वै वर्णो ब्राह्मणः असुर्यः शूद्रः।
5. *Āp. Dh. S.* I. 1.1.7.
   शुश्रूषा शूद्रस्येतरेषां वर्णानाम्।
   also, *Gaut. Dh. S.*
   परिचर्या चेतरेषाम्। तेभ्यो वृत्तिं लिप्सेत।
6. *Mbh. Śānti P.* 60.28.
   प्रजापतिर्हि वर्णानां दासं शूद्रमकल्पयत्।
7. *Gaut. S. XI.* 1.
   राजा सर्वस्येष्टे ब्राह्मणवर्जम्।
8. *Mitākṣarā on Yāj.* S. II. 302
   ब्राह्मणस्य पुनः न शारीरो दण्डः इति निषेधात्....
9. *Mbh. Anu.* P. 59.33
   दूराच्छूद्रेणोपचर्यो ब्राह्मणोऽग्निरिव ज्वलन्।

10. *Pad. P.* I. 32.201, IV. 14. 1, *Kūr P.* II.26.36, *Nār.P.* I.6.59, *Bh.P.* II.5.1.
11. Vām. P. I. 15.64.
    स्वानि वर्णाश्रमोक्तानि धर्माणीह न ह्रापयेत्
    also, *Gar. P.* I.213.3.
12. *Bh. P.* 1.40.31.
    ब्राह्मण्यजातिर्नृषु नास्ति काचित्।
13. *Br. P.* 115.12.57[ab]
    कारणानि द्विजत्वस्य वृत्तमेव तु कारणम्।
14. *Ibid.* 58[ab]
    वृत्ते स्थितश्च शूद्रोऽपि ब्राह्मणत्वं च गच्छति।
15. *Bh. P.* 1.41.15[cd]
    शूद्रब्राह्मणयोस्तस्मान्नास्ति भेदः कथंचन।
16. *Ibid.* 1.41.41
    न ब्राह्मणाश्चन्द्रमरीचिशुभ्रा न क्षत्रियाः किंशुकपुष्पवर्णाः।
    न चेह वैश्या हरितालतुल्याः शूद्रा न चाङ्गारसमानवर्णाः।।
17. *Ibid.* 1.41.45.
    एवं प्रजानां हि किलैक एव पित्रैकभावन्नं च जातिभेदः।
18. *Rv.* X.85.46.
    सम्राज्ञी श्वशुरे भव सम्राज्ञी श्वश्रां भव।
    ननान्दरि सम्राज्ञी भव सम्राज्ञी अधि देवृषु।।
    also, *Av.* XIV. 1.3
19. *Ait. Br.* VII.3.13
    सखा ह जाया कृपणं हि दुहिता ज्योतिर्हि पुत्रः परमे व्योमन्।
20. *Śat. Br.* V.1.6.10
    अर्धो ह वैष आत्मनस्तस्माद्यावज्जायां न विन्दते अर्धो ह
    अथ यदैव जायां विन्दते ऽथ प्रजायते तर्हि सर्वो तावद् भवति।
21. *Āp. Dh.* S.6.14.16 ff
    जायापत्योर्न विभागो दृश्यते। पाणिग्रहणाद्धि सहत्वं कर्मसु तथा पुण्यफलेषु।
22. *Hārīta Dh.* S.
    q. by P.V., *Kane History of Dharmaśāstra*, Vol. I., Pt. I. B.O.R.I., Poona, 1990, revised and enlarged edition, first published in 1930, p. 132
23. *Nār. S.* XI. 19
    अपत्यार्थं स्त्रियः सृष्टाः स्त्री क्षेत्रं बीजिनो नराः।
24. *Jaimini* V. 1.24.
    अतुल्या हि स्त्री पुंसा। यजमानः पुमान् विद्वांश्च।
    पत्नी स्त्री चाविद्या च।
25. *Mbh. Anu.* p. 134.51[ab]
    पतिर्हि देवो नारीणां पतिर्बन्धुः परा गतिः।
26. *Manu S.*V. 154

विशीलो कामवृत्तो वा गुणैर्वा परिवर्जितः।
उपचर्यः स्त्रिया साध्व्या सततं देववत् पतिः।।

27. *Dakṣa*. S. IV. 12
अनुकूला न वाग्दुष्टा दक्षा साध्वी पतिव्रता।
एभिरेव गुणैर्युक्ता श्रीरेव स्त्री न संशयः।।

28. *Rām*. II. 24.4[cd]
इह प्रेत्य च नारीणां पतिरेको गतिः सदा।

29. *Ait. Br.* VII. 10
अपत्नीकः कथमग्निहोत्रं जुहोति। श्रद्धा पत्नी सत्यं यजमानः श्रद्धा सत्यं तदित्युत्तमं मिथुनम्।

30. *Manu* S. IX. 81.[d]
सद्यस्त्वप्रियवादिनी।

31. *Bh. G.* IX. 32[ab]
स्त्रियो वैश्यास्तथा शूद्रास्तेऽपि यान्ति परां गतिम्।

32. *Mat*. p. 210. 17
पतिर्हि दैवतं स्त्रीणां पतिरेव परायणम्।
also, *Mārk*. p. 16,64

33. *Vyā.S.* II. 53
मृतं भर्तारमादाय ब्राह्मणी वह्निमाविशेत्।
जीवन्ती चेत् त्यक्तक्लेशा तपसा शोधयेद्वपुः।।

34. *Śat. Br.* XI. 4.3.2
स्त्री वैषा यच्छ्रीर्न वै स्त्रियं हन्ति।
also., *Mbh. Ādi* p. 172. 41

35. Altekar A.S. *The Position of Women in Hindu Civilisation,* The Culture Pub. House, Benares, 1938, p. 276

36. *Manu* S. IX. 3
पिता रक्षति कौमारे भर्ता रक्षति यौवने।
रक्षन्ति स्थविरे पुत्रा न स्त्री स्वातंत्र्यमर्हति।।
Vas. S. V. 2
पिता रक्षति कौमारे भर्ता रक्षति यौवने।
पुत्राश्च स्थविरे भावे न स्त्री स्वातंत्र्यपर्हति।
also, *Yāj. S.* I.85

SECTION-VII

GRAMMAR AND LINGUISTICS

VII.1

RELATIVE VALUATION OF THE CONCEPTS OF ŚRADDHĀ AND MEDHĀ WITH THE GRAMMARIAN PATAÑJALI

S.D. Laddu

0. Introductory

0.0 The concepts *śraddhā* and *medhā* occur throughout Sanskrit literature, from the earliest times beginning with the Vedas.

0.1 The term *medhā* (occurring in the *Kaṭha Upaniṣad* 2.23, the *Bṛhadāraṇyaka Up.*, in the *Medhājanana* Rite of the *Āśvalāvana, GṛhyaSūtra* 1.15.2, 1.21.4, and so on) has been commonly translated as "intellect" or "intelligence". The term *śraddhā* occurring in the *Ṛgveda* 10.151 *śraddhā-sūkta,* the *Chāndogya Up.* 7.22.1): has been translated variously as "faith/desire/devotion"; and the resulting confusion was pointed out by G.S.Pendse.[1] But that has[2] been resolved recently by M.A.Mehendale as: being particular denotations of the term, to be so understood in particular context only.

0.2 We are not concerned here with all the different occurrences, whether lexical or literary, of the two terms. We propose here to draw attention to their occurrences in early Sanskrit Grammatical literature alone.

1. With the Munitraya of Sanskrit Grammar

Pāṇini in his *Sūtras* refers to these two terms each twice or thrice (*śraddhā* : 1.4.66, 3.2.158, 5.2.101; *medhā*: 5.2.121, 5.4.1 Kātyāyana in his *Vārttikas* refers to *medhā* once (5.2.109.3); and

Patañjali in his *Mahābhāṣya*[3] refers to *śraddhā* four times (I.341.23, I.436.19, 23, II.362.10) and twice to *medhā* (I.436.19, II.397.18).

2. With Patañjali

2.1.1 The context in which Patañjali refers to these two terms together has been provided under the *Sūtra alpāctaram* (2.2.34), and this falls within the fields of : (1) *pūrvanipāta* "primary placement" (by *anuvṛtti* of *pūrvam* from the *Sū. upasarjanaṁ pūrvam,* 2.2.30), and (2) a Dvandva compound (by *anuvṛtti* from the Sū. *dvandve ghi,* 2.2.32). Thus, the context here comes to be: "the first member of a Dvandva compound".

While further specifying one of the conditions, the *Vārttika abhyarhitam* (2.2.34.4) is noted for the first placement within a Dvandva compound.

Patañjali illustrates the Vt. with two examples : *mātāpitarau* and *śraddhāmedhe* (I.436.19). Pertinent to our discussion is the second example : *'śraddhāmedhe'*

2.1.2 Be it noted, incidentally, that this latter example (*sraddhāmedhe*) has been provided by Patañjali *alone*, it being not found later among the *Prakriyā* works on Pāṇini's *Aṣṭādhyāyī*. The *Rūpamālā* and the *Rūpāvatāra* here give no example at all, while the *Vaiyākaraṇa-Siddhānta-Kaumudī* notes only *tāpasaparvatau* by way of example of this Vt.- So, it can be said to be *peculiar* to the *Mahābhāṣya* of Patañjali.

2.2.1 A question may be asked here : What is this '*abhyarhita*' (or *abhyarhitatva)* mentioned, in the Vt. 2.2.34.4 ?— It is a derivative (a past passive participle) from the root *arh* 'to merit, to be worthy', strengthened with the prefix *abhi*, and means: 'what is much honoured or respected'.

And, from the elaboration given by Kaiyaṭa in his *Pradīpa* (for 'much respect that is due to what is the first member of a Dvandva compound') on the first of the two examples, *mātāpitarau* (viz. *'garbhadhārāṇadinā pitrapekṣaya mātābhyarhitā'),* it can be inferred that '*abhyarhita*' stands for "very much respected."

2.2.2 Thus, obviously for the second example, *śraddhāmedhe,* the superiority of *śraddhā* over *medhā* is secured through its first placement within a Dvandva compound. Here, the *factor* of superiority has been stated by the two scholiasts, Kaiyaṭa (in *Pradīpa)* and Haradatta (in *Padamañjarī*), in almost identical terms in their respective works :

satyāṁ śraddhāyām arthakriyākāriṇī medhā,
iti śraddhāyā abhyarhitatvam / (- Pradīpa);

satyāṁ śraddhāyām arthakriyākāriṇī medhā,
iti abhyarhitatvaṁ Śraddhāyāḥ (-Padamañjarī)

2.3 Now, what is meant by *'arthakriyākārin'* ?

In the *Kāvyaprakāśa* of Mammaṭa in the second *Ullāsa* we come across the line :

"yady api arthakriyākāritayā pravṛttinivṛttiyogyā vyaktir eva, tathāpi ...."

This, by the explanation supplied by the editors A.B.Gajendragadkar and S.N. GaJendragadkar[4], comes to stand for : ability of doing an action calculated to serve the purpose or end.

If this is accepted, Kaiyaṭa and Haradatta can be taken to mean: "Given *śraddhā* or Faith, then alone *medhā* or Ability to do an efficacious activity is possible".

2.4 The picture according to the two scholiasts then seems to be :

śraddhā (Deep Faith) is the Basis, and

medhā (Intelligence or Reasoning Faculty) is the resulting Activity.

Such is Patañjali's thinking, according to them.

3. May this then be supposed to be the "Message" of Patanjali :

'To value Faith or Devotion above Intellect" ?

FOOTNOTES

1. *The Vedic Concept of Śraddhā* (Pune, 1978), p. 14.
2. *Prācheen Bhārat: Samāj āni Saṁskrti* (in Marathi) (Prājña Pāṭhaśālā Maṇḍal, Wai, 2001) : *'śraddhā'*, (pp. 19-23).
3. Third Edition of Kielhorn, by K. V. Abhyankar, (Bhandarkar Oriental Research Institute, Pune) in 3 Vols, 1962-1972 (with references to : Volume, Page and Line).
4. Revised ed. (1959), Notes :, p. 171.

VII.2

ON LANGUAGE

N.B. Patil

The evolutionists say that man appeared on the scene of evolution some 50, 000 years before. It took him centuries to achieve the present state of culture and civilization. With certain biological changes, particularly in the cranium, he developed certain faculties. His social and rational behaviour changed from what it was in those distant millenia. We say that man is a social and rational being. Both these traits could not have developed without language. Language is the basic factor in man's socialisation. It permeates his thoughts, mediates his relations with others and even creeps in his dream.

Insights about language are of immense intellectual significance. These have relevance in many disciplines. Language is largely a mental phenomenon. Our thoughts, our concepts necessarily assume linguistic forms. Linguistics is comparatively a later discipline. It is a scientific study of languages. It is a pure science. This means that linguistics will not prescribe, how a language should be but will simply describe what it is. Linguistics has developed in six branches. The foremost is (l) Descriptive Linguistics : This is the study of a language at one point of time. It studies its structure, vocabulary, syntax etc. (2; Historical Linguistics. This is a diachronic study of a language. It studies the changes that take place in a language through a period of time. This presupposes the study of Descriptive Linguistics as well. This study is of immense use for the students of culture. (3) Anthropological Linguistics. This is an investigation into the languages of human groups as a part of the study of their culture. (4) Psycho-Linguistics. : This is the study of language acquisition and language behaviour,—also psychological mechanism for such behaviour. (5) Socio-linguistics : This branch studies the functioning of the language in a society. (6) Applied Linguistics : Here, the results of all linguistic studies are put to practical use.

Descriptive Linguistics had for several decades laid an emphasis on sound systems of languages. They paid little attention to meaning and syntactical relations in sentences. While syntax is a way of combining words to form grammatical sentences, Semantics is the science of the meaning of sentences.

In India, the tradition of semantic studies is a part of ancient history. In the wake of the Vedas, semantic, syntactical and grammatical studies evolved. This itself developed in the philosophy of grammar. This sharpened philosophical speculations and the result was the rich philosophical literature in ancient India.

As we all know, language is very special to human species. Animals can communicate their feelings which are almost human; but they cannot articulate. The higher mammals, such as whales, dolphins, elephants etc. also indicate their feelings . Even among lower species such as ants, bees etc. they have their own systems of communication, which satisfy their social and community needs. But these systems are not languages. Acquisition of a language is purely a human prerogative.

Language learning is not a genetical trait. A normal child not reared in isolation learns the language of those who are near it and interacts with it. This interaction plays an important part in the child's acquisition of the mother tongue. Children pick up languages, other than their mother tongue, through their peers as well. Adults cannot learn other language or languages with the same facility, as that of a child.

Language is a social phenomenon whose form is determined by biological and geographical (this includes climatic) factors. The relation between word and its form and its meaning is arbitrary, except in languages with pictorial scripts. It is a wonder how the word symbols developed in various languages, except with regard to certain onomatopoeic words. In many languages world over, the words for father and mother such as Papa, Pa, Dad, Daddy, Mom, Ma, Mommy are somewhat similar.

Is it possible to think without the aid of words or languages? Thought is a conscious mental activity. It is said that this activity, though facilitated by language, may not entirely depend upon it. Music, for example, is a mental activity. It will be seen that words or a language is immaterial for musical activity. This is more so when music is instrumental. Similarly, sculpture. It speaks for itself and its message is ultralingual. Just as instrumental music can be without lyrics, a sculpture also emits its message without recourse to any language. It is also true that at times, we do not find words to express our profound feelings and extremely abstract thoughts. But all the same it is true that words facilitate thinking as they serve as counters or symbols and we can easily manipulate them. They are quite helpful in expressing abstract ideas such as justice, liberty, education, democracy etc.

LANGUAGE AND SOCIETY

It is believed that there are about more than 5000 languages spoken all over the world. We cannot arrive at the exact number, in spite of the advancement of Information Technology, as we do not have all the voluminous information from all parts of the world to arrive at the accurate estimate. Again, though we have some idea of what we mean by the term 'language', the facts of language use are such that it is often extremely hard in practice to decide when this term is properly applied. While geographical boundaries can be marked with certainty, marking of language boundaries is not so simple. The languages like English, French, Russian or Hindi can be traced all over the world.

The Linguistic Survey of India (Grierson) records 179 languages and 544 dialects. There could not be any survey after Independence. The Census Reports, however, record the languages of the states. Grierson's figures cease to have any relevance today. The fact is that India is a multilingual country and we have a polyglot population. The major languages in India are 18 and these are 1. Assamese; 2. Bengali; 3. Gujarati. 4. Hindi; 5. Kannad; 6. Kashmiri; 7. Konkani; 8. Malayalam; 9. Manipuri; 10. Marathi; 11. Nepali; 12. Oriya; 13. Punjabi; 14. Sanskrit; 15. Sindhi; 16. Tamil; 17. Telugu and 18. Urdu. These are mentioned in Schedule VIII of the *Constitution of India*. It has been the policy of our Government to develop all these languages. Every state has its official language as well. The efforts at the state and the central levels in developing these languages are 'commendable. The fact, however, remains that all the states could not so far impart higher education in regional languages. That is why we could not have an all round democratic progress .

The main purpose of developing regional languages is to enable them to function as the languages of administration in the respective states. This is the *sine qua non* of a meaningful democracy.

Language is an important component of culture. Neglect of one's own language would alienate one from one's own culture. So it is our bounden duty to develop our languages and raise them to the status of media of higher education. In a polyglot country like India, we have necessarily to become multi-lingual. The Northerners should love Southern languages and *vice versa*. This will help integration and would ensure national solidarity.

SECTION-VIII

PRAKRIT AND JAINISM

VIII.1

SOMAPRABHA-ĀCĀRYA AND HIS CONTRIBUTION

Prof. M. L. Wadekar

Introductory

The Jain *Tīrthaṅkaras* and *Ācāryas* have contributed immensely to the fields of Indian Philosophy, Literature, Art and culture. Many scholarly treatises, Poetic compositions, Commentaries on different works, Artistic Paintings and sculptures are available, which are their contributions at the several periods of Indian history. Their contribution in propagation and preservation of Manuscripts by way of their continuous copying and circulation activities, is also noteworthy. Hemacandrācārya's contribution to the fields of Jain philosophy, literature, grammar, lexicography, *yoga* etc, is quite distinct and well-known. Here in this paper Somaprabhācārya-a well-known Jain Scholar-Ācārya and his contribution to Sanskrit, Prakrit and Apabhraṁśa literature in the form of his literary compositions is considered.

Biographical details

Fortunately, ample biographical information about this *ācārya* is available from his various works. He was a Vaiśya of Prāgvāṭa (Porvad) community. His father's name was Sarvadeva and that of his grandfather was Jinadeva. Jinadeva was a Prime-minister of some Prince and was a greatly respected person of his time. In his early childhood, Somaprabha took up initiation in Jain Religion. He was a great versatile scholar and intelligent fellow, who attained mastery over all the different lores and rose to the position of "*Ācārya*". He was also well-versed in logic, poetics and religious discourses. It is to be noted that *ācārya* Somaprabha was a contemporary of King Kumārapāla and his preceptor Hemacandra. Only eleven years after the death of king Kumārapāla, Somaprabhācārya is said to have composed the *Kumārapālapratibodha* in 1195 A.D.[2] (*Śaśijalanidhisūryavarṣe*). This work is said to be composed by the author while dwelling in the house of the poet Siddhapāla. He was the son of Poet-King Śrīpāla of the Prāgvāṭa (Porwad) community. It was written for the benefit of Hariścandra and Śrīdevī-son and daughter of Sheth Abhayakumāra-son of Nemināga. The three learned disciplies of Hemacandra namely, Mahendramuni, Vardhamāna and Guṇicandra, had listened to it from the beginning to the end. The author's other work, namely, *Sumatināthacarita* was also composed by him in the same house.

The entire genealogical tree of the preceptors of Somaprabhācārya's lineage could be represented in the following manner. This information is available in the *Kumārāpālapratibodha* and other works of different scholars. It should be noted that each of these preceptors has contributed separate scholarly treatises on the Jain philosophy. Jagaccandrasūri, the founder of the ascetic assembly known as *Tapāgaccha* was successor of Somaprabhācārya. According to *Paṭṭāvalis,* Somaprabhācārya held the 43rd position in lineal succession from Mahāvīra.

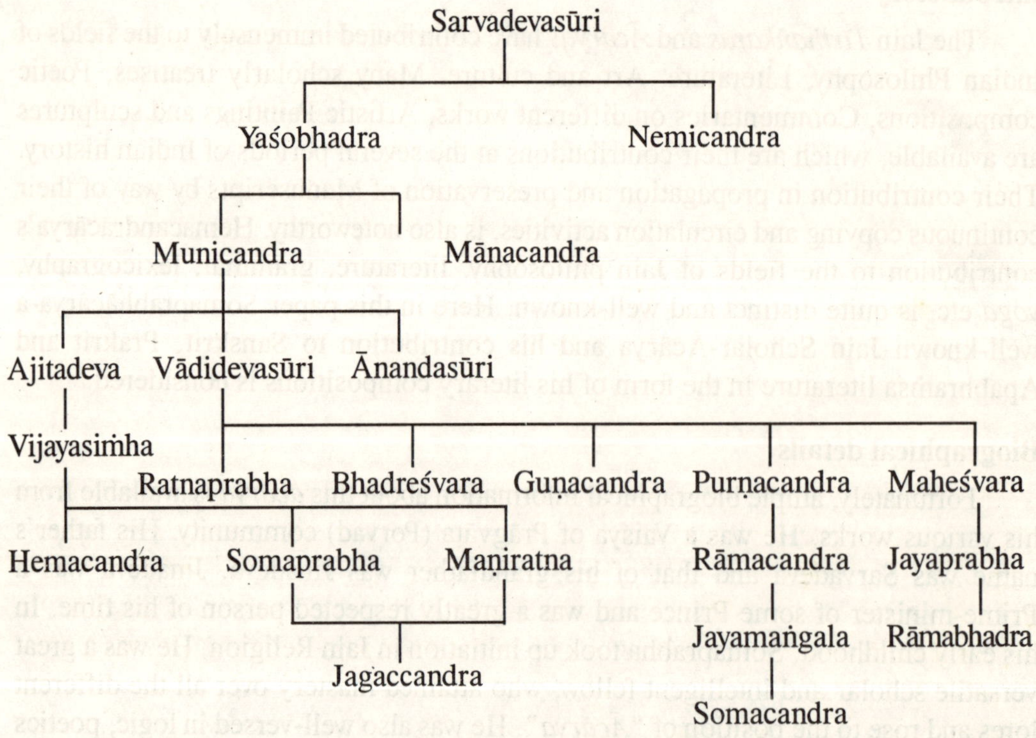

Contribution of Somaprabhācārya

Somaprabhācārya has contributed four different works, written in Sanskrit, Prakrit and Apabhraṁśa languages; this shows that he was not only well-versed in all these languages, but also had good command over prosody and grammar. His four works in their chronological order are (1) *Sumatināthacarita* (2) *Sūktimuktāvalī* (3) *Śatārthakāvya* (4) *Kumārapālapratibodha*.

(1) *Sumatināthacarita*—It is a work, describing the life of Sumatinātha the fifth *Tīrthaṅkara* of the Jain Religion. Written mainly in Prakrit language, it incorporates in about 9000 and a half verses, the legends and stories, pertaining to Jain tenets and philosophy. The *Praśastis* at the end of this work are similar to those found at the end of the work *Kumārapālapratibodha*. The manuscripts of this work are found in Jain Bhāṇḍāras at Patan.

(2) *Sūktimuktāvalī*—This seems to be an anthology, compiled by the author . It is also known as *Somaśataka* or *Sindūraprakara*. It begins with the word *Sindūraprakara*, hence it is so-called. It as the name *'Somaśataka'* suggests contains one hundred verses. Similarly, it is also called *Sūktimuktāvalī,* as it comprises of verses of good sayings. It is written in the style of *Nītiśatāka* of Bhartṛhari and contains short and pithy verses on different topics of morality like *Ahiṁsā, Satya, Asteya, Śauca, Sadācāra, Daiva, Karma*. etc. It is written in simple language and is very famous among the scholars. Some of the verses of it are found quoted in the *Kumārapāla-pratibodha*. This is published in 1917 by Shri Jain Bhaskarodaya Press, Jamnagar. A Ms. of '*Sindūraprakaraṇ Sāvacūrṇiḥ*' is available in Oriental Institute, Baroda (Vide. Acc. No. 2981). One more Ms. '*Sindūraprakaraḥ Sārthaḥ*' is also available in Oriental Institute, Baroda (Vide Acc. No. 4717, dt. *Saṁ,* 1786).

(3) *Śatārthakāvya*—It is a *kāvya,* as the title itself suggests, having hundred meanings. Here, there is only one verse in the *Vasantatilakā* metre, but is explained by the author in hundred different ways. This exhibits the extra-ordinary scholarship and the unusual command over Sanskrit language. From this work itself, the author was given the title '*Śatārthika*', by many different writers e.g.—

सोमप्रभो मुनिपतिर्विदितः शतार्थी-मुनिसुन्दरसूरिकृत-गुर्वावलिः। ततः शतार्थिकः ख्यातः श्रीसोमप्रभसूरिराट्-गुण रत्नसूरिकृत-क्रियारत्नसमुच्चयः।

The verse of hundred meanings is as follows—

कल्याण-सारस-वितान-हरेक्ष-मोह-
कान्तारवारणसमानजयाद्यदेव।
धर्मार्थकामद-महोदयवीरधीर-
सोमप्रभावपरमागमसिद्धसूरे।।

At the beginning of the commentary, explaining this verse in hundred ways, the author has composed five verses in which an Index to these hundred explanations, intended by him is given. At the beginning, the verse is explained in the context of 24 *Tīrthaṅkaras*. Then it is expounded referring to Vedic deities like Brahmā, Viṣṇu etc. This is also elucidated as alluding to his contemporaries like Vādidevasūri and Hemacandra. The four Chalukya kings of Gujarat, namely-Jayasiṁhadeva, Kumārapāla, Ajayadeva and Mūlarāja, the poet Siddhapāla, best citizens of the time, his two preceptors—Ajitadeva and Vijayasiṁha are also referred to through the exposition of the verse. Some disciple of Somaprabhācārya has written a *Praśasti* on him which is given at the end. From this *Praśasti* also, we get ample personal information about Somaprabhācārya which is quite similar to the one, found at the end of the work - *Kumārapālapratibodha*. Two Mss. of this work are available in the Oriental Institute Baroda (vide. Acc. nos. 2942 and 13192 entitled *"Śatārthī* (*Śatārthavṛtta-Kāvyāvacūriḥ*) by Somaprabhācārya.

(4) *Kumārapālapratibodha*—This is the most voluminous work of the author, as the tittle suggests, containing teachings of Jain philosophy and good conduct imparted by Hemacandrācārya to Kumārapāla mainly in Prakrit language, but some stories are in Apabhraṁśa language also. This shows the command of the author over all the three languages and his mastary over metres thereof. It has five *prastāvas (chapters) and total* 8800 verses (i.e.) *granthasaṅkhyāpramāṇa)* It contains many stories, explaining importance of good conduct and Jain Philosophical tenents. The work is not only important from the point of view of exposition of Jain doctrine but also is an important Prakrit work. It is well-honoured by the subsequent authors, writing about Kumārapāla. Since the author was a contemporary of Kumārapāla and had very authentic and close acquaitance with both of them and their activities, the work has great value as a historical treatise also. From this work, the valuable account of Kumārapāla's succession to the throne, his desire to know the true religion, Hemacandra's early life, Hemacandra as *ācārya*, relation between Hemacandrācārya and Kumārapāla, Kumārapāla's celebration of Jain festivals, Kumārapāla's pilgrimage to Saurastra temples, his building of steps over Girnar Hills, his building of charitable Institutions —*Satrāgāra, Poṣadhaśālā,* Kumārapāla's total conversion to Jainism, his daily timetable, his faith in *Namaskāramantra*-is available. The *Kumārapālapratibodha* is published as Gaekwad's Oriental Series No. 14 by the Oriental Institute, Baroda in 1920.

This valuable contribution of this great Somaprabhācārya—43rd in the rank—to the Sanskrit, Prakrit and *Apabhraṁśa* languages and literature and to the propagation of Jain philosophy and rightous conduct should always be taken notice of.

FOOTNOTES

* Oriental Institute, M.S. University of Braoda, Vadodara

1. प्राग्वाटान्वयनीरराशिरजनीजानिर्जिनार्चापरः
संजातो जिनदेव इत्यभिधया चूडामणिर्मन्त्रिणाम्।
यस्यौदार्य-विवेकविक्रमदयादाक्षिण्यपुण्यैर्गुणैः
साम्यं लब्धुमहर्निशं जगदपि क्लिश्यन् न विश्राम्यति।।
तस्मात्मजः सुजनमण्डलमौलिरत्न-
मुज्जृंभितेन्द्रियजयोऽजनि सर्वदेवः।
एकस्थसर्वगुणनिर्मितकौतुकेन
धात्रा कृतोऽयमिति यः प्रथितः प्रथिव्याम्।।
सूनुस्तस्य प्रथमकमलादर्पणः पुण्यकामः
कौमारेऽपि स्मरमदजयी जैनदीक्षां प्रपन्नः।
विश्वस्यापि श्रुतजलनिधेः पारमासाद्य जज्ञे
श्रीमान् सोमप्रभ इति लसत्कीर्तिराचार्यवर्यः।।
यो गृह्णाति समश्रुतं वहति यस्तर्केऽद्भुतं पाटवं
काव्यं यस्त्वरितं करोति तनुते यः पावनीं देशनाम्।
योऽबध्नात्सुमतेश्चरित्रभरितां सत्सूक्तिपंक्तिं परां
श्रीसोमप्रभसूरिरेष (तिलके) वृते शतार्थं व्यधात्।।

—Concluding verses of *Sumatināthacarita*

2. इति सोमप्रभकथिते कुमारनृपहेमचन्द्रसंबद्धे।
जिनधर्मप्रतिबोधे प्रस्तावः पंचमः प्रोक्तः।।
शशिजलनिधिसूर्यवर्षे शुचिमासे रविदिने सिताष्टम्याम्।
जिनधर्मप्रतिबोधः क्लृप्तोऽयं गूर्जरेन्द्रपुरे।।
प्रस्तावपंचकेऽप्यात्राष्टौ सहस्राण्यनुष्टुभाम्।
एकैकाक्षरसंख्यातान्यधिकान्यष्टभिः शतैः।।

—Concluding verses of *Kumārapālapratibodba*

VIII.2

UPAKATHĀ-S IN KARAKAṆḌUCARIU —A CRITICAL STUDY

Dr. Gauri Mahulikar

Philologically, *Prākrit* represents third stage in the development of *Sanskrit*. *Prākrit-s* are'mostly a compromise between the spoken dialect *(Apabhraṁśa)* and *Sanskrit*. Though *Prākrit* is different from *Apabhraṁśa*, the demarcating line between the two is very thin. Most of the literature in *Apabhraṁśa* is in verse form.[1] It can be classified thus'[2]—

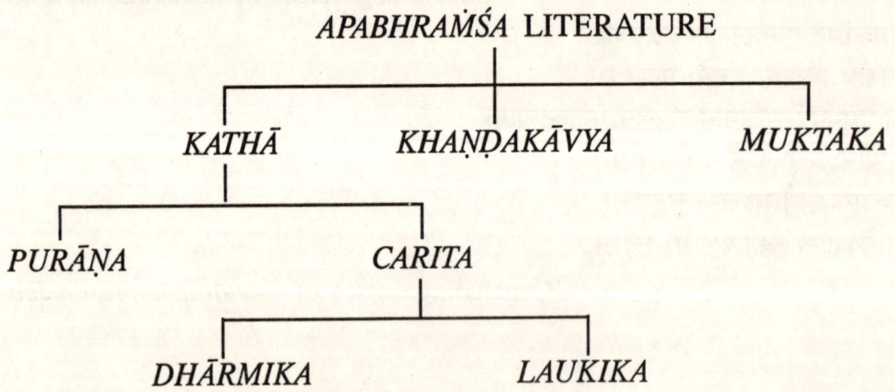

Laukikacarita or mundane has for its hero, the son of a king or a *vaiśya* who is romantic and heroic. The story abounds in hyperbole and supernatural elements. *Karakaṇḍacariu*, a famous *carita* text of the Jains, written by sage Kanakāmara, is a *laukikacarita*. Tradition declares that *Kanakāmara* wrote it in one *Āśāpurī* city in 11th century A.D. Dr. Hiralal Jain, in his critical edition of *Karakaṇḍacariu,* gives five different places of this name, located from *Andhra Pradesh* to *Panjab* and finally concludes that it must be a city near *Bhopal,* in *Madhya Pradesh*[3].

Karakaṇḍu seems to be a very popular figure. As many as eight books glorify him. *Raidhu* wrote one in *Apabhraṁśa,* during the tenure of king Dungarsimha of Gwalior[4] but unfortunately it is not available. There are four books in *Sanskrit* on his biography.[5] Brahma Jinadesa wrote it in *Gujarati* during 15th century. This paper has for its basis, the one written by Muni Kanakāmara, in *Apabhraṁśa* during 11th century.

Karakaṇḍacariu is in ten *sandhis*. The story of *Karakaṇḍa / Karakaṇḍu / Karaṇḍa /Karaṇḍu,* a *pratyekabuddha,* has for its background the cave temples of Terāpur near *Osmanabad*. The main story is supported and supplemented by ten narratives / subordinate stories *(upakathā-s)*. Four out of these occur in the second *sandhi,* forming one group and the rest are scattered in *sandhis* six to ten.

The first narrative highlights the importance of knowledge. It is a story of two friends, a brahmin and a trader staying in the city of Kānyakubja. They once came to Chaula region to acquire wealth. While returning, they heard the drum beatings proclaiming that the daughter of the king was forcibly carried away by a demon, and that one who rescued her would get a fitting reward. Both the friends accepted the challenge. Since both were learned and wise, they went near the demon and humbled him with the recitation of the *mantra-s*[7]. The text does not specify the *mantra-s*. It seems that the town was devoid of learned men. Of course what is emphasized here is the influence of knowledge and the principle that a wise always commands respect.

Exactly reverse is the narrative of two foolish friends, stating that the friends nearly met death because they didn't know how to subdue a demon with the help of *mantras*. Both the stories appear childlike; but then entire *Pañcatantra* is meant for the training and education of the dull-witted princes of king *Amaraśakti*. A fool is condemned to such an extent that parents prefer to be childlless than have a dull son.[8] On the other hand, *jñāna* is glorified[9]. The one who has wisdom, has power as well. If a small creature like rabbit can defeat a mighty lion, is it impossible for a wise man to subjugate a demon? Third story deals with the consequences of mean company. The mean always gets swayed by the other and misunderstands; whereas the noble is firm and faithful. This universal truth is communicated in the next narrative. Aravinda, king of Benaras, once fell into a dry well/pit and was afflicted by hunger and thirst. A passer-by merchant saved his life, offering him three fresh juicy fruits. The king appointed him as his minister. Once, to test the king, the minister, abducted the royal prince, removed his ornaments and presented the same to a harlot. The king got worried and assured great reward to one telling him the whereabouts of his son. Greedy harlot told the king that it was the new minister who murdered his son. King calmly replied that he had paid off the debt of one fruit, but he should be excused for the other two. The minister was pleased and restored the son to the king. True friendship or association with the noble can withstand all hardships and calamities. This is a typical folk story element. The first four stories thus state some moral norms, ideals. 'Good yields good', 'as you sow, so do you reap', is the common thread in these stories, which is everybody's childhood treasure.

Karakaṇḍacariu, being written by a Jain sage, their philosophy of cleansing the mind off all the thoughts and desires, is preached through a narrative of two Mathura based brothers, *Mādhava and* Madhusūdana[10]. Mādhava, poverty striken and jealous of his brother's fortunes, took to austerities and died with the desire of causing sorrow to Madhusūdana. He was born as Madhusūdana's son and died at an early age, pushing his father into inconsolable grief. An ascetic, narrating this story to Karakaṇḍa, said that such relations come through rival desires, and therefore, they should be conquered .If a person passes away having some unfulfilled wishes, he takes birth in one form or the other and fulfills those. This is a deep-rooted Indian belief that is expressed here. The *Bhagavadgītā* stated it much earlier as a piece of philosophical truth.

Karakaṇḍa's wife Madanāvatī was carried away by a wild elephant, who was in fact a Vidyādhara, cursed to that effect. Karakaṇḍa was unhappy and dejected. His guardian *khecara,* therefore, narrated to him a story of Naravāhanadatta, the popular hero of many stories of *Kathāsaritsāgara (Kss),* written by *Somadeva.* Sage Kanakāmara seems to be greatly impressed by Kss as well as *Kādambarī* of Bānabhaṭṭa. Story within story is the common structural pattern of both these works and the same is maintained in *Karakaṇḍacariu.* The account of Madanamāra, who was caused to be a parrot by an ascetic girl, reminds us of Mahāśvetā turning Vaiśampāyana into a parrot. This story told by the ascetic seems to serve the purpose of consoling the pious king Karakaṇḍa and assuring him that he would certainly get reunited with his wife Madanāvatī in course of time

The next story gives an interesting motif of exchange of a good omen.[11] Once a poor and hungry brahmin saw an ascetic in the forest. Considering it as a good omen he started dancing joyfully, stretching his arms. The tendency to believe in omens seems to be inherent in human race. Beholding a good omen Śrīdatta set out in search of his wife, says, Somadeva. (Kss.ll.2.152.) A prince, passing by asked him the cause of his ecstasy. When the brahmin told him about the good omen of seeing a sage and the possibility of obtaining royal fortune as a result of it, the prince said," Oh master, give me this omen and take in exchange my ornaments and horse". As a result of the good omen, the prince soon became a king and reigned happily for many years. Good omens portend joy and evil omens, misery.

The idea of exchanging an omen is as good as transfer of merit, or even transfer of sin.[12]

The eighth narration occurs in the eighth *sandhi*. It is a long story of king Aridamana of Avantī.[13] It is narrated by Goddess Padmāvatī to *Rativegā,* wife of Karakaṇḍa and daughter of Simhaleśvara. Karakaṇḍa, with his wife, boarded a huge boat and set out through sea route. In the midst of the ocean,.a large, hostile fish appeared. The monster came up running with wrath. Karakaṇḍa jumped into the water with sword in his hand. The king killed the fish, but was carried away by an irresistible *khechara* woman. Rativegā then invoked goddess Padmāvatī, drawing a beautiful circle and worshipped her with flowers and fruits. The whole process of worship and the subsequent description of the goddess are vividly presented by Kanakāmara.[14] Padmāvatī then assured Rativegā that she would be reunited with her husband and so on. What is curious to note is that worship of *Padmāvatī* and of Jina occur here hand in hand. Kanakāmara has certainly tried to have a harmonious combination or assimilation of two religious faiths. Again the goddess holding over her head the fivefold hood of a serpent and exercising a mysterious influence reminds one of the statues of Jina with similar descriptions.

The story of Aridamana, has a parrot speaking like human beings. This reminds us of the parrot brought in the court of king Śūdraka. Somadeva speaks of one caged parrot in the hands of a low caste woman. The bird is well versed in four Vedas, skilled in all the arts and remembering his past life.[15] The parrot in *Kādambarī* escaped by the oversight of the fowler, but, the one in *Karakaṇḍacariu* is more grown up and wise and shows great skill in planning the escape of the entire pack of parrots from the clutches of the bhillas. This is borrowed from the fable of Chitragrīva, the pigeon king, occurring in *Pañcatantra*. The last narration is regarding a religious practice, by which young Sumitrā, daughter of king of Ujjayini, could change her miserable female sex, in the subsequent birth. She was born as a brahmin boy, who accomplished difficult tasks for the king, then he took to austerities and entered the portals of heaven. He was then born as *Arjuna*.[16] This narration highlights two points; 1) female birth is miserable, it is to be got rid of and 2) the importance of fast from first day of the month to the fifteenth day.[17]

The fast and its completion as stated in the book is similar to any religious fast described in the *Purāṇas*.The person completing his vow should be dressed in bright garment, he should place a jar in front devoutly, covering it with a new cloth and worship it with all the materials of worship offered into it. Then placing a religious book there and observing sleeplessness (*jāgaraṇa*) he should bestow gifts on the deserving recipients. Then one should present sixteen canopies and flags jingling with small bells, to a Jina temple. The reward assured is obtainment of all desired happiness. This is the usual *arthavāda* told in every religious vow. The main purpose of this work is to emphasize various *vrata-s like, Aṇuvrata, Guṇavrata, Śikṣāvrata* and *Mahāvrata.*[18] Jainism always preached the noble moral virtues like *Ahimsā* (non-violence). *Asteya (non* stealing), *Amarṣa, (*non falsehood), *Apargraha*, non-possession) and *Brahmacarya* (celibacy).These are meant to be observed both by the householder as well as an ascetic. Right faith and righteous living, holy conduct, ways of charity and pious thoughts, get rid of the inflow of *Karma*. *(Samvara bhāvana* and *Nirjara bhavana*).[19] This results into detachment and dispassion to worldly things.

Irrespective of any religion, such moral issues attract all pious and devout people. This, perhaps, is the reason why the story of *Karakaṇḍa* is found in the Buddhist *Jātaka* also. The *Kumbhakāra Jātaka, says* that king Karaṇḍa of Dantapura in *Kaliṅga* region got enlightenment through a mango tree.[20] The king saw one mango tree laden with fruits and the other one barren. Everybody was snatching the fruits of the tree and they soon rendered it in a pitiable condition; whereas the barren one stood there gracefully. Karaṇḍu stood at the root of the tree, reflected on three properties, viz. impermanence, suffering and unreality and thereafter perfecting spiritual insight, became *Pacceka-buddha.* The story occuring in Devendra's commentary on *Uttarādhyayana Sūtra,* is elaborate and the cause of dejection of Karakaṇḍa here, is a mighty bull, who lost all his pride and fighting spirit because of old age. Looking at the bull Karakaṇḍu thought that all subjects in this world are short-lived, perishable and as evanescent as rainbow, as unstable as streak of lightening. Reflecting in similar maner, he experienced spiritual awakening and became *Pacceka-buddha.*[21]

Tradition accepts four *Pacceka-buddhas; Karakaṇḍu* of Kaliṅga, Naggai of *Gāndhāra,* Durmukha of Pāñcāla and *Nimi* of Videha.[22]

General points of appreciation :

This 11th century work exhibits all the literary and poetic beauties prevalent in those times. In the fourth *sandhi* there is a description of lake, a lotus from which was offered everyday to a giant anthill. The lake is personified. It was greeting Karakaṇḍa as it were, through the chirping of the birds, was proclaiming its mind through the flying of fish, as if laughing in the form of foamy bubbles, singing through the humming of bees and so on. The lake was as if a noble person, agreeable and worthy of a visit:[23] The onomatopoeia is abundantly used by Kanakāmara.The description of the fight between *Karakaṇḍa* and king Dhādivāhana in third *sandhi* is beautiful and rhythmic. It is fun reading it in *Apabhraṁśa* as many words resemble modern Mararhi words.[24]

Elephant motif, which is a folk motif and also an auspicious motif in Jainism, occurs thrice in this work. First, when queen Padmāvatī is carried away in the forest by a mad elephant.(1.12) Secondly, Karakaṇḍa is luckily made the king of Dantipura when the royal elephant showers water over him with a jar of water held in its trunk. In folk tales, often an heir to *a* childless king is chosen in this manner. (11.21) Third instance is when a white elephant worships the gigantic anthill at Terapur in Osmanabad with a lotus everyday. (IV.4)

FOOTNOTES

1. Dasgupta. S. N. *A History of Indian Literature* Vol. I. Calcutta, 1947, p.683.
2. Joshi. Lakshmanshastri. *Marathi Vishvakosha.* Vol. I., p. 280.
3. Jain. Hiralal. *Karakaṇḍacariu* 2nd edition. Varanasi. 1964, p. 10
4. *Jain-jñanakośa*. Caturbai Jain Granthamala Trust. Vol. 4 Aurangabad, 1974, p. 15.
5. *Ibid.,* p. 262.
6. *Ibid.* Vol. 2., p. 251.
7. *Karakaṇḍacariu.* 11.10-12
8. *Pañcatanra,* MLBD. Delhi. 1990. *Kathāmukha.* 4 -7
9. Ibid. *Mitrabheda.* verse 237. 1. 135.
   यस्य बुद्धिर्बलं तस्य निर्बुद्धेस्तु कुतो बलम्।
   न तच्छस्त्रैर्न नागेन्द्रैर्न हयैर्न पदातिभिः। कार्यं संसिद्धिमभ्येति यथा बुध्द्या प्रसाधितम्।।
10. *Karakaṇḍacariu* VI. 4-5.
11. *Ibid.* VII. 2
12. For detailed discussion of this concept, see, Mahulikar. Gauri, "*Atharvaveda* VI. 112 & 113 : A Comparative Study". *Annals* of B.O.R.I., Vol. *LXXXl* (2000). Pune, p. 251-256.
13. *Karakaṇḍacariu* VIII. 1-16.
14. *Ibid* VII. 12-13
15. KSS.X.15, 16
16. *Ibid.* X 15.16
17. *Ibid.* X. 15, 16.
18. *Ibid.* X. 15.6
19. *Ibid.* IX, 13, 14.
20. Jain Hiralal, *Op. Cit.*, p. 228, Appendix A1
21. *Ibid.,* p. 237.
22. *Ibid.,* p. 228.

करण्डु नाम कलिंगानं गन्धारानं च नग्गइ।
निमिराजा विदेहानं पंचालानं च दुम्मुखो।।

23. *Karakaṇḍucariu* IV. 7.

24. *Ibid.* III. 18.18.

उद्दंडसुंड गय गुलुगुलंत कुडिलाणण वरहय हिलिहिलंत।
संचल्लिय रहवर घरहरंत फारक्कहिं फरियहिं फरहंत। .... etc. III. 13.
धरणियलु तडतडिउ ते कुम्भु कडगडिउ।
भुवणयलु खलभिलिउ गिरिपवरु टलटलिउ।
मयरहरु झलझलिउ घरणिंदु सलवलिउ।
खगणाहु परिसरिउ सुरराउ शरहरिउ। III. 18.

VIII.3

SUANDHADAHAMĪKAHĀ— A PENTALINGUAL LEGENDARY STORY

Dr. Siddharth Yeshwant Wakankar

Summary of the Paper

The Story-literature is the mirror of the richness of a nation. Every Nation has its own contribution to this field. India is very rich in its treasure of stories in Brahmanical (Hindu), Buddhist and Jaina religious traditions. The *Pañcatantra*, the *Hitopadeśa* etc. are perennial sources of stories. The Bauddha *Jātakas* and the Jaina stories also have their own importance in the development of this kind of Narrative literature.

Here, in this paper, I have dealt with a very rare story which glorifies the Sugandhadaśamīvrata, which is observed from the fifth day to the ninth day, with its *pāraṇā* or *udyāpana* on the tenth day of the first (bright) half of the month of Bhādrapada. The speciality of this story is : this *vrata* is observed in order to get rid of the stinking smell emanating from the mouth of a person, as a result of the sin incurred on account of giving bitter food to a Jaina *muni*. This story is narrated in five different languages, viz. Apabhraṁśa, Sanskrit, Gujarati, Hindi and Ṃarathi and that too by only the Jaina authors. This is the only story that has come to my notice which is written in five languages. The other speciality of this story is : the hardships undergone by the unfortunate step-child due to the harassment at the hands of her step-mother and step-sisters are similar to those experienced by the similarly unfortunate child in the western counterpart, viz. Cinderella. This particular parallel from the story of the western world is discussed here, with a view to bringing this interesting story to the notice of the scholars. I ventured to write on this story mainly because, the late Prof. Dr. Jagadish Chandra Jain, one of the greatest authorities on Jainism in modern times, also has not mentioned this story in his Hindi as well as English books on Jaina Narrative Literature and thus, has remained much unknown or very little-known to the scholars. The paper also shows its popularity with the Jaina authors and the spread of this in the story literature of the western world, with obvious local variations/tinge in keeping with their culture.

The richness of a Nation is reflected in its Story Literature. Every Nation has its own atmosphere, conducive to some kind of story-literature, peculiar to itself, conforming to its environs and perception of life. Owing to intercourse with other peoples, the story-literature of every nation gets influenced and it almost becomes very difficult to gauge the exact extent to which a particular nation borrows from some other nation or loans to some other people. At times, it does become a bone of contention to prove the borrower. Without going into much details about this kind of a controversy, I intend to bring to the notice of the scholars one very rare *Kathā-* which originated in India as far as the antiquity of its story is concerned, but, had its reflection in the Western World, especially, in the story literature of France, Germany and England. The *Kathā* in question is the famous SUANDHADAHAMĪKAHĀ alias the SUGANDHA-DAŚAMĪKATHĀ. It is a vow which is observed from the fifth to the tenth day of the bright half of the month of Bhādrapada and is meant to get rid of the stinking smell either of the body or the mouth of a person who receives it as a punishment to the sin he/she commits by giving bitter food to a Jaina-*muni. This is the only Kathā which is described in five languages, viz. Apabhraṁśa, Sanskrit Gujarati, Hindi and Marathi,* and that too, only by the Jains. Before we turn our attention to the actual story, let us give some details about these five Texts.

(1) **Apabhraṁśa :** This work available in four manuscripts has two *Sandhis* and twenty-one *Kaḍavakas*. One of the Mss.is dated V.S.1676(-56=1619AD). The author is Udayacandra of the Mathura Sangha who stayed near Mathura and Bharatpur along with his *śiṣyas*, in the reign of the King Ajayapala of the Yaduvaṁsa and flourished roughly in 1150 A.D., that is, middle of the twelfth century.

(2) **Sanskrit :** This work contains 161 verses couched in the Anuṣṭup metre with the exception of the last verse which is in Mālinī metre author. The Śrutasāgara, flourished in the V. S.1530 (i.e. 1472 A.D.).

(3) **Gujarati :** This is termed as a *Rāsa* by the author Jinadāsa Brahmachārī (C.1450A.D.) himself. There were three Mss.of this work from the Senagaṇa Digambara Jaina Mandir, Nagpur and it contains 205 verses. The author belonged to the Balātkāra Gaṇa of Idar, North Gujarat.

(4) Hindi : It is composed by Khuśālacandra Kālā" from Sanganer in Rajasthan and contains 143 verses.

(5) Marathi : This work containing 136 verses is available in only three Mss.Two Mss.are from the Sena Gaṇa Bhandar, Nagpur and the third one comes from the private collection of Shri B.S.Mahajan from Nagpur. One of the Mss.is illustrated.The author, Jinasāgara (Middle of the 18th cen.) stayed at Shirad and other places in the Parbhani Dist.in Maharashtra.

Leaving aside the linguistic study of these five texts for some other occasion, I just turn to the narrative structure of this *Kathā*. The *Kathā* has three parts, viz. 1st and 3rd parts have the story while the 2nd part gives the details about the actual ritual of the vow. I furnish below the broad outline:

The First Tale :

The King Padmanābha of Varanasi, along with his Queen Śrīmatī, proceed to enjoy the sports of the Spring Season. On the way, they come across Sudarśanamuni and the King asks his Queen to offer food to the *Muni* by taking him to the palace. The Queen gets angry on the *Muni,* because his arrival deprived her of the pleasures. Consequently, she gives him food consisting of bitter gourd. The *muni* consumes it and later on dies. After serving him the food, the Queen again joins the King. As it turned out, the King developed avarice towards his Queen, who looked ugly with her face giving stinking smell. On his return in the evening, the King came to know about the death of the *Muni*, due to the food given by the queen. He banishes her from the kingdom. She meets with miserable end and passes through a series of rebirths like that of a śūkarī, gardabhī, Cāṇḍālakanyā, Brāhmaṇakanyā etc. In the last birth as a Brāhmaṇakanyā, named Durgandhā, she recollects her past sin (*jātismaraṇa*), atones for it when at a suitable time, Sudarśanamurni presents the details of the Sugandhadaśamīvrata, its *Vidhāna* and *Udyāpana* too. She duly observes the same and adopts renunciation and submits to the *Sannyāsamaraṇa* and is then reborn as Tilakamatī in the next birth.

The Second Tale :

Tilakamatī, the beautiful daughter of the merchant Jinadatta of Ratnapur, had a captivating scent to her body. Unfortunataly, she loses her mother in the childhood and the father remarries and gets a daughter through the second wife. She is named as Tejomatī.The step-mother loves her daughter, but, harasses the step-child by making her undergo all sorts of hardships. The father, as usual, is unaware of all this. In the meanwhile, the King Kanakaprabha sends merchant Jinadatta to a distant land for purchasing precious Jewels.Before leaving, the merchant advises his wife to marry off the daughters, even in his absence, if suitable matches are available.

The obedient wife deceitfully arranges the marriage of Tilakamatī and takes her to the cemetery saying that it was their family-custom that the bride-groom comes to the cemetery to take the hand of the bride. Saying so, she makes her stay there throughout the night and herself returns home and announces to the relatives that Tilakamatī has eloped with some one and thus marries her own daughter to the groom in the presence of the relatives gathered there. The King Kanakaprabha sees a lone and beautifully decked girl at the cemetery at night and getting curious goes there and after learning her story, marries her there, introducing himself as a Mahiṣīpāla(a cowherd/King) and promises her that he will visit her every night and again leave her before the sunrise. The mother offers a room to her step-daughter on her return home and the Mahiṣīpāla-as promised-regularly visits her at night and offers Royal costumes etc. The step-mother suspects that the son-in-law must be a thief and informs her husband about this after he returns from his errand. Pleading his innocence, the merchant returns the Royal things to the King, who in turn asks him to find out the culprit. Thereafter, the father approaches his daughter and asks the name of his son-in-law, but, the daughter innocently says that she neither knows his name nor has she seen the face of her husband in broad day-light and hence she cannot know him, except by the touch of his feet which she used to wash. Then a feast was arranged where she was supposed to identify the thief by washing the feet of every guest with her eyes blind-folded.The thief, however, turns out to be the King himself. Then the King gives out the truth and then openly marries Tilakamatī-thus, she becomes a Queen, after undergoing all sorts of hardships. All this ending in happiness is due to her observing the Sugandhadaśamīvrata.

Before giving our observations on this narrative, we think it better to furnish some details about the actual *Vrata* known as Sugandhadaśamī.

The *Vrata* starts on the *Śuddha Pañcamī* of the month of Bhādrapada and is to be observed for five days (upto *Navamī*).During that period, the Jina is to be worshipped by means of flowers, fruits, scents etc. Every item/thing should be in a collection of ten types or kinds. A fast is to be observed with concentration and this is to be observed for ten years. After this *Vidhāna*, the *Udyāpana* is given as under: The Jina Temple should be decorated with all possible things. Then books, clothes etc. are to be given in gift to ten *Munis*. If a person follows this strictly in consonance with the ritual, he/she acquires a lot of merit and experiences all sorts of happiness.

Critical Comments :

The outline in brief helps us to get an idea of the Philosophy of the Jainas. The inviolable law of *Karman* functions automatically and maintains the moral balance in the world. The principle of "as you sow, so would you reap" works, making the

Soul migrate through births-human, sub-human, hellish, divine etc. The tinge of religious surmons, dogmatic details and didactic discourses through a monk who is endowed with a vision of the Three Times play their own part. The spirit of asceticism dominates and the tendency to make every character retire from this world to attain a better status in the next birth also is important. All these traits are to be met with in this *Kathā*. A particular character gets favour from a *Siddha* person due to some favour or good deed done to him OR a person suffers-due to the wrath of a *Siddha* person-from the stinking smell of the body and other bodily ailments or physical tortures, getting rid of these owing to the favour of some *Siddha* person or by observing some vow (*vrata*)-all these are the traits to be seen in every religious sect/system. In this regard, we may cite the famous example of Matsyagandhā/ Gandhavatī or Yojanagandhā from the *Mahābhārata*. So, we may safely say that this motif is purely of Indian origin and it was used by the Jains also. Such a motif is also to be found in other Jain works. I just furnish their references without going further into the details: The *Nāyādhammakahā*-16; the *Sāvayapannatti* (*Śrāvakaprajñapti*) of Haribhadrasūri (c.750 A.D.), verse no.93 and the commentary thereon; the *Harivaṁśapurāṇa* of Jinasena (Śaka 707-735);the *Pradyumnacarita* (*Sarga* 8, verses 140-160) of Mahāsena and the *Kathākośa* (No.108) of Hariśeṇa. When we come to the second Tale, we find surprising parallels in the stories of the Western World. I here refer to the famous story of Cinderella-which is very much popular with the children. The similarity of a motherless child, harassed by her step-mother and step-sisters, depriving her of all the pleasures of childhood, making her wear tattered clothes and work hard for the happiness and comfort of others, especially, the step-relatives, the innocence of the father about the hard life of his daughter through the earlier wife etc. are all the similar traits that are common to such stories. The only difference in these two types is : The Indian story does not have any supernatural element, to help the distressed child.The typical trait of a chaste wife washing the feet of her husband clinches the issue. There are no parties or festivals in the Indian version of the story. On this background, we can compare the Western story, especially, French, German and English which is given under: The French story is found in the 1st part of the 41st Volume of the "*Cabinet des Fees*" by Charles Parrault (1628-1703 AD). The German story appears with the title Ashen-puttele (The Āsh-puppet) in "*Kinder und Hausmarchen*"-a collection of folk-tales in three Volumes by Jacob Ludwick Grim (1785-1863 AD). A brief account of these stories is given hereunder:

French Story :

The wife of a rich man dies, leaving behind a very beautiful daughter. The rich man marries a widow who had two daughters. Then start the troubles of the daughter from the earlier wife, viz. harassment by the step-relatives, absence of happiness, physical torture, mental disturbance and imbalance etc. Once a dance festival is arranged in the palace. The step-child is not allowed to attend it, hence, she laments. A fairy listens to her lamentations, gives her magical things which enable her to attend the dance festival, the fairy, however, puts her a condition that she should return home before 12 at night, otherwise, her magical things, including her charming dress, slippers etc. would vanish. For two days, she dances with the Prince who is attracted towards her. On the third night, however, both of them were so engrossed in dancing that she forgets the time-limit set by the fairy and after the stroke of twelve she loses her magical things and is obliged to return home in a hurry. In her frenzy, one of her two glass-slippers slipped from her foot and she returns home with the other slipper with her. The Prince orders for the search of the wearer of the dropped slipper and in the end, comes to this unfortunate girl. The slipper exactly fits her foot and thus she becomes the wife of the Prince, after showing the other slipper (which she had retained and preserved). The irrefutable proof suddenly changes her fortune and the harassed orphan girl becomes the wife of the Prince.

German Story :

It is almost similar to the above in many instances, esp. its beginning, but, differs in its development. The father of this motherless child goes to a big fair and asks his three daughters (one from the earlier wife and two from the present, i.e. second wife) as to what they desire. The two sisters ask for dresses and ornaments and the earlier child asks for a twig of the tree which will touch his head on his way. The father obliges the daughters with their desired objects. The motherless child plants the twig in her garden on the grave of her mother and regularly sprinkles it with her tears, so that it becomes (grows into) a big tree which is frequently visited by a bird who later on becomes her friend. This bird visiting the Hazel tree enables her to attend the dance festival at the palace. The Prince is enamoured of her charms and dances with her throughout the night and offers to give her lift upto her residence. She politely refuses it. The Prince was so much fascinated by her charms that he chases her, but, she disappears in her garden, but, not before losing her one slipper. As per the order of the prince, that slipper was tried on the foot of the girls in the family. The step-mother tries to deceive the Prince squeezing the foot of her first daughter and fitting the slipper in her foot. The Prince rides with her, but, the bird on the Hazel tree, warns him that he is deceived. He returns to the house of the girl. Then the mother cuts the toe of her second daughter's foot and makes her wear the slipper, which surprisingly fits. The Prince sets with this girl and again the bird on the Hazel tree warns the prince that he is again fooled. Then the step-child was given a chance to wear the slipper and lo the slipper exactly fits her foot. In this way, the Prince along with Ashenputtele, starts for his palace and the bird says that now your choice is correct and thus, Ashenputtele becomes the wife of the Prince.

In both these stories, there is the supernatural element of a fairy helping the child with magical things and a bird obliging the child to attend the festival. The second wife of the merchant plays the havoc and the dance festivals etc. play their part in the western stories. The Indian version, however, does not possess any such miraculous things or the help of any supernatural element, and the Sugandhadaśamīkathā naturally evolves in the sense that the King sees the unfortunate step-child in the cemetery all alone and that too at night and goes to inquire there and after knowing the truth, marries her. His being a Mahiṣīpāla is also true, the word having a pun on it, in keeping with the tendency of the Indian authors. Moreover, the wife washing the feet of her husband is also purely Indian in nature.

Thus, we can say that the Western story is more romantic and fabulous, while, the Indian story is more natural and idealistic in keeping with our cultural tradition.

The fact that the original Suandhadahamīkahā was composed in the middle of the twelfth century and has been a source for adaptation in different Indian languages through the Jaina tradition is sufficient to prove its antiquity as compared to the story available in the Western countries from the seventeenth century onwards. The literary evidence is a solid and irrefutable proof-if any is needed at all-that this story did originate in India and then travelled to the western world through the interaction with the foreigners, just like the other cultural things like the Board-games like Chess and Snakes and Ladders etc.which successfully transcended the boundaries of nations and now have become common to all the nations with local differences and variations.

I conclude this paper with a sincere hope that this brief resume will go a long way in arousing the interest of scholars in the comparative study of story-literature of the Orient and the Occident.